Human Footprints on the Global Environment

Human Footprints on the Global Environment

Environment

Threats to Sustainability

Edited by Eugene A. Rosa, Andreas Diekmann, Thomas Dietz, and Carlo Jaeger

The MIT Press
Cambridge, Massachusetts
London, England

For information about special quantity discounts, please email special_sales @mitpress.mit.edu.

This book was set in Sabon by SNP Best-set Typesetter Ltd., Hong Kong. Printed on recycled paper and bound in the United States of America.

Library of Congress Cataloging-in-Publication Data

Human footprints on the global environment : threats to sustainability / edited by Eugene A. Rosa...[et al.].
    p. cm.
Includes bibliographical references and index.
ISBN 978-0-262-01315-4 (hardcover : alk. paper)—ISBN 978-0-262-51299-2 (pbk. : alk. paper) 1. Environmental policy—International cooperation. 2. Sustainable development–International cooperation. I. Rosa, Eugene A.
GE170.H84   2010
363.7'0526—dc22

                                                        2008054057

10 9 8 7 6 5 4 3 2 1

Contents

Acknowledgments

Rachel Shwom provided valuable assistance in the early stages of producing the manuscript. Amy Mazur provided valuable criticisms of certain chapters and both she and Linda Kalof provided guidance about the publishing process. Amy Smith has done a heroic job of moving the last several versions of the manuscript toward production, catching many errors and inadvertent inconsistencies along the way. And, of course, our chapter authors have done a superb job not only in synthesizing vast and complex literatures but also in being patient and attentive in revising their contributions.

Preface: Footprints Small and Colossal

During the Pliocene epoch, three early hominids walking across the Laetoli plains in East Africa were showered with ashes when the volcano Sadiman erupted. As they continued to walk, the light rain that was falling cast each of their footprints into a mixture of muddy ash. A little later, the impressions dried, leaving a fossil record of their trek. Three and a half million years later, archaeologist Mary Leakey discovered the prints.

These three sets of fossilized footprints found in what is now known as Northern Tanzania are remarkable because they have been preserved for so long. Literal footprints such as these are typically ephemeral, soon obliterated by wind, rain, or the trampling of later walkers. In the past much of the human ecological footprint was similarly ephemeral, absorbed by the natural cycles of ecosystem replenishment.[1]

Modern-day humans (*Homo sapiens sapiens*), like their ancient ancestors, leave traces of their presence wherever they roam or settle. But these footprints are not just temporary marks in ash and dirt. More than our ancestors, we, unavoidably leave durable footprints on the ecosystems we inhabit and exploit. Since primeval times protohumans and humans alike have impacted the ecosystems that sustain them (Redman 1999). But unlike their ancestors, modern humans have, with remarkable acceleration, expanded enormously the size and depth of their ecological footprints. The impact of these footprints in the contemporary period of twenty-first-century modernity can best be described as colossal; they dwarf by a considerable margin the footprints of all predecessors in recent or distant history. And colossal footprints are spreading around the globe, revealing such ostensible impacts as numerous species extinctions, deforestation on a grand scale, soil degradation and erosion, air and water pollution, and strong signs of a warming climate.

The growing impacts of modern human's colossal footprints now threaten the sustainability of the entire planet. Indeed, with remarkably few exceptions—for example, the political scientist Bjørn Lomborg (2001) and the science fiction writer Michael Crichton (2004)—there is widespread concern among all students of environmental change about the sustainability of the planet in the light of current trends in the use of nature's capital and services. Among scientists, policymakers, and other close observers, there is a virtual epistemic consensus over this concern. These communities have labeled the collection of these changes global environmental change (GEC) and have initiated worldwide coordinated research programs to better understand how the planet is changing and why.

What accounts for the colossal size of contemporary footprints? What are their key characteristics? What are the human forces driving their rapid growth? What can be done about curbing this rate of growth? Where does such growth most threaten the ecological sustainability of societies? What cultural and institutional practices are available for avoiding, mitigating, or managing ecological crises? These core questions summarize and frame the cumulative findings of the variety of sciences researching GEC.

But, ironically, they are questions not about the long expanse of historical time or the natural cycles and dynamics of GEC, but about the anthropogenic drivers of environmental change around the globe—the human causes of GEC. These human dimension questions are not the types of inquiries that researchers and scientists in the traditional global change sciences—rooted in physics, chemistry, and biology—are prepared to address. These are questions for the social sciences.

Yet a second irony is the fact that the social sciences, while better prepared to address these GEC-related questions, have been chary to do so, making them latecomers to GEC research. However, in the last few years, this reluctance has gradually given way to focused research. There are now major theoretical and empirical programs addressing key questions regarding the human dimensions of global change. The important goal of this volume is to collect the fruits of these labors, to organize them, and to present them in one place. Here we bring together core findings on the human dimensions of GEC to illustrate the advances that have been made in this critical area of study.

In this volume, chapters written by world-renowned experts on a wide range of environmental topics address key facets of the core questions identified earlier. Together, these contributions not only cover the breadth of current work on the human dimensions of global environmental change, and provide well-articulated depth on the key findings from these research programs, but the chapters also point to the directions for fruitful human dimensions research.

Eugene A. Rosa
Moscow, Idaho

Thomas Dietz
Grand Isle, Vermont

Notes

1. There have been exceptions, of course. The Pleistocene era witnessed the extinction of megafauna everywhere except Africa (Martin and Klein 1984). In the case of the Americas, it remains a continuing debate as to whether the extinctions were caused by a precipitous change in climate at the end of the last glaciation (approximately ten thousand to thirteen thousand years ago), or by the appearance of human hunters in the new world. Not in dispute is the fact that Native North Americans sometimes substantially altered the ecosystems they exploited (Krech 1999). And much of the Amazon basin may have been reshaped by human action (Balee 1998). But despite these important events, the scale of the human footprint at present is without precedent in our history on the planet.

References

Balee, W. L. 1998. *Advances in historical ecology.* New York: Columbia University Press.

Crichton, M. 2004. *State of fear.* New York: HarperCollins.

Krech, S. III. 1999. *The ecological Indian: Myth and history.* New York: W. W. Norton.

Lomborg, B. 2001. *The skeptical environmentalist.* Cambridge, UK: Cambridge University Press.

Martin, P. W., and R. G. Klein, eds. 1984. *Quaternary extinctions: A prehistoric revolution.* Tucson: University of Arizona Press.

Redman, C. L. 1999. *Human impact on ancient environments.* Tucson: University of Arizona Press.

1

Global Transformations: PaSSAGE to a New Ecological Era

Eugene A. Rosa and Thomas Dietz

The magnitude of the threat to the ecosystem is linked to human population size and resource use per person. Resource use, waste production and environmental degradation are accelerated by population growth. They are further exacerbated by consumption habits, certain technological developments and particular patterns of social organization and resource management.

—Joint Statement by Fifty-Eight of the World's Scientific Academies, New Delhi, India, October 1993

Discovery of Global Scale and Environmental Change

Scale matters. The 1980s ended with an unprecedented awakening to the global scale of environmental impacts, previously thought to be confined to the local and regional levels. The awakening, underscored in the epigram to this chapter, resulted in a conceptualization of environmental threats worldwide, expressed in the universally accepted term *global environmental change* (GEC). While GEC embeds many uncertainties, one thing is absolutely certain: the magnitude of change is doubtlessly due to the actions of the planet's dominant species, *Homo sapiens sapiens*; that is, to humans. Hence, an understanding of the causes of GEC is a function of understanding the range of choices and actions humans undertake.

This volume has two primary goals. The first is to assess our state of knowledge about the dynamics of coupled human and natural systems, with an emphasis on their human dimensions. This goal is centered on these questions: How and where has our understanding of the human dimensions of the human-nature link advanced over the past two decades? And what have been the key contributions from the social sciences in pushing the frontiers of this understanding? The second goal aims to bring into sharp relief not only the key gaps in our understanding, but also the opportunities, challenges, and limitations for further advances in knowledge. What are the promising routes to a higher ground of knowledge about the role of human systems in the wide array of global environmental processes? And what limitations are there in producing such knowledge?

Defining Global Environmental Change (GEC)

Human societies are systems integrated with and dependent upon natural ecosystems for sustenance and survival. Known to the ecological and social sciences from their inception, this link has been brought center stage by the many ostensible threats to ecosystems due to transformations of environments around the globe. Indeed, this indispensable link has recently been given a refined conceptualization and a name: coupled human and natural systems, or CHANS (Liu et al. 2007a, 2007b). CHANS represents not only a coupling of the two systems, but also the recognition that the two systems "interact reciprocally and form complex feedback loops" (Liu et al. 2007a, 1513).

GEC is CHANS on growth hormones. In the past, and still in a few places around the world that are in the process of vanishing, CHANS were fairly isolated and, therefore, circumscribed dynamic systems. Band and tribal societies often developed sustainable CHANS in isolation from other human systems or intrusions. While lingering perhaps as a memory of a rhapsodized past, such social systems no longer exist. There is literally no place on earth that is entirely isolated.[1] Neither nuclear clouds, nor the warming of the planet, nor other ecological threats know geographic boundaries. The study of GEC is the study of CHANS in the context of dynamic global processes.

The idea of GEC is generally agreed to consist of two complementary dynamics: *cumulative* effects (that are local in domain but so widely replicated that in sum they have global consequences) and *systemic* effects (that occur on large spatial scales or alter the function of large systems; Turner et al. 1990). Cumulative effects include tropical deforestation, desertification, damaged local ecosystems, species losses, and resource exhaustion, while systemic effects include ozone depletion and global climate change. Both types of effects are traceable to human activities.

The human dimensions of GEC raise the question of whether human practices and institutions have seriously disrupted carbon, ocean, climate, biotic, and other biogeochemical cycles. If so, what are the specific human drivers responsible for the disruptions? Which disruptions make societies most vulnerable, and where? Have human practices, old and new, led to species extinction, biodiversity loss, and overuse of nature's capital and services? What opportunities and strategies are available for preempting, mitigating, or adapting to environmental changes at the global level—large or small?

An early marker of the awakening that environmental impacts were global was the highly influential report of the World Commission on Environment and Development (WED), *Our Common Future* (WED 1987). Known as the "Brundtland Report," after the commission's chair, Gro Harlem Brundtland of Norway, the report sounded the alarm that present global trends in resource use and environmental impacts could not continue indefinitely. They would need to be reversed. And, the Brundtland Report further argued, many of the critical environmental trends could not be solved within the confines of the nation-state—instead, they must be tackled from the vantage point of global cooperation. The WED's assessment of the state of the world was hardly sanguine, but, nevertheless, the report ended on an optimistic, though cautionary, note that centered on the idea of sustainability, of taking actions to counteract the feedback from the reciprocal interaction of CHANS that could dangerously reduce nature's capital and services. The WED's creatively ambiguous definition of sustainable development read: "the ability of humankind...to ensure that it meets the needs of the present without compromising the ability of future generations to meet their own needs."

Other indicators soon followed. Perhaps the most significant were the emergence of a variety of institutions devoted to global environmental change, such as the founding of the Intergovernmental Panel on Climate Change (IPCC) in 1988 and the Human Dimensions Programme of GEC in 1990 (becoming in 1996 the International Human Dimensions Program); and the beginning of sustained attention by the U.S. National Research Council/National Academy of Sciences (NRC/NAS) to the human dimensions of GEC. The standing NRC/NAS Committee on the Human Dimensions of Global Change published the germinal report *Global Environmental Change: Understanding the Human Dimensions* in 1992 (Stern, Young, and Druckman), referred to as the GEC92 hereafter.[2] This report codified and highlighted human dimensions as an important and separate field of study, provided an initial state-of-the-art assessment of social scientific knowledge about global change, and proposed an early research agenda for advancing the field.

The foundation of GEC92 is consonant with the core idea of CHANS, namely that human and environmental systems are inextricably connected in webs of mutual causation. Because of this mutuality the range of human responses to global change typically alter both kinds of systems—further underscoring the pivotal importance of proximate human drivers.[3] GEC92 also underscored the intersection of human with physical and biological processes and of the need to understand how they interact, often via complex feedback. That intersection recurs in two conceptual locations. One is where proximate human (anthropogenic) actions produce direct and relatively immediate environmental changes. The other is where changes to physical and biological systems directly and indirectly affect the natural capital and services that determine what humans value and what they can do. The GEC92, a systematic review of the literature existing then on the human driving forces, made it clear that, despite the immense contributions of individual scholars, sustained research traditions were difficult to find. Since GEC92's publication, the social science literature on GEC has grown in both volume and sophistication, and is on the verge of becoming fully interdisciplinary and well articulated.

Proximate Driving Forces
GEC92 distilled the key proximate anthropogenic drivers implicated in global environmental change from a multilayered synthesis of the social science literature. There were five social variables identified as key human forces: (1) population change, (2) economic growth, (3) technological change, (4) political-economic institutions, and (5) attitudes and beliefs (Stern, Young, and Druckman 1992, 75). This identification catalyzed the course of social science research and, accordingly, directly shaped the choice of topics we have covered in the chapters of this volume. It also provides a baseline against which to measure the cumulative social science knowledge of the past fifteen years. Hence, the majority of substantive chapters in this volume are devoted to a state-of-the art assessment of what scholars in the social sciences know about these drivers, or what they need to learn. The chapters do not cover all these topics, nor do they exhaust the subject matter relating to the included topics—indeed, they are not intended to do so. Rather, our volume has a more refined scope, to present selected, vanguard exemplars of analyses of

those topics. The chapters, in our judgment, are representative of the more mature lines of human dimensions research.

Missing from this volume—as it is more generally in analyses of global change—is detailed coverage of the third social variable from our list of five drivers: technological change. It is omitted not because it lacks importance, but because of the difficulty of harnessing the complex and proximate effects of technological change. On the one hand, this unmet challenge is reflected in the glacial growth in our understanding of technology's role in GEC. That lacuna, in turn, accounts for its absence from this volume. On the other hand, it simultaneously pinpoints one of the most serious gaps in human dimensions research and the one, perhaps, most desperately in need of concerted attention.

While the GEC92 provided a template for the topics covered in these chapters, it is important to understand the geophysical and historical context leading to that template, to understand what led us to the processes it summarizes. Hence, in the remainder of this chapter we outline key features of the linked human and natural systems of the earth that illuminate the past and present role of human impacts on the planet. We also situate the current state of anthropogenic forces on that system in a larger context: that of an accelerated Pace, Scale, and global Spread of environmental impacts driven by a process of Autocatalysis, Globalization, and the interconnectedness of Ecosystems around the globe. The acronym PaSSAGE provides a summary of these processes and an aid to remembering them.

To begin, we sketch the long history that set the stage for these processes. We then delineate the narrower context of contemporary global processes sparked by human actions or impacting them.

The Biosphere

The biosphere is the global envelope of all life. The biosphere[4] comprises not only the dynamics of large, linked physical processes such as the carbon cycle, the hydrological cycle, short- and long-term atmospheric dynamics, and geological change, but also the global ecosystem comprising the dynamics of living systems of all the species of life on the planet. It appears that earth's evolutionary history has alternated between long periods of relative balance among these dynamics followed by cataclysmic disruptions. In the modern era the biosphere is threatened with one such major disruption. But unlike previous planetary catastrophes—excursions brought about by the impact of asteroids, changes in solar radiation, or major geological disruptions—the current one is due to an entirely new force, the actions of the biosphere's dominant species: *Homo sapiens sapiens*. Humans are changing the global environment in unprecedented ways.

Knowledge, Agency, and Uncertainty

All species are reliant on ecosystems. CHANS are uniquely different from nonhuman ecosystems because of the self-referential capacity of humans: the extensive ability to plan, organize, and create systematic solutions to repeatable problems—to create institutions. Contemporary societies have a unique advantage over their predecessors in that we have a repertoire of success and failures of past societies and, therefore, the opportunity to learn from them (Diamond 2005). The chapters in this volume are intended not only to summarize key developments in global human dimensions research, but also to underscore the many uncertainties that remain to be addressed. One of the most compelling themes to have emerged is the recognition that uncertainties about the human drivers of GEC trump, by a considerable margin, the uncertainties in biophysical processes. The greater uncertainties shrouding human ecosystems are a function of two key factors: complexity and reflexivity. Humans, more than all other species, elaborate their ecosystems and act reflexively within them. What might be reasonable strategies for addressing these uncertainties?

Then, of course, there is the even more intractable form of uncertainty: meta-uncertainty. There are, no doubt, key factors for which our knowledge is uncertain but we do not know how uncertain it is. In some cases we may even be unaware that our knowledge of it is uncertain. Our hope is that this volume not only will point to the direction for future research on the human dimensions of CHANS, but also will become a foundation for addressing this hierarchy of uncertainties.

The Context of Time: Its Arrow, Its Cycles[5]

Cataclysmic disruptions to the entire planet are recorded in geologic time. In contrast, human impacts are recorded in historical time. The idea of historical time, the concept for interpreting human experience through the fourth dimension favored for centuries in the West, captures the unique "irreversible sequence of unrepeatable events" (Gould 1987,

194) experienced by the human species. *Time's arrow* is the widely adopted metaphor to capture the concept of this lens of retrospection. But more than metaphor, time's arrow also reflects one of the universe's most basic processes and most basic markers of time—the law of entropy, the relentless process toward disorder. The second law of thermodynamics, the most ostensible manifestation of entropy, bears directly on the sustainability of the principal sources of fuel available to humans around the globe.[6]

But the physical world does not follow unique and unidirectional time sequences alone. It is also punctuated with repeatable and, to some degree, predictable processes over time: *time's cycles*. The cycles of time are presumed to have no clear direction, no vector of progress. Ecosystems, for example, are understood to reflect the reasonable predictability of dynamic cycles. Global environmental change can be understood as the total collection of these evolutionary processes and cycles. Perhaps more importantly, it can also be understood as the linking together of countless CHANS around the globe into what might be called a mega-CHANS. Similarly, GEC can be viewed as the extension of human systems into an ever-widening natural system—nature in a global sense. In perhaps the broadest way to frame it, GEC is borne of the interaction and interpenetration of these two sequences—as the trajectory of time's arrow interacting with time's cycles—and the consequences of this coupling for ecological sustainability.

The principal driving forces of GEC, as noted, are the proximate anthropogenic drivers reflecting practices and institutions emerging from time's historical trajectory. A key challenge—indeed, *the* challenge for GEC—is whether these anthropogenic arrows have markedly disrupted time's cycles, and whether the entropic forces of human history have disrupted—perhaps irreversibly—global cycles.

As we will see, most work on CHANS has focused on the last half century. It is during this period, sometimes called "the Great Acceleration," that many forms of environmental change became manifest and trade—the flow of information, politics, and human migration—became truly global. Of course, as the term *acceleration* implies, these processes were under way well before the mid-twentieth century. But their pace clearly intensified after World War II. This manifest global transformation in human and natural systems has prompted the research reviewed in this volume. But while the majority of scholarship has focused on the Great Acceleration, there is widespread acknowledgment that longer time scales can provide essential insights into the large dynamics of coupled human and natural systems at the global, regional, and local levels. For example, the Integrated History and Future of People on Earth project (Costanza, Graumlich, and Steffen 2007; http://www.aimes.ucar.edu/activities/ihope.shtml) considers CHANS at scales of ten thousand, one thousand, and one hundred years. Data are often much more sparse at such longer scales than for inquiries focused on the more recent path. But long time scales also may reveal dynamics that cannot be observed with less diachronically extensive data. In the long run, better integration of long-term extensive and short-term intensive analysis is bound to yield powerful insights. For the moment, however, most research focuses on the Great Acceleration and that is reflected in this volume.

Scientific Worldview: Tipping the Balance of Nature

Examining CHANS on a global level, the focus of GEC, represents a remarkable reinterpretation of one of science's most deeply embedded presuppositions, the firm belief in the balance of nature. For well over a century one of the most pervasive and persistent scientific worldviews presupposed nature to be in near-perfect balance, a balance virtually impervious to internal and external disturbances—and certainly impervious to the actions of members of the puny hominid species we call *humans*. For example, the gases that envelop the planet, warm its surface, and protect it from harmful radiation were generally in balance in between occasional excursions from one equilibrium to another—thereby exercising a moderating influence that makes life possible on Earth (but not on Earth's closest neighbors, Mars and Venus).

Human disturbances to that balance were axiomatically dismissed in the past as perturbations that were local in scope and transitory in time. Humans had no measurable impacts on the larger dynamics or their balance. In this worldview, time's cycles could be read in the continuous balance of nature. Time's arrow could be read as transitory and circumscribed in its disturbances, not only insignificant in the larger picture of the natural world, but also clear evidence that the natural balance always prevailed (Weart 2003). In a sense, the cycles were epicycles in the grand design and neither the cycles nor the arrow were susceptible to human influence in any consequential way.

This deeply held presupposition about the balance of nature provides an engaging backdrop for understanding GEC. With that backdrop one can view the scientific focus on GEC as a scientific mind shift, as a fundamental change in the overarching conceptualization of nature, as a replacement of a dominant worldview with an entirely different one.

GEC, by replacing the worldview presupposing natural balance, underscores the recognition of disturbances to nature's balance on a global scale. Growing evidence shows that global physical cycles may no longer be in the balance that has characterized them for the last dozen or so millennia. The global CHANS—that is, the global hydrological, carbon, climatic, and oceanographic cycles—are no longer seen as forces in equilibrium but as systems disturbed by the overreaching of the human species. Are such disturbances simply the circumscribed and localized manifestations of time's cycles on a larger scale? Growing evidence suggests the answer to this question is "no." Interestingly, the evidence pointing toward that conclusion comes from a hybridization of the scientific method.

Hybrid Scientific Method: Residual Framing and Inferences

The textbook ideal of scientific investigation that follows iteration between theory development and experimentation to test theory is denied to GEC research. The experimental method remains the gold standard of scientific investigation; however, scientists cannot manipulate the earth in its entirety.[7] Hence, the consistent and convergent indicators showing that the global environment has been markedly altered, especially in recent centuries, provide an exemplary scientific puzzle that raises the question: What is causing these changes? While the question is endemic to science, the approach to answering it is not. It places before us an asymmetrical scientific problem to which we can apply considerable knowledge about changes to the dependent variable (environmental change), but remarkably meager knowledge about the independent variables (specific causes) producing those changes or their causal pathways. While progress has been made over the past two decades in expanding knowledge of both the dependent and independent variables, the gap remains because progress has been uneven.

Physical science research addresses this limitation with an approach that might be called *residual framing* and *inference*, which seeks to identify whether current geochemical and other cycles have deviated significantly from long-term global and geological cycles (presumed "natural patterns"), and examines disruptive physical events such as volcanic activity and changes in solar radiation. This approach then reasons that residual or remaining differences between long-term and current patterns must, therefore, be due to anthropogenic drivers, that is, to human activities. Hence, the physical sciences have identified and are assessing the variety of natural-cycle disruptions and discontinuous environmental changes now occurring at a global level. To the extent these cycle disruptions deviate significantly from past patterns and where they cannot be explained by changes in "natural" processes the disruptions provide prima facie evidence that the chain of causal links leads back to human activities—to proximate anthropogenic drivers, to human activities as the fundamental causes of environmental change at a global level. For example, climate modelers—literally using some of the most powerful computers in the world—are determining how much of the current changes in the global climate are attributable to dynamic natural processes and how much, through a process of inference from the residual framing approach, is attributable to anthropogenic sources.

This inferential chain of reasoning has led to an epistemic agreement among scientists that proximate anthropogenic drivers now either match or surpass natural processes as the causal agents of environmental changes across the planet. Humans appear to be disrupting global ecological cycles in unprecedented ways. What are the human domains and dynamics that are disrupting the replenishing cycles of nature? How do these dynamics operate at a global level? The extensive record of human history offers one tool for addressing these questions.

Archaeological Science: Nothing New?

Humans, even our protohuman predecessors, have transformed the global environment since the beginnings of historical time.[8] Ecological transformations across the planet have occurred in the past—and many times. Hence, at first blush the current dynamic of ecological change due to human activity appears to be, literally, nothing new under the sun—or the other stars, or the planets, or the moon.

The question that naturally follows is: Are contemporary environmental dynamics merely an extension of past challenges? Or are they uniquely more challenging, and if uniquely more challenging, do the lessons of those bygone eras and the scientific tools at our disposal make us better prepared to avoid the repeated ecological disasters of the past? Does the available scientific evidence sustain the initial observation that humans have disrupted the global environment in unprecedented ways?

Human impacts on ecosystems are a clearly documented feature of prehistory.[9] For example, Central and South American rain forests show evidence of human habitation as far back as ten thousand to twelve thousand years ago (Rice 1996).[10] And evidence of disturbances to these rain forests appears in Panama as early as eleven thousand years ago and in Amazonia by eight thousand years ago (Roosevelt et al. 1996).

History provides additional supporting evidence. Ice core samples from Greenland, at summit elevations of 3,200 meters above sea level, have revealed the presence of serious air pollution in the ancient world due to lead emissions. Lead production, owing to improvements in technology, became common around 3000 BC and then increased dramatically as a byproduct from the making of silver coins in Greek and Roman times, reaching eighty thousand metric tons per year about two thousand years ago (Hong et al. 1994).[11] The plumes of lead emissions were apparently carried thousands of miles across Europe and into the Atlantic by circulation in the middle troposphere. Similarly, core samples of copper concentrations, first produced from native copper seven thousand years ago, show heightened elevations of pollution from Roman and medieval times, especially in Europe and China (Hong et al. 1996). Hence, long-distance transport of air pollutants, a major issue in the early twentieth century, is in fact a problem that is seven millennia old.

Perhaps the most dramatic and certainly most ironic historical example of ecological collapse comes from the Fertile Crescent. This disaster was dramatic because it occurred in a region of such favorable climatic and biotic conditions (e.g., the crescent was once replete with forests) that it was not only the site of the origins of agriculture, but also of civilization itself. The collapse was ironic because the term *Fertile Crescent* is still used to identify that region, when in fact its fertility has long been lost to history.

Accompanying the ecological collapse of the Fertile Crescent was the collapse of the region's world cultural leadership as well as its millennia-long lead over Europe in social organization and cultural sophistication.

Why then did the Fertile Crescent [currently the Mesopotamian marshlands in Southern Iraq and extending into Iran, Syria, and Turkey]...lose [its] enormous lead of thousands of years to late-starting Europe? The major factor behind these shifts becomes obvious as soon as one compares the modern Fertile Crescent with ancient descriptions of it. Today, the expression "Fertile Crescent" and "world leader in food production" are absurd. Large areas of the former Fertile Crescent are now desert, semidesert, steppe, or heavily eroded or salinized terrain unsuited for agriculture.[12]...[The] Fertile Crescent and eastern Mediterranean societies had the misfortune to arise in an ecologically fragile environment. They committed *ecological suicide* by destroying their own resource base. (Diamond 1997, 410–411; emphasis added)

Hence, human history repeatedly has seen periods when ecological conditions presaged the coming and going of particular civilizations. But it has witnessed no era where the human species (*Homo sapiens sapiens*) was threatened in toto, where the human race itself was threatened with extinction due to a global overexploitation of ecological resources.

The pattern of ecological collapse has repeated itself many times in the prehistoric and historic past. Archaeologist Charles Redman, from his examination of a variety of archaeological case studies[13] around the globe, summarizes the fundamental causal process of these collapses: "This seemingly self-destruction [of environments] occurs repeatedly— individuals, groups, and entire societies make decisions that are initially productive and logical, but over time have negative and sometimes disastrous environmental implications" (1999, 13–14).

This record of past disasters is, nevertheless, partly counterbalanced by past success stories where societies managed to address environmental challenges and exist for lengthy periods of time. And societal successes can be found across diverse environments from ninth-century New Guinea, to sixteenth-century Germany, to seventeenth-century Shogun Japan (Costanza, Graumlich, and Steffen 2007; Diamond 2005).

Can contemporary societies take ecological lessons from past societies—from those that failed as well as those that succeeded? Are modern societies little more than a "fast-forward" of ancient societies? If so, is it the successful societies they emulate in an accelerated mode? Or are they emulating collapsed societies? Are modern societies, by using nature's capital faster than it can be replenished, exceeding their carrying capacities, placing them on the road to "overshoot" carrying capacity and perhaps even to ecological disaster? If such disasters are a feature of the global future will they occur everywhere and at the same pace?

Smooth Transition or Sharp Break?

A key aspect in the answers to these questions lies in one defining distinction between human systems and those of all other species. Humans are more effective than other species as ecosystem shapers than as ecosystem adaptors. Hence, they have ultimately modified their environments more than have any other of the planet's creatures. The modern era, on the one hand, doubtlessly represents an extension of the evolutionary process of cyclical adaptation. On the other hand, it may mark an unequivocal break with the past—a passing of history into a *new ecological era*. The dynamics of contemporary CHANS, highlighting humans as ecosystem shapers and ecosystem adaptors, reilluminates the central question of GEC: *to what extent has time's arrow so penetrated time's cycles that the dynamics of both are threatened, thereby threatening the sustainability of the biosphere for contemporary societies?*

A New Era, a New Identity?

The marked global increase in key environmental consequences has, for a number of careful observers, signaled a sharp break with the past. This, in turn, has led some distinguished scholars to give special designations to the human species and to this new ecological era. Each designation is driven by the observation that global environmental changes threaten the carrying capacity of the planet, meaning, the number of people Earth can support.[14] Distinguished sociologist and human ecologist William Catton (1980) was one of the first to warn of this break. Wishing to highlight the magnitude of human threats to global carrying capacity, Catton (1987) designated humankind as *Homo colossus* whose diverse and excessive appetites make it the world's most "polymorphous species." And it is this specie's voraciousness that portends the overshooting of the global ecological system.[15]

Similarly, Nobel Laureate Paul Crutzen[16] and ecologist Eugene Stoermer (Crutzen and Stoermer 2000) have redefined the term *Anthropocene* to describe the period that began roughly at the time James Watt perfected the steam engine in the latter part of the eighteenth century and continues today.[17] The refinement by Crutzen and Stoermer emphasizes the impacts on the environment of industrialization and modernization. This telescoping of the modern era, this alignment with the age of modernity, underscores the astounding increase in the pace of anthropogenic exploitation of the earth's resources over the past three centuries.

Global Processes: AGE Drives GEC

Three fundamental, large, pervasive processes are driving GEC: autocatalysis (A), globalization (G), and the interconnectedness of ecosystems (E), of CHANS, around the globe—AGE for short.

Autocatalysis

Historical precedent offers at least one conceptual tool for understanding the predicament of modern societies: autocatalysis. From the beginning of human history, many of the fundamental changes impacting the environment have followed an "autocatalytic process—one that catalyzes itself in a positive feedback cycle, going faster and faster once it has started" (Diamond 1997, 111). For example, in ancient civilizations intensified food production, the development of occupational specializations, and the emergence of societal complexity stimulated each other through this autocatalytic process. Large populations, specialized and better organized, could further intensify food production and exploit other resources leading to even larger populations, new specializations, and new forms of resource exploitation.

This historical process not only extends into the modern age, it is a principal cause of GEC. Ecologically, autocatalysis is a dynamic process of accelerated, cumulative ecological impacts. The unavoidable and sobering fact is that such a process cannot continue indefinitely. Yet modern societies, by accelerating the pace of autocatalysis (through the five social variables, or driving forces, noted earlier), are de facto ignoring this reality and producing a considerable threat to their sustainability.

Globalization

The world is undergoing one of the most profound social and political changes ever to have occurred: globalization.[18] The term *globalization*, the worldwide spread of communication and commerce, of interpenetrating networks of production processes, risks, and ecosystems, and the emergence of new international challenges and regimes attracts a variety of definitions. Among these, Held and colleagues provide a characteristic and insightful one describing globalization as the "widening, deepening, and speeding up of worldwide interconnectedness in all aspects of contemporary social life" (1999, 2). While the idea of globalization is grounded in economic, social, and political processes, its main features—widening, deepening and speeding up—mean the increased spread, scale, and pace of global ecological processes. Globalization also means, as previously noted, the interpenetration of CHANS near and far, resulting in a mega-CHANS. In short, globalization underscores basic transformations on a global scale manifest in the speed of transactions, their extensive and broad reach, and the deepening patterns of their ecological interconnectedness.

A Global CHANS

Ecological interconnectedness, the third process of GEC, comprises ecological connections and interdependencies on a global scale. Ostensible features of this process are the worldwide extraction and distribution of nature's capital, the use of nature's services over broad reaches, as well as the worldwide distribution of labor. One consequence of globally linked CHANS is that ecological problems in one part of the world have the potential to affect many other parts. One publicized example of the ecological consequences in one part of the world due to resource demand in another part is the so-called *hamburger connection*. It is claimed that nearly 40 percent of the forest cover in Central America has been destroyed to make room for the pasture needed to raise beef cattle for North America's fast-food industry (Myers 1981).

Global Dynamics: Outcomes of AGE

The three AGE processes have led to the ecological outcomes that define GEC. In particular, autocatalysis, globalization, and ecological interconnectedness have, as noted, led to an accelerated *pace* of the global ecological metabolism, an increased *scale* of ecological impact, and the global *spread* of impacts, or PaSS for short. Combined with AGE, the acronym becomes the PaSSAGE described earlier.

The pace of ecological metabolism refers to the acceleration in the rate of demand on nature's capital and services and to the marked rate of increase in human-generated environmental impact, referred to as "the Great Acceleration" (Hibbard et al. 2007). The historical pace of evolutionary processes is being superseded even in the most remote parts of the globe by a dynamic comprising systems of rapidly changing variables that may be approaching thresholds where the magnitude of their effects shift, all driven by human action that continues to accelerate with ever more profound effects.

Scale refers to demonstrable, often dramatic increases in the magnitude of the drivers of ecological impacts or in the impacts themselves. Corresponding to the systemic domain of GEC, as described previously, they are processes that occur on large spatial scales or alter the function of large systems.

The term *spread* refers to growth in the size of the distributional demands for nature's capital and services and to the growth in the distribution of environmental impacts, such as the global transfer of environmental degradation or diseases. Corresponding to the cumulative-effects domain of GEC, similarly described, many activities are already global in spread.

PaSSAGE

There is little question that the processes driving GEC (AGE: auto-catalysis, globalization, and ecological interdependency), its overall dynamic, and each element of outcome (PaSS: pace, scale, and spread) sets today's global ecological challenges apart from all past challenges. The pace of past environmental change—time's arrow—was glacial and the scale and spread of ecosystem impacts—time's cycles—were local or regional in scope. In the past few centuries how things have changed.[19]

It is important to underscore a crucial point that may be obvious, but whose importance cannot be diminished with overstatement. Neither GEC's elements of autocatalysis, globalization, and ecological inter-dependency nor their global outcomes of pace, scale, and spread are entirely independent of one another. Nor do either the elements or the outcomes always follow patterns of linear, temporal influence. Rather, many interpenetrate in dynamic and synergistic ways, some of which impact sustainability positively, others negatively.

Our outline of the conceptual and definitional features of GEC pace, scale, and spread provide the abstractness and generalization necessary to illuminate the discussion of anthropogenic drivers. But understanding their operation and effectiveness requires concrete examples for each GEC outcome.

Pace

Three quantitative indicators reaffirming the accelerated pace of eco-logical change are the rates of atmospheric CO_2 concentration (currently 35 percent above that in 1750, the beginning of the industrial age) and climate change, the rapid increase in the human population, and the rate of species extinction.[20] While these three indicators paint a far from complete picture of the accelerated pace of change, their availability and quantification provide an exemplary sketch.

CO_2 Concentrations   No one doubts the importance of climatic condi-tions in shaping the possibilities of what humans could and did do on earth (Rosa and Dietz 1998). The various ice ages are a blunt testament to those connections. So, too, are the ecological adaptations of native cultures around the globe. For the vast expanse of human history, over thousands of years, the concentrations of several trace gases critical to shaping the earth's climate—carbon dioxide (CO_2), methane (CH_4), and nitrogen oxides (NOx)—have remained fairly stable.

Then, beginning in the late eighteenth century,[21] atmospheric concentrations of these gases began to increase rapidly, reaching today's 35-percent-larger concentration. The coincidence of gas concentrations and the rapid expansion of industrial activities—dependent, as they were, on unprecedented amounts of fossil fuels—provide the obvious and widely accepted hypothesis that human activities had, for the first time, disturbed the approximate equilibrium of the earth's basic cycles. Time's arrow, due to the entropic increases from the burning of fossil fuels, impacted the slow cycle of fossil fuel creation and accumulation. Perhaps this well-documented spike upward in the concentrations of greenhouse gases is the most apparent indicator of the vast spread of environmental impact, the globalization of threats to CHANS.

Climate Change   The accelerated pace of cumulating CO_2, the principal greenhouse gas, may be partly revealed in the most recent estimates of global climate change. The trend in global temperature over the past eighteen thousand years is estimated to be an increase of about 5°C (9°F)[22]—with estimates of a much greater warming, perhaps 10°C, 20°C, or 30°C at higher altitudes. The twentieth century alone accounts for a land-area warming of 0.74 ± 0.18 degrees Celsius (IPCC 2007). Thus, while it took eighteen millennia to produce the 5°C warming, a sizable proportion of it came in the last century alone. Since the beginning of the industrial era, emissions have accounted for five times the change in climate due to solar variation (IPCC 2007). Projections suggest that future warming from greenhouse gases may occur at an even faster pace. For example, it is expected that the climate will warm by an average of 3°C (between 1.7°C and 4.0°C) by the end of this century. The pace of warming trends is as worrisome as their magnitude, since a quickened pace produces effects that are less predictable and more pronounced and for which adaptation is constrained.

Population Growth   As of this writing, there are 6.8 billion people on Earth (United Nations 2005). It took many millennia, until around 1810, for the world population to reach one billion persons. It then took only just over a century to add another billion to the total, only three and a half decades to add a third billion, only a decade and a half to add a fourth, a mere thirteen years to add a fifth, and then twelve years to add the sixth billion in 2000 (the shortest amount of time to add a billion in human history). It is anticipated that world population will reach seven billion by about 2015, taking fifteen years to add the most recent billion, indicative of a gradual reduction in the pace of growth. Nonetheless, population is expected to continue to grow, reaching between eight and eleven billion by 2050. For the vast majority of human history, the world population grew relatively slowly. In the modern era it grew exponentially. Indeed, the world added an astounding 4.4 billion persons in the twentieth century alone.

UN projections, based upon a median fertility scenario, expect that world population will stabilize sometime after 2200 at ten billion persons—a more than 50 percent increase over the current population size. Hence, while the human population is expected to grow in the twenty-first century at a considerably slower pace than it did in the twentieth, the total number of people placing demands on environmental capital and services will be of unprecedented scale and, consequently, will present an unprecedented assault on global ecosystems.

While the growth rate of the human population is slowing and expected to stabilize, the declining size of households and the subsequent growth in their number continues at a rapid pace (Liu et al. 2003). The increase in households typically manifests itself in urban sprawl (a serious threat to biodiversity conservation) and places increased demands on infrastructure needs. The decline in the size of households also represents a significant increase in the consumption of resources. Along with the scale of the global population, these trends raise the question of whether there will be sufficient resources to satisfy the growing demands they embed.

Species Extinction   The vast majority of species that have ever walked the earth are extinct. The bulk of these extinctions, however, are due to either astronomical or terrestrial cataclysms in geological history or to slow rates of extinction through evolutionary processes. In modern times the rates of extinction are extraordinarily faster, for some species groups one thousand to ten thousand times the evolutionary rate of extinction that existed prior to the appearance of the human species. It is estimated that as many as 137 species disappear each day, amounting to over fifty thousand species each year (Raven and McNeely 1998; Dowdeswell and Heywood 1995; Wilson 1992).

These dramatic rates of species extinction are a serious challenge to ecological sustainability because they represent disturbing assaults to symbiotic relationships among species and to complex species interdependencies, including the dependence of CHANS on the many ecosystem goods and services provided or enhanced by plant and animal species. Indeed, species extinction may be the most ostensible evidence of time's arrow disrupting time's cycles. And the primary cause of this accelerated pace is clear—habitat destruction by expanded land use, by the introduction of exotic species into ecosystems, by overexploitation of some species for commercial purposes, and, in some places, by pollution. In the future, it is expected that climate change will also be a major contributor.

Much of this change has occurred over the last half century. As the UN's recent Millennium Ecosystem Assessment (see table 1.1) puts it:

The structure and functioning of the world's ecosystems changed more rapidly in the second half of the twentieth century than at any time in human history. More land was converted to cropland in the 30 years since 1950 than in the 150 years between 1700 and 1850. Cultivated systems (areas where at least 30 percent of the landscape is in croplands, shifting cultivation, confined livestock production, or freshwater aquaculture) now cover one quarter of earth's terrestrial surface. (UNEP 2005a, 2)[23]

Scale

What about scale consequences? In pioneering research, Vitousek and colleagues (1997) carefully estimated the scale of ecosystem impacts around the globe by examining the dominant influence of human actions in producing those impacts. As for the accuracy of their estimates of scale, the authors write: "The numbers have large uncertainties, but the fact that they are large is not at all uncertain" (1997, 495). Figure 1.1 summarizes their findings.

Land Use   Land use and its transformations represent the single most influential human impact worldwide and is the primary driving force in the loss of biodiversity. Between one-third and one-half of the global land surface has been altered by humans. Other key transformations include the growing percentage of fully exploited marine fisheries (including the 22 percent of fisheries already overexploited or depleted), the 35 percent increase in CO_2 concentrations compared to the preindustrial era, and the use of more than half of all accessible surface fresh water.

Table 1.1

Comparative table of systems as reported by the millennium ecosystem assessment (C.SDM)

Note that the boundaries of these systems often overlap. Statistics for different systems can therefore be compared but cannot be totaled across systems, as this would result in partial double-counting.

System and subsystem	Area[a] (million sq. km.)	Share of terrestrial surface of Earth (percent)	Population Density (people per sq. km.) Urban	Population Density (people per sq. km.) Rural	Growth rate (percent 1990–2000)	GDP per capita (dollars)	Infant mortality rate[b] (deaths per 1,000 live births)	Mean NPP (kg. carbon per sq. meter per year)	Share of system covered by PAs[c] (percent)	Share of area transformed[d] (percent)
Marine	349.3	68.6[e]	–	–	–	–	–	0.15	0.3	–
Coastal	17.2	4.1	1.105	70	15.9	8.960	41.5	–	7	–
Terrestrial	6.0	4.1	1.105	70	15.9	8.960	41.5	0.52	4	11
Marine	11.2	2.2[e]	–	–	–	–	41.5	0.14	9	–
Inland water[f]	10.3	7.0	817	26	17.0	7,300	57.6	0.36	12	11
Forest/ woodland	41.9	28.4	472	18	13.5	9,580	57.7	0.68	10	42
Tropical/ subtropical	23.3	15.8	565	14	17.0	6,854	58.3	0.95	11	34
Temperate	6.2	4.2	320	7	4.4	17,109	12.5	0.45	16	67
Boreal	12.4	8.4	114	0.1	-3.7	13,142	16.5	0.29	4	25
Dryland	59.9	40.6	750	20	18.5	4,930	66.6	0.26	7	18
Hyperarid	9.6	6.5	1,061	1	26.2	5,930	41.3	0.01	11	1
Arid	15.3	10.4	568	3	28.1	4,680	74.2	0.12	6	5
Semiarid	22.3	15.3	643	10	20.6	5,580	72.4	0.34	6	25
Dry subhumid	12.7	8.6	711	25	13.6	4,270	60.7	0.49	7	35
Island	7.1	4.8	1,020	37	12.3	11,570	30.4	0.54	17	17
Island states	4.7	3.2	918	14	12.5	11,148	30.6	0.45	18	21

Mountain	35.8	24.3	63	3	16.3	6,470	57.9	0.42	14	12
300–1,000 m	13.0	8.8	58	3	12.7	7,815	48.2	0.47	11	13
1,000–2,500 m	11.3	7.7	69	3	20.0	5,080	67.0	0.45	14	13
2,500–4,500 m	9.6	6.5	90	2	24.2	4,144	65.0	0.28	18	6
>4,500 m	1.8	1.2	104	0	25.3	3,663	39.4	0.06	22	0.3
Polar	23.0	15.6	161[g]	0.06[g]	-6.5	15,401	12.8	0.06	42[g]	0.3[g]
Cultivated	35.3	23.9	786	70	14.1	6,810	54.3	0.52	6	47
Pasture	0.1	0.1	419	10	28.8	15,790	32.8	0.64	4	11
Cropland	8.3	5.7	1,014	118	15.6	4,430	55.3	0.49	4	62
Mixed (crop and other)	26.9	18.2	575	22	11.8	11,060	46.5	0.6	6	43
Urban	3.6	2.4	681	–	12.7	12,057	36.5	0.47	0	100
GLOBAL	510	–	681	13	16.7	7,309	57.4	–	4	38

Source: UNEP 2005a, 31.

a. Area estimates based on GLC2000 dataset for the year 2000 except for cultivated systems where area is based on GLCCD v2 dataset for the years 1992–1993 (C26 Box1).

b. Deaths of children less than one year old per 1,000 live births.

c. Includes only natural protected areas in IUCN categories I to VI.

d. For all systems except forest/woodland, area transformed is calculated from land depicted as cultivated or urban areas by GLC2000 land cover data set. The area transformed for forest/woodland systems is calculated as the percentage change in area between potential vegetation (forest biomes of the WWF ecoregions) and current forest/woodland areas in GLC2000. Note: 22 percent of the forest/woodland system falls outside forest biomes and is therefore not included in this analysis.

e. Percent of total surface of Earth.

f. Population density, growth rate, GDP per capita, and growth rate for the inland water system have been calculated with an area buffer of 10 kilometers.

g. Excluding Antarctica.

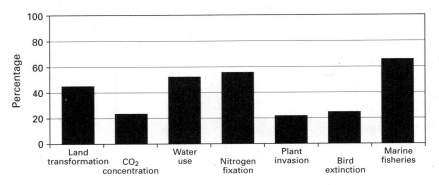

Figure 1.1
Human dominance or alteration of several major components of the Earth system, expressed as (from left to right) percentage of the land surface transformed; percentage of the current atmospheric CO^2 concentration that results from human action; percentage of accessible surface freshwater used; percentage of terrestrial nitrogen fixation that is human-caused; percentage of plant species in Canada that humanity has introduced from elsewhere; percentage of bird species on Earth that have become extinct in the past two millennia, almost all of them as a consequence of human activity; and percentage of major marine fisheries that are fully exploited, overexploited, or depleted.
Source: Vitousak et al. 1997, 495, reproduced with permission.

Other examples abound. Since 1700, the actions of humans have converted 19 percent of the world's forests and woodlands to cropland and pasture, resulting in a sizable redistribution of land uses across the globe (Richards 1990). This recent historical shift alone triggered not only changes in land uses, but also changes in biogeochemical cycles including hydrological cycles as well as in ecosystems—in short, changes in the earth system itself.

Spread

Energy Consumption   Three centuries ago nations in the West started an industrial revolution that continues to spread around the globe. The fundamental practice launching the revolution was the shift in reliance from direct use of solar energy, burning of wood hydrocarbons, and direct use of photosynthetic energy fixation to a reliance on fossil hydrocarbons. In essence, the industrial revolution was a revolution in the use of fossil fuels that created a deep dependence on that form of energy— a dependence that remains unabated. The global use of fuel hydrocarbons "has increased nearly 800-fold since 1750 and about 12-fold in the twentieth century" alone (Hall et al. 2003, 318). And the use of fossil fuels has spread everywhere. The leading form of fossil fuel, oil, is consumed by literally every nation (nearly two hundred in total) around the globe (Hall et al. 2003) and in nearly every nation, demand for fossil fuels is growing, quite rapidly in many cases.

The continued high levels of fossil fuel consumption and increased global demand threaten nature's capital in a variety of significant ways. Consumption reduces the availability of this resource for future generations (by how much is a hotly debated issue), markedly contributes to global climate change, and is responsible for smog and particulates as well as toxic substances that are harmful to health.

Deforestation   One of the most obvious spreads of ecological impact around the globe is the loss of forest cover. Deforestation, once virtually concentrated in the temperate zones, has now reached all climatic zones, especially the South—which contains 77 percent of the New World's tropical forests (Rudel 1989). Globally, the 3.4 billion hectares (a hectare equals approximately 2.41 acres) of forestland that existed in 1980 had declined by 5 percent to 3.2 billion hectares just fifteen years later (FAO 1997).

The spread of deforesting practices is especially pronounced in the tropics where, for example, the amount of deforested land increased from 7.5 million hectares per year in 1979 to 13.2 million hectares in 1991, an increase of over 75 percent or an annual increase of 4.5 percent per year (Bawa and Dayanandan 1997). Worldwide, tropical forests are being lost at a rate of 14 to 16 million hectares per year. Examples of the most rapid spread of tropical deforestation include Brazil, where the Amazon region alone contains 40 percent of the world's remaining tropical rain forest. Over the last twenty-five years, Brazil has lost forest cover equivalent to the size of Germany (Mertens et al. 2002).

Closed-canopy forests (unbroken forests consisting of virgin, old-growth, and naturally regenerated woodlands) are especially valuable in countering soil erosion, desertification, and the impacts of climate change. The remaining closed-canopy forests are concentrated in only fifteen countries, nearly all in the South, making them especially vulnerable to population and development pressures (UNEP 2001).

To deforestation can be added the spread of other impacts: desertification (the conversion of arable land into desert-like conditions), soil erosion (the decline in the fertility, depth, and structure of arable land),

and salinization (where water tables rise close to the surface, water evaporates, leaving a salty residue in the soil; cf. Harrison 1993).

Urban Sprawl   One of the key factors that accounts for the spread of deforested areas—as well as species loss, other forms of land degradation, and the destruction of coastal zones—is another form of spread: urban sprawl (Ewing et al. 2005).[24] The growing concentration of the human population into urban areas accompanied by the rise of megacities (cities with populations over ten million) is a long-standing, persistent demographic trajectory that is expected to continue indefinitely (United Nations 2004). Three and a half billion people now live in urban areas, over one-half of the entire human population as of mid-2007 (Wimberley and Kulikowski 2007), and will increase to over two-thirds of the population by 2030. The continued expansion of urban housing and infrastructure into open areas comes at the expense not only of their material requirements, but also of other forms of natural capital, including forest cover, and the species that are dependent upon them.

Chemicals Everywhere   Remarkably enough, as noted, traces of lead and copper were discovered in Greenland that could be tracked to the golden ages of Greece and Rome and to the Northern Sung dynasty of China (tenth to twelfth century). In modern times, the problem of chemical pollution in this remote place not only persists but also is markedly worse. Body burdens (measurable amounts of chemicals in the body) of two hundred hazardous compounds have been found among the ninety thousand Inuit natives who occupy Eastern Canada and Greenland. These compounds are implicated in birth defects, lowered intelligence, and a wide variety of other health problems. Samples of the breast milk of mothers reveal PCBs (Polychlorinated biphenyls) and levels of mercury twenty to fifty times higher than levels found in the urban areas of the United States. Furthermore, the flame-retardant chemical PBDEs (Polybrominated diphenyl ethers) have been found in Inuit blood (Courtney et al. 2000).

Other evidence also indicates that chemicals have spread far and wide. A number of modern chemical marvels, taken for granted by countless users around the globe, were developed from several types of perfluoronated compounds, such as perfluorooctane sulfate (PFOS) and perfluorooctanoic acid (PFOA). Known by such brand names as Teflon, Scotchgard,[25] Stainmaster, and Gore-Tex, these chemicals have been detected around the globe—literally. They have been found in polar bears roaming the Arctic Circle, in dolphins swimming in the Mediterranean Sea off the coast of Italy, and in gulls flying above Tokyo. Furthermore, they have been detected in the Great Lakes, the source of drinking water for nearly forty million U.S. residents. Perfluoronated compounds have been linked to cancer, development problems, liver damage, and other health problems in a number of animal studies as well as studies showing more direct implications in the health of humans (cf. Alexander et al. 2003; Butenhoff et al. 2002; Ciriolo et al. 1982; Kliewer, Lehmann, and Wilson 1999; Kroll et al. 2000).

The Spread of Germs   One of the subtler, but potentially more devastating consequences of GEC is its impacts on human well-being. Climate change, for example, is very likely to increase the incidence and the spread of disease. Throughout history "diseases have been the biggest killers of people, [and therefore] have also been decisive shapers of history" (Diamond 1997, 197).

Recent history recapitulates—in fast-forward time—this recurrent feature of all of human history. There is clear evidence that the increased warmth and dryness of a recent ENSO (El Niño Southern Oscillation) season led to vegetation growth that sustains desert rodents. This prompted not only a growth in the rodent populations, carriers of the Hantavirus, but also a spread of rodents into human habitats. The net effect was an outbreak of an acute respiratory disease with a high death rate (the Hantavirus Pulmonary Syndrome) among humans (CCSP 2003). It is reasonable to suspect parallel processes with global warming. For example, a receding of permafrost and snowcaps will likely expand the area of mosquito breeding, which will result in the spread of mosquito-borne diseases including malaria, dengue fever, yellow fever, as well as viruses (various types of encephalitis, West Nile virus, and others).

The fast-forward of modern disease, exhibiting all the features of PaSSAGE, shows itself in the rate and consequences of disease spread: the pace of transmission is much faster, the numbers of those exposed is much greater (a vast increase in scale), and due to the variety and ease of international travel the expanse of exposure is much higher (a vast increase in spread). There is a very real potential for climate change to cause ecological changes that can be costly not only to human health, but also to human wealth and quality of life. Extreme events can have ripple effects that disrupt economies, communities, agricultural production, trade, tourism, and even the social fabric itself.

A variety of ostensible global impacts is traceable to the processes of GEC, a combination of pace, scale, and spread. What are the drivers of those processes?

Humans as Shapers of Environment and History

Jared Diamond summarizes his influential examination of the entire history of the human species succinctly: "Environment molds history" (1997, 352). Few would disagree. But to complete the causal chain, we need to add that "humans mold environments." And the residual framing approach of scientific evidence has clearly demonstrated that CHANS and the global environment are being molded in unprecedented ways.

CHANS are Janus-like. They are reciprocal, feedback systems where, on the one hand, human practices and institutions determine the availability of natural capital and services to sustain human populations. But on the other hand, the resulting changed ecosystems determine the range of options and institutions available to humankind. CHANS are dynamic, serving as both the medium and outcome of human actions—planned and unplanned. Put more succinctly, humans shape the natural ecosystems that support life but are also, in turn, shaped by those ecosystems.

Proximate Anthropogenic Drivers

The National Research Council/National Academy of Sciences report GEC92 (Stern, Young, and Druckman 1992) summarized the epistemic agreement over the probable proximate anthropogenic (or human) drivers of GEC. That scientific consensus has provided the useful checklist of factors that guided the selection of chapters in this volume: population, affluence and consumption (especially of energy and materials), technological change, changes in land cover and land use, institutional actions and responses, and culture. Recurrently, population dynamics and environmentally significant consumption, combined with direct modifications of natural systems, account for the vast majority of effects on the global environment that are traceable to human activities (Dietz, Rosa, and York 2007; Rosa, York, and Dietz 2004; York, Rosa, and Dietz 2003a, 2003b). What follows is a sketch of the dynamics of these dominating forces driving GEC: population, consumption, and technological efficiency.

Population   Human population—all its dynamics—is one of the most direct and enduring forces behind land use change, energy use, and basic levels of consumption—placing increased demands on living space, food production, water use, and the flora and fauna of the planet. It has been so since the early beginnings of the human species. Archaeologist Charles Redman observed that, "in every case study," in his book of the human impacts on ancient environments, "the growing number of people is a factor creating an imbalance between society and the environment" (1999, 164).

Consumption   There is little doubt (Dietz, Rosa, and York 2007; Rosa, York, and Dietz 2004; York, Rosa, and Dietz 2003a) that consumption is a key driver of environmental degradation, and that the patterns of consumption represent a sword that cuts in two directions. On the one hand, the economic fruits of modernity mean that a growing share of the world's population can look forward to material and social comforts that have historically eluded them. And improvements in sanitation, health, and education—indicators of virtually all definitions of social progress—mean that a larger share of the world's population enjoys a quality of life unreachable only a generation ago.

On the other hand, these improvements come with an environmental cost. In the short run, reductions in mortality lead to increased population growth, the key driver of impacts. Over the longer term, improvements in health, education, and opportunities fuel demographic transitions that result in slowdowns in population growth. But the increase in longevity is ineluctably an increase in the number of years individuals continue to consume—adding further to aggregate consumption, despite the decline in the rate of consumption growth as a population moves toward stabilization.

During the modern era the industrial nations were the primary benefactors of increased consumption and were the primary producers of many environmental impacts. In this era of high modernization, other nations, such as China and India, are experiencing rapid economic growth, catapulting them abruptly into the high-consumption club. As we already noted, the pace of population growth is slowing, meaning that it will eventually peak. Nevertheless, the level of that peak will reach heights unknown to history. The slowed rate of population growth could ultimately mean reduced stress to the environment. However, such reduction could be counterbalanced or, worse, trumped by the rapid growth in consumption associated with the emergence of a global middle class (Myers and Kent 2003). Perhaps there is no better example of this than China.

China   While having reduced its rate of population growth dramatically, China continues to be the most populous nation on earth.[26] It also has one of the fastest growing economies. As a result, more and more of the 1.3 billion Chinese can afford to purchase a wider array of goods. In 2003, China consumed one-half of the world's cement production, one-third of its steel, nearly one-fourth of its copper, and nearly one-fifth of its aluminum. Traditionally a large exporter of coal, China is now consuming almost all of its production while simultaneously becoming the second-largest importer of oil after the United States (Goodman 2004). And China, the fastest-growing car market in the world with purchases of 4.4 million vehicles in 2002, has replaced Germany as the third largest automobile market in the world, ranking only behind the United States and Japan (Eisenstein 2004).

What is perhaps most troubling about China's new wealth is that its rapid growth in consumption may be the harbinger of what could follow among the other poorer countries of the world (e.g., India) that are now experiencing increased economic prosperity. Indeed, the Chinese may be the paradigmatic example of what Myers and Kent (2004) refer to as "the new consumers," the rising tide of people around the world with growing incomes to satisfy their pent-up demand for goods. While there are many uncertainties over the magnitude of stress this sort of rising consumption will place on ecosystems, that there will be significant stress is entirely certain.

Technological Efficiency   As economies mature, their structures undergo transformation. A number of observers (Mol and Sonnenfeld 2000; Grossman and Kruger 1995; Graedel and Allenby 1995) believe that changes in the structure of advanced economies will result in reduced impacts to the environment. One of the features of the most advanced economies is a decline in the extractive and manufacturing sectors, whose dominance is replaced by a rapidly growing service sector. Owing to this shift, some observers anticipate a demonstrable decline in the environmental impacts of mature economies despite continued economic growth.

Electronic Age   That expectation is challenged on several grounds. One such challenge comes from the growth in the personal computer market. The most significant technological change enabling and supporting a service economy is the personal computer, whose unit sales totaled one billion (nearly one computer for every six people in the world) by the end of 2002 (Kuehr and Williams 2003). But, contrary to expectation, computers seriously impact the environment. The manufacture of each computer requires an astounding amount of energy and materials. One desktop computer and monitor, averaging fifty-three pounds, requires at least ten times its weight in fossil fuels and chemicals, making it more materials intensive than an automobile or refrigerator[27] (Kuehr and Williams 2003).

The materials burden of the desktop computer is magnified by the facts that computers have a short lifespan and that many of the chemicals in their manufacture, such as lead, are toxic. Many of these toxic chemicals pose serious risks not only during their manufacturing stage, but also when they are discarded. And contrary to optimistic predictions of "paperless" offices a few decades ago, personal computers have led to a marked increase in paper consumption (Senior 2007).

The examples reviewed here are merely the pixels of a much larger picture. What are the contours of that picture?

Human Dimensions of GEC: The Big Picture

Human dimensions of GEC are a conceptual framing of global CHANS that produces questions about the role of humans in ecological change on a global scale. As noted, there has been a scientific consensus for over two decades about the probable anthropogenic drivers or human factors that account for global environmental change. Given that long-standing consensus, it becomes appropriate to ask: what is our state of knowledge about the human dimensions of GEC? Over the last decade or so, major international research programs have greatly enhanced our understanding of global CHANS.

For the first time, it is realistic to speak of a science of sustainability that is devoted to "coupled human-environment systems" (Clark 2007) or CHANS, with their dominance by human dimensions. One of the clearest indicators of the institutionalization process was the decision by the U.S. National Academy of Sciences to devote a section of its prestigious journal, *Proceedings of the National Academy of Sciences*, to sustainability science (Clark 2007). Another prestigious scientific society, the American Association for the Advancement of Science, established a resource website on sustainability that highlights research and programs investigating CHANS (http://sustainabilityscience.org).

GEC, the global context of CHANS, has generated formally organized and coordinated research programs, mostly through the International Human Dimensions Programme (http://www.ihdp.org/). Other research programs were the spontaneous convergence of researchers scattered about the globe addressing common intellectual themes. Still other research represents a refocusing of traditional disciplinary interests on GEC topics. In this volume, we offer a carefully selected sample of "state of the science" reviews of these these major research efforts.

The remaining chapters are devoted to some but not all of the consensual themes of GEC's human dimensions: population, consumption, land cover and land use, institutional actions, and culture. The chapters provide a broad, exemplary picture of these themes while also summarizing our cumulative understanding of this complex topic, offering an unprecedented vantage point for understanding CHANS and how they are networked and interrelated globally.

We have not attempted to assemble examples of all types of human dimensions research. Our goal, instead, has been to be simultaneously more modest, by limiting the breadth of coverage, and more ambitious, by bringing the greater depth of well-developed, illustrative works to the attention of the larger scientific and policy audiences. These works exemplify core issues addressed by interdisciplinary research that combines social science and ecology.

The authors in this volume do not always speak exactly the same language, or always share assumptions about the dynamics of the human dimensions of GEC, or hold the same opinions of which methods are most appropriate for understanding global CHANS. But aligning rather than ignoring the disparate approaches is exactly the goal of the volume. GEC work in the physical and biological sciences has been an enterprise of a truly global community, as it must be to study worldwide phenomena. We believe the same is true for the social sciences. To understand the human dimensions of global environmental change requires a framing that brings the various traditions together so that currently disparate approaches can be forged into a common language to ensure an authentic global effort.

In examining approaches to understanding CHANS, we find a strong divide between the Continental and North American research traditions in the social sciences. Rather than ignore this work, or represent only one side of this divide exclusively, as is often done, we include two chapters that combine the two traditions (chapter 6 by McCay and Jentoft and chapter 7 by Kasperson, Kasperson, and Turner) and one exemplar of the Continental tradition (chapter 2 by Beck). Our intentions are to inform readers and begin facilitating communication between traditions that normally do not talk to one another and to promote research that becomes more synthetic and richer than would otherwise be the case.

Galison (1997), a distinguished historian of science, notes that even in as seemingly narrow a field as high-energy physics, researchers from different disciplines or specialties have distinct languages. Hence, they must first develop a "pidgin" language so that they can communicate across specialty areas. The inclusion of a chapter representing the Continental tradition in the social sciences is an initial effort to lay out the parent languages from which such a pidgin can be formed. The remaining chapters tap the consensual themes of research—population; consumption; land cover and use; institutional actions, culture, and consequences—in the human dimensions of GEC as well as methodological issues relevant to understanding these themes. By reading across them one learns not only the state of social science thinking on these issues, but also the conceptual language and alternative approaches being brought to bear on this complex topic. This is a necessary step in the essential task of developing the integrated approaches needed to understand GEC.

Research Traditions and Directions: The Substantive Chapters

Continental social science, not only a dominant perspective in mainland Europe, but also a major force in parts of the United Kingdom and its Commonwealth as well as South America and elsewhere, differs from American social science in its very foundations. The Continental tradition emphasizes the view that humans are neither passive recipients of environmental knowledge and options, nor merely objects to be studied via scientific methods by those interested in human-nature dynamics. Rather, this tradition notes that values, beliefs, norms, attitudes, and stories about the environment are all actively—and in many cases, strategically—constructed. As such they become the focus of investigation, not the "objective" conditions of nature.[28] This view is one of the cornerstones of much of the Continental approach and often a source of tension between the Continental and Anglophone traditions, since it has implications for epistemology especially. An exemplar of the Continental tradition is the theorizing of German sociologist Ulrich Beck in chapter 2.

Risk Worldview

A fundamental characteristic of GEC is the extent to which our understanding of the biosphere and related human influences is fraught with uncertainty. For more than two decades, uncertainty has been understood as a central feature of all environmental issues. A substantial literature has emerged to address uncertainty, reconceptualized as risk. This literature ranges from highly sophisticated toxicology and exposure modeling to sociological studies of risk organizations and psychological studies of how perceptions of uncertainty are shaped and move through society. Perhaps the most provocative and influential line of argument within this growing literature on risk is the idea that risk itself has become a major foundation of twenty-first-century society, displacing to some extent older foundations such as class, social location, fundamental belief systems, or ethnic identity.

In chapter 2, Ulrich Beck, the major architect of this new "risk worldview," recapitulates and extends in new directions his original "risk society" argument (Beck [1986] 1992). He not only distinguishes his theoretical argument from competing continental perspectives (e.g. cultural theory) but, more important, also provides a conceptual lens to focus our understanding of fundamental, reinforcing changes in social structures and human ecosystems. The emergence of PaSS, reflecting the human system part of CHANS, generated a remarkable increase in the magnitude and scale of risks and their spread around the globe. PaSS created a "world risk society" that bifurcates modernity into two distinct phases: in the first phase, modernity comprises all the features characteristic of rational calculus (Jaeger et al. 2001); in the second, modernity comprises risks and vulnerabilities that elude rational calculus. Furthermore, Beck articulates the pervasive socialization of nature and its transformation from an ontological entity into an idealization. Owing to this idealization ecological debates are no longer about nature per se, but about competing cultural and political concepts of nature. It follows, then, that concerns about global environmental change are unavoidably bound up with a panoply of constructed representations of nature, facilitated by the media and political actors. Here Beck explains how global climate change, one of GEC's principal systemic changes, is so bound up.

Population and Consumption

In contrast to the grand sweep of Continental thinking is a research program devoted to understanding the anthropogenic drivers of GEC. An advanced and systematically developed line of research, this program, labeled "STIRPAT," focuses on other primary drivers of human impacts on the environment, especially those of population and consumption (www.stirpat.org). STIRPAT is a CHANS-focused approach devoted to the question of why nation-states and other entities differ in their impact on the environment. With the nation-state as its principal unit of analysis to date, STIRPAT provides a suite of macrofindings that should complement the microfindings from the case studies that now dominate CHANS research (Liu et al. 2007a). STIRPAT research draws on theory in ecology and social science and on methods in the social sciences, where macrocomparative analysis is a long-established tradition. But it also attends to the tradition in the physical and natural sciences of using relatively simple accounting equations to understand the driving forces of global change, and deploys emerging measures of human environmental impact. The resulting research is referred to as Structural Human Ecology (SHE). In chapter 3, Thomas Dietz, Eugene A. Rosa, and Richard York, principal STIRPAT architects, review SHE's approaches and theories and STIRPAT results to date. Their findings are consistent with general arguments that are centuries old, but are much more disciplined and robust, and point to population size and consumption as key factors resulting in environmental impacts.

Land Use and Land Cover

One of the most important and stimulating challenges of the last decade of work on human dimensions of global change is finding ways to integrate questions and methods from the social sciences with those of the physical and biological sciences. A particularly advanced and systematically developed topic in this line of investigation is research on land-use and land-cover change.

Changes in how land is used and resulting changes in landscape cover and ecology are among the most profound of human influences on the earth, and are major drivers of climate change, deforestation, biodiversity losses, and alteration of biogeochemical cycles. So it is not surprising that an international program of research on Land Use Cover and Change (LUCC) was the first of the systematic human dimensions programs to emerge. In chapter 4, Emilio F. Moran reviews the progress in our understanding of land use change over the last decade. He shows that the cumulative literature on the topic underscores how decisions concerning the use of land and other resources are nested in the context of community practices, spatial distributions of populations, state policies, and international forces. He anticipates a considerable refinement in this literature over the next decade with a deeper understanding of the structure of landholding, the influence of tax and insurance regulations, the cost of alternatives for protecting land resources, and effective management practices.

Institutional Structures and Practices

One culmination of the long, repeated historical process of institution building is the nation-state. Except for Antarctica, all inhabitable areas of the globe are defined and ruled by territorially defined states—approximately two hundred in total. Because the nation-state is so pervasive, it is easy to forget that the idea of the nation-state, now the universal, large-scale political form, is of relatively recent origin, a product of modernization. As recently as 1500 AD, only a small fraction (less than 20 percent) of the world's land area was territorially bounded into states.

International Environmental Regimes   That the nation-state is the principal agent of collective decision making leads to one unequivocal challenge of GEC: global impacts to CHANS do not respect national borders. For example, air pollution generated by coal-fired plants in the Midwest of the United States does not stop upon reaching the Canadian border, and nor does air pollution generated in East Asia stop at the Pacific Ocean but travels freely over water to contribute to air quality problems on the West Coast of the United States.

This incongruity between the ecological boundaries of GEC and the political boundaries of collective action doubtless represents one of the most difficult institutional challenges of GEC. It has led to the increased importance of international environmental agreements of the sort Oran R. Young reviews in chapter 5. Here the research is an organized and systematic effort to understand how institutional regimes, especially at the international level, come into play and what effect they have. Young provides an assessment (what he terms a "mid-term" report) of the extent to which the creation and growth of international regimes is an effective response to the challenges of GEC. He concludes with both hope and caution. Hope lies in the effectiveness of emergent regimes in mitigating a number of GEC problems. Caution lies in the realization that neither a common model nor a "simple recipe" is the appropriate strategy to pursue. Rather, the most effective international environmental regimes will be those that evolve from in-depth understanding of individual cases.

Common Pool Resources

The research agenda of international institutionalism intersects with a centuries-old problem concerning the tension between unlimited human demands and nature's finite resources. At least since the writings of classical economist David Ricardo in the eighteenth century, scholars have pondered this problem of "diminishing returns." In modern times the question is at the heart of a decades-old research program on the human governance of common pool resources. This modern version of the problem was largely stimulated by a germinal article with a provocative title, "The Tragedy of the Commons," in the journal *Science* (1968). In this article, biologist Garrett Hardin argued that the solution to the problem of a growing population pushing against finite resources could not be found in technical solutions.

A rich tradition of contemporary research, more synthetic than in the past, has drawn attention to a variety of nuances to the problem and to a range of solutions that eluded Hardin's overly simplistic version (Dietz, Ostrom, and Stern 2003). Bonnie J. McCay and Svein Jentoft, in chapter 6, label Hardin's approach as "thin" and abstract, resulting in various tenuous conclusions. They provide a "thick" or ethnographically rich alternative that reveals the limitations of Hardin's abstractness while uncovering numerous adaptive institutions that affect the resilience of the environment. They show that local and regional resources around the globe are threatened by cumulative environmental change—change that is governed at least in part by local behavior, but is also influenced by globalization. With this foundation McCay and Jentoft go on to review our substantial knowledge of commons and do so in a way that respects both the Anglophone and Continental traditions of scholarship.

Ecological Consequences: Vulnerability

Scholars have become increasingly aware of at least one lesson of history—that CHANS in many circumstances are particularly vulnerable to environmental change (Kasperson, Kasperson, and Turner 1995; Gunderson and Holling 2002; Turner, Kasperson et al. 2003; Turner, Matson et al. 2003). Indeed, many past societies did not ease into stages of ecological insustainability, but experienced abrupt collapse (Diamond 2005). This recognition has produced a spontaneous tradition of research that engages both the Continental and American social scientific traditions and focuses on the comparative vulnerability of societies around the world. The critical importance of determining the types, locus, and scale of human vulnerability to environmental change has led to increased efforts to coordinate and promote this research. Chapter 7, by Jean X. Kasperson, Roger E. Kasperson, and B. L. Turner II, provides an overview of the theoretical underpinnings and the state of the science in this rapidly changing and very critical area.

But more important, the idea of vulnerability explored by Kasperson, Kasperson, and Turner provides the dynamic link between time's cycles and time's arrow in CHANS. The ecological cycles of societies lacking the resilience to overcome the stresses of vulnerability are prone to "criticality," a level of endangerment whereby time's arrow overwhelms nature's regenerative cycles (Kasperson, Kasperson, and Turner 1995). This crucial point is summarized by Kasperson, Kasperson, and Turner: "'Criticality' is a function of the speed and intensity of environmental degradation, the vulnerability of people and ecosystems affected, and coping capacities and resilience... environmental criticality emerges historically through a series of stages in which the decisive attributes are the regenerative capacities of affected ecosystems and the buffering and mitigative costs incurred by affected societies."

In sum, the concept *vulnerability* provides a basis not only for earmarking threatened ecosystems but also for understanding the unsustainable transformation of CHANS globally—Mega-CHANS.

What Lies Ahead?

The elaboration of the pivotal issues we have outlined lies in the chapters that follow. In them, the authors provide a state-of-the-art assessment of how far human dimensions research has come in the past several decades. They also map out the most promising paths to take toward a fuller understanding of the complex challenges of coupled human and natural systems in the context of global environmental change.

Acknowledgments

This chapter was improved considerably by the comments of Lauren Richter, Christopher Dick, Shushanik Makaryan, Kennon Kuykendall, and Mick Wilks.

Notes

1. The ecological communities surrounding deep ocean geothermal vents—"smokers"—and deep underground microbial communities may be the exceptions that prove the rule.

2. GEC92 is often referred to as the "Rainbow Book" in the human dimensions community because of its multicolored dust jacket.

3. We follow GEC92 in referring to key aspects of human action as "proximate human drivers" or "proximate anthropogenic drivers." The Millennium Ecosystem Assessment (UNEP 2005a; Alcalmo et al. 2003) refers to these factors as *indirect drivers* while using the term *direct drivers* to refer to factors such as land-use change, species introduction, and use of technology. In the MEA, direct drivers are defined as factors that "unequivocally influence ecosystems" and include climate variability and change, plant nutrient use, land conversion, and biological invasions and diseases. The GEC92 and the MEA frameworks are internally consistent but care must be taken in moving across them to avoid confusion of terms.

4. The term *biosphere* is generally associated with Russian geologist Vladimir Ivanovich Vernadsky ([1924] 1998) from the title of his book *The Biosphere*.

5. In adopting the terms *time's arrow* and *time's cycles*, we mimic Stephen Jay Gould's (1987) phrasing and framing of history in long glances.

6. Origination of the phrase "arrow of time" rests with physicist Sir Arthur Eddington who, holding the second law of thermodynamics to be supreme, pointed to it as the only unassailable indicator of evolution of the physical world (Eddington [1935] 1958).

7. In this regard, global environmental research is like astronomy or many of the social sciences where the theory-to-experiment-to-theory cycle that exemplifies scientific research cannot be applied because it is not possible to conduct controlled experiments on the key phenomena being studied.

8. For example, *Homo erectus* used fire at least four hundred thousand years ago, long before the appearance of our species, *Homo sapiens sapiens* (Gouldsblom 1992).

9. More extensive analysis of such linkages can be found in Costanza, Graumlich, and Steffen (2007).

10. Roughly at the end of the Pleistocene Era.

11. Rome had its share of other environmental problems due to its growing population and rising standard of living. Demand increased for timber—as building material, fuel for cooking, energy for industrial purposes, and heat source for private and public buildings. Farmers eagerly cut trees for timber to meet this demand, thereby accelerating deforestation while increasing arable land available for cropping (Gouldsblom 1992). Adding to Rome's environmental problems was its considerable air pollution traceable to chariot traffic on the city's dusty streets and to the smoke from the funeral pyres on the outskirts of the city. Tainter and Crumley (2007) discuss how the dynamics of the Roman Empire were driven in part by climate change, so the feedback between the Empire and the natural environment ran in both directions.

12. Landsat assessments in 2003 showed that 90 percent of the Mesopotamian marshlands have disappeared (UNEP 2003). A United Nations Environment Programme project, funded by the government of Japan, reflooded the marshlands resulting in a 40 percent recovery of the marshlands in just two years (UNEP 2005b).

13. Archaeological records are essential to understanding the impacts of past societies and civilizations on ecosystems because they often cover a sufficient amount of time to provide a basis for differentiating human impacts from impacts due to natural cycles.

14. Note that while the human-carrying capacity of the planet is difficult to define and estimate, the human population has already exceeded a third of all estimates of carrying capacity ever developed (Cohen 1995).

15. There are numerous examples where societies and civilizations (Easter Island is the paradigmatic example) have overshot their ecological limits in the past, resulting in their own demise. What is different in Catton's framework is his analysis of ecological exploitation at a global scale.

16. Crutzen shared the 1995 Nobel Prize in Chemistry with Mario Molina and Sherwood Rowland for basic discoveries of the effects of chlorofluorocarbons (CFCs) on the earth's ozone layer.

17. The entire Holocene (Recent Whole) era, consisting of the last twelve thousand years or so, is sometimes labeled as the Anthropocene (meaning recent *Homo sapiens sapiens*) to reflect, somewhat incorrectly, the emergence, survival, and dispersal of humans around the globe. Actually humans had evolved and dispersed all over the world prior to twelve thousand years ago. Furthermore, ecological disasters up to three centuries ago tended to be isolated and localized, not a threat across the globe.

18. While there is widespread agreement over the idea of globalization, there is considerable debate on when the process of globalization began. Held et al. (1999) identify three schools of thought pursuing the idea: hyperglobalization,

"skeptics," and transformationalists. Hyperglobalizers view globalization as the signature of an entirely new, unprecedented era where far-reaching transformations around the world are rendering the institutions and culture of modernism obsolete. Skeptics, observing similar patterns in the not-too-distant history, draw a much different conclusion and argue that not much is changing. Transformationalists view globalization as the efflorescence of a slow, long-term historical process. An even more far-reaching transformationalist view is that of world-systems theory (WST), which sees globalization as the extension of processes that had their origins in the sixteenth century (Wallerstein 2004). Yearley (2007) discusses the links between globalization and global environmental change, although he addresses neither the distinctions among theories of globalization offered by Held et al. (1999) nor the widely accepted conceptualization of global environmental change developed by Turner et al. (1990). Gallagher (2009) provides an excellent review of the conceptual links between globalization and environmental change, and reviews the evidence for the major claims.

19. Vitousek et al. (1997, 498) summarize their estimates of global human impacts this way: "The rates, scales, kinds, and combinations of changes occurring now are fundamentally different from those at any other time in history: we are changing the Earth more rapidly than we are understanding it."

20. Hibbard et al. (2007) provide further evidence of these recent rapid changes.

21. The beginning of "The Anthropocene" (Crutzen and Stoermer 2000).

22. This seemingly low value may appear innocuous, but it is anything but. This is precisely the average surface temperature of the globe that brackets the climate of the ice ages and the warm interglacial periods.

23. The problem is exacerbated in parts of the world that follow shifting cultivation practices, such as slash-and-burn agriculture. With increasing population pressure and with increased demand for raw materials, fallow periods are cut short, thereby reducing the replenishment of the soil and accelerating the rate of soil erosion.

24. The impacts of urbanization on deforestation are not uniform throughout the world. In Africa, for example, deforestation appears to be driven as much by rural population growth as by urbanization (Bawa and Dayanandan 1997).

25. In 2000 the 3M company, maker of Scotchgard, phased out the PFOS-based version of the product and substituted a formula free of PFOSs.

26. Expected to be overtaken by India in the next several years.

27. In particular, a desktop computer with a seventeen-inch CRT monitor requires at least 530 pounds of fossil fuels, fifty pounds of chemicals, and 3,330 pounds of water to manufacture. The amount of materials required for its manufacture equals roughly the weight of a sports utility vehicle (Kuehr and Williams 2003).

28. For continental theorists, noting that no place on earth is without a human footprint, the term *natural* no longer means a passive, pristine environment. There are no natural environments, only socialized ones.

References

Alcalmo, J., N. J. Ash, C. D. Butler, J. B. Callicot, D. Capistrano, S. R. Carpenter, J. C. Castilla, et al. 2003. *Ecosystems and human well-being: A framework for analysis.* Washington, DC: Island Press.

Alexander, B. H., G. W. Olsen, J. M. Burris, J. H. Mandel, and J. S. Mandel. 2003. Mortality of employees of a perfluorooctanesulphonyl fluoride manufacturing facility. *Occupational Environmental Medicine* 60:722–729.

Bawa, K. S., and S. Dayanandan. 1997. Socioeconomic factors and tropical deforestation. *Nature* 386:562–563.

Beck, U. [1986] 1992. *Risk society: Towards a new modernity.* London: Sage.

Butenhoff J., R. York, A. Seacat, and D. Luebker. 2002. Perfluorooctanesulfonate-induced perinatal mortality in rat pups is associated with a steep dose-response. *Toxicologist* 144:264–268.

Catton, W. R., Jr. 1980. *Overshoot: The ecological basis for revolutionary change.* Urbana: University of Illinois Press.

Catton, W. R., Jr. 1987. The world's most polymorphous species: Carrying capacity transgressed two ways. *Bioscience* 37:413–419.

CCSP (Climate Change Science Program). 2003. *Strategic plan for the U.S. Climate Change Science Program.* Washington, DC: U.S. Climate Change Science Program.

Ciriolo, M. R., I. Mavelli, G. Rotilio, V. Borzatta, M. Cristofari, and L. Stanzani. 1982. Decrease of the superoxide dismutase and glutathione peroxidase in liver of rats treated with hypolipdemic drugs. *FEBS Letters* 144:264–268.

Clark, W. C. 2007. Sustainability science: A room of its own. *Proceedings of the National Academy of Sciences* 104:1737–1738.

Cohen, J. E. 1995. *How many people can the Earth support?* New York: W. W. Norton.

Costanza, R., L. J. Graumlich, and W. Steffen, eds. 2007. *Sustainability or collapse? An integrated history and future of people on Earth.* Cambridge, MA: MIT Press.

Courtney, D., C. D. Sandau, P. Ayotte, E. Dewailly, J. Duffe, and R. J. Norstrom. 2000. Analysis of hydroxylated metabolites of PCBs (OH-PCBs) and other chlorinated phenolic compounds in whole blood of Canadian Inuit. *Environmental Health Perspectives* 108:611–616.

Crutzen, P. J., and E. F. Stoermer. 2000. The Anthropocene. *IGBP Newsletter* 41 (May): 17–18.

Diamond, J. 1997. *Guns, germs, and steel: The fate of human societies.* New York: W. W. Norton.

Diamond, J. 2005. *Collapse: How societies choose or fail to succeed.* New York: Viking.

Dietz, T., E. A. Rosa, and R. York. 2007. Driving the human ecological footprint. *Frontiers in Ecology and the Environment* 5:13–18.

Dietz, T., E. Ostrom, and P. C. Stern. 2003. The struggle to govern the commons. *Science* 302 (5652):1907–1912.

Dowdeswell, E., and V. H. Heywood. 1995. *Global biodiversity assessment.* Cambridge: Cambridge University Press.

Eddington, A. [1935] 1958. *The nature of the physical world.* Ann Arbor: University of Michigan Press.

Eisenstein, P. A. 2004. China goes car crazy. June 14. http://www. thecarconnection.com/ Auto_News/Daily_Auto_News/China_Goes_Car_Crazy. S173.A7231.html.

Ewing, R., J. D. Kostayack, D. Chen, B. Stein, and M. Ernst. 2005. *Endangered by sprawl: How runaway development threatens America's wildlife.* Washington, DC: National Wildlife Federation, Smart Growth America, and NatureServe.

FAO (Food and Agricultural Organization). 1997. *State of the world's forests 1997.* Rome: United Nations/FAO.

Galison, P. 1997. *Image and logic: A material culture of physics.* Chicago: Chicago University Press.

Gallagher, K. P. 2009. Globalization and the environment. Forthcoming in *Annual Review of Environment and Resources* 34.

Goodman, P. S. 2004. Booming China devouring raw materials: Producers and suppliers struggle to feed a voracious appetite. *The Washington Post*, May 20, A1.

Gould, S. J. 1987. *Time's arrow time's cycle: Myth and metaphor in the discovery of geological time.* Cambridge, MA: Harvard University Press.

Gouldsblom, J. 1992. *Fire and civilization.* London: Penguin Books.

Graedel, T. E., and B. R. Allenby. 1995. *Industrial Ecology.* Englewood Cliffs, NJ: Prentice-Hall.

Grossman, G., and A. Krueger. 1995. Economic growth and the environment. *Quarterly Journal of Economics* 110:353–377.

Gunderson, L. H., and C. S. Holling, eds. 2002. *Panarchy: Understanding transformations in human and natural systems.* Washington, DC: Island Press.

Hall, C. A. S., P. Tharakan, J. Hallock, C. Cleveland, and M. Jefferson. 2003. Hydrocarbons and the evolution of human culture. *Nature* 426:318–322.

Hardin, G. 1968. The tragedy of the commons. *Science* 162:1243–1248.

Harrison, P. 1993. *The third revolution: Population, environment, and a sustainable world.* New York: Penguin Books.

Held, D., A. McGrew, D. Goldblatt, and J. Perraton. 1999. *Global transformations: Politics, economics, and culture.* Stanford, CA: Stanford University Press.

Hibbard, K. A., P. J. Crutzen, E. Lambin, D. Liverman, N. J. Mantua, J. R. McNeill, B. Messerli, and W. Steffen. 2007. Group report: Decadal-scale interactions of humans and the environment. In *Sustainability or collapse? An integrated history and future of people on Earth*, ed. R. Costanza, L. J. Graumlich, and W. Steffen, 341–375. Cambridge, MA: MIT Press.

Hong, S., J-P. Candelone, C. C. Patterson, and C. F. Boutron. 1994. Greenland ice evidence of hemispheric lead pollution two millennia ago by Greek and Roman civilizations. *Science* 265:1841–1843.

Hong, S., J-P. Candelone, C. C. Patterson, and C. F. Boutron. 1996. History of ancient copper smelting pollution during Roman and Medieval times recorded in Greenland ice. *Science* 272:246–249.

IPCC (Intergovernmental Panel on Climate Change). 2007. *Climate change 2007 synthesis report*. Report of Working Group I, of the Fourth Assessment. http://www.ipcc.ch/.

Jaeger, C., O. Renn, E. A. Rosa, and T. Webler. 2001. *Risk, uncertainty, and rational action*. London: Earthscan.

Kasperson, J. X., R. E. Kasperson, and B. L. Turner II, eds. 1995. *Regions at risk: Comparisons of threatened environments*. Tokyo: United Nations University Press.

Kliewer, S. A., J. M. Lehmann, and T. M. Wilson. 1999. Orphan nuclear receptors: Shifting endocrinology into reverse. *Science* 284:757–760.

Kroll, T. G., P. Sarraf, L. Pecciarini, C. J. Chen, E. Mueller, B. M. Spiegelman, and J. A. Fletcher. 2000. PAX8-PPARγ1 fusion in oncogene human thyroid carcinoma. *Science* 289:1357–1360.

Kuehr, R., and E. Williams, eds. 2003. *Computers and environment: Understanding and managing their impacts*. United Nations University, Tokyo: Kluwer Academic Publishers.

Liu, J., G. C. Daily, P. R. Ehrlich, and G. W. Luck. 2003. Effects of household dynamics on resource consumption and biodiversity. *Nature* 1359:1–4.

Liu, J., T. Dietz, S. R Carpenter, M. Alberti, C. Folke, E. Moran, A. N. Pell, P. Deadman, T. Kratz, J.Lubchencko, E. Ostrom, Z. Ouyang, W. Provencher, C. L. Redman, S. H. Schneider, and W. W. Taylor. 2007a. Complexity of coupled human and natural systems. *Science* 317:1513–1516.

Liu, J., T. Dietz, S. R. Carpenter, C. Folke, M. Alberti, C. L. Redman, S. H. Schneider, E. Ostrom, A. N. Pell, J. Lubchencko, W. W. Taylor, Z. Ouyang, P. Deadman, T. Kratz, and W. Provencher. 2007b. Coupled human and natural systems. *Ambio* 36:639–649.

Mertens, B., R. Poccard-Chapuis, M-G. Piketty, A-E. Lacques, and A. Venturieri. 2002. Crossing spatial analyses and livestock economics to understand deforestation processes in the Brazilian Amazon: The case of Sao Felix do Xingu in South Para. *Agricultural Economics* 27:267–294.

Mol, A. P. J., and D. Sonnenfeld, eds. 2000. *Ecological modernization around the world*. London: Frank Cass.

Myers, N. 1981. The hamburger connection: How Central America's forests become North America's hamburgers. *Ambio* 10:3–8.

Myers, N., and J. Kent. 2003. New consumers: The influence of affluence on the environment. *Proceedings of the National Academy of Sciences* 100:4963–4968.

Myers, N., and J. Kent. 2004. *The new consumers: The influence of affluence on the environment.* Washington, DC: Island Press.

Raven, P. H., and J. A. McNeely. 1998. Biological extinction: Its scope and meaning for us. In *Protection of global biodiversity: Converging strategies,* ed. G. D. Lakshman and J.A. McNeely, 13–32. Durham, NC: Duke University Press.

Redman, Charles L. 1999. *Human impact on ancient environments.* Tucson: University of Arizona Press.

Rice, D. S. 1996. Paleolimnological analysis in the Central Petén, Guatemala. In *The managed mosaic: Ancient Maya agricultural resource use,* ed. S. L. Fedick, 193–206. Salt Lake City: University of Utah Press.

Richards, J. F. 1990. Land transformations. In *The Earth as transformed by human action,* ed. B. L. Turner, W. C. Clark, R. W. Kates, J. F. Richards, J. T. Mathews, and W. B. Meyer, 163–178. Cambridge: Cambridge University Press.

Roosevelt, A. C., M. L. da Costa, C. Lopes Machado, M. Michab, N. Mercier, H. Valladas, J. Feathers, et al. 1996. Paleoindian cave dwellers in the Amazon: The people of the Americas. *Science* 272:373–384.

Rosa, E. A., and T. Dietz. 1998. Climate change and society: Speculation, construction, and scientific investigation. *International Sociology* 13:421–455.

Rosa, E. A., R. F. York, and T. Dietz. 2004. Tracking the anthropogenic drivers of ecological impacts. *Ambio* 33:509–512.

Rudel, T. K. 1989. Population, development, and tropical deforestation: A cross-national study. *Rural Sociology* 54:327–338.

Senior, K. 2007. Facing up to our paper addiction. *Frontiers in Ecology and the Environment* 5:4.

Stern, P. C., O. R. Young, and D. Druckman. 1992. *Global environmental change: Understanding the human dimensions.* Washington, DC: National Academies Press.

Tainter, J. A., and C. L. Crumley. 2007. Climate, complexity, and problem solving in the Roman Empire. In *Sustainability or collapse? An integrated history and future of people on Earth,* ed. R. Costanza, L. J. Graumlich, and W. Steffen, 61–75. Cambridge, MA: MIT Press.

Turner, B. L., II, R. E. Kasperson, P. Matson, J. J. McCarthy, R. W. Corell, L. Christensen, N. Eckley, J. X. Kasperson, A. Luers, M. L. Martello, C. Polsky, A. Pulsipher and A. Schiller. 2003. A framework for vulnerability assessment in sustainability science. *Proceedings of the National Academy of Sciences* 100:8074–8079.

Turner, B. L., II, R. E. Kasperson, W. B. Meyer, K. M. Dow, D. Golding, J. X. Kasperson, R. C. Mitchell, and S. J. Ratick. 1990. Two types of global environmental change: Definitional and spatial-scale issues in their human dimensions. *Global Environmental Change* 1:14–22.

Turner, B. L., II, P. A. Matson, J. J. McCarthy, R. W. Corell, L. Christensen, N. Eckley, G. K. Hovelsrud-Broda, J. X. Kasperson, R. E. Kasperson, A. Luers, M. L. Martello, S. Mathiesen, R. Naylor, C. Polsky, A. Pulsipher, A. Schiller, H. Selin, and N. Tyler 2003. Illustrating the coupled human-environment system: Three case studies. *Proceedings of the National Academy of Sciences* 100:8080–8085.

UNEP (United Nations Environment Programme). 2001. *An assessment of the status of the world's remaining closed forests.* UNEP/DEWA/TR 01–2. Nairobi, Kenya: United Nations Environmental Program.

UNEP (United Nations Environment Programme). 2003. "Garden of Eden" in Southern Iraq likely to disappear completely in five years unless urgent action taken. Division of Communications and Public Information, UNEP News Release. March 22. http://www.unep.org/Documents.Multilingual/Default.asp?ArticleID=3920&DocumentID=298.

UNEP (United Nations Environment Programme). 2005a. *Ecosystems and human well-being: Synthesis, report of the Millennium Ecosystem Assessment.* Washington, DC: Island Press.

UNEP (United Nations Environment Programme). 2005b. *Support for environmental management of Iraqi marshlands.* Tokyo: United Nations Environmental Program.

United Nations. 2004. *World urbanization prospects, the 2003 revision.* New York: United Nations, Population Division.

United Nations. 2005. World population prospects: The 2004 revision. *POPULATION Newsletter.* New York: United Nations, Population Division.

Vernadsky, V. I. [1924] 1998. *The biosphere: Complete annotated edition.* New York: Springer.

Vitousek, P. M., H. A. Mooney, J. Lubchenko, and J. A. Melilo. 1997. Human domination of Earth's ecosystems. *Science* 277:494–499.

Wallerstein, I. 2004. *World-systems analysis: An introduction.* Durham, NC: Duke University Press.

Weart, S. 2003. *The discovery of global warming.* Cambridge, MA: Harvard University Press.

Wilson, E. O. 1992. *The diversity of life.* Cambridge, MA: Harvard University Press.

Wimberley, R., and M. Kulikowski. 2007. World population becomes more urban than rural. Raleigh, NC: North Carolina State University. http://news.ncsu.edu/releases/2007/may/104.html#content.

World Commission on Environment and Development (WED). 1987. *Our common future.* Oxford: Oxford University Press.

Yearley, S. 2007. Globalization and the environment. In *The Blackwell companion to globalization*, ed. G. Ritzer. Malden, MA: Blackwell Publishing. Blackwell Reference Online. http://www.blackwellreference.com/public/ (accessed 29 August 2008).

York, R. F., E. A. Rosa, and T. Dietz. 2003a. Footprints on the Earth: The environmental consequences of modernity. *American Sociological Review* 68: 279–300.

York, R. F., E. A. Rosa, and T. Dietz. 2003b. STIRPAT, IPAT, and ImPACT; Analytic tools for unpacking the driving forces of environmental impacts. *Ecological Economics* 46:351–365.

2

World Risk Society as Cosmopolitan Society: Ecological Questions in a Framework of Manufactured Uncertainties

Ulrich Beck

In theorizing a "world risk society," I distinguish between a first form of modernity (modern, industrial, national society) in which society demanded that risks were calculable and subject to management, and a second form of modernity (postindustrial, post-risk-calculation, post-national society) in which there are manufactured dangers that run out of control (Beck 1992, 2008; Beck and Lau 2005). My focus is not on natural hazards, such as earthquakes, which have always plagued human settlements, but on *un*natural, human-manufactured uncertainties and hazards that move beyond political boundaries—these are the sort of difficulties we are increasingly confronted with today. Indeed these new uncertainties—such as those that result from climate change and global financial turbulences but also from transnational terrorist networks—are not simply beyond boundaries, but are de-bounding because they transcend existing boundaries and eventually transform them. They do so spatially (e.g., across nation-state boundaries), temporally (e.g., they are long-tailed, and in some cases, seemingly infinite), and socially (e.g., they create social trouble regarding attributions of liability, accountability, responsibility, and response-ability).

Seen through the lens of the first modernity, these new manufactured uncertainties are but negative side effects of accountable and rational activity: "residual risks" that can be subject to cost-benefit analysis and future control through advances in science and technology. Seen through the lens of the second modernity, these new manufactured uncertainties delegitimate institutional authority, erode scientific rationality, create distrust in technologies, and insinuate radical doubt about the future. They abolish the four pillars of risk calculus: compensation, limitation, security, and classification. They contribute to a stronger emphasis on the responsibility of individuals, organizations, and communities to embrace more risk. They also engender a precautionary approach to a wide range of risks that have catastrophic potential. This "age of unintended consequences" has to be distinguished from the expectation of intentional catastrophes. The terrorist power of uncertainty is especially strong because we do live in a risk society. Thus the different types of global risks—ecological, technological, economical, and terrorist risks—enforce and at the same time contradict each other.[1]

This chapter will focus on one—but only one among others—of the key dimensions of the dynamic of world risk society, namely, environmental crises, and, in particular, climate change and its diverse consequences. It will have little to say about "nature" or the "destruction of nature" or about "ecology" or "environmental destruction," but all the more about world risk society. This concept is chosen with systematic intent. For I want to propose a concept for the sociological analysis of environmental questions that allows us to grasp them not as problems of the environment in the sense of the surrounding world [*Umwelt*], but as problems affecting the inner world [*Innenwelt*] of society. In place of the seemingly self-evident key concepts of nature, ecology and environment, which underline the difference from the social, I propose a conceptual framework that goes beyond the opposition between society and nature and shifts the focus to the *uncertainty fabricated* by human beings: risk, catastrophe, side effects, insurability, individualization, and globalization.

It is often objected that the concept of a world risk society encourages a kind of neo-Spenglerism and hinders political action. Precisely the opposite is the case. As a world risk society, society becomes *reflexive* in a three-fold sense.[2] First, it itself becomes an issue: global threats found global commonalities; indeed, a (virtual) global public sphere is taking shape. Second, the perceived globality of the dangers produced by civilization itself triggers a politically manipulable impulse toward the revitalization of national politics and the development of cooperative international institutions. For example, at the end of 2006, then British Prime Minister Tony Blair and his designated successor Gordon Brown discovered and awakened the "political giant" lurking in climate change when they proclaimed their vision of a "green Great Britain" and "green capitalism." This was made possible by the so-called "Stern Report" (Stern 2006), which offers eloquent warnings against the dire *economic* consequences of irreversible climate change. Third, politics is losing its sharp contours: constellations of a global and direct "subpolitics" are forming that relativize and circumvent the coordinates and coalitions of national politics and could lead to worldwide "alliances of mutually exclusive convictions." In other words, a "cosmopolitan society" can take shape in the perceived danger confronting world risk society.

Elements of a Theory of Environmental World Risk Society

The Indeterminacy of the Concepts of Nature and Ecology

The concept of ecology has enjoyed an impressively successful history. Nowadays, responsibility for the condition of nature is laid at the door of ministers and managers. Evidence that the side effects of products or industrial processes pose a threat to human life or to its natural bases can cause markets to collapse, destroying political confidence as well as economic capital and faith in the superior rationality of experts. This (in many respects highly subversive) success disguises the fact that ecology is an utterly vague concept; everyone offers a different answer to the question of what should be preserved.[3]

Wrote the German poet Gottfried Benn:

Once again I realised what humbug nature is. Even when snow does not melt, it provides hardly any linguistic or emotional themes: you can fully grasp its indisputable monotony without leaving the house. Nature is empty and desolate; only philistines see anything in it, poor devils who have to keep going on about it. For example, forests lack any thematic material and everything below 1,500 metres is old hat since you can see and experience Piz Palü in the cinema for a mark.... Steer clear of nature! It messes up your thoughts and has a notoriously bad effect on your style! *Natura*—female, of course! Always looking to tap the male's semen, to copulate with him and tire him out. Is nature even natural? It begins something and then lets it drop, as many interruptions as beginnings, changes of direction, failures, desertions, contradictions, flashes, meaningless deaths, experiments, games, appearances—the textbook example of the unnatural! And it is also uncommonly laborious, marching up the hill and down again: ascents that cancel each other out, vistas that become blurred, previously unknown lookout points that are immediately forgotten—in short, idiocy. (1986, 71)

The use of the word *nature* immediately invites the question: what cultural model of nature is being assumed? Is it nature in its current state, driven to exhaustion by industry? Or the country life of the 1950s (as it now appears in hindsight or as it appeared to country dwellers at the time)? Mountain solitude before the appearance of the book *Hiking in the Solitary Mountains?* The nature of the natural sciences or the longed-for nature (in the sense of silence, mountain streams, inner peace) as extolled in the tourist brochures of the supermarkets of global solitude? The "hard-headed" image of nature of businessmen for whom industrial operations on nature can always be made good or the image of "hypersensitive" individuals stirred by nature for whom even the most insignificant changes cause irreparable damage?

Nature—especially nature—is not nature but is more than ever a concept, a norm, a recollection, a utopia, an alternative plan. Nature is being rediscovered and pampered at a time when it has ceased to exist. The ecological movement is a reaction to the global condition of a contradictory fusion of nature and society that has superseded both concepts in a relationship of mutual connections and violations of which we do not as yet have any notion, let alone a concept. Attempts in the environmental debates to use a natural condition as a standard against its own destruction rest, and always rested, on a *naturalistic misunderstanding*. For the nature invoked no longer exists (Beck 1992, 1994; Oechsle 1988). What do exist and cause such a political stir are different forms of socialization and different symbolic mediations of nature (and the destruction of nature), cultural concepts of nature, and conflicting notions of nature and their (national) cultural traditions, which determine ecological conflicts throughout the world beneath the surface disputes among experts, the technical formulae, and threats.[4]

But if nature in itself cannot be the analytic reference for the environmental crisis and for a critique of the industrial system, what can play this role? There are a number of possible answers to this question. The most common is: the *science* of nature. Technical formulae—levels of toxins in the air, water and food; climatological models; or the cybernetic conceptions of feedback loops in the science of ecosystems—are supposed to decide what levels of damage and destruction are tolerable. This approach, however, has at least three drawbacks. First, it leads directly to "ecocracy," which differs from technocracy only in its higher intensity—namely, global management—crowned with a robust good conscience. Second, it ignores the meanings of cultural perceptions and of intercultural conflict and dialogue. Third, scientific models themselves involve ecological questions and implicit cultural models of nature (e.g., that of System Theory, which contrasts with the understanding of nature of early natural conservation).

Thinking in natural scientific terms is a precondition for perceiving the world as ecologically endangered in the first place. Thus environmental awareness is the exact opposite of a "natural" attitude; it is an extremely scientific view of the world, in which, for example, the abstract models of climatologists influence everyday behavior. And particularly urgent is the question of what kind of staging, indeed "visualization," is necessary and possible in order to overcome this abstractness and render climate change and its apocalyptic consequences "visible."

Yet no expertise can ever answer the question: how do we want to live? What people are prepared to accept and what they won't accept cannot be deduced from any technical or ecological diagnosis of threats. It must instead be made the topic of a global dialogue between cultures. This is the aim of a second perspective, that of *cultural* sciences. It states that the scale and urgency of the ecological crisis fluctuate in accordance with intracultural and intercultural perception and evaluation. What kind of truth is it, one might ask with Montaigne, that is accepted in Europe but is regarded as deception and illusion in the United States? From this perspective, dangers do not exist "in themselves," independently of our perceptions. They become a political issue only when everyone becomes aware of them; they are the products of social stagings that are strategically defined, covered up, or dramatized with the aid of scientific materials. It is no accident that two Anglo-American social anthropologists—Mary Douglas and Aaron Wildavsky (1982)—presented this analysis already in 1982 in their book *Risk and Culture*. Douglas and her coauthor argue (in a deliberate affront to the emerging environmental consciousness) that there is no effective difference between the dangers of early history and those in developed civilization, except in how they are culturally perceived and how they are organized in world society.

However correct and important this view may be, it remains unsatisfactory. First, it highlights the (mistakes of a) sociology that reduces everything to society and ignores the characteristic "both/and" quality of the immateriality (social staging) *and* the materiality of risk (physical change and destruction). Second, we know that people in the Stone Age did not have the capacity for nuclear and ecological self-destruction and that the threats posed by lurking demons did not exhibit the same political dynamic as the manmade risks of climate change.[5] *Act now or the world as we know it will be lost forever!*—this is the conclusion drawn by the Stern Report, which provides very concrete and dramatic illustration of the apocalyptic impacts of climate change.

If global warming increases by one degree Celsius (by comparison with the preindustrial temperature of the earth)—in 2000 it had already reached 0.8 degrees—small glaciers (e.g., in the Andes) will melt; the water supply of fifty million people will be in jeopardy; three hundred thousand human beings will die annually of malaria, diarrhea, and so forth; and 10 percent of the animal species will become extinct.

Global warming of two degrees Celsius will mean an unimaginable sixty million malaria fatalities in Africa alone and the world sea level will rise by seven metres.

If the temperature of the earth rises by three degrees Celsius, 40 percent of all animal species will become extinct and Southern Europe will be threatened by a devastating drought.

If four degrees Celsius is reached, agriculture will collapse, first in Australia and Africa but in other regions of the world as well.

Finally, if the temperature increases by five degrees Celsius, London, New York, and Tokyo are in danger of being inundated by the sea, the glaciers in the Himalayas will disappear, and there will be mass migrations and movements of refugees.

What time scale are we dealing with here? Since 1980 alone, global warming has increased from 0.2 to 0.8 degrees. Some studies conjecture that the temperature will increase by five or six degrees if emissions continue to increase at their present rates and the warming effect may even be accelerated by the escape of CO_2 gas from the ground.

The Stern Report by the former World Bank economist Nicolas Stern (2006) is undoubtedly an extremely skillful piece of staging. In order to counteract the abstractness of climate change and render the invisible visible, the anticipation of catastrophes is heightened in thematic and geographical terms by means of empirical indicators that touch cultural nerves (malaria, water shortage, dying agriculture and animal species, not to mention the demise of London, New York, and Tokyo). Yet this is not all. The point of the message is that climate change represents the greatest market failure ever, greater than the economic costs of two world wars and the Great Depression of the 1920s *together*! This impending *economic* catastrophe can only be averted at enormous cost. But this is relatively small, and the money in question is a good investment because it will avert the threatened economic catastrophe. Is this a representation of "reality" or a work of "fiction"? Is it "realist" or "constructivist"? After all, climate change is not (yet) a reality. It is a risk, something that threatens to become a reality, a future projected into the present, an *anticipation* bearing all the hallmarks of uncertainty, whose aim is to change present actions, specifically those of governments, managers, and ultimately all human beings throughout the world. What, then, is meant by reality when we speak of the "reality of the impending catastrophe"?

The Realism-Constructivism Debate

This is the starting point of the theory of world risk society. There are two possible answers to the question of the justification for this concept, one *realist* and one *constructivist* (for an interpretation and critique, see Wynne 1996). In the realist view, the consequences and dangers of developed industrial production "are" now global. This *are* is supported by natural scientific data. In this view, the development of productive forces is interlinked with the development of destructive forces and together they are giving rise to the novel conflicts dynamics of a world risk society—in the shadow of latent side effects. Aside from the 1986 Chernobyl reactor disaster, this dynamic is reflected at the beginning of the twenty-first century in global warming, which is an ideal, typical illustration of the fact that environmental destruction "knows no boundaries."

The realist perspective conceives of the world risk society in terms of global socialization that is enforced by man-made threats. The new situation enhances the importance of international cooperation and institutions. To global dangers, therefore, correspond—"realistically"—global modes of perception, forums of public debate and action, and, finally, assuming the supposed objectivity generates sufficient practical impetus, transnational actors and institutions.

The strength of realism can be seen in its clear historical sequential model, in which industrial society has gone through two distinct phases. In the first phase, class or social questions were paramount, in the second phase, ecological questions. Yet it would be a gross simplification to assume that the environmental question is supplanting the class question. Clearly, environmental, labor market, and economic crises overlap and may well aggravate one another. Such a phase model becomes more persuasive, however, if it represents the globality of ecological questions as following upon the issues of poverty and class that dominated the national phase of industrial capitalism. Often suspected of naivety, this realism thus represents—or even generates—a considerable spur to power to carry through a policy that counteracts the catastrophic impacts of global warming.

Yet even a superficial examination of such realist justifications of a world risk society reveals how untenable they are. In the first place, the unreflected realist viewpoint forgets or suppresses the fact that realism is nothing other than sedimented, fragmented, mass-mediated collective consciousness. Of course, as Bryan Wynne (1996) has shown, public knowledge concerning risk is often not expert but lay knowledge that has been refused social recognition.[6] Nevertheless ecological images and symbols are by no means scientifically confirmed as intrinsically certain knowledge. They are culturally perceived, constructed, and mediatized; they are part of the social knowledge "fabric," with all of its contradictions and conflicts. The catastrophic consequences of climate change must, as we have seen, be *made visible*, that is, they must be effectively staged in order to generate pressure for action. The explanatory power of realism is a function of the exclusion of all considerations that support the interpretative superiority of constructivist approaches. How, for example, is the borrowed self-evidence of "realistic" dangers actually *produced*? Which actors, institutions, strategies, and resources are key to its *fabrication*? These questions can be meaningfully posed only from a constructivist perspective.

On the social-constructivist view, world risk society is not a function of the globality of problems (as diagnosed by science) but of *"transnational discourse coalitions"* (Hajer 1995) that place the global threat to the environment on the public agenda. These coalitions were forged and gained power only in the 1970s and 1980s. In the 1990s, and especially since the Rio Earth Summit, they began to reshape the discursive landscape around global planetary problems and now, at the beginning of the twenty-first century, are reaching a new acme with the green turn of the New Labour government, the European Union, and perhaps the United States. Necessary preconditions are the institutionalization of the environmental movement; the construction of networks and transnational actors, such as the IUN, WWF, and Greenpeace; and the establishment of environment ministries, and national and international laws and treaties; and the rising of environmental industries and "big science: to the task of global management of world problems. Moreover, these actors must also be *successful* and continually assert themselves against powerful opposing coalitions.

Thus far, the diagnosis of a world risk society has met with three kinds of counterarguments:

First, it is argued that the relevant (lay and expert) knowledge concerning global risks is far from clear. It appeals to future events that have not yet occurred and hence uses assertions that can at present be neither proven nor refuted. Thus critics repeatedly refer to discrepancies between the actual state of expert knowledge and the public dramatization of threats and crises.

Second, the global definition of environmental problems is criticized as a kind of Western *ecological neo-imperialism*, especially by actors and governments in the so-called Third World. The claim is that Western states thereby assure themselves of a lead in knowledge and development over poorer countries, while at the same time covering up their own primary responsibility for the threats to global civilization.

This is why, in conceptualizing the dynamics of inequality in world risk society, it makes sense to distinguish between *self-endangerment* and *endangerment by others* (Beck and Holzer 2004). In Europe, environmental crises are perceived in the first instance as a creeping change that takes the form of a latent self-endangerment through the impacts of industrial modernization. For Third World countries it is nothing new that, within the context of a world system that systematically (re)produces inequality (Wallerstein 1974; Frank 1969), modernization in the so-called First World hinders their development. However, such theories reflect a reductive economic analysis of the interrelations. Regions are unequally affected not only by the impacts of failed modernization but also by the "side effects" of *successful* modernization, as the theory of world risk society emphasizes.

Third, it is objected that the global character of ecological questions leads to a perversion of "nature conservation" into its opposite, a kind of global world-management. In this way new monopolies of knowledge are established, the high-tech "global climate models" (the "global circulation models" of the International Panel for Climate Change [IPCC]), with their inbuilt policies and claims to interpretation and control (specifically, those of the natural and computer sciences).

Furthermore, it is becoming apparent that world risk society is by no means synonymous with overcoming ethnonational conflicts of perception and evaluation. On the contrary, it seems to herald the outbreak of new antagonisms (e.g., in disputes over "levels" of danger, or who is "responsible" for them and over the need for counter-measures), which in turn give rise to winners and losers in the national and in the global context.

However contradictory the essentialist-realist and constructivist approaches may be in their points of departure and their methods and basic assumptions, in their diagnoses they agree on a central issue. They both justify speaking in terms of world risk society. This certainly should not lead us to play down the differences. It is particularly striking that realism places the emphasis on *world risk* society, whereas constructivism, by contrast, stresses world risk *society* (where the concept of society in this context is indeterminate). In the constructivist optic, transnational actors already have to have *imposed* their discursive politics if the globality of environmental issues is to determine social perceptions and calls for action. On the realist view, by contrast, this globality is grounded *solely* in the assumed intrinsic power of objective dangers. One could say that realism conceives of the ecological problematic as closed, whereas constructivism stresses its *openness* in principle. For some, the *dangers* (the doomsday scenarios) of world risk society are the central focus; for others, it is the *opportunities*, that is, the contexts in which actors can operate. For some, global dangers must first give rise to international institutions and treaties; for others, talk of global environmental dangers already presupposes successfully operating supranational discourse coalitions. However, realism recognizes something that constructivism easily loses sight of, namely, the *irreversibility of the damage and destruction* that stand in an inverse relation to their public thematization, on the motto: those who deny climate change contribute to its acceleration.

But a further, indeed a farther-reaching question arises here: are realism and constructivism mutually exclusive in every respect in their approaches to world risk society? This is true only if naive versions are assumed on both sides. For just as there is belief in nature and reality as they really exist, so too there is belief in a purely constructivist form of constructivism. As long as we remain at this level, we will fail to recognize the interpretative content of reflexive realism, and hence its potential role in strategies of power. Such a reflected form of realism highlights sources that first make "constructions of reality" into a reality; it examines how self-evidence is generated, questions are curtailed, alternative interpretations are shut up in "black boxes," and so on.

Thus, if one mistrusts simple oppositions, one can oppose a naive constructivism to a reflexive realism or situate them on the same level. Naive constructivism fails to recognize the different varieties of constructivist realism and as such remains rooted in a so-called realist self-misunderstanding of its strict constructivism. It fails to appreciate that durable stagings of reality that are supposed to guide action must repudiate their constructed character because otherwise they will be conceived as *constructions* of reality and not as *reality tout court*. Furthermore, naive constructivism underestimates the materiality or the

Table 2.1
Theoretical and epistemological positions

Epistemology	Theory	Theorists
Strong (naive) realism	Human ecology	Catton and Dunlap 1978; Dunlap 1997
	Environmental sociology	Huber 1995; Jänicke 1985
	Ecological modernization	Spaargaren and Mol 1991
Weak (critical/ reflexive) realism	Green social theory	Dickens 1992; Burns and Dietz 1992; Dietz and Burns 1992; McLaughlin and Dietz 2008; Rosa 1998
Weak constructivism (constructivist realism)	Reflexive modernization	Beck 1992, 1994, 1999, 2005, 2008; Giddens 1990; Eder 1996
	Actor network theory	Latour 2004
Strong (naive) constructivism	Rational choice theory	Esser 1990
	Cultural theory	Douglas 1986; Douglas and Wildavsky 1982
	Autopoietic systems theory	Luhmann 1993; Ewald 1991
	Governmentality	Rose 2000; Ericson, Doyle, and Barry 2003)

Source: Adapted from Strydom 2002, 47.

"natural," scientifically diagnosed inherent constraints of global threats, which are by no means inferior to the materiality of economic constraints. Constructivist analyses that lose sight of the difference between destruction as *event* and *discourse* concerning this event can downplay dangers in a cognitivist manner.

In a "realist constructivism," by contrast, the essentialist meaning in discourse concerning nature and the destruction of nature is replaced by *expert and anti-expert knowledge* (as in Wynne 1996 and Hajer 1995). The latter, in criticizing mainly Anglo-American discourse and cultural theory, developed a politically and analytically more radical approach to this dimension of knowledge. In the process, the naturalist-essentialist content of discourse concerning the destruction of nature takes an—only apparently paradoxical—turn toward the action-related theory of actors and institutions. "Discourse coalitions" that stretch across the boundaries of classes, nation-states and systems now take center stage. They are, as it were, discursive landscape architects: they create, design, and alter "cognitive maps," "narrative frameworks," and "taboos." Reality becomes the project and product of action, with an, until now, unclarified ambiguity in talk of the production [*Herstellen*] of reality assuming major importance. This may be meant primarily in a cognitive sense, thus referring only to the construction of knowledge, or it may include action (decision, work, production) and thus refer to material change through production or the purposeful shaping of realities. Although it is often difficult to demarcate these two aspects of the meaning of production from one another, nevertheless they refer to different modes of the "creation of reality" or of the "shaping of the world." The point is no longer merely how realities are created in world risk society (e.g., through corresponding reports concerning threats in the mass media); there is also the question of how reality in itself is (re-)produced through discourse politics and coalitions within institutional contexts of decision, action, and work.

Consequently, constructions of reality can be distinguished as to whether they are more or less real. The closer they are to and in institutions (understood as institutionalizations of social practices), the more powerful and closer to decision and action they are, and the more real they become or appear. Essentialism, when scrutinized and analyzed by the sociology of knowledge, turns into a kind of strategic institutionalism geared to power and action. In a world risk society dynamic that reduces everything to decisions, reality in itself arises out of structures of action, ingrained decision and work routines, in which modes of perception are realized or redrawn. The way in which people continue to speak of nature and the destruction of nature may be an indicator of the paradoxical strategy of the construction of deconstruction. The appearance of construction is thereby (more or less) reflexively and powerfully destroyed and the appearance of reality in itself is produced.

Institutional Constructivism

With these points in mind, we can make the theory of world risk society more concrete. It shares in the rejection of the dualism of society and nature that Bruno Latour (1993; 2004), Donna Haraway (1991), and Barbara Adams (1995) effect with such intellectual flair.[7] The only question is: how do we deal with nature *after* it ends? This question is answered in the theory of world risk society along the lines of an *institutional constructivism.* "Nature" and the "destruction of nature" are institutionally produced and defined (in conflicts between lay people and experts) within industrially internalized nature. Their essential content correlates with institutional power of action and organization. Here production and definition are two aspects of the material *and* symbolic production of (the destruction of) nature; they refer, if you will, to discourse coalitions within and between fundamentally different, global action networks. It remains to be examined in detail *how*, and with what discursive and industrial resources and strategies, these differences in the naturalness of nature, its destruction and re-naturalization, are produced, suppressed, normalized, and integrated within institutions and in the conflict between cognitive actors.

The theory of world risk society translates the question of the destruction of nature into another question: how does modern society deal with self-produced uncertainties? The point of this formulation is to distinguish between decision-dependent *risks* that can in principle be brought under control and *threats* that have escaped or neutralized the control requirements of industrial society, in at least two forms.

First, the norms and institutions developed within industrial society—risk assessment, insurance principle, the concept of an accident, disaster prevention, preventive aftercare (Ewald 1991; Bonss 1995)—can fail. Is there a convenient indicator of this? The answer is yes, there is, for the controversial industries and technologies often are those that either do not have private insurance or have only inadequate private insurance. This holds for atomic energy, genetic engineering (including research), and other sectors of high-risk chemical production. What goes without saying for motorists—never use your car without insurance protection— has apparently been suspended for whole industrial branches and cutting-edge technologies, where the dangers involved present too many problems.

Second, the pattern of decisions in industrial society and the globality of their aggregate side effects belong to two different eras. Whereas decisions bound up with the scientific, technical-economic dynamic are organized at the national level and at the level of individual enterprises, the resulting threats make us all members of a world risk society. The task of ensuring the health and safety of citizens can in world risk society no longer be performed at the national level in spite of the divisions and power struggles that exist in tackling climate change, and the financial crisis could be a springboard for creating a more cooperative world.

This is the "cosmopolitan moment" of the ecological crisis (Beck 2008). With the appearance of ecological discourse, the end of "foreign policy," the end of the "domestic affairs of another country," the end of the national state is becoming an everyday experience. At the same time, a central strategy in the production of difference and indifference becomes discernable. The established rules for allocating responsibility—causality and blame—are breaking down. This means that their indefatigable application in administration, management, and the administration of justice now produces the opposite result: dangers grow *as a result of* being made anonymous. In other words, the old routines of decision, control, and production (in law, science, administration, industry, and politics) cause the material destruction of nature *and* its symbolic normalization. The two complement and aggravate one another. To put it more concretely, it is not the rule violation but the rule itself that "normalizes" the death of species, rivers, and lakes.

This circular movement between symbolic normalization and permanent material threat and destruction is captured by the concept of "organized irresponsibility." The state administration, politics, industrial management, and research work out the criteria of what is rational and safe, with the result that the hole in the ozone layer grows larger, allergies become endemic, and so on.

Alongside (and independent of) the material explosiveness, discourse-strategic action potentially renders *politically* explosive the dangers that are normalized in the circuits of legitimation of administration, politics, law, and management and spread uncontrollably on a global scale. To speak with and against Max Weber (1972): rational bureaucracy transforms universal culpability into acquittal, and as an unintended side effect threatens the very basis of its claim to rational control.

The key idea of the theory of world risk society, therefore, is that the transformation of the unseen side effects of industrial production into global ecological flashpoints is not strictly a problem of the "environing" world—it is not a so-called environmental problem—but instead a radical institutional crisis of the first (national) phase of industrial modernity. As long as these new developments are understood within the conceptual horizon of industrial society, they continue to be seen as negative side effects of seemingly justifiable and calculable action ("vestigial risks") and their tendency to subvert systems and delegitimize basic principles of rationality goes unrecognized. Their central political and cultural significance becomes apparent only within the conceptual horizon of world risk society and they underscore the need for reflexive self- and re-definition of the Western model of modernity.

In this phase of the discourse of world risk society, it gradually becomes apparent that the threats triggered by technological-industrial development are neither calculable nor controllable as measured by existing institutional yardsticks. A prime example of this is the climate change debate. It requires crass ignorance or decidedly selective vision to overlook the link between an ominously rising temperature curve and increasing greenhouse gas emissions, notwithstanding the uncertainty of the correlation. That the established national institutions have no answer to this is also in the meantime a truism. This forces us to reflect on the bases of the democratic, national, and economic models of the first modernity and to examine existing institutions (for externalizing the effects in the economy, law, science, and so on) and the historically devalued bases of their rationality. This is a truly global challenge, out of which new global flashpoints and even wars can emerge—though also supranational institutions of cooperation, conflict regulation, and consensus building.

The economy is also undergoing radical change. Once upon a time, in the entrepreneurial paradise of early capitalism, industry could launch projects *without* submitting to special controls. Then came the period of state regulations when business activity was subject to labor legislation, safety regulations, tariff agreements, and so on. In the world risk society, all of these agencies and regulations can be observed without this guaranteeing security. Even managers who observe the regulations may suddenly find themselves placed in the dock of global public opinion as "environmental polluters." Manufactured insecurity thus appears in the core areas of action and management founded on economic rationality. The normal reactions of industry and politics are to block demands for effective change and to condemn as irrational or hysterical the storm of protest that breaks out in spite of official assurances. The way is now open for a series of errors. Proudly confident of representing reason in a sea of irrationalism, people tumble headlong into the trap of extremely heated risk conflicts (see Lau 1989; Nelkin 1992; Hildebrandt et al. 1994; Holzer and Sørensen 2003; Voss, Bauknecht, and Kemp 2006).

In world risk society, business projects become *political* matters, in the sense that large investments presuppose long-term consensus. Such consensus, however, is no longer guaranteed—indeed it is jeopardized—by the old routines of simple modernization. What could formerly be negotiated and implemented behind closed doors under the guise of "practical constraints"—waste disposal, for example, and even production methods or product design—is now in danger of being exposed to the crossfire of public criticism.

The most important consequence is the politicization of formerly taken-for-granted presuppositions and institutions. Who has to "prove" what under conditions of manufactured uncertainty? What should be regarded as sufficient proof? Who should decide on compensation? The legal system does not found social peace any longer because it generalizes and legitimizes threats to life—and the threat to politics.

Indicators, Conditions of Emergence, and Forms of Expression of a Global Subpolitics

On the Concept of Global Subpolitics

Anyone who speaks of world risk *society* must also address how global threats lead to action. Here two arenas or actors can be distinguished: first, globalization *from above* (e.g., through international treaties and institutions) and, second, globalization *from below* (e.g., through new transnational actors operating outside of the system of parliamentary politics who challenge established political organizations and interest groups). There is compelling evidence of the existence and operation of both arenas. Thus the majority of international accords on the environment were reached over an extremely short period, in other words, over the past three decades.

Richard Falk identifies a number of political arenas in which globalization from above is pushed through:

The response to threats against strategic oil reserves in the Middle East, the efforts to expand the GATT framework, the coercive implementation of the nuclear nonproliferation regime, the containment of South-North migration and refugee flows.... The legal implications of globalization-from-above would tend to supplant interstate law with a species of global law, but one at odds in most respects with "the law of humanity." (1994, 137)[8]

It is repeatedly objected that global environmental politics represents, at best, the proverbial drop in the bucket. However, we must also consider whether in years to come we will witness an ecological conversion and whether policy on climate change will be raised to the level of "serious politics" because governments whose hands are tied by the institutions of the nation-state discover new opportunities for strategic action and an unexpected source of legitimation in a global alliance

around climate change. Already over the past decade a number of spec-
tacular global boycott movements operating across cultural borders have
made clear that the impotence of official policy when faced with industrial interests is an impotence vis-à-vis the classical institutional divisions.
For in the meantime, agencies of a globalization *from below* have also
appeared on the scene in the shape of nongovernmental organizations
(NGOs) such as Robin Wood, Greenpeace, Amnesty International, and
Terre des Hommes. Here one can discern the initial contours of a "global
citizenship"—or, as we would say, a new constellation of global subpolitics is emerging. The principal conclusion is that this constellation
can give rise to a differentiation between governance and the nation-
state. The first concrete indicators of this are new alliances between civic
groups and national governments, which are seizing their chance and are
sweeping everything else (opposition, their own errors and omissions)
away in the name of "Save the World." In this respect, the concept of
global subpolitics deepens the cosmopolitan moment of world risk
society. We must now explain how this is possible.

The victory march of industrial modernity heralds the universal
success of rational form of political administration. The common sense
of this era is supported by an everything-under-control mentality, which
extends even to the uncontrollability that it itself produces. However,
the imposition of this form of order and control brings about its opposite, namely, the return of uncertainty and insecurity. Global climate
problems arise as "second-order dangers" (Bonss 1995). In this way,
society opens up into the (sub)political as a result of the side-effects of
global dangers. All fields of action—the economy and science, private
life and the family, and politics—face a decisive turning point: they need
a new justification; they must be renegotiated and rebalanced. How
should this be conceptualized?

Crisis is not the right concept, any more than dysfunction or disintegration, for it is precisely the *triumphs* of unbridled industrial
modernization that call it into question. This is what is meant by
"reflexive modernization": theoretically, self-application; empirically,
self-transformation; politically, loss of legitimacy and a power vacuum.
This can be clarified by a figure of thought of Thomas Hobbes. As is
well known, he argued for a strong, authoritarian state, but he also
specified *one* individual right of civil resistance. If the state creates or
permits life-threatening conditions, with the result that a citizen must
"abstain from the use of food, medicine, or any other thing, without

which he cannot live" then, according to Hobbes, "hath that man the Liberty to disobey" (Hobbes 1968, 269).

Analysed in terms of social policy, therefore, the ecological crisis involves a *systematic violation of basic rights* whose long-term socially destabilizing effects can scarcely be overestimated. For dangers are being produced by industry, externalized by economics, individualized by the legal system, legitimized by the natural sciences, and downplayed by politics. That this is undermining the power and credibility of institutions only becomes apparent when the system is put to the test by Greenpeace, for example, and, in a completely different way, by al-Qaeda. The result is the subpoliticization of world society.

The concept of subpolitics refers to the *decoupling of politics from government*; it underlines that politics is also possible beyond the representative institutions of the nation-states. This holds for transnational corporations as much as for the managers of global uncertainty in international organizations, social movements, or, in the opposite sense, the terrorist network that breaks the state's monopoly on violence. Thus the concept of subpolitics directs attention to indicators of a global self-organization of non-state politics that has the potential to mobilize all areas of society. Subpolitics means *direct* politics—that is, *selective* intervention, sometimes even individual participation in political decisions, bypassing the institutions of representative will formation (political parties, parliaments), often without legal backing or in deliberate violation of all law. In other words, subpolitics means the shaping and transformation of society from below, irrespective of the political aims of this intervention. The state, business, science, law, the military, professions, everyday existence, the private sphere—in short, the basic institutions of the first modernity—become caught up in the storms of global political controversies. Interestingly, this differentiation between state politics and subpolitics does not lead automatically or exclusively to depoliticization, as is often assumed. Rather, it now becomes possible to forge new transborder alliances in order to implement highly legitimate civic goals that afford governments new opportunities for action in domestic policy against the opposition, business, the mass media, and the electorate. Accordingly, in a future "cosmopolitan doctrine of government," the overlapping of domestic and foreign policy—in particular, the extension of the state's domestic room for maneuver through its involvement in global affairs (climate change policy)—must assume central importance. Such alliances do not fit into the traditional spectrum of party-political differences, however. Thus the subpolitics of world society can certainly find expression in ad hoc "coalitions of opposites" (of parties, nations, regions, religions, governments, corporations, and social movements). The decisive point is that, in one way or another, subpolitics sets politics free by changing the rules and boundaries of the political so that global politics becomes more open and more amenable to new goals, issues, and interdependencies.

I will illustrate this point, first, with an example of a symbolically staged mass boycott, and in subsequent sections I continue with the subpolitics of climate change.

In the summer of 1995, Greenpeace, the latter-day crusader for good causes, initially succeeded in getting Shell to dispose of a scrapped oil rig on land rather than sink it in the Atlantic. The multinational activist organization then tried to halt a resumption of French nuclear tests by publicly pillorying President Jacques Chirac for a deliberate breach of international treaties. Many asked whether it signalled the end of fundamental rules of international politics when an unauthorized actor like Greenpeace could conduct its own world domestic politics without regard for national sovereignty or diplomatic norms.

What such resistance to Greenpeace overlooked was that the multinational oil company was brought to its knees not by Greenpeace but by a mass public boycott set in motion by a worldwide televised indictment. Greenpeace itself did not rock the political system; rather, it revealed the resulting vacuum of power and legitimacy.

Everywhere there are signs of this coalition model of global subpolitics or direct politics. Alliances of forces presumed incapable of allying with one another are coming into being. Thus the then German chancellor, Helmut Kohl, joined the Greenpeace protest as a citizen who also happened to be the head of government and supported Greenpeace's action against then British Prime Minister John Major. Suddenly political elements in everyday action—for example, filling one's car with gas—were discovered and put into effect. Car drivers banded together against the oil industry (which is really something to savor). In the end, the state joined in with the illegitimate action and its organizers. In this way the state used its power to legitimize a deliberate, extra-parliamentary rule violation, while for their part the protagonists of direct politics explicitly sought to escape—through a kind of "ecological self-administered justice"—the narrow framework of indirect, legally sanctioned authorities and rules. Finally, the anti-Shell alliance marked a sea change between the politics of the first and second modernity. National governments sat in the audience while the unauthorized actors of the second modernity orchestrated the events.

In the case of the worldwide movement against President Chirac's decision to resume nuclear testing, a spontaneous global alliance arose of governments, Greenpeace activists, and the most diverse protest groups. The French miscalculation was reflected in two aspects of the situation: (a) the Mururoa decision coincided with commemorations of the fiftieth anniversary of the United States dropping atomic bombs on Hiroshima and Nagasaki; and (b) this decision was unanimously condemned by a meeting of the ASEAN Forum, in which, to top it all, the United States and Russia took part. All this pointed to a momentary alliance of direct politics spanning national, economic, religious, and political-ideological differences. The result was a global coalition of conflicting symbolic and economic forces. A special feature of this politics of the second modernity is that in practice its "globality" does not exclude anyone or anything—not only in a social sense, but also morally and ideologically. It is, thought through to its conclusion, a politics *without opponents or opposing forces*, a kind of *enemyless* politics.

The political novelty, therefore, was not that David had beaten Goliath but that David *plus Goliath*, acting at a global level, successfully joined together, first against a multinational and then against a national government and one of its policies. What was new was the worldwide alliance between extraparliamentary and parliamentary forces, citizens and governments, for a cause that is legitimate in the higher sense: saving the world.

Something else also became apparent. The post-traditional world only appears to be dominated by individualization. Paradoxically, the challenges posed by global threats provide it with a source of new global morality and activism and new forms (and forums) of protest—though also new hysteria. Status or class-consciousness, belief in progress or decline—all of this could be replaced by the humanity-wide project of saving the world environment. Global threats found global risk communities, at least ad hoc ones at particular historical moments.

This is also new. Politics and morality are acquiring priority over expert rationality. Whether one can go beyond single issues to constitute a coherent environmental politics through such politicization is quite another matter. This probably marks the limits of global subpolitics.

Conversely, the trend toward subpoliticization should not be considered as irrational at all because it bears the hallmarks of republican modernity in contrast to the representative, national-parliamentary democracy of parties. The activities of multinationals and of national governments are being exposed to the pressure of global public opinion. Striking and decisive here is the individual-collective participation in global action networks: citizens are discovering that the act of purchasing can function as a vote that they can always use in a political way. In boycotts, the active consumer society thus links up and forms an alliance with direct democracy, on a global scale.

In this way, the cosmopolitan society constitutes a global nexus of responsibility in which individuals, and not only their organizational representatives, can participate directly in political decisions. This explains the discussions of and calls for "technological citizenship" in the United States. The issue is the recovery of basic democratic rights in the face of the "anonymous rule" of technological developments. In Andrew Zimmerman's view (1995, 88), social autonomy is being hollowed out by technological autonomy, whereas in the first modernity, the well-being and "freedom" of the citizen were a function of the well-being and freedom of technical systems. Philip Frankenfeld's contrasting approach attempts to justify the demand for technological participation:

The status of technological citizenship may be enjoyed at the national, state, local, or global level or at levels in between. Hence one can be a technological citizen of…the Chernobyl ecosphere, of the plastic explosives production and use "noosphere"—which is global in scale—of a particular nuclear-free zone in the noncontiguous network of them, of the realm covered by the non-proliferation treaty….However, one *would* be a technological citizen of *any* of these spheres of impact *if* their inhabitants deigned to create a set of agencies, a cocoon of protections or benefits, or a cocoon of rights and responsibilities granting subjects status in relation to impacts of technologies with a specific overarching purpose. (1992, 463, qtd. in Zimmerman 1995, 89; see also van Steenbergen 1994; Archibugi and Held 1995)

As normatively overarching goals of citizenship, Frankenfeld cites: "(1) autonomy, (2) dignity, (3) assimilation—vs. alienation—of members of the polity." Citizenship therefore includes "1. rights to knowledge or information; 2. rights to participation; 3. rights to guarantees of informed consent; and 4. rights to limitation on the total amount of endangerment of collectivities and individuals" (Frankenfeld 1992, 462, 465).

But where are the sites, and what are the instruments and the media of this direct politics of a "global technological citizenship"? The political site of world risk society is not the street but *television* and the Internet—in short, the old and the new media. Its political subject is not the working class and its organization, the trade union. Its function is assumed by the *staging of cultural symbols in the mass media*, where the accumulated bad conscience of the actors and consumers of industrial society can be assuaged.

This thesis can be illustrated from three directions. First, destruction and protest are symbolically mediated in the abstract omnipresence of dangers. Second, in acting against ecological destruction, everyone is also their own enemy. Third, the ecological crisis is breeding a cultural Red Cross consciousness. Those who inscribe this on their banner are admitted into the ecological nobility and rewarded with an almost unlimited credit of trust—which has the advantage that, in case of doubt, one's information and not that of the agents of industry is believed.

Herein lies a crucial limitation of direct politics. Human beings are like children wandering around in a "forest of symbols" (Baudelaire 1993). In other words, we have to rely on the symbolic politics of the media. This holds especially on account of the abstractness and omnipresence of destruction that keep world risk society going. Tangible, simplifying symbols, in which cultural nerve fibers are touched and alarmed, here take on central political importance. These symbols have to be produced or forged in the open fire of conflict provocation, before the strained and terrified public of television viewers. The key question is: who discovers (or invents), and how, the symbols that disclose the structural character of the problems while at the same time fostering the ability to act? The latter should be all the more successful, the simpler and neater is the staged symbol, the fewer are the costs of public protest actions for the individual, and the more easily everyone can thereby relieve their consciences. In this way, even errors in information, such as those committed by Greenpeace in the anti-Shell campaign, can be glossed over.

Simplicity has many meanings. The first is *transmissibility*: we are all environmental sinners; just as Shell wanted to dump its oil rig in the sea, "we all" itch to toss soda cans out of the car window. This is the everyman situation that makes the Shell case (as socially constructed) so "transparent." However, there is the essential difference that the size of the sin seems to increase the likelihood of official acquittal. The second meaning is *moral outrage*: "the big shots" can sink an oil rig filled with toxic waste in the Atlantic with the approval of the government and its experts, while "we small fry"—especially in Germany—have to divide every teabag into three parts, paper, string, and leaves, and dispose of them separately in order to save the world. The third meaning is *simple alternative actions*: in order to damage Shell, you had to and could fill up your car with "morally clean" gasoline from one of its competitors. And the fourth meaning is *sale of ecological indulgences*: the bad conscience of the original inhabitants of industrial society lent the Greenpeace boycott importance because it meant that a kind of personal *ego te absolvo* could be granted at no personal cost.

Far from aggravating a general sense of meaninglessness in the modern world, global ecological threats give rise to a horizon of meaning dominated by avoidance, resistance, and assistance, a moral climate that intensifies with the scale of the perceived danger and in which the roles of hero and villain acquire a new political significance. The perception of the world within the coordinates of environmental and industrial self-endangerment combine morality, religion, fundamentalism, desperation, tragedy, and tragicomedy—always connected with their opposites: salvation, assistance, and liberation—into a universal drama. In this worldwide comedy, business is free to assume the role of either the villain of the piece or the hero-rescuer. This is the very background that enables Greenpeace to hog the limelight with the cunning of weakness. Greenpeace practices a kind of *judo politics* whose goal is to mobilize the superior strength of environmental miscreants against themselves.

The Greenpeace people are multinational media professionals who know how self-contradictions between pronouncements and violations of safety and surveillance norms can be presented so that the great and powerful (corporations, governments), blinded by power, stumble into the trap and thrash around telegenically for the entertainment of the global public. Henry David Thoreau and Mahatma Gandhi would have been delighted to see Greenpeace using the instruments of the media age to stage worldwide mass civil disobedience. Greenpeace is at the same time a veritable forge of political symbols in which cultural transgressions and symbols of transgression are produced with the artificial means of black-and-white conflicts, which can concentrate protests and turn them into a lightening rod for the collective guilty conscience. This is how new certainties and new outlets for rage are constructed in the enemyless democracy of Europe after the end of the East-West conflict. This is and remains part of the global fairground of symbolic politics.

Isn't all this an absurd distraction from the central challenges of world risk society?

If we focus not on single issues, however, but on the new political constellation, then the stimulation of experiencing success becomes apparent. In the playful merging of opposites into transcultural global resistance, cosmopolitan society feels its direct power. Everyone knows that nothing is as infectious as success. Anyone who wants to track down what is exciting or thrilling soon discovers that here mass sport and politics fuse with one another on a global scale. It is a kind of political boxing match with active audience participation, all around the world. No normal television entertainment can compete with that; not only does it lack the extra kick of the real, but also the ecological aura of world salvation that no longer meets with opposition. At any event, *this* case study makes clear that the widespread talk of the end of politics and democracy or of the demise of all values—in short, the whole canon of cultural criticism—is foolish because it is blind to history. People only need the slightest touch of the coattails of such tangible success and they are swept away.

As awareness of the risks spreads, world risk society becomes self-critical. Its foundations, coordinates, and ready-made coalitions are thrown into turmoil. Anyone who wants to understand why must inquire into the cultural and political significance of manufactured risks. Risk too is externalized, concentrated subjectivity and history. It is a kind of collective obsessional memory of the fact that our decisions and mistakes are behind what now confronts us. Global risks are the embodiment of the errors of the whole industrial era; they are a kind of collective return of the repressed. In their conscious investigation may lie an opportunity to break the spell of industrial fatalism. If someone wanted to build a machine to counteract the mechanization of society, they would have to use the blueprint of ecological self-endangerment. It is a reification that cries out to be overcome. This is the admittedly tiny chance for global (sub)politics in world risk society.

If the need for a worldwide environmental politics from above is also included, then it becomes apparent that we are condemned to reinvent the political.

Subpolitics from Above: Global Climate Policy and the Potential Emergence of the "Cosmopolitan State"

The global character of risks (climate change) is giving rise to uncertainty—the framing of the global problem, possible organizational

responses, legal underpinnings, global economic preconditions and implications, and so on—which is being processed by a whole ensemble of
institutions such as the International Monetary Fund, the World Bank,
the World Trade Organization (WTO) and the Organization for Economic Co-operation and Development (OECD). The directors of these
institutions, who represent the incarnation of "globalization from above,"
know each other and often move from one organization to the other.
They have close contacts with the national think tanks and decision-
making bodies from which they are mainly recruited. Thus a good nick-
name for such experts in matters global would be Mr. or Mrs. Network.
They are embodiments of the global interdependence and "discourse
coalitions" previously discussed. Viewed from the one angle, they sit
between the stools in their professional activity but, from the other, they
sit on several stools. Under conditions of indeterminate global risks, they
are constantly confronted with the contradictions between the different
national definitions of their work or the various definitions in terms of
global regions. This sets them free from the "national framings" and
enables them to define the shared goals of their work pragmatically and
in an ongoing mutual dialogue. It is they who also decide whether what
they do explodes the national premises, while for that reason perhaps
also being in the global *and* national, hence cosmopolitan, interest. This
means that here it is possible (though not necessary) that conceptual
factories for forging a cosmopolitan subpolitics may emerge that escape
the constraints of the national-definition relations of risk politics. The
climate report of the former head of the World Bank, Nicholas Stern
(2006), written at the behest of the British government, which presented
it with great pomp, is an outstanding illustration of this point.

The Stern Report's major accomplishment as a work of "stage management" is not only that it transformed the "rationale" of the climate
problem but also that it made it into an economic and political policy
issue. For years scientists have been presenting compelling reasons why
global warming must finally meet with decisive action. Stern's study has
now added the decisive economic argument. Not so long ago, the associated rational construct—in other words, the way in which catastrophic
climate change was "framed"—boiled down to the alternative of balancing high costs today against a vague risk in the distant future. How much
of our current prosperity must we sacrifice to prevent our planet from
possibly overheating some time in the future? That was the *staging of a
dilemma* that permitted chauvinistic national politicians and sceptical
voters to do nothing. The Stern Report turns the argument from its head

onto its (economic) feet. The costs of taking measures against global warming today are minor in comparison to the costs of doing nothing. In the future doing nothing could rob the global economy of 20 percent of its performance—annually. Thus the new rationale is that what the world invests in climate protection today will be repaid with compound interest in the future. This robs the opponents of the cost argument—there's no excuse left.

If the newly staged rationale is to acquire historical force, however, we need more than a successful demonstration of the lack of economic alternatives to preventive climate protection. In addition, an alliance of global economic actors must be forged, one of whose major goals is to commit the nations and governments that are anxious about their sovereignty to the new vision of multistate cooperation. The lingering doubt concerning one's own argument must be shielded against internal critics. Let us begin with this last point.

Definition relations are relations of domination that confer collective validity and legitimation on the stagings of risk. In the national constitution of the first modernity they are geared to "progress." This means that in the distribution of the burdens of proof, *laissez-faire*—something is safe until it has been proven dangerous—enjoys priority over the principle of *precaution*: nothing is safe until it has been proven harmless. The Stern Report substitutes the principle of precaution for the laissez-faire distribution of the burdens of proof, not as the result of an official pronouncement and debate or a vote among scientists but through the power of publicly staged arguments. Thus the relations of definition were "revolutionized" in that now, when faced with manufactured uncertainty and the threat to the planet, the principle that had previously held, "When in doubt, opt for doubt," was replaced by the opposite principle, "When in doubt, opt against doubt." In view of the threat facing humanity, the irreducible uncertainty of any prognosis of catastrophe is played down, as it were, and the option of hiding behind the protective shield of burdens of proof that cannot be satisfied is removed.

The *anticipation dilemma* of self-endangering civilization is either to succumb, because the feared decline regrettably could not be proved, or not to succumb but to expose oneself to the scornful mirth of a scientifically staged global panic echoing through the centuries.

Stern stage manages the magical power of large numbers. Economists, being economists, will expose his calculations to scrupulous doubt. But the methodology of uncertainty—namely, presenting ranges of possible scenarios rather than absolute prognoses—has in the meantime won the agreement of renowned colleagues.[9]

In general, we should expect methodological misgivings from within the profession gradually to lose their countervailing staging power insofar as the global economy itself sees decisive political action to counter climate change as a source of new opportunities for markets and growth, as is clearly increasingly the case. The onetime major adversaries of the ecology movement—the oil multinational Shell and the energy companies, and so on—have long since wrapped themselves in a green cloak and are busily looking for ways out of the carbon dioxide business. These are not born again do-gooders acting of humanitarian interest. Business continues to pursue short-term goals that threaten long-term harm to human beings and the environment as (shall we say?) "acceptable costs of doing business." Yet the global consensus on climate protection that is now within reach is also creating new markets, "enforced markets," as can typically occur in the context of acknowledged global risks. The economic attraction here is that safety and precautionary principles prescribed by the state enforce the (ultimately even worldwide) "consumption" of carbon dioxide-free and energy-efficient technologies. Under a regime of "green capitalism" composed of transnationally structured ecological enforced markets, ecology no longer represents a hindrance to the economy. Rather, the opposite holds: ecology and climate protection could soon represent a direct route to profits.

Ultimately, state politics can be reinvented by actively embracing a policy of climate protection in an alliance with civic groups. In the first place, the attribute *global* and the honorific term *climate protection* promise elevated status and weighty responsibility and entice heads of government, ground down in the mills of domestic politics, with the prospect of statesmanlike stature. In the case of Great Britain, there is the additional factor that the term *global climate protection* revives pleasant memories of the past glories of the British Empire in a humanitarian guise.

The cosmopolitan state has internalized the cosmopolitan outlook in institutional form to the extent that it has ceased to invoke the national outlook and, by actively cultivating connections with other states and civic movements, has taken advantage of the room for maneuver opened up by the globalization of the economy and culture (Beck 2005, 217–235). This means in concrete terms that the cosmopolitan room for maneuver of the state must be conceptualized and explored at both the conceptual and the political level independently of the received notions of sovereignty and autonomy. In that case the sovereignty or the autonomy of the state would no longer be the primary focus but instead its *practical capacities* in the broadest sense, hence the ability of states to cooperate in solving global problems (Grande and Risse 2000, 253).

To put it even more concretely, the state's recovered cosmopolitan scope for action *extends* its influence in the domestic *and* the foreign domains through action and governance in transnational networks to which other states—but also NGOs, supranational institutions, and transnational corporations—belong. Thus the cosmopolitan state, freed from scruples concerning sovereignty, uses the unrecompensed cooperation of other governments, nongovernmental organizations, and globally operating corporations to solve "national" problems.

Hence the room for maneuver of cosmopolitan states that could be generated by overcoming climate change can no longer be derived from the institutional capacities of national governments. The "doctrine of government" trapped in methodological nationalism is becoming false. It ignores the cosmopolitan extension of power in the national political domain. Reduced to a formula, the scope for action of the cosmopolitan state would be the *sum* of the scope for action of each of the national governmental institutions and bureaucracies *plus* the deliberate use of the cooperative capacities of transnational networks.

Of course, this optimistic construction could easily collapse under its own weight. It is fragile because the costs and benefits of an active climate change policy are not equally distributed, either internationally or nationally, and because the burning question of justice in a radically unequal world is at the heart of the distribution conflicts. The costs will hit existing generations hardest whereas the benefits will fall to the grandchildren of our grandchildren. The wealthiest countries must demonstrate the greatest willingness to compromise even though they are not the most vulnerable to the impacts of global warming. In order to strike the required "global deal," the agreement of the United States is most urgently needed, even though it would have to pay China, its archrival, gigantic sums in order to make that country carbon dioxide-free—at a historical juncture when this huge country is preparing to overtake the United States economically and to become the center of world power. The counterargument is easy to foresee: the poor must pay for the high-flying dreams of rescuing the world. Thus there are many reasons for resignation. But a large-scale political experiment of historic dimensions has begun that will exert a great fascination, as a global drama or also as a global comedy, and probably both.

Outlook: Does World Risk Society Have an Enlightening Function?

Anybody who confronts global risk must appreciate unintentional irony. The grand narrative of global risk and its social and political effects tells of the unintentional satire and the optimistic futility with which the basic institutions of modern society—science, the state, the economy, and the military—seek to anticipate what cannot be anticipated. We had to await the events of the second half of the twentieth century to learn what Socrates meant by his puzzling statement "I know that I know nothing." Ironically, our continually perfected scientific-technological society has granted us the fatal insight that we do not know what we do not know. But this is precisely the source of the dangers that threaten humanity. The perfect example of this is the debate over the coolant CFC (Böschen et al. 2004). In 2004, around forty-five years after its discovery, the chemists Rowland and Melina put forward the hypothesis that CFCs destroy the ozone layer of the stratosphere and that as a result the world is increasingly exposed to ultraviolet radiation. Their conclusion was that a chain of unpredictable side effects would lead to a dramatic increase in the cancer risk among human beings. When the substance CFC was invented, however, nobody could have known or even suspected that this "miracle agent" would have such devastating effects.

Those (like the U.S. government) who believe in non-knowing aggravate the threat of a climate catastrophe. Or, in more general terms, the more emphatically world risk society is denied, the more it becomes a reality. The disregard for the globalizing risks heightens the globalization of risk.

The greatest military power in history constructed a defense system costing countless billions of dollars to protect it against missile attacks. Must it not also count as a bitter irony when the sense of security and self-confidence of the United States are deeply shaken by an attack that, by any risk logic, was extremely improbable—namely the use of commercial passenger aircraft piloted by suicide attackers as missiles—since this action destroyed the symbols of American world power? The irony of risk here is that rationality—which means past experience—misleads us into measuring risk against completely inappropriate standards and into treating them as calculable and controllable, whereas catastrophes always occur in situations of which we know nothing and that as a result we cannot anticipate.

Risk is ambivalence. In the modern world, taking risks is inescapable for individuals and governments. At the turn of the twenty-first century, all actions must face global risks. But against the view that we are help-less in the face of obscure powers, we have to ask: what is the ruse of history that also belongs to world risk society and comes to light with its realization? In a word: does world risk society have an *enlightening function* and what form does this take? Does the dynamic of world risk society—contrary to the secular apocalyptic interpretation expressed in the social sciences—set free a "cosmopolitan moment," and how could this be understood and justified?

The experience of being at the mercy of global risks represented a shock for the whole of humanity. Nobody predicted such a development. Nietzsche had a premonition when he spoke of an "age of comparison" in which different cultures, peoples, and religions can enter into relations with each other and live side by side. Even though he did not say as much, he was aware of the historical irony that not only physical but also ethical destructive power made it possible for modern human beings to overcome the nation-state and the international order and thus to go beyond the heaven and hell of modernity.

When risk is perceived as omnipresent, three reactions are possible: *denial, apathy* or *transformation*. The first is a hallmark of modern culture, the second finds expression in postmodern nihilism, the third constitutes the cosmopolitan moment of world risk society. What this means can be explained by appealing to Hannah Arendt. The moment of existential threat—herein lies the fundamental ambivalence of global risks—unintentionally (and often also imperceptibly and ineffectually) opens up the (mis)fortune of a possible new beginning (which is no excuse for false sentimentality). How can and should one live in the shadow of global risks? How can one lead one's life when old certainties come to naught or prove to be lies? Arendt's answer anticipates the irony of risk: the expectation of the unexpected means that the taken-for-granted can no longer be taken for granted. The shock of danger is a call for a new beginning. Where there is a new beginning, there are new possibilities of action. For example, people forge relations across estab-lished borders. Freedom means strangers acting in concert. Freedom is founded on this ability to make new beginnings.

Arendt writes: "Politics rests on the fact of human plurality," and hence its task is to organize and regulate the cultural coexistence of people who encounter one another as equals. Drawing on the customary interpretation of human beings as a *zoon politikon* (Aristotle) according to which the political is an intrinsic part of human nature, Arendt stresses that politics does not have its source *in* the human being but *between* human beings—more precisely, between human beings who belong to different worlds and who create a joint space of action through their actions. In view of the catastrophic experiences of the twentieth century—indeed, almost as a response to them—Arendt emphasizes that "human beings themselves, in a most miraculous and mysterious way, are endowed with the gift of performing miracles," namely, they can act, take initiatives, make a new beginning. "The miracle of freedom resides in this ability to make new beginnings, which resides in turn in the fact that every human being, by being born into the world which existed before him and continues to exist after him, is himself a new beginning" (Arendt 1998, 34).

Arendt thought that the republican idea of a new beginning under conditions of freedom was realized at just a few historical moments, in the Athenian polis and with the American Founding Fathers, though also following the Holocaust. At the beginning of the twenty-first century we must add to these the cosmopolitan moment of world risk society. Paradoxically enough, sociology—a child of the first modernity—does not share this sceptical self-confidence in the possibility of a new beginning against the background of the expectation of catastrophic risks, a confidence that makes possible a wholesale reinvention of the basic institutions of the modern national society (Beck 1997). On the contrary, a certain nostalgia that has never disappeared is built into the foundations of European sociological thought. Perhaps this nostalgia can be overcome through the theory of world risk society. My aim is a new, non-nostalgic critical theory whose task is also to reconceptualize the past of modernity from the standpoint of the threatened future. It is not correctly described as utopianism or pessimism; only the concepts of irony and ambivalence accurately describe it. Instead of an either/or, I am looking for a new both/and: a way of bringing two contradictory postures, self-destruction and the capacity for a new beginning, into equilibrium. To what extent are global risks a force in present and future world history that escapes any control while simultaneously opening up new opportunities for action for states, NGOs, and the like (Beck 2008)?

Notes

1. I developed this theory in my book *World at Risk* (2008).

2. On reflexive modernization, see the contrasting positions of Ulrich Beck, Anthony Giddens, and Scott Lash in their book, *Reflexive Modernization* (Beck, Giddens, and Lash 1994) and the results of the continuing Munich Collaborative Research Centre on Reflexive Modernization collected in Beck and Bonss 2001 and Beck and Lau 2004.

3. See the historical analysis of basic concepts and theories of nature and the concept of "nature after the end of nature" in Böhme 1991; for an account of the both universal and subculturally specific images of nature among environmental activists, industrial managers, and so on, from the perspective of cultural theory, see Schwarz and Thompson 1990; and on the general images of nature in modern society, see Hitzler 1991, van den Daele 1992, and Gill 2003.

4. This is bringing to a close a long period in the history of sociology in which—in strict accordance with its original division of labor with the natural sciences—it could abstract from nature as the other, the environment, what is already given. This disregarding of nature corresponded precisely to a certain relation to it. The classical sociologist August Comte stated this explicitly. He expressly wanted the relationship of national conquest to be replaced with one of natural conquest by the rising bourgeois-industrial society, in order to defuse conflicts within society. Right up to the present day this theme has lost none of its significance. Abstraction from nature thus presupposes domination over nature. In this way, the "process of consuming nature"—which is how Karl Marx understood the labor production process—could be driven onward. When people speak today of "ecological citizenship," arguing that basic rights must be extended to animals, plants, and so on, they are expressing the emergence of this relationship of subordination and abstraction into its polar opposite.

5. Moreover, it is difficult to square the claims of cultural theory to transhistorical, context-independent validity with its interest in precision, relativity, and cultural construction. In which cultural context does this almost unthinking universalism originate? It is hard to give an answer without alluding to Eurocentrism.

6. "In the 1970s local claims were made by ordinary people living near the Sellafield nuclear reprocessing complex, that excess childhood leukemias were occurring in the area.... This issue came to the attention of TV researchers, and a national documentary programme was eventually broadcast in 1983." In the end, however, the excess cancers around Sellafield "were almost routinely referred to as having been *discovered* by the Black Committee" (Wynne 1996, 49).

7. Latour's *We Have Never Been Modern* (1993) is, however, one of the most outstanding and challenging works to have appeared for years on the sociology of technology. Perhaps even more important is his book *Politics of Nature* (2004), which has revolutionized political ecology.

8. On the framework conditions for creating international regimes, see Zürn 1995 (49–56) and Voss, Bauknecht, and Kemp 2006.

9. For example, Martin Rees, the president of the Royal Society, stated: "This should be a turning point in a debate which has pitted short-term economic interests against long-term costs to the environment, society and the economy" (2006, 7).

References

Adams, B. 1995. *Timewatch: The social analysis of time.* Cambridge, UK: Polity Press.

Archibugi, D., and D. Held, eds. 1995. *Cosmopolitan democracy.* Cambridge, UK: Polity Press.

Arendt, H. 1998. *The human condition.* Chicago: University of Chicago Press.

Baudelaire, C. 1993. *Flowers of evil.* Oxford: Oxford University Press.

Beck, U. 1992. *Risk society: Towards a new modernity.* London: Sage.

Beck, U. 1994. *Ecological politics in an age of risk.* Cambridge, UK: Polity Press.

Beck, U. 1997. *The reinvention of politics.* Cambridge, UK: Polity Press.

Beck, U. 1999. *World risk society.* Cambridge, UK: Polity Press.

Beck, U. 2005. *Power in the global age.* Cambridge, UK: Polity Press.

Beck, U. 2008. *World at risk.* Cambridge, UK: Polity Press.

Beck, U., and W. Bonss, eds. 2001. *Die Modernisierung der Moderne.* Frankfurt am Main: Suhrkamp.

Beck, U., A. Giddens, and S. Lash. 1994. *Reflexive modernization.* Cambridge, UK: Polity Press.

Beck, U., and B. Holzer. 2004. Wie global ist die Weltrisikogesellschaft? In *Entgrenzung und Entscheidung: Was ist neu an der Theorie reflexiver Modernisierung?,* ed. U. Beck and C. Lau, 421–439. Frankfurt am Main: Suhrkamp.

Beck, U., and C. Lau 2005. Second modernity as a research agenda: Theoretical and empirical explorations in the "meta-change" of modern society. *British Journal of Sociology* 56 (4):525–557.

Benn, G. 1986. *Das Gottfried Benn Brevier.* Munich: Fischer.

Böhme, G. 1991. *Die Natur im Zeitalter ihrer technischen Reproduzierbarkeit,* ed. G. Böhme. Frankfurt am Main: Suhrkamp.

Bonss, W. 1995. *Vom Risiko: Unsicherheit und Ungewißheit in der Moderne.* Hamburg: Bund.

Böschen, S., C. Lau, A. Obermeier, and P. Wehling. 2004. Die Erwartung des Unerwarteten. Science Assessment und der Wandel der Risikoerkenntnis. In

Entgrenzung und Entscheidung: Was ist neu an der Theorie reflexiver Modernisierung, eds. U. Beck and C. Lau, 123–148. Frankfurt am Main: Suhrkamp.

Burns, T. R., and T. Dietz. 1992. Socio-cultural evolution: Social rule systems, selection and agency. *International Sociology* 7 (3):259–283.

Catton, W. R., and R. E. Dunlap. 1978. Environmental sociology. *The American Sociologist* 13:41–49.

Dickens, P. 1992. *Society and nature*. London: Harvester Wheatsheaf.

Dietz, T., and T. R. Burns. 1992. Human agency and the evolutionary dynamics of culture. *Acta Sociologica* 35:187–200.

Douglas, M. 1986. *Risk acceptability according to the social sciences*. London: Routledge and Kegan Paul.

Douglas, M., and A. Wildavsky. 1982. *Risk and culture*. Berkeley: University of California Press.

Dunlap, R. 1997. The evolution of environmental sociology: A brief assessment of the American experience. In *The international handbook of environmental sociology*, ed. M. Redclift and G. Woodgate, 21–39. Cheltenham, UK: Edward Elgar.

Eder, K. 1996. *The social construction of nature*. London: Sage.

Ericson, R.V., A. Doyle, and D. Barry. 2003. *Insurance as governance*. Toronto: University of Toronto Press.

Esser, H. 1990. "Habits," "frames" und "rational choice." *Zeitschrift für Soziologie* 19 (4):231–247.

Ewald, F. 1991. Insurance and risk. In *The Foucault effect*, ed. G. Burchell, C. Gordon, and P. Miller, 197–210. Hemel Hempstead: Harvester Wheatsheaf.

Falk, R. 1994. The making of global citizenship. In *The condition of citizenship*, ed. B. van Steenbergen, 127–140. London: Sage.

Frank, A. G. 1969. *Latin America: Underdevelopment or revolution*. New York: Monthly Review Press.

Frankenfeld, P. 1992. Technological citizenship: A normative framework for risk studies. *Science, Technology, and Human Values* 17 (4):459–484.

Giddens, A. 1990. *The consequences of modernity*. Cambridge, UK: Polity Press.

Gill, B. 2003. *Streitfall Natur*. Opladen: Westdeutscher Verlag.

Grande, E., and T. Risse. 2000. Bridging the gap. Konzeptionelle Anforderungen an die politikwissenschaftliche Analyse von Globalisierungsprozessen. *Zeitschrift für Internationale Beziehungen* 7:235–266.

Hajer, M. A. 1995. *The politics of environmental discourse*. Oxford: Oxford University Press.

Haraway, D. 1991. *Simians, cyborgs and women: The reinvention of nature*. London: Routledge.

Hildebrandt, E., U. Gerhardt, C. Kühleis, S. Schenk, and B. Zimpelmann. 1994. Politisierung und Entgrenzung: Am Beispiel ökologisch erweiterter Arbeitspolitik. *Soziale Welt*, Special Issue 9:429–444.

Hitzler, R. 1991. Zur gesellschaftlichen Konstruktion von Natur. *Wechselwirkung* 50:43–48.

Hobbes, T. 1968. *Leviathan*. Harmondsworth: Penguin.

Holzer, B., and M. P. Sørensen. 2003. Rethinking subpolitics: Beyond the "Iron Cage" of modern politics? *Theory, Culture & Society* 20 (2):79–102.

Huber, J. 1995. *Nachhaltige Entwicklung*. Berlin: Stigma.

Jänicke, M. 1985. *Preventive environmental policy as ecological modernization and structural policy*. Berlin: Wissenschaftszentrum.

Latour, B. 1993. *We have never been modern*. Cambridge, MA: Harvard University Press.

Latour, B. 2004. *Politics of nature: How to bring the sciences into democracy*. Cambridge, MA: Harvard University Press.

Lau, C. 1989. Risikodiskurse. *Soziale Welt* 3:418–436.

Luhmann, N. 1993. *Risk—A sociological theory*. New York: De Gruyter.

McLaughlin, P., and T. Dietz. 2008. Structure, agency and environment: Toward an integrated perspective on vulnerability. *Global Environmental Change* 18: 99–111.

Nelkin, D., ed. 1992. *Controversy: Politics of technical decisions*. London: Sage.

Oechsle, M. 1988. *Der ökologische Naturalismus*. Frankfurt am Main: Campus.

Rees, M. 2006. Final piece in the jigsaw. *The Guardian* (Manchester), October 31, 7. http://www.guardian.co.uk/environment/2006/oct/31/greenpolitics.climatechange.

Rosa, E. 1998. Metatheoretical foundations for post-normal risk. *Journal of Risk Research* 1:15–44.

Rose, N. 2000. Government and control. *British Journal of Criminology* 40 (2):321–339.

Schwarz, M., and M. Thompson. 1990. *Divided we stand: Redefining politics, technology and social choice*. New York: Harvester Wheatsheaf.

Spaargaren, G., and A. P. J. Mol. 1991. Ecologie, Technologie en Sociale Verandering. In *Technologie en Milieubeheer*, ed. A. P. J. Mol, G. Spaargaren, and A. Klapwijk, 185–207. Den Haaf: SDU.

Steenbergen, B. van, ed. 1994. *The conditions of citizenship*. London: Sage.

Stern, N. 2006. Stern review on the economics of climate change. HM-Treasury. http://www.hm-treasury.gov.uk/.

Strydom, P. 2002. *Risk, environment and society: Ongoing debates, current issues and future prospects.* Buckingham, UK: Open University Press.

van den Daele, W. 1992. Concepts of nature in modern societies. In *European social science in transition,* ed. M. Dierkes and B. Biervert, 526–560. Frankfurt am Main: Campus.

Voss, J-P., D. Bauknecht, and R. Kemp, eds. 2006. *Reflexive governance for sustainable development.* Northampton, MA: Edward Elgar.

Wallerstein, I. 1974. *The modern world system,* vol. 1. Cambridge, UK: Cambridge University Press.

Weber, M. 1972. *Wirtschaft und Gesellschaft.* Tübingen: Mohr.

Wynne, B. 1996. May the sheep safely graze? In *Risk environment and modernity: Towards a new ecology,* ed. L. B. Szerszynski and B. Wynne, 4483. London: Sage.

Zimmermann, A. D. 1995. Towards a more democratic ethic of technological governance. *Science, Technology and Human Values* 20 (1):86–107.

Zürn, M. 1995. Globale Gefährdungen und internationale Kooperation. *Der Bürger im Staat* 45 (1):49–56.

3

Human Driving Forces of Global Change: Dominant Perspectives

Thomas Dietz, Eugene A. Rosa, and Richard York

Introduction

The spread of environmental impacts across planet Earth has attracted the title global environmental change (GEC). As described in chapter 1, the spread is global in two fundamental ways (Turner et al. 1990). First, some changes, such as depletion of stratospheric ozone or increases in the concentration of greenhouse gases (GHGs), are systemic due to changes in systems that function at a planetary level. Second, some changes, such as deforestation or the dispersion of nonnative species, are local in their occurrence and impact but are happening throughout the globe and, therefore, are cumulative. Environmental change in the twenty-first century can be labeled global because many of the forces that drive it are shaped by processes that are in themselves global, such as the emergence of global political institutions, dispersed production and international trade, the diffusion of common risks, the diffusion of information via the World Wide Web, and the worldwide spread of consumer culture.[1]

That the drivers of environmental change, like so much else in the twenty-first century, are globalized hides a critical point about how we study anthropogenic environmental change. A striking feature of globalization is the wide variation in environmental impacts across the planet. The basic question, then, is: What causes larger impacts in some places than in others?[2] Why, for example, are pollution levels so much higher in states of the former Soviet Union than in, say, the United States, the European Union, or Japan? The general answer to the question is already known, namely, that the variation is the result of a large range of social, economic, cultural, and political factors. But this answer begs an operational question: which units should be the focus of analysis—individuals, households, communities, organizations, nations, or the entire global social system?

A critical insight of the social sciences is that units of analysis are nested within each other: each unit is either embedded in more aggregate units or embeds less aggregate units or both. A household is made up of individuals, as is an organization. A community comprises individuals, households, and organizations. A nation comprises individuals, households, communities, and organizations (including local and regional forms of government). Trying to understand causal processes at any level of analysis while taking adequate account of more and less aggregate levels is a fundamental challenge in the social sciences (Gibson, Ostrom, and Ahn 2000; Berkes et al. 2006; Wilbanks 2006; Young 2002). The challenge is magnified when the goal, as here, is to understand coupled human and natural systems (CHANS), since human systems are never isomorphic with ecological systems. In figure 3.1 we illustrate this point by showing the variety of units examined by ecologists and by social scientists. Both ecologists and social scientists conceptualize the systems they study as hierarchical, but with complex embeddings. Unfortunately, the boundaries of the biophysical units seldom correspond to the boundaries of the social units. Taken together the embedding and the boundary challenges frame some of the most difficult methodological issues in studying why human impacts on the environment vary across individuals, households, communities, organizations, and nations.

Chapter Purpose

Our purpose in this chapter is to critically review major perspectives from ecology and the social sciences about the interconnected CHANS of GEC. In particular our emphasis is on perspectives that posit reasons for the variation across nation-states in the environmental threats to sustainability and the impacts they generate. There is a substantial and rich literature exploring cross-national variation in environmental risks and impacts. There are, however, two limitations in this literature that we should note at the outset. First, the amount of discourse across disciplinary boundaries is meager. Economists seldom cite sociologists and vice versa, ecologists seldom cite anthropologists and vice versa, and so on. Second, empirical work has seriously lagged behind theoretical developments and discourse approaches. As a result, the field is less cumulative than it could be and there are few critical tests of multiple theories

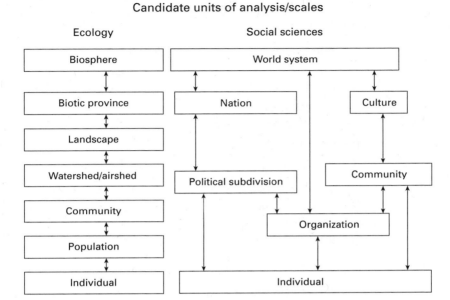

Figure 3.1
Units of theoretical and empirical analysis in ecology and the social sciences.

based on well-specified models or extensive data. Thus, we focus on explicating and juxtaposing theoretical arguments about the drivers of anthropogenic environmental change, with the goal of aligning them in a way that allows us to see where cross-fertilization is occurring among them, where gaps in theory remain, and how to better connect theory to empirical test. By juxtaposing and critically evaluating current theories, we also hope to encourage work that compares, integrates, and tests a full repertoire of current theories.

The various perspectives we review differ sharply regarding the causes and consequences of human alteration of the environment. Debates center on the importance of the factors that drive environmental change, on the functional form of the relationships, and on the valence of the effects—whether degrading or mitigating. These are matters that, at least in principle, can be resolved through scientific investigation. However, there are also dramatic paradigm differences among perspectives about the value of the natural environment and about the normative prescriptions they offer for appropriate human interaction with the environment.

These debates center on the types of environmental alteration with which humans should be concerned and we will review them as well.

The Nation-State: Theoretical and Empirical Issues

In this chapter our approach to understanding environmental variations is principally at the level of the nation-state. A key assumption common across the theoretical and empirical perspectives we review is that the nation-state is a universally adopted large-scale political unit that plays an important role in shaping the actions of institutions, organizations, and individuals, and thus the nation-state is a meaningful unit of analysis. All permanently inhabitable areas of the globe are defined and ruled by a territorial defined state. The globe's approximately two hundred nation-states are a product of early modernization, while globalization is a product of late modernization. This political reality is also a practical reality since the most available, reliable, and thorough data for analyses is provided at the nation-state level. Trade, migration, international politics, war, scientific discourse, and other interactions that constitute globalization are the focus of much of the research that compares nations; therefore, working with nation-states by no means distracts attention from the processes that connect nations—rather, it highlights them.

Over the last decade or so, a rich theoretical and empirical literature examining the differences in environmental impacts across nations has emerged, driven by concerns that are still evolving. The literature draws on the larger traditions of cross-national comparative work in the social sciences, especially in sociology, economics, and political science. But before we review these works, it is important to consider some general points about the nation-state as a unit of analysis and as the focus of problems being addressed.

The Nation-State as the Unit of Analysis
Using the nation-state as a unit of analysis attracts a methodological caution about inferences from aggregate measures. Sociologists and political scientists are keen to avoid the well-known "ecological fallacy," which occurs when one measures a social phenomenon at an aggregate level such as the nation-state but draws conclusions at a lower level of aggregation, such as the individual. This problem was first identified in a study of voting in Oregon (Ogburn and Goltra 1919). Data were available on vote outcomes and gender composition for local areas, but

the primary question being asked was about the behavior of individuals—in particular, did women vote differently from men? Using aggregate data one can draw valid conclusions about the correlation between the percentage of women in a district and the overall vote. But in general one cannot draw defensible conclusions about the voting patterns of women from such data and thus cannot answer the question that motivated this classic study (King 1997).

Methodological concern over the ecological fallacy sometimes leads to rejection of all analysis at the aggregate level. But such wholesale rejection is not justified. Humans create structures and institutions that are both the medium for and outcome of individual choices. While a focus on the individual may be a fruitful undertaking, in some contexts there are unequivocal reasons to look at human activities at multiple levels of aggregation.

The nation-state is one logical choice for such analysis. It is a leading political entity, an arena of political contestation for social movements and other organizational entities, and the prime actor in international political systems. Thus the nation-state, while not a functionally integrated "actor" in the same sense as the individual, nonetheless has observable emergent properties that result from the actions of more microlevel units including individuals. We can use these emergent properties to describe the nation-state in useful ways. For example, it is useful and meaningful to examine a national political economy with its flows of good and services and the resulting extraction of resources from the environment and deposition of materials and waste energy into it. Here the nation-state exercises its political and economic autonomy as a legally recognized "individual," a persona ficta.

Critical questions arise over how to theorize the relationship between the individual and more aggregate units. This is the classic challenge of "population thinking," which is a central theme not only in the social sciences but also in ecology and evolutionary theory (Mayr 1959; McLaughlin 1998; Sober 1980). In the social sciences, Vayda (1988) has promoted the idea of "progressive contextualization" (see also Dietz and Rosa 2002; Rosa and Dietz 1998). A human action with demonstrable environmental consequences becomes the starting point for theorizing and empirical analysis. One might ask why does a small landholder cut a tree, or a suburbanite drive a car to work? Microlevel explanations for such phenomena begin with the social psychology of decision making. But individual values, beliefs, and rules for making decisions are shaped by socialization and by the social, political, and economic contexts in which decisions are made and routines and habits carried out. To put it differently, decisions are shaped by families, communities, organizations, and markets, which in turn are shaped by (and shape) larger aggregations such as the nation-state. Understanding the macrolevel factors that influence microlevel behavior is a critical challenge in all anthropogenic research programs that are not naively reductionist and oblivious to context.

A priori one can imagine an ideal research design that would be based on large samples of individuals from each of many nations. The goal would be to have substantial variation across individuals within a nation and also across the contexts in which those individuals act via variation across nations. Such data could address a key question: How much is variance across individuals explained by characteristics of the individual, by characteristics of the nation in which the individual lives, and by the interaction between the two? Multilevel modeling methods provide guidance over how to conduct statistical analyses that address such questions (Steenbergen and Jones 2002).

The problem with these approaches is that their demands can be taxing and seldom met by data available on coupled human and natural systems. There must be sufficient data on individuals in each context examined to allow statistical analysis at that level as well as data on enough contexts to support statistical analysis at aggregate levels. For example, the World Fertility Survey, which is often seen as one of the best examples of such multilevel research, included samples of several thousand women in each of forty-one countries. This was a massive and highly regarded undertaking, yet forty-one is still a relatively small number to capture statistical differences across countries (Cleland, Scott, and Whitelegge 1987). Research on the human dimensions of global change has not been well funded, so we lack the kind of data sets that allow this "gold standard" of methodology to be applied for many key questions. And as Steenbergen and Jones (2002) note, multilevel analysis is also very theory intensive—it serves best when we actively engage with theoretical arguments that take seriously both the individual and the context. This is a major challenge for all work on human dimensions of global change and for work on driving forces in particular. As we will see, there are many macrolevel theories that ignore or at least do not clearly articulate the microlevel processes that logically underpin them. Most microlevel theories may have macrolevel implications, but such implications typically are not much explored. Thus very few theories have sketched a cross-scale analysis of the sort that must ultimately be developed.

The most prominent empirical approach to studying the driving forces of environmental change is the single context case study. Researchers collect data at one or a few sites, for example at a few villages within a region. This allows robust understanding of factors (e.g., values, beliefs, decisions rules, and position within the local social structure) that vary across individuals within that particular context. But it leaves the researcher with only speculation about how those factors might act in different political, economic, social, and cultural contexts. Context clearly matters (Dietz and Henry 2008). But the intensive analysis of one or a few sites cannot reveal such contextual effects directly. As a result, there is growing interest in moving analysis from a single place or region to comparative analyses.

Two approaches are being deployed to address this problem. One is to develop a moderate number of comparable cases by using common research approaches at multiple sites, which are chosen to facilitate comparison of the influences of key structural factors. Examples of this approach include the multiscale assessments conducted as part of the Millennium Ecosystem Assessment (MEA) (http://www .millenniumassessment.org/en/Products.Global.Multiscale.aspx) and the International Forest Resources and Institutions Program (FRI) (www .umich.edu/~ifri).

Resources limit the size of such studies and constrain which sites can be included. For example, there were eighteen approved and twelve associated assessments in the MEA while there are two hundred sites in ten countries in the IFRI data set. These are among the most ambitious projects of this type. The sample sizes in such comparative designs often are much smaller. Cross-site comparisons based on this approach are of great value, but still do not capture the full power of multilevel analysis.

Comparative analysis of cases from existing literature is a second approach. Researchers collect information from the literature on independent studies on the same topic and create a database for comparing across studies and contexts. This approach has a strong precedent in the Human Relations Area Files that compiles information from a wide collection of ethnographies (http://www.yale.edu/hraf/). Such comparisons can use purely qualitative methods, the hybrid qualitative/quantitative methods suggested by Ragin (2000) or standard quantitative statistical methods, including meta-analysis. These approaches have yielded important results in several areas of human ecology (e.g., Palloni 1994; Agrawal 2002; Bardhan and Dayton-Johnson 2002; Beierle and Cayford 2002; Rudel 2005). But they have important limits. First, without explicit coordination, it can be very difficult to establish comparability across studies conducted by different researchers in different regions at different times for different purposes. Second, when this approach has been deployed, even the most thorough search for previous studies can yield only modest sample sizes for statistical analysis (around one hundred cases seems to be a common upper bound). Missing data for many cases on at least some variables often reduces the working-sample sizes to the point that key questions cannot be addressed.

Each of these approaches—single-context studies, comparative analyses of a moderate number of cases, efforts to build databases from the existing literature—represents a pillar in efforts to understand the human dimensions of global change in general and the driving forces of global environmental change in particular. Cross-national comparisons also have much to contribute to understanding GEC. Not all important variation is captured by individual or household differences within a single context, and so we need comparisons in which culture, economic institutions, and social structures differ. Although multilevel analysis is very powerful, data sets that combine substantial variation across both individuals and context, as we have snoted, are rare and often suffer from lack of comparability, sharp limits in sample size, or limited measurement of variables central to theory. So comparisons across nation-states are a useful complement to other approaches because of their precise focus on context and political reality.

What Are We Trying to Explain?

Theoretical arguments about GEC typically are conceptualized at a very general level and do not differentiate across types of environmental impacts. But for empirical and theoretical progress to obtain, some care about the particular impacts to be explained is necessary.

First, it is useful to differentiate between impacts and stressors. Most of the theories we review make reference to impacts, and we use that term when we discuss these theories. But a closer look shows that most empirical studies use measures of stressors as the object of explanation. Stressors are proximate causes of threats to ecosystems. Impact implies a measurable change in the structure or function of an ecosystem, usually a change that affects ecosystems services of concern to humans. So, for example, release of GHGs to the atmosphere is a stressor on the climate system, but the actual changes in that system (impacts) are the result of a complex interplay of chemistry, physics, and biology across the planet.

Adding nitrogen to an aquatic ecosystem also is a stressor. The response of the ecosystem, the impact, is a result of the ecosystem dynamics that result from the increased nitrogen.

It is easier to examine stressors than impacts because the measures of stressors are more readily available, and because the models crucial to analyzing impacts require the integration of understandings from the physical, biological and social sciences that are so complex they tax our current scientific abilities. One of the goals of research on CHANS is to examine ecosystem responses to anthropogenic stressors and the resulting feedback to human systems. The Millennium Ecosystem Assessment, inter alia, has pursued this framework (Alcamo et al. 2003; Reid et al. 2005). Nevertheless, most theory and empirical work to date focuses on stressors, not impacts, even though the term *impact* is commonly used in the literature.

Second, there has been extensive attention paid to some stressors and little to others. Too often, the practical issue of data availability rather than theoretical considerations has driven the choice of a dependent variable. For example, the stressors most often examined have been GHG emissions, especially CO_2 emissions; local pollutants, especially air pollutants; and land-cover changes, especially deforestation. These are important factors, but they are often chosen simply because they are the ones for which we have reliable data. Other critical stressors, such as alterations of the nitrogen cycle or introductions of exotic species into ecosystems, have been examined less frequently, typically for lack of reliable data. As we will note in the final chapter of this volume, further advances in our understanding of anthropogenic environmental change will require data collection efforts that place the needs of the social sciences on a par with those of the physical and biological sciences. Until such efforts provide a basis for analysis, we must remember that our results are skewed by data availability.

Third, some lines of research explore aggregate measures of anthropogenic stress while others examine a single stressor only (e.g., local pollution or greenhouse gas emissions, as already noted). For example, a number of studies have focused on explaining cross-national variations in the ecological footprint (EF) (Jorgenson 2003; Rosa and York 2002; York, Rosa, and Dietz 2003, 2005). The ecological footprint is a measure of consumption that aggregates across types of stressors.[3] It takes into account GHGs; consumption of forest products, products of grazing, agriculture, fish and other seafood; and the amount of land used for living space and infrastructure (housing, roads, public buildings, etc.). The aggregation occurs across types of consumption by translating each into the land area required to sustain that consumption, assuming global average levels of productivity. The EF can be applied at any level of aggregation—it can be calculated for individuals, households, communities, organizations, nations, or the entire planet. EF has both strengths and limits. We will examine them because they illustrate the issues that must be considered in deploying an impact measure (or actually a stressor) in theoretical and empirical analysis.

Trade-Offs   There are many trade-offs among environmental stressors. For example, a nation can reduce its GHG emissions by greater reliance on hydroelectric and nuclear power, but those forms of energy production have environmental impacts (such as high-level nuclear wastes) that are ignored when GHG emissions are the sole focus of analysis. EF attempts to avoid this problem by aggregating multiple types of stressors into a single measure, although in its present form it neglects some important ones, such as toxics substances and water shortages, because there is no natural capacity to deal with these problems and so no clear way to translate them into the land-area metric used in the footprint.

Locus of Impact   When making comparisons across nations, a common approach is to allocate stressors to nations where impacts occur. This is a logical choice for some purposes. But it masks the effects of consumption in one country that, through international trade, is driving impacts in another country. The EF is allocated based on consumption, so, for example, a tree cut in one country to provide wood in another is allocated to the forest EF of the country where the wood is consumed.

Logic of Weighting   In creating an aggregate measure of impact or stressors from multiple indicators, a formula must be used to convert all indicators into a common metric. In such a formula, each indicator is multiplied by a weighting factor. For example, in developing an overall estimate of GHG emissions, most researchers multiple the emissions of a specific GHG by a weight that reflects both the photochemical ability of that compound to "trap" heat and the typical length of residence of a molecule of the compound in the stratosphere. A carbon dioxide molecule is given a weight of 1, so all other compounds are compared to it. For example, in this metric, methane has a weight of 25, indicating that each molecule of methane emitted has 25 times the impact on radiative forcing (the amount of energy trapped by the atmosphere) as a molecule of carbon dioxide. The EF converts all impacts into hectares of land at average global productivity. The underlying logic is to estimate how much productive land and sea area would be required to support a pattern of consumption. This seems a defensible logic and it can be operationalized for many critical environmental stressors. But one can imagine alternative procedures for aggregating stressors, although we are unaware of other attempts to do so based on a systematic assessment of environmental processes (Parris and Kates 2003).

Level of Aggregation   Finally, it is worth noting that measures of stress can be decomposed almost ad infinitum. As noted the EF is an attempt to aggregate all major stressors into a single measure. This has the advantage of taking account of trade-offs across stressors. But stressors may differ in their relationship to drivers, so analysis at both an aggregate and a disaggregate level are important for a full understanding. For example, GHG emissions are a component of the EF. GHG emissions can be decomposed into their constituent gases: CO_2, CH_4, CFCs, and so on. The gas emissions can then be decomposed into their sources and then into the activity/use that drives each source. CO_2 from fossil fuel consumption is a result of diverse energy uses: transportation, industrial and commercial, residential, and so on. Each use can then be decomposed. For example, one can decompose transportation in turn by purpose (recreation, commuting, other household uses, commercial uses, etc.) or by mode (single-occupant driving, car pooling, public transport, etc.). The goals of the analysis should determine which of these levels is most appropriate.

A few scholars have begun to explore the drivers of sustainability rather than of anthropogenic environmental stressors. Of course, the measurement of sustainability is fraught with difficulty, as might be expected for a concept that is so polysemous (Parris and Kates 2003). De Soysa and Neumayer (2005) have examined the genuine savings rate, a measure of sustainable development used by the World Bank. The genuine savings rate adjusts the net savings of a nation by subtracting costs associated with depleting natural resources and damaging the environment and by adding increases in human capital. Dietz, Rosa, and York (2009) have suggested that rather than attempting to measure sustainability per se, a more appropriate initial approach would be to consider the relationship between human well-being and environmental stressors; to ask how the use of ecosystem services are connected to the human condition. A number of other measures of sustainability, such as the Genuine Progress Indicator or other adjustments to national economic accounts (Hecht 2005), may offer advances in our understanding of sustainability, but have not yet been explored in this literature.

Theories of Environmental Change

Ecologists' Perspectives

Next, we delineate the intellectual roots of the human dimensions of environmental stressors by comparing two ecological perspectives, that of Paul Ehrlich and John Holdren, on the one hand, and Barry Commoner, on the other hand. Their ideas played a particularly influential and lasting role in shaping contemporary debates about the human effect on the environment. We also briefly note the integrative model proposed by Peter Richerson and Robert Boyd. Then, we turn to social science perspectives and general social science insights that seek a deeper understanding of human shaping of the environment.

The early 1970s witnessed the incipient stages of recognition that environmental impacts are global in scale. This recognition launched a debate over the driving forces behind environmental change between Paul Ehrlich and John Holdren on one side and Barry Commoner on the other. A well-known formula, I = PAT (where Impacts are a function of Population, Affluence, and Technology), emerged out of this debate. It has been influential ever since in discussions of CHANS.[4] Due to the widespread recognition and adoption of the IPAT formulation and the fact that Ehrlich, Holdren, and Commoner frame their discussions of human alteration of the environment in the IPAT context, we briefly summarize this approach. We then go on to other ecological perspectives.

The basic IPAT formula proposes that anthropogenic environmental impact (I) is the multiplicative product of three key driving forces: population (P), affluence (A), and technology (T). In mathematical terms, the formula is represented by the equation I = PAT. Straightforwardly enough, population is the number of people; affluence is operationalized as the per capita consumption of resources;[5] and technology is the impact per unit of production or consumption. Technology is conceptualized broadly and, therefore, includes not only "hardware" or infrastructure, but also other factors that affect impact per unit of production or consumption, such as culture and social organization. Nor is technology to be interpreted as a continuum of complexity or sophistication from "primitive" to "advanced" (i.e., technology in the IPAT context is not necessarily synonymous with technological development or modernization).

The Intergovernmental Panel on Climate Change (IPCC) uses IPAT in its analyses of greenhouse gas emissions, where it is known as the "Kaya identity" (Kaya 1990; Yamaji et al. 1991). While emissions scenarios grow increasingly more sophisticated (Carpenter et al. 2005; De Vries 2007; IPCC 2005; Raupach et al. 2007; U.S. Climate Change Science Program 2007), the logic of IPAT/Kaya remains at their core. Some analyses of the environmental Kuznets curve, which we discuss subsequently, employ a similar decomposition of affluence and technology (Bruvoll and Medin 2003; Stern 2002; Zhang 2000).

IPAT, of course, is an oversimplification, as are all models (Dietz and Rosa 1994). On this and other grounds it has attracted criticism from a number of social scientists. Fischer-Kowalski and Amann (2001) offer particularly thoughtful of these criticisms. The first part of their critique, echoing that of others, argues that, as an accounting equation, IPAT has limited value in theory testing. They go on to note the utility of a stochastic version of the model,[6] but point to the care that must be taken in conceptualizing and operationalizing the variables used. In particular, they note that T can be a "catch all" for everything that is not population or affluence, and they call for a much more sophisticated conceptualization of all the variables in the model than is usually deployed. In particular, they argue for the use of materials flows as an appropriate impact measure.

IPAT attracts another critique from MacKellar and colleagues (1998) who point to the lack of social science content in IPAT as well as note some technical problems in many applications of IPAT. They argue that the IPAT formulation does not allow for nonproportional and threshold effects; can be ambiguous about whether the appropriate unit of analysis is the individual, the household, or a larger geopolitical entity; and does not take account of causal interactions among the driver variables. Schnaiberg (1980), Rosa and Dietz (1998), and Forsyth (2003) propose similar arguments. In the most thorough review of IPAT to date, Chertow (2001) noted that, in the usual application of IPAT, technology is simply the term left to balance the equation. This diverts attention from the possibility that technological change can lead to reductions in impact, a point to which we will return. To summarize, the consensus of the social science literature is that IPAT per se, as an accounting equation, is not of much value for the kind of causal analysis that underpins much social science research. Several alternatives to IPAT have been offered (Dietz and Rosa 1994; Fischer-Kowalski and Amann 2001) that suggest more robust ways of approaching empirical analysis. Further, the critiques appropriately argue that each of the variables in IPAT needs to be carefully theorized and elaborated. It is to this issue that we now turn, outlining the major theoretical positions in the literature.

Paul Ehrlich and John Holdren   Paul Ehrlich and John Holdren, as well as Anne Ehrlich, are generally identified as advocating the position that population is the primary, or even sole, factor responsible for environmental disruption. However, this is not an entirely accurate representation of their position. The Ehrlichs and Holdren argue that affluence and technology make substantial contributions to impacts too (Ehrlich and Holdren 1970a, b, 1971, 1972; Ehrlich and Ehrlich 1990, 2004). They clearly recognize a striking variation in the impact of individuals, with those living in affluent Western nations contributing disproportionately to environmental change. They also recognize that the effects of one factor are contingent on the other factors, and that population, affluence, and technology are interdependent—changes in one factor may lead to changes in the other factors (e.g., where a demographic transition leads to greater individual consumption). However, Ehrlich and Holdren single out population as being especially important because it tends to grow exponentially and can thereby rapidly multiply impacts. From this perspective population has the greatest potential variability of all driving forces, and therefore deserves special attention.[7]

It is claimed that Ehrlich and Holdren underemphasize technology, although their acceptance of the IPAT formulation is a clear recognition of technology's influence on impacts as a multiplier. Their key point is that technology cannot overwhelm the other factors because the limitations of physical laws simply do not allow for near-zero or negative impacts per unit of production (Holdren and Ehrlich 1974). In contrast to Commoner's position, which we will outline, Ehrlich and Holdren do not see environmental problems as having emerged in the modern era but as the contemporary manifestation of long historical processes. In particular, they argue that humans have affected the environment since their emergence as a species, a point documented by many others (Diamond 2005; Krech 1999; Ponting 1991).

Ehrlich and Holdren have a broad view of what constitutes an environmental impact and, therefore, the IPAT formula "represents not one calculation but many" (Holdren and Ehrlich 1974). Their point is that any single impact (or stressor)—for example, a certain type of pollution—will not necessarily change proportionally in response to quantitative changes in P, A, and T, because changes in technology may shift impacts from one type of impact to another. Hence, "I" represents all impacts taken together, with the consequence that a focus on only one type of impact can be misleading, since that type of impact may decrease due to an increase in a different type of impact (e.g., replacing fossil fuel power plants with nuclear power plants). Their focus on impact is typically on what are now called natural capital and ecosystem services, meaning the life-sustaining processes inherent in healthy ecosystems—such as the filtering services provided by wetlands (see, e.g., Alcalmo et al. 2003; Reid et al. 2005). Similarly, they count as impact the extinction of species, deforestation, soil erosion, resource depletion, environmental pollution, and climate alteration regardless of the immediate effect these environmental changes have on human welfare. This is not to say that ecological impacts do not affect humans; quite the contrary due to the coupling of human and natural systems. Ehrlich and Holdren obviously believe that ultimately they will, but they recognize that the effect on humans may be indirect, delayed, subtle, diffuse, and not fully visible in the short run. For example, the loss of plant species limits future options for human utilization of biological diversity (such as developing new drugs from plant products), but may present no immediate problem to humans.

Also, there may be a decoupling of human welfare and ecosystem health, but Ehrlich and Holdren recognize this to be temporary—a short-lived phenomenon only. In the long run human sustainability is always coupled to ecosystems. A clear analogy explaining this phenomenon is the consequence of repeated withdrawals from a savings account (Ehrlich and Ehrlich 1990). If one only withdraws interest on the account one can spend the entire withdrawal and still preserve the capital balance. But if withdrawals are greater than the earned interest, then one can maintain this balance only for a limited time; continuous overwithdrawals inevitably lead to exhaustion of the account. In the same sense, if one exploits renewable resources faster than they are replenished, or continues to extract nonrenewable resources, eventually limits will be reached and scarcity will follow. In this way nature's capital and services are being drawn down relentlessly, with the consequence that human welfare will eventually suffer due to the impending ecological bankruptcy.

Barry Commoner   Barry Commoner, co-originator of the IPAT identity, treats the right-hand side components of the IPAT equation (population, affluence, technology) differently from Ehrlich and Holdren. In his original (Commoner, Corr, and Stamler 1971) and subsequent (1992) writings on the subject, he has emphasized the importance of technology, and in particular the technology choices societies make, while deemphasizing the role of population and affluence. He is quite explicit in this position: "Most of the sharp increase in pollution levels is due not so much to population or affluence as to changes in productive technology" (Commoner 1971, 177).

He further argues that environmental impacts have grown much faster than population and per capita consumption (affluence), and therefore cannot be explained adequately by those two variables. Because technological development, particularly since World War II, has increased the environmental impact per unit of production and has generated new types of impacts (e.g., nuclear waste) that are particularly pernicious, technology is the primary driver of impacts. Furthermore, technology has more variability than other causal factors, and therefore explains most of the variability of impacts. Technological improvement is, therefore, where ameliorative attention should be directed (Commoner 1971, 1972a, b; Commoner, Corr, and Stamler 1971).

Commoner has focused almost exclusively on pollution as an indicator of impact. His conceptualization of environmental impacts is, therefore, much narrower than that of Ehrlich and Holdren. Although acknowledging the existence of other types of impacts (1972b), he has not devoted the same level of analytical effort to them as he has to the impacts of technological change. While concerned about the impacts of pollution on ecosystem services (1971), Commoner is more generally concerned with how pollution affects human welfare. His examination of environmental impacts clearly is centered not on ecosystems for their own sake, but on how environmental change affects humans. In this sense his perspective more directly focuses on how ecosystem services affect human welfare—a pivotal goal of human dimensions research in general and of the Millennium Ecological Assessment in particular.

One of Commoner's important contributions to debates about the environment is his emphasis on political factors, especially on the existence of unequal power in society, in shaping environmental impacts. Key technological decisions are made by a handful of elite actors who are primarily concerned with private profits rather than either ecosystem health or the public good (Commoner 1971, 1992). Thus, the apparent basis of his oppositional viewpoint to that of Ehrlich and Holdren stems largely from his concerns about social injustice. He clearly thinks it inappropriate to "blame" poor people in developing nations (where fertility rates are high) for the environmental crisis, when affluent nations (where fertility rates are low), which consume resources at levels many times that of poor nations, are the overwhelming source of impacts. Also, elites in affluent nations exercise extraordinary control over economic and technological development. Commoner's sensitivity to social justice issues has made his work influential in many social science circles and beyond. Eagen (2007) provides an intellectual biography of Commoner that delineates the evolution of his thinking as well as his conflict with Ehrlich and Holdren.

The Cultural Revolution of Richerson and Boyd   Peter Richerson, a limnologist and cultural evolutionist, and Robert Boyd, a mathematical anthropologist, are best known for their work on the theory of cultural evolution (Richerson and Boyd 2005). They have extended that work with a theoretical analysis of the interplay among population, economic growth, environmental deterioration, and wealth and poverty (Richerson and Boyd 1997–1998). Their initial formulation complements other theories that focus on human systems. Their goal is to create a simple mathematical model of CHANS that emphasizes the interactions among human population change, affluence, technological change, and environmental impacts. In modeling language these variables are all endogenous. Since one of the major criticisms of models such as IPAT is that the complexity of feedback between factors is ignored, the Richerson and Boyd approach of making them depend on one another is an important theoretical step. Our focus here is on the drivers of global change, so for simplicity we review only which variables are included in their model, not their complex interactions.

Richerson and Boyd offer an innovative conceptualization of affluence that sharply contrasts to standard economic definitions, such as those underpinning Julian Simon's work and the environmental Kuznets curve to be discussed. They define affluence as the difference between the actual human population and the maximum sustainable population that could be supported using the technology deployed by the population. Affluence is, therefore, something like carrying capacity. It follows, then, that Richerson and Boyd define environmental damage as changes that reduce carrying capacity for humans. This idea has some clear parallels to recent work comparing the ecological footprints of nations to their actual land area (Wackernagel and Rees 1996; Wackernagel et al. 2002). Environmental damage can be traced to exogenous changes in the environment (e.g., volcanism, earthquakes, nonanthropogenic climate change), to the technology deployed, to the size of the human population, or to the product of population and per capita affluence.

The system of equations used to describe these interactions can be applied separately to different social classes, allowing an explicit treatment of social stratification—a capability that permits tests of arguments by Commoner, and of social theorists such as Schnaiberg and structural theorists such as Blühdorn (discussion of both follows) who connect environmental impacts with issues of social justice.

Richerson and Boyd have published only a single paper describing this promising model. Its parameters have not been estimated empirically nor have there been analytical or simulation studies to examine the statics and dynamics of their system of equations. But their approach is clearly a promising start to a line of research that integrates many of the subtleties of the social theories described here, links the social sciences with the ecological sciences, and provides the formalism of a mathematical model.

Social Science Perspectives

There is a disjuncture between the social science disciplines with strong traditions of macrocomparative analysis of nation-states (sociology, political science, and economics[8]) and the social science disciplines that have taken the environment as a core part of their concerns (anthropology, geography). As a result, macrocomparative studies of national environmental impacts did not become common until the 1990s. Most of the theories deployed to explain cross-national variation in environmental impacts have emerged from theoretical traditions that either focused on the environment but not the nation-state or on the nation-state but not the environment. However, we begin our review with Julian Simon, a theorist who was eager to debate Ehrlich and Holdren and thus, implicitly, the theories we have just reviewed.

Julian Simon   One of the sharpest counterpoints to the ecological perspective was the work of economist Julian Simon, who viewed population as the driving force behind human effects on the environment. However, unlike Ehrlich and Holdren, he argued that population growth contributes not to degradation of the environment, but to its enhancement. As population increases total human intellectual capital increases, with the effect that the greater supply of human minds leads to more creativity and innovation, which in turn leads to improvements in technology and greater efficiency of production (1981, 1996). Furthermore, the technological "advances" spurred by population growth lead to a higher quality of life for humans through the expansion of production, which in turn, leads to more resources available for investment in technology. Simon recognized that population growth increases demand for resources, but this is of minor importance because the increased demand for resources is more than offset by the contribution of a growing number of bright new people, who improve technology, making more resources available for productive use, and who advance science to discover or create new resources.

Simon's perspective on what constitutes environmental degradation differs significantly from the ecological perspective of Ehrlich and Holdren, Commoner, and Richerson and Boyd. The key feature of Simon's view that distinguishes it from that of ecologists is his unabashed anthropocentrism. According to Simon, extinction and pollution are not impacts in and of themselves. Environmental alteration is only an impact, and therefore detrimental, when human welfare is clearly affected. He considers, for example, the availability of safe drinking water, amount of agricultural production, and life expectancy to be the factors of primary concern, as opposed to conditions of interest to ecologists such as the vitality of ecosystems, the sustainability of their services, and biological diversity (1981, 1996). If some obscure tropical plant with no immediate value to human welfare became extinct it would not constitute an impact in Simon's formulation.

One key distinction between Simon's view and the ecological perspective lies at the junction between ecology and mainstream economics; scarcity in Simon's formulation is measured relative to economic markets, not to absolute availability in the environment. The idea of natural capital or ecosystem services is absent from Simon's formulation. Simon accepted the long-standing economic principle of infinite substitutability, believing that if a resource is completely depleted a substitute can always be found.[9] While many ecologists consider dependence on oil to be unsustainable because the absolute inventory in the world inevitably decreases, Simon disagreed. He argued that oil was becoming more plentiful because new technology makes more of it accessible and, therefore, more available in the market. Even if global climate change occurred, Simon would not have considered it to be detrimental unless it affected prices, human health, or human welfare. Therefore, demonstrating that population growth is responsible for increases in CO_2 emissions, deforestation, and extinction rates would not embarrass Simon's position. For these reasons, Simon concluded that the quality of the environment is improving, not deteriorating as claimed by many ecologists (1981, 1996).[10]

Ester Boserup   Danish economist Ester Boserup's perspective on the human relationship to the environment was quite similar to Simon's and antedated his by more than a decade. Boserup too viewed population as the driving force of technological innovation. She developed a five-stage dynamic sequence: increases in population growth placed pressure on resources that, in turn, spurred technological innovation resulting in economic growth that, in a feedback sequence, spurred further innovation and further growth. However, her claims were not as far reaching as those of Simon (she primarily focused on agriculture), and she refused to make projections about the future (Boserup 1965, 1980). Her model was only intended to explain what happened in the distant past, and in particular, during the Northern African agricultural revolution circa 10,000 years BP. Also, she did not necessarily claim, as did Simon, that humans improve environments, but simply that they do not degrade them (Boserup 1965). With the exception of these noted differences, her perspective overlapped considerably with Simon's.

Boserup's ideas regarding the relationship between scarcity and technological innovation have been expanded and tested by the induced innovation school in agricultural economics (Binswanger and Ruttan 1978; Hayami and Ruttan 1987a, b). Clifford Geertz's (1963) concept of "agricultural involution" is similar in orientation. He argued that in Indonesia population growth increases demand for food and thus leads to shortages and increases in food prices. This in turn led to technological change that then raises productivity.

Allan Schnaiberg Sociologist Allan Schnaiberg's view of the political economy of the environment rests squarely on a core idea—that capitalism is built upon a treadmill of production (1980; Gould, Pellow, and Schnaiberg 2008). In this conceptualization, economic elites seek to maximize profits by expanding the scale of production, while externalizing the costs of that production (e.g., avoiding the costs of the pollution they generate). The profits generated from production are invested in technology to further increase profits via improved efficiency, which displaces workers. Workers are therefore trapped into supporting even further increases in production in order to create new jobs, to compensate for the loss of jobs in the previous round of investment and mechanization. This cycle of production leading to more production—the treadmill—continues because of the dependency of all sectors of society (business, labor, and government) on continued economic growth to solve problems of business cycles, as well as to avoid problems associated with the unequal distribution of economic benefits (which are often created by growth itself). Schnaiberg draws upon the concept of crisis in capitalist economies developed by the "Monthly Review" school of Marxist political economy (Baran 1957; Baran and Sweezy 1966; Sweezy and Magdof 1972) and first applied to the environment by Anderson (1976). Another sociologist, James O'Connor (1994) makes an argument parallel to Schnaiberg and Anderson, adding that exploitation of the environment constitutes the "second contradiction" of capitalism.

The treadmill of production is the primary cause of environmental disruption since it assaults the environment in two reinforcing ways: it extracts resources from and deposits wastes into the environment. The pressures to continue growth militate against efforts to protect the environment. Therefore, growth-dependent economic systems, especially capitalist-industrial economies, are intrinsically unsustainable, since production requires natural resources that are finite. In Schnaiberg's view there is no easy solution to this fundamental conflict between economy and environment. The only way to curb environmental deterioration is to overthrow the economic structure and logic supporting the treadmill and to install no-growth systems.

An important point common to Schnaiberg and Commoner, distinguishing them from the other theorists, especially Simon, is their emphasis that technological choice is influenced by political and economic power and by the role of profit seeking. Simon seems to have equated profit, economic growth, and human welfare, and only considered the environment to be of importance to the extent that it constrains these.

Thus for Simon, decisions that maximize private profit must be good for the environment. In contrast, Commoner and Schnaiberg note that profits can flow from the externalizing of costs of production by privately appropriating the environment for use as a source of raw materials or a sink for wastes. Neoclassical environmental economists (e.g., Randall 1987; Freeman 1993), tracing their analysis back to Coase (1960) and Pigou (1920), also make this point about externalizing costs. The difference is that Schnaiberg and Commoner emphasize the importance of political power in determining which costs of production are externalized and which are not. Indeed, one of Schnaiberg's key arguments about the treadmill of production is that the benefits of hiding the environmental costs of production are to some degree shared by capital, organized labor, and government. The resulting political coalition makes it difficult to mobilize support to force firms to internalize these costs. The modernization theorists we consider next draw a quite different conclusion—that broad and effective coalitions to protect the environment arise in advanced industrial societies, leading to reduced environmental impact with further growth.

Environmental Improvement with Advanced Modernization

Several contemporary theories argue that the modernization of technological infrastructure and the social changes that are assumed to accompany economic growth will lead to reduced environmental impact.

Ecological Modernization and Kuznets Curves   The most prominent of these theories of modernization is ecological modernization theory (EMT),[11] which proposes that, as industrial society matures, organizations and institutions are restructured along the lines of ecological rationality—making decisions that take account of, and minimize, environmental impacts. This leads to a reduction in human impacts on the environment even as economic and population growth continues. Technological innovation, market forces, government regulation, and political pressure (e.g., the action of NGOs and social movements) drive this process. According to EMT, continued industrialization is necessary to reduce environmental impacts. "Superindustrialization" (Cohen 1999, 105; Spaargaren and Mol 1992) can occur, where production systems become environmentally efficient—they minimize the quantity of resources they use and wastes they emit. EMT stresses that a reduction in impacts is not due to changes in technology alone (in the hardware sense) but also to changes in social organization. Advances in technology historically have led to increasing environmental impacts, but this pattern will likely change in the future, with decreases in the amount of environmental impact per unit of affluence. This increase in environmental rationality eventually becomes incorporated into national political and economic policy, with environmental protection becoming a core responsibility of the state (Frank, Hironaka, and Schofer 2000) and even a source of economic growth (Giddens 1998).

EMT implicitly assumes environmental impacts may follow an inverted U-shaped curve, with impacts first increasing with economic development but then leveling off and finally decreasing. Environmental economists have proposed a similar theory called the environmental Kuznets curve (EKC), after the work of Nobel Laureate Simon Kuznets. Kuznets (1955) argued that as an economy develops, inequality first tends to increase along with affluence, but eventually the degree of inequality levels off and then declines with further increases in affluence. Grossman and Krueger (1995) extended this argument to claim that there is a parallel relationship between economic growth and environmental impacts. These two literatures, EKC and EMT, rest on parallel logics but are unmindful of one another with neither literature typically citing the other. One key difference between them is that extensive empirical tests of the EKC theory, using cross-national data, have been conducted. Another is the vast difference in publicity accorded each. The World Bank's 1992 World Development Report (International Bank for Reconstruction and Development 1992) popularized the concept of the EKC, leading to an explosive growth in the literature. In contrast, EMT has relied on a handful of in-depth case studies, a key point attracting criticism of EMT (York and Rosa 2003).

Early empirical studies by economists looking for the EKC found the expected nonlinear (inverted U) relationship between affluence and certain per capita environmental impacts. This was particularly the case for pollutants that had local consequences, such as most forms of water and air pollution. However, recent studies using panel data and more powerful statistical methods have questioned the validity of the EKC found for local air pollutants and similar stressors (Perman and Stern 2003; Stern 2004). Furthermore, empirical work focused on global stressors, such as total resource consumption and the emission of greenhouse gases, typically finds that pressure on the environment rises consistently with economic growth (York, Rosa, and Dietz 2003). Contrary to the predictions of the EKC, the general conclusion of the empirical work is that impacts consistently rise with growing affluence—sometimes disproportionately. The early results showing a decline in environmental impact with increasing affluence may have masked some critical differences across nations (Dasgupta et al. 2002), a result anticipated by the world systems theorists we will discuss.

Over the last few decades the most rapid economic growth has taken place in middle-income countries. Their increase in affluence is accompanied by increases in environmental impacts. In contrast, some of the most affluent nations are experiencing relatively slow growth, accompanied by reduced environmental impact. This pattern may be due to consumer choices, technological decisions, or governmental policies that led to reduced per capita impacts (a result often called environmental efficiency). But it may also be due to the shift of polluting industries and to the importation of natural resources to less affluent nations. These richer nations, despite slowed economic and population growth, may be the beneficiary of this ameliorative trend because it only takes modest changes in technology and institutions to keep pace with the slowed increases in population and affluence. This is not the case in more rapidly growing nations. Since the more affluent nations had the largest economies, their relative decline in some types of impact may be outliers dominating the overall pattern resulting in the appearance of an EKC. It is also important to recognize that consumption in the affluent nations is likely a major source of impacts in less developed countries. Thus environmental improvements in rich countries may be a reflection of the inequalities of the global economy—a point consistent with world systems theory (WST) and to which we soon return. As Commoner and Schnaiberg would have it, choice of technology is important in driving environmental impacts and there is little evidence that middle-income countries are choosing low-impact technologies.

The implications of these results for ecological modernization theory are not entirely clear because EMT is far less precise in its operational measures of change than the EKC. Certainly, one interpretation of EMT emphasizes the secular trend toward increased environmental efficiency that recent analyses have detected in the most affluent nations. It now appears that any such trend is restricted to a subset of nations, a result not consistent with a broad application of EMT. So if EMT does have a case for reduced impacts, it is restricted to a handful of affluent nations, while the arguments of Commoner and Schnaiberg, developed in the U.S. context, continue to have broad applicability.

Industrial Ecology   Industrial ecology (IE) is an engineering approach that emphasizes production efficiency.[12] IE uses natural ecosystems as a template for reshaping the infrastructure and processes of production. Natural systems generate zero permanent impacts because the detritus of one species is a resource for some other species whose detritus, in turn, is a resource for a third species, and so on. Ausubel and Wernick and their colleagues (Ausubel 1996, 2000; Ausubel and Waggoner 2008; Wernick 1997; Wernick, Waggoner, and Ausubel 2000) have analyzed historical improvements in various technologies that have led to substantial decreases in environmental impact—providing a practical "how" to underpin the "why" of EMT and the EKC. They suggest these technological improvements provide a basis for optimism, but they say little about the societal processes that drive such changes—an expected limitation given this work is grounded in the physical sciences, especially engineering.

Postmaterialist Values   The EKC and IE perspectives largely ignore, while the EMT sketches out, the institutional and cultural changes that drive reductions in impact posited by these theories. None of these theories have attempted to connect the macrochanges theorized with individual values. Given the substantial body of research on environmental values, such macro-micro links would be pivotal (Dietz, Fitzgerald, and Shwom 2005). Political scientist Ronald Inglehart (1995) attempts to fill this gap. He has argued that increased concern with the environment is part of a general values shift away from materialist values, focused on economic growth and national security, toward postmaterialist values focused on quality of life and individual freedoms. He posits a societal transition driven by economic growth. His concepts are grounded in Maslow's hierarchy of needs—a universal set of psychological needs that range from basic survival needs to higher human aspirations as economies develop. Successive cohorts become less concerned with the survival needs low on Maslow's hierarchy and more concerned with higher-order needs. A number of studies have attempted to test this theory, and the evidence, while mixed, seems mostly to refute it—individual concern with the environment is not strongly predicted by affluence (e.g., Brechin 1999; Brechin and Kempton 1997; Dunlap and Mertig 1997; Dunlap and York 2008). However, a few studies (Franzen 2003; Diekmann and Franzen 1999) found that national levels of affluence are positively related to individual environmental concern. Gelissen (2007) uses multilevel analysis to examine both individual-level and national-level effects. As we have noted previously, this seems the most appropriate way to test theory about human driving forces. He finds general support for the postmaterialist thesis at both the individual and national level. Marquart-Pyatt (2007) has argued that some of the differences across these analyses may be the result of differences in the measurement of environmental concern across studies, which suggests that it may be difficult to draw general conclusions.

Arguments have been offered that focus on the political and institutional structures that must emerge to achieve the environmental benefits posited by modernization theories. Much like the EMT theorists, Murphy (2000) emphasizes a "new politics of pollution" in which the state is held more directly responsible for environmental protection Copeland and Taylor (2003) and Neumayer (2002b) raise similar points, while Ehrhardt-Martinez, Crenshaw, and Jenkins (2002) emphasize the importance of strong democracy.

Blühdorn (2007; Blühdorn and Welsh 2007) has offered a strong critique of EMT, and by implication, EKC and postmaterialist theory (PMT). Drawing on Gorz's (1980) arguments about the resilience of the neoliberal state and its ability to incorporate challenges while retaining the same basic logic of production and growth, Blühdorn asserts that a system that integrates democracy, consumerism, and capitalism remains dominant, with infinite economic growth and wealth accumulation as its fundamental paradigm. In his view, in contemporary neoliberal states a rhetoric of sustainability is incorporated into government and private decision making along with a call for "win-win solutions" that allow economic growth as well as reduced environmental impact. But to Blühdorn these are not a solution to environmental problems but a diversion from them, one that blocks any moves toward sustainability.

Roca (2003) makes an argument bridging from the logic of self-interest in environmental decision making that underpins the EKC to the structural theories we review next. In his view it is relatively easy to displace adverse environmental impacts to disadvantaged social groups within societies, across societies, and over time to future generations. Thus a "rational" actor need not consider adverse impacts because they have been displaced to other groups, other nations, or other eras. The idea of displacement of environmental impacts across nations underpins a major line of macrocomparative theory to which we now turn.

Structural Theories   World systems theory starts with the idea that the globe is highly structured, comprising an integrated economic, political, and social system. WST and related perspectives were originally developed to understand the long-term historical processes that led to the apparent differential patterns of economic and social change across nations. WST was driven by the question of why some countries enjoyed progress while others stagnated or retrogressed. The theory, first applied to the environment by Bunker (1984, 1985), was further developed by Roberts and Grimes (2002) who argued that WST can provide an integrated theory of environment and development, a goal parallel to that of Richerson and Boyd. How does the broad compass of WST address the issue of environmental impacts?

The contribution of world systems theory to understanding the human drivers of environmental impacts is its emphasis on a fundamental sociological insight: system integration matters. The central tenet of WST is that the world is not merely a loose collection of independent nations, but rather an integrated system structured around a single economy organized into three sectors: the core, the periphery, and the semiperiphery. The core dominates the system economically, politically, and militarily. As a result, core nations such as the United States, the major Western European states, and Japan, and the firms headquartered in them, set favorable terms of trade for themselves. The result is typically unfavorable for nations in the periphery and semiperiphery. In some cases the system is also of great advantage to client elites in the peripheral and semiperipheral nations. These structural differences across nations drive impacts and adverse environmental consequences from the core to the semiperiphery and periphery. If Commoner and Schnaiberg, on the one hand, and the various modernization theorists, on the other, are focusing on effects within a nation, the WST theorists remind us that effects take place across nations—among coupled social systems. Profit maximizing, technological choice, the treadmill of production and hyperindustrialization each can be achieved, at least in part, by displacing adverse environmental effects from one nation to another, from the core to the periphery, for example.

In a series of papers, Roberts and Grimes (1997, 2002) have shown just that. They found that the EKC (and patterns consistent with other modernization theories) is only found in affluent nations in the core who have improved their energy efficiency since the oil crises of the 1970s. They found that there has been no increase in efficiency in the semiperiphery and the periphery of the sort predicted by modernization theories, nor, they argue, is there likely to be since global forces that militate against such salutary effects shape the political economies of noncore nations. These results anticipated important findings in recent critiques of EKC, such as those of Blühdorn and Roca previously discussed. Of course, proponents of the EKC and EMT could reasonably argue that only core nations have acquired the requisite level of affluence and social infrastructure to make the transition toward a sustainable society with relatively low impacts. Hence, debate continues.

Structural theories underscore the political effects of economic domination. Core nations, multinational corporations from the core, and international organizations dominated by the core have the power to shape institutions and decisions in the semiperiphery and periphery. For the semiperipheral and peripheral nations this is termed dependency. Inherent, then, in WST is the question of who is responsible for environmental impacts. The impacts occurring in one nation may be the result of resource demand and political power in another. World trade allows production and consumption to be spatially separated as never before. Thus environmental stressors and even the technologies used to extract and transform resources can be shaped by a nation's position in the world system. In addition, WST, like Schnaiberg, focuses on the need for capital accumulation to keep the global political economy functioning and to prevent crises. The demand for capital accumulation, therefore, drives environmental degradation. Importantly the accumulation of wealth occurs in the core while environmental degradation occurs primarily in the periphery and semiperiphery. Thus core nations where capital accumulation occurs are often spared local environmental impacts that occur in the periphery and semiperiphery (Frey 1994, 2006).

Structural theories also emphasize the effects of international relations on the internal politics, economics, and social structure of a nation. They reject the notion that some nations are "underdeveloped"—a term that implies a growth trajectory that will be followed by all nations. Instead, they suggest that the peripheral and semiperipheral nations are developed in ways that serve the interests of more powerful nations and national and global elites—a type of dependency symbiosis. One implication is that a driver of environmental impacts may differ across nations, having one effect in the core and a different, even opposite effect in noncore nations. This point has been made theoretically and demonstrated empirically in a number of studies (Burns, Kick, and Davis 2003; Jorgenson 2004, 2009; Kick et al. 1996; Roberts and Grimes 1997).

Perhaps the most empirically studied theoretical prediction of WST is dependence on the export of raw materials for noncore economies.

Bunker was the first to explore the environmental implications of export dependence (Bunker 1985, 1984, 1996). The argument is that such dependence slows economic growth, deters the changes emphasized by modernization theorists, and traps the economy into activities with high environmental impact (Jorgenson, Rice, and Crowe 2005; Neumayer 2002a; Røpke 1994; Shandra et al. 2004). It has also been suggested that a focus on export commodities, by increasing the dependency of the state on both national and global elites, weakens the state and, as a consequence, limits its ability to promote environmental protection (Crenshaw and Jenkins 1996; Ehrhardt-Martinez 1998a, b). The adverse environmental consequences of commodity concentration and export have been emphasized in a number of studies of deforestation (Allen and Barnes 1985; Kick et al. 1996; Rudel 1989) and recently of water pollution (Shandra, Shor, and London 2009).

Environmental economists have made a parallel argument. The division of labor that results from international trade can tend to concentrate heavily polluting industries, such as those based on resource extraction and some forms of manufacturing, in lower income (peripheral and semiperipheral) nations. At the same time the presumably less damaging service-sector industries and some forms of manufacturing concentrate in countries with substantial human and manufactured capital—typically the core (Arrow et al. 1995; Hettige, Lucas, and Wheeler 1992; Stern, Common, and Babbier 1996; Suri and Chapman 1998).[13]

Direct foreign investment in the national economy also is frequently invoked as a mechanism of dependence that blocks environmental improvements. It is not in the self-interest of foreign investors to incur the costs of pollution reductions and other externalities. Hence, according to this argument, they will favor nations with weak environmental protections to locate polluting facilities and will exert influence to keep those protections weak (Inman 1992; Shandra et al. 2004). Foreign debt (Inman 1992) and externally imposed structural adjustment policies (Kahn and MacDonald 1994) have also been suggested as pressures that may force a government to focus on revenue generation and preclude policies that protect the environment. However, others have argued that multinational firms headquartered in the core may carry their production practices or standards developed to meet government regulations at home to their subsidiaries in the developing world in order to avoid the costs associated with revamping established production facilities. The adoption of this practice may be viewed as a sort of modernization theory applied via corporate engagement in noncore countries (Garcia-Johnson 2000).

For more than a decade, there has been a sharp debate about the impact of trade on the environment. In many ways this debate parallels the theoretical one between modernization and structural theorists, with some arguing that trade will lead to environmental benefits for all while others argue that trade has adverse environmental impacts, at least in the poorest nations and perhaps in all nations. While public debate on this topic is intense, the number of formal theoretical arguments and empirical studies devoted to it is more modest. As noted, several scholars have suggested that international trade weakens the political structures and attendant policies in exporting nations. This constrains the capacity of these nations to mitigate impacts (Lopez 1994, 2003). This can lead to a "race to the bottom" where countries with low incomes and in desperate need of industry recruit heavily polluting industries by limiting environmental regulations. The consequence is a lack of effective political structures for environmental protection (Copeland and Taylor 2003; Frey 2003).

In contrast, modernization theorists argue that engagement in the global political economy reduces environmental impacts (Bhagwati 2004; Frankel 1999). This view, traceable to classical economist David Ricardo, suggests that an openness to trade forces greater efficiency in resource use, reduces government subsidies to inefficient uses (Birdsall and Wheeler 1993; Brack 1995; Yu 1994) and encourages national engagement in international treaties (Neumayer 2002b). For example, de Soysa and Neumayer (2005) present evidence that trade and direct foreign investment when coupled with effective democracy reduce environmental impacts. However, Jorgenson (2009) finds that foreign direct investment leads to less environmental efficiency in economic output per unit of gross domestic product and higher overall CO_2 emissions. Longo and York (2009), in one of the few studies that have examined water consumption, found that increased trade decreased water consumption in the agricultural sector but increased it in the nonagricultural sector.[14]

While WST and other structural theories are in many ways diametrically opposed to the various forms of modernization theory, it can be difficult to specify clear hypotheses that would allow critical empirical tests of the theories. For example, WST suggests that core nations will use their power to increase their wealth. Thus the theory predicts that there will be a strong correlation between a nation's position in the world systems and affluence, and in empirical work this relationship is often so strong that measures of affluence such as gross domestic product per capita cannot be distinguished from position in the world system. Theorists using WST have argued that any improvements in environmental efficiency will be found only among core nations. As noted previously, this is consistent with most empirical results. But modernization theorists could argue that the effects they postulate will only occur at high levels of affluence or modernization, thus reconciling the seemingly contradictory results with their position.

A continuing disappointment is the lack of dialogue between the modernization and structural literatures. Most scholars in both traditions seldom compare theories or engage in critical comparative tests of the sort that would be useful in honing our general understanding of the drivers of environmental change. There are a few exceptions that demonstrate the feasibility of such comparative work. McKinney, Fulkerson, and Kick (2009) in an examination of bird species diversity (a measure of impact rather than a stressor) found support for world systems theory and partial support for treadmill of production theory and population pressure, but no support for ecological modernization theory. York, Rosa, and Dietz (2003) found significant influences of ecological factors and the treadmill of production on the ecological footprint, but no support for ecological modernization theory.

Culture and Institutions   Although the theories covered so far have received the most attention in the environmental and social science literature, other ideas about the driving forces of anthropogenic environmental change have emerged. While not as thoroughly developed, they deserve some consideration since they may better specify or refine the causal processes underlying ecological, modernization, and structural perspectives. In particular, these theories emphasize culture and institutions more directly than the theories already reviewed.

Gender and Militarization   Seager (1993) and Lough (1999) have drawn on ecofeminist theory to suggest that environmental impacts are driven by patriarchy and by militarization. They argued that those male-dominated societies tend to be more militaristic and that both militarism and gender inequity have adverse consequences for the environment, ceteris paribus. Since increasing gender inequality and militarization often accompany peripheral status in the world system and intermediate levels of development, Lough and Seager's arguments can be interpreted as providing an alternative explanation for the empirical results obtained from work driven by modernization and structural theories—that the driving force is in part empowerment of women. Norgaard and York (2005) found that nations where women have greater representation in the political sphere are more likely to support environmental treaties, giving some empirical support to the implications of the previously mentioned theories. However, work linking gender inequality to cross-national differences in actual environmental impact is still largely absent from the literature. There also is some preliminary empirical support for the idea that nation-states dominated by the military will generate larger environmental impacts than other nations (Jorgenson, Rice, and Crowe 2005; York 2008). These provocative ideas are certainly worthy of further exploration.

Institutional Forms   Structural theories and the parallel arguments of Commoner and Schnaiberg point to the conflict between elites and nonelites over costs to the environment. It might be expected that these tendencies can be overcome only by intervention, such as effective action by a government or an environmental movement. This requires reasonably open communications channels, a sufficient scientific infrastructure to monitor environmental conditions, and the resources and organizational ability to translate such concerns into effective political action.

It follows that responsive political institutions seem essential to environmental protection. As noted, a number of scholars have discussed the importance of democratic processes in protecting the environment (Congleton 1996; de Soysa and Neumayer 2005; Midlarsky 1998; Shandra et al. 2004). However, other scholars have suggested that democracy alone, while necessary, is not sufficient to reduce environmental impacts. Didia (1997), for example, argued that not only democracy, but also press freedom and political stability are important to environmental protection. Ehrhardt-Martinez, Crenshaw, and Jenkins (2002), elaborating on the issue, have shown that the political capacity of the state is also an important condition since a democratic state might still be ineffectual.

Many scholars have acknowledged the importance of the environmental movements, and in particular links to international social movement organizations (SMOs) in facilitating sound environmental policies and actions (Princen and Finger 1994; Shandra et al. 2004). Frank and his colleagues (Frank 1997; Frank, Hironaka, and Schofer 2000) have claimed that the emergence of a "world society" with its global system of governmental and nongovernmental environmental organizations is a prime driver of the environmental politics of nation-states. Buttel (2000) raised concerns that participation in this system may be only symbolic, but Schofer and Hironaka (2005) present evidence that such participation is consequential for reducing CO_2 and CFC emissions and Shandra, Shor, and London (2009) show participation in the international polity reduces water pollution.

Values, Beliefs, Norms, and Worldviews   As we have noted, Inglehart has offered a theory linking individual values and macrolevel social change. To recapitulate, Inglehart posits that times of affluence and peace lead to a rise in postmaterialist values that favor environmental protection. While the majority of studies investigating this argument have found disconfirming evidence, it remains the only theory that links the micro to the macro in a systematic way. "Cultural theory" also has been applied to debates about environmental policy, although not in a way that links it directly to macrolevel structural change. Cultural theory posits four basic ways of organizing, perceiving, and justifying social relations: egalitarianism, hierarchy, individualism, and fatalism (Douglas 1987; Gross and Rayner 1985; Thompson, Ellis, and Wildavsky 1990). In a series of papers, Rayner and collaborators have argued that the predisposition of individuals and organizations to view the world through one or another of these lenses leads them to differing policy narratives that imply alternative causes for environmental problems and suggest different approaches to solving them (Rayner 1991; Rayner and Malone 1997; Rayner, Lach, and Ingram 2006; Verweij et al. 2006). Thus worldviews influence policy outcomes and ultimately environmental impacts. However, to date this approach has not been integrated with macrocomparative approaches to yield any hypotheses about cross-national differences in environmental impact. Nor have approaches to individual-level values, beliefs, norms, and worldviews been linked to macrolevel processes, as noted, either due to both a lack of theory or a lack of data that would allow for simultaneous consideration of individual- and structural-level effects. The sole exception, as we have discussed, is Gelissen's (2007) multilevel analysis of postmaterialist theory.

The imitation of Western consumption patterns by those in the rest of the world, especially the emerging "global middle class" has been proposed as a key driver of environmentally significant consumption (Myers and Kent 2003; Wilk 1997). The argument is that in many societies, prestige and status are associated with what are perceived as Western life styles, including the use of automobiles and increased consumption of beef. This pattern of consumption generates substantial environmental stress. While globalization researchers have devoted considerable attention to consumption (Goodman 2007), the "emulation" hypothesis has not been subject to empirical testing.[15]

Demographic Changes

Malthus was not the first—or the last—to raise concerns about population and environment; although it is he who is most often associated with the view that increasing human population leads to resource exhaustion (Dietz and Rosa 1994). Concerns about population size have been central to the development of several of the theories reviewed, but population has been given only modest attention in the current cross-national comparative literature. Aspects of a human population other than size have been proposed as drivers of environmental change. Dietz (1996–1997), elaborating Frey and Al-Mansour (1995), noted a key link between institutional arrangements and population growth. Rapid population growth, whether as a result of migration or natural increase or both, can retard the development of social institutions of the sort required for environmentally sound democracy. Institutions can be overwhelmed by sheer numbers of people and they can also become ineffective when they are not designed to handle a new diversity of values, beliefs, and norms.

There are a variety of arguments about environmental impacts due to urbanization, some theorists arguing that it may be harmful to the environment, others arguing that it may ameliorate environmental problems. For example, Marx's theory of metabolic rift claims that the displacement of workers from agricultural production to the industrial labor force of urban centers contributed to environmental degradation during the industrial revolution (Foster 1999). This finding receives some support from empirical studies of contemporary nation-states (York, Rosa, and Dietz 2003). However, Ehrhardt-Martinez and her colleagues have countered that urbanization may lead to environmental efficiencies resulting in an EKC for urbanization with early stages of urbanization being resource intensive followed later by more benign stages (Ehrhardt-Martinez 1998a, 1998b; Ehrhardt-Martinez, Crenshaw, and Jenkins 2002). They also point to an interaction between urbanization and growth in the service sector, where growth in both is necessary for the realization of reductions in environmental impact.

A number of researchers examining deforestation and reforestation have posited a nonlinear effect due to rural population size. Presumably rapid rural population growth leads to accelerated and substantial rural immiseration and environmental destruction. But eventually population growth slows and with it the pace of deforestation, leading to reforestation (Allen and Barnes 1985; Ehrhardt-Martinez 1998a, 1998b; Rudel 1989; Rudel and Roper 1997; Tole 1998). What produces this pattern? One explanation according to Ehhardt-Martinez and colleagues is that migration of young men to urban areas, part of a larger dynamic process, reduces pressure on forests and other resources in rural areas, whatever the consequences to urban areas and to other aspects of the environment. Finally, several studies have suggested that an increase in the number of households, rather than population size itself, drives consumption and thus environmental impact (Cramer 1997, 1998; Dietz and Rosa 1994; Liu et al. 2003). The idea here is that consumption is driven more by the household unit than by the gross number of individuals. As societies become more affluent there is tendency toward smaller household size and toward more households for a given population size.

Ecological Factors

With some exceptions (Diamond 1999, 2004; Lenski 1986, 2005; Lenski and Nolan 1984; Nordhaus 2006), social scientists have been resistant to the idea that the physical and biological environment is coupled with social systems and social processes. In large part this was a justifiable response to theories of environmental determinism that dominated early developments in the social sciences. But this resistance to environmental influence is ever more difficult to maintain in the context of growing knowledge about CHANS and about GEC, where large-scale impacts are increasingly evident. It is clear that climate, energy sources, soils, topography, and biogeography set the parameters of what societies can and will do (Diamond 1999, 2004). Nordhaus (2006) recently demonstrated the importance of physical factors in economic activity. Ecological conditions also exert influences on institutions and culture over very long time spans (Sieferle [1982] 2001). The availability of energy resources shapes the form and capacity of production as well as the institutions that grow around such basic processes (Rosa and Machlis 1983). For example, climate influences energy consumption, which in turn influences GHG emissions and the ecological footprint (York, Rosa, and Dietz 2003).

Progress is taking place in understanding these couplings. As we have noted in chapter 1, the remaining open challenge for work on GEC is to better understand the feedbacks between anthropogenic environmental change and the influence of the biophysical environment on human systems—the dynamic core of CHANS.

Early efforts to develop theories linking human and natural systems had a tendency to adopt a functionalist/systems analytic approach that was popular in both the social sciences and ecology during the late 1960s. A number of scholars judged that approach to be problematic (McCay and Vayda 1975; Richerson 1977). Most of the theories we have reviewed either focus on societal conflicts rather than on functionalist approaches (treadmill of production, world systems theory and other structural approaches, for example) or at least do not explicitly invoke functionalist systems analysis. However, Blühdorn's approach, as discussed, draws on Luhman's system theory, and some arguments of ecological modernization theory emphasize what seems to be a homeostatic process at the societal level through which societal environmental problems are corrected. As we move toward theory appropriate for understanding CHANS, attention will have to be given to what some have termed *metatheoretical* issues regarding the fundamental assumptions about social and ecological processes that underpin models and hypotheses. Rudel (2009) has begun an interesting investigation of the degree to which the classical ecological concept of succession might be useful in theorizing about CHANS.

Conclusions

Theoretical arguments over the human driving forces of environmental change are over three decades old, and can be traced to the beginnings of earnest research on the subject. The key questions have centered on what elements of human systems are most influential in altering natural systems—the first stages of the CHANS dynamic. Unfortunately, until quite recently progress was stalled by theoretical debates that talked past one another and by limited empirical tests of theories. In large part this was due to the absence of a common vocabulary across perspectives and to the paucity of data sets spanning the disciplines that would allow researchers to address these issues. Here we have systematically reviewed leading perspectives on the human dimensions, the driving forces behind environmental change with the goal of moving beyond the lingering impasse by aligning the perspectives around common objectives. For example, ecological modernization theory, the environmental Kuznets curve argument, postmaterialist theory, and recent analyses grounded in industrial ecology all argue for a decrease in environmental impacts among the most affluent societies, while each emphasizes different elements of this transition. We can hope that the elements emphasized here can be brought together in an integrated framework. In contrast, Schnaiberg, Commoner, Ehrlich and Holdren, and the world systems theorists all predict further environmental degradation, although they differ over the dynamics driving these changes. There is hope here, too, that a focus on common elements can lead to progress toward their integration.

Our alignment of perspectives with a common interest in the human dimensions of environmental impacts—perspectives unaccustomed to dialogue—has drawn into relief not only the subtleties of their commonalities, but also remaining gaps in our understanding of this exceedingly complex topic. To dwell on these gaps would detract attention from the larger picture showing that a great deal has been accomplished in the last dozen years or so in our understanding of coupled human and natural systems and the anthropogenics of GEC. As increased attention is given to the understanding of CHANS, the carefully developed extant theories, if not yet fully integrated, provide a solid and essential basis for better bridging future work in the social and ecological sciences.

Notes

1. Work in the tradition we review here focuses on roughly the last fifty years, which some have called the "Great Acceleration" that occurred after World War II. Most of the work we review focuses on the dynamics of this period. However, in considering coupled human and natural systems (CHANS), much longer time scales are also of great importance. For example, the ongoing Integrated History and Future of People on Earth (IHOPE) project (Costanza, Graumlich, and Steffen 2007; http://www.aimes.ucar.edu/activities/ihope.shtml) seeks to understand CHANS at four scales: 10,000 years, 1000 years, 100 years, and the future. The kinds of analyses that are possible with these longer time scales yield insights that are complementary to those pertaining to the shorter time scales and more detailed data available across the last half-century. We anticipate that important progress will come from the dialogue among scholars working across temporal scales, even as later in the chapter we argue for dialogue across spatial scales.

2. There are, of course, important feedbacks between natural or biophysical and social systems, but theory here is even less developed than is theory about the drivers of human impacts of the biosphere (but see the work of Richerson and

Boyd 1997–1998 discussed later). As we noted in chapter 1, the emerging literature on coupled human and natural systems (Liu et al. 2007a, b) emphasizes these links. Successful theories of human-environment interactions will ultimately have to take account of both causal directions—human impacts on biophysical systems and impacts of biophysical systems on social systems. In this chapter, for simplicity, we look only at theories of how human actions affect the environment.

3. EF was introduced by Wackernagel and Rees (1996). Details on its calculation can be found at www.footprintnetwork.org. EF can be interpreted as a means to calculate threats to sustainability since it measures the potential depletion of natural capital and services, not actual impacts.

4. Ehrlich and Holdren were the first to conceptualize the IPAT model (1970a, b) and provide its current acronym (1972) while Commoner (1971; Commoner, Corr, and Stamler 1971) gave the equation its algebraic form.

5. Gross domestic product (GDP) per capita is the most commonly used measure of affluence in the literature we review. GDP is, equivalently, the sum of value added by all producers in an economy; the monetary value of all final uses of goods and services in an economy; or the sum of the primary incomes of producers (Hecht 2005). GDP is a central concept in the System of National Accounts used to monitor the economy of modern nation states and therefore reliable data on GDP are available for most nations. But it must be recognized that GDP may not be a precise match for what is meant by affluence in theories of anthropogenic drivers.

6. Fischer-Kowalski and Amann refer to a research program York, Rosa and Dietz have developed by modifying IPAT into a model more amenable to testing realistic hypotheses. Called STIRPAT, for Stochastic Impacts by Regression on Population, Affluence, and Technology, our approach emphasizes disaggregating P, A, and T into theoretically meaningful components and specifying a multiplicative regression model (linear in the logs) that captures the interaction effects of variables (e.g., that the effect of population depends on the level of affluence of the nation in question). See www.stirpat.org for details. The website provides a bibliography of applications of IPAT and STIRPAT. Zhageni and Billari (2007) have extended STIRPAT into a set of stochastic differential equations they have used to examine the costs of reductions in CO_2 emissions.

7. Over the thirty years since the Ehrlich and Holdren/Commoner debate began, rates of population growth have declined in most nations (Cohen 1995). In the early twenty-first century, variation over time and across nations in A and T seems to be greater and more uncertain than anticipated changes in P from natural increase. However, migration both within and between nations can lead to regional population change that far outstrips the pace of population growth from natural increase and is much harder to forecast. Elsewhere (York, Rosa, and Dietz 2002), we have addressed the need to recognize the potential variability and rate of change (what we term "plasticity") of population, affluence, and technology, so as to assess their potential influence on impacts.

8. Environmental and resource economics is nearly as old as the discipline of economics itself. But research in development economics and in macroeconomics where cross-national analyses are commonplace has not taken up the environment as a focus until recently.

9. Simon's argument might be characterized as a form of "weak sustainability" since he believes in perfect substitutability across forms of capital, and indeed emphasizes human capital (in population numbers) as "the ultimate resource" (Simon 1981).

10. Bjorn Lomborg (2001) has taken up Simon's arguments that environmental problems are exaggerated but offers no new theoretical arguments on human driving forces so we do not review his work in any detail.

11. German theorist Joseph Huber and German political theorist Martin Jänicke generally are considered key founders of EMT. Nevertheless, EMT has grown and changed substantially due to the input of many theorists writing on this topic. For the sake of conciseness, the work of Arthur P. J. Mol (1995, 1996; Mol and Spaargaren 2000) and Gert Spaargaren (1997), two leading academics in the field, will serve as the focus of this analysis.

12. Known as industrial metabolism in Europe.

13. It is important to note that in a core nation the service sector may represent a larger fraction of the economy than in a peripheral or semiperipheral nation, while the core nations still can have a manufacturing and even a resource-extraction sector that is larger in absolute terms than those in semiperipheral nations (Roca 2003).

14. Gallagher (2009) provides a detailed review of recent research examining the effects of globalization on the environment.

15. Brulle and Young (2007) show that advertising expenditures in the United States are related to some types of consumption. As they note, the critical next step is to link shifts in consumption patterns to changes in environmental stressors.

References

Agrawal, A. 2002. Common resources and institutional stability. In *The drama of the commons*, ed. E. Ostrom, T. Dietz, N. Dolsak, P. C. Stern, S. Stonich, and E. Weber, 41–85. Washington, DC: National Academies Press.

Alcalmo, J., N. J. Ash, C. D. Butler, J. B. Callicot, D. Capistrano, S. R. Carpenter, J. C. Castilla, R. Chambers, K. Chopra, A. Cropper, G. C. Daily, P. Dasgupta, R. de Groot, T. Dietz, A. K. Duraiappah, M. Gadgil, K. Hamiltion, R. Hassan, E. F. Lambin, L. Lebel, R. Leemans, L. Jiyuan, J.-P. Malingreau, R. M. May, A. F. McCalla, A. J. McMichael, B. Moldan, H. Mooney, S. Naseem, G. C. Nelson, Niu Wen-Yuan, I. Noble, O. Zhiyun, S. Pagiola, D. Pauly, S. Percy, P. Pingali, R. Prescott-Allen, W. V. Reid, T. H. Rickets, C. Samper, R. Scholes, H. Simons, F. L. Toth, J. k. Turpie, R. T. Watson, T. J. Wilbanks, M. Williams,

S. Wood, Z. Shidong, and M. B. Zurek. 2003. *Ecosystems and human well-being: A framework for analysis.* Washington, DC: Island Press.

Allen, J. C., and D. F. Barnes. 1985. The causes of deforestation in developing countries. *Annals of the Association of American Geographers* 75:163–184.

Anderson, C. H. 1976. *The sociology of survival: Social problems of growth.* Homewood, IL: Dorsey Press.

Arrow, K., B. Bolin, R. Costanza, P. Dasgupta, C. Folke, C. S. Holling, B.-O. Jansson, S. Levin, K.-G. Mäler, C. A. Perrings, and D. Pimentel. 1995. Economic growth, carrying capacity and the environment. *Science* 268:520–521.

Ausubel, J. H. 1996. Can technology spare the Earth? *American Scientist* 84:166–178.

Ausubel, J. H. 2000. The great reversal: Nature's chance to restore land and sea. *Technology in Society* 22:289–301.

Ausubel, J. H., and P. E. Waggoner. 2008. Dematerialization: Variety, caution, and persistence. *Proceedings of the National Academy of Sciences, USA* 105:12774–12779.

Baran, P. A. 1957. *The political economy of growth.* New York: Monthly Review Press.

Baran, P. A., and P. M. Sweezy. 1966. *Monopoly capital: An essay on the American economic and social order.* New York: Monthly Review Press.

Bardhan, P., and J. Dayton-Johnson. 2002. Unequal irrigators: Heterogeneity and commons management in large-scale multivariate research. In *The drama of the commons,* ed. E. Ostrom, T. Dietz, N. Dolŝak, P. C. Stern, S. Stonich, and E. U. Weber, 87–112. Washington, DC: National Academies Press.

Beierle, T. C., and J. Cayford. 2002. *Democracy in practice: Public participation in environmental decisions.* Washington, DC: Resources for the Future.

Berkes, F., W. V. Reid, T. Wilbanks, and D. Capistrano. 2006. Conclusions: Bridging scales and knowledge systems. In *Bridging scales and knowledge systems: Concepts and applications in ecosystem assessment,* ed. W. V. Reid, F. Berkes, T. Wilbanks, and D. Capistrano, 315–331. Washington, DC: Island Press.

Bhagwati, J. 2004. *In defense of globalization.* New York: Oxford University Press.

Binswanger, H. P., and V. W. Ruttan. 1978. *Induced innovation: Technology, institutions and development.* Baltimore, MD: The Johns Hopkins University Press.

Birdsall, N., and D. Wheeler. 1993. Trade policy and industrial pollution in Latin America: Where are the pollution havens? *Journal of Environment and Development* 2:137–149.

Blühdorn, I. 2007. Sustaining the unsustainable: Symbolic politics and the politics of simulation. *Environmental Politics* 16:251–275.

Blühdorn, I., and I. Welsh. 2007. Ecopolitics beyond the paradigm of sustainability: A conceptual framework and research agenda. *Environmental Politics* 16:185–205.

Boserup, E. 1965. *The conditions of agricultural growth.* Chicago: Aldine Publishing Company.

Boserup, E. 1980. *Population and technological change: A study of long-term trends.* Chicago: University of Chicago Press.

Brack, D. 1995. Balancing trade and the environment. *International Affairs* 71: 497–514.

Brechin, S. R. 1999. Objective problems, subjective values, and global environmentalism: Evaluating the postmaterialist argument and challenging a new explanation. *Social Science Quarterly* 80:783–809.

Brechin, S. R., and W. Kempton. 1997. Beyond postmaterialist values: National versus individual explanations of global environmentalism. *Social Science Quarterly* 78:16–20.

Brulle, R. J., and L. E. Young. 2007. Advertising, Individual Consumption Levels, and the Natural Environment, 1900–2000. *Sociological Inquiry* 77:522–542.

Bruvoll, A., and H. Medin. 2003. Factors behind the environmental Kuznets curve: A decomposition of changes in air pollution. *Environmental and Resource Economics* 24:27–48.

Bunker, S. G. 1984. Modes of extraction, unequal exchange and the progressive underdevelopment of an extreme periphery: The Brazilian Amazon, 1600–1980. *American Journal of Sociology* 89:1017–1064.

Bunker, S. G. 1985. *Underdeveloping the Amazon: Extraction, unequal exchange and the failure of the modern state.* Urbana: University of Illinois Press.

Bunker, S. G. 1996. Raw material and global economy: Oversights and distortions in industrial ecology. *Society and Natural Resources* 9:419–429.

Burns, T. J., E. L. Kick, and B. Davis. 2003. Theorizing and rethinking linkages between the natural environment and the modern world-system: Deforestation in the late 20th century. *Journal of World-Systems Research* 9:357–390.

Buttel, F. H. 2000. World society, the nation-state, and environmental protection. *American Sociological Review* 65:117–121.

Carpenter, S. R., P. L. Pingali, E. M. Bennett, and M. B. Zurek. 2005. Ecosystems and human well-being: *Scenarios, Volume 2.* Washington, DC: Island Press.

Chertow, M. 2001. The IPAT equation and its variants: Changing views of technology and environmental impact. *Journal of Industrial Ecology* 4: 13–29.

Cleland, J. G., C. Scott, and D. Whitelegge, eds. 1987. *The world fertility survey: An assessment.* Oxford: Oxford University Press.

Coase, R. 1960. The problem of social costs. *Journal of Law and Economics* 3:1–44.

Cohen, J. E. 1995. Human population grows up. *Scientific American* 293:48–55.

Cohen, M. 1999. Sustainable development and ecological modernization: National capacity for rigorous environmental reform. In *Environmental policy and societal aims*, ed. D. Requier-Desjardins, C. Spash, and J. van der Straaten, 103–128. Dordrecht: Kluwer.

Commoner, B. 1971. *The closing circle*. New York: Knopf.

Commoner, B. 1972a. The environmental cost of economic growth. In *Population, resources and the environment*, ed. R. G. Ridker, 339–363. Washington, DC: US Government Printing Office.

Commoner, B. 1972b. A bulletin dialogue on "The Closing Circle": Response. *Bulletin of the Atomic Scientists* 28 (5):17, 42–56.

Commoner, B. 1992. *Making peace with the planet*. New York: New Press.

Commoner, B., M. Corr, and P. J. Stamler. 1971. The causes of pollution. *Environment* 13 (3):2–19.

Congleton, Roger D. 1996. The political economy of environmental protection: *Analysis and evidence*. Ann Arbor: University of Michigan Press.

Copeland, B. R., and M. S. Taylor. 2003. Trade, growth and the environment. *Journal of Economic Literature* 42:7–71.

Costanza, R., L. J. Graumlich, and W. Steffen, eds. 2007. *Sustainability or collapse? An integrated history and future of people on Earth*. Cambridge, MA: MIT Press.

Cramer, J. C. 1997. A demographic perspective on air quality: Conceptual issues surrounding environmental impacts of population growth. *Human Ecology Review* 3:191–196.

Cramer, J. C. 1998. Population growth and air quality in California. *Demography* 35:45–56.

Crenshaw, E. M., and J. C. Jenkins. 1996. Social structure and global climate change: Sociological propositions concerning the greenhouse effect. *Sociological Focus* 29:341–358.

Dasgupta, S., B. Laplante, H. Wang, and D. Wheeler. 2002. Confronting the environmental Kuznets curve. *Journal of Economic Literature* 42:7–71.

de Soysa, I., and E. Neumayer. 2005. False prophet, or genuine savior? Assessing the effects of economic openness on sustainable development, 1980–99. *International Organization* 59:731–772.

De Vries, B. 2007. Scenarios: Guidance for an uncertain and complex world? In *Sustainability or collapse? An integrated history and future of people on Earth*, ed. R. Costanza, L. J. Graumlich, and W. Steffen, 379–397. Cambridge, MA: MIT Press.

Diamond, J. 1999. *Guns, germs and steel*. New York: W. W. Norton.

Diamond, J. 2004. *Collapse: How societies choose to fail or succeed*. New York: Viking.

Didia, D. 1997. Democracy, political instability and tropical deforestation. *Global Environmental Change* 7:63–76.

Diekmann, A., and A. Franzen. 1999. The wealth of nations and environmental concern. *Environment and Behavior* 31:540–549.

Dietz, T. 1996–1997. The human ecology of population and environment: From Utopia to Topia. *Human Ecology Review* 3:168–171.

Dietz, T., A. Fitzgerald, and R. Shwom. 2005. Environmental values. *Annual Review of Environment and Resources* 30:335–372.

Dietz, T., and A. Henry. 2008. Context and the commons. *Proceedings of the National Academy of Sciences, USA* 105:13189–13190.

Dietz, T., and E. A. Rosa. 1994. Rethinking the environmental impacts of population, affluence and technology. *Human Ecology Review* 1:277–300.

Dietz, T., and E. A. Rosa. 2002. Human dimensions of global change. In *Handbook of environmental sociology*, ed. R. E. Dunlap and W. Michelson, 370–406. Westport, CT: Greenwood Press.

Dietz, T., E. A. Rosa, and R. York. 2009. Environmentally efficient well-being: Rethinking sustainability as the relationship between human well-being and environmental impacts. *Human Ecology Review* 16:113–122.

Douglas, M. 1987. *How institutions think.* London: Routledge.

Dunlap, R. E., and A. G. Mertig. 1997. Global environmental concern: An anomaly for postmaterialism. *Social Science Quarterly* 78:24–29.

Dunlap, R. E., and R. York. 2008. The globalization of environmental concern and the limits of the post-materialist values explanation: Evidence from four cross-national surveys. *The Sociological Quarterly* 49:529–563.

Eagan, M. 2007. *Barry Commoner and the science of survival: The remaking of American environmentalism.* Cambridge, MA: MIT Press.

Ehrhardt-Martinez, K. 1998a. Social determinants of deforestation in developing countries: A cross-national study. *Social Forces* 77:567–586.

Ehrhardt-Martinez, K. 1998b. Social determinants of deforestation in developing countries—Correction. *Social Forces* 78:860–861.

Ehrhardt-Martinez, K., E. M. Crenshaw, and J. C. Jenkins. 2002. Deforestation and the environmental Kuznets curve: A cross-national investigation of intervening mechanisms. *Social Science Quarterly* 83:227–243.

Ehrlich, P. R., and A. H. Ehrlich. 1990. *The population explosion.* New York: Simon and Schuster.

Ehrlich, P. R., and A. H. Ehrlich. 2004. *One with Nineveh: Politics, consumption, and the human future.* Washington, DC: Island Press.

Ehrlich, P. R., and J. P. Holdren. 1970a. Hidden effects of overpopulation. *Saturday Review* 53 (31):52.

Ehrlich, P. R., and J. P. Holdren. 1970b. The people problem. *Saturday Review* 53 (27):42.

Ehrlich, P. R., and J. P. Holdren. 1971. Impact of population growth. *Science* 171:1212–1217.

Ehrlich, P. R., and J. P. Holdren. 1972. A bulletin dialogue on the "Closing Circle": Critique: One-dimensional ecology. *Bulletin of the Atomic Scientists* 28 (5):16–27.

Fischer-Kowalski, M., and C. Amann. 2001. Beyond IPAT and Kuznets curves: Globalization as a vital factor in analysing the environmental impact of socio-economic metabolism. *Population and Environment* 23:7–47.

Forsyth, T. 2003. *Critical political ecology.* New York: Routledge.

Foster, J. B. 1999. Marx's Theory of Metabolic Rift: Classical foundations for environmental sociology. *American Journal of Sociology* 105:366–405.

Frank, D. J. 1997. Science, nature and the globalization of the environment, 1870–1990. *Social Forces* 76:409–437.

Frank, D. J., A. Hironaka, and E. Schofer. 2000. The nation-state and the natural environment over the twentieth century. *American Sociological Review* 65:96–116.

Frankel, J. A. 1999. *The environment and globalization.* Cambridge, MA: National Bureau of Economic Research.

Franzen, A. 2003. Environmental attitudes in international comparison: An analysis of the ISSP surveys 1993 and 2000. *Social Science Quarterly* 84:297–308.

Freeman, A. M., III. 1993. *The measurement of environmental and resource values.* Washington, DC: Resources for the Future.

Frey, R. S. 1994. The international traffic in hazardous wastes. *Journal of Environmental Systems* 23:165–177.

Frey, R. S. 2003. The transfer of core-based hazardous production processes to the export processing zones of the periphery: The maquiladora centers of Northern Mexico. *Journal of World-Systems Research* 9:317–354.

Frey, R. S. 2006. The flow of hazardous exports in the world-system. In *Globalization and the environment*, ed. A. Jorgenson, and E. Kick, 133–149. Leiden, The Netherlands: Brill Academic Press.

Frey, R. S., and I. Al-Mansour. 1995. The effects of development, dependence and population pressure on Democracy: The cross-national evidence. *Sociological Spectrum* 15:181–208.

Gallagher, K. P. 2009. Globalization and the environment. Forthcoming in *Annual Review of Environment and Resources* 34.

Garcia-Johnson, R. 2000. *Exporting environmentalism: U.S. multinational chemical corporations in Brazil and Mexico.* Cambridge, MA: MIT Press.

Geertz, C. 1963. *Agricultural involution: The processes of ecological change in Indonesia.* Berkeley: University of California Press.

Gelissen, J. 2007. Explaining popular support for environmental protection: A multilevel analysis of 50 nations. *Environment and Behavior* 39:392–415.

Gibson, C. C., E. Ostrom, and T. K. Ahn. 2000. The concept of scale and the human dimensions of global change: A survey. *Ecological Economics* 32: 217–239.

Giddens, A. 1998. *The third way: The renewal of social democracy.* Cambridge, UK: Polity Press.

Goodman, D. J. 2007. Globalization and consumer culture. In *The Blackwell companion to globalization,* ed. G. Ritzer. Malden, MA: Blackwell Publishing. Blackwell Reference Online. http://www.blackwellreference.com/subscriber/tocnode?id=g9781405132749_chunk_g978140513274919 (accessed September 1, 2008).

Gorz, A. 1980. *Ecology as politics.* Boston: South End Press.

Gould, K. A., D. N. Pellow, and A. Schnaiberg. 2008. *The treadmill of production: Injustice and unsustainability in the global economy.* Boulder, CO: Paradigm Press.

Gross, J. L., and S. Rayner. 1985. *Measuring culture.* New York: Columbia University Press.

Grossman, G. M., and A. Krueger. 1995. Economic growth and the environment. *Quarterly Journal of Economics* 110:353–377.

Hayami, Y., and V. W. Ruttan. 1987a. *Agricultural development: An international perspective.* Baltimore, MD: The Johns Hopkins University Press.

Hayami, Y., and V. W. Ruttan. 1987b. Population growth and agricultural productivity. In *Population growth and economic development: Issues and evidence,* ed. D. G. Johnson and R. G. Lee, 57–101. Madison: University of Wisconsin Press.

Hecht, J. E. 2005. *National environmental accounting: Bridging the gap between ecology and economy.* Washington, DC: Resources for the Future.

Hettige, H., R. E. B. Lucas, and D. Wheeler. 1992. The toxic intensity of industrial production: Global patterns, trends and trade policy. *American Economic Review* 82:478–481.

Holdren, J., and P. Ehrlich. 1974. Human population and the global environment. *American Scientist* 62:282–292.

Inglehart, R. 1995. Public support for environmental protection: Objective problems and subjective values in 43 societies. *PS: Political Science and Politics* 15:57–71.

Inman, K. 1992. Fueling expansion in the third world. *Society and Natural Resources* 6:17–39.

International Bank for Reconstruction and Development. 1992. *World development report 1992: Development and the environment.* New York: Oxford University Press.

IPCC (Intergovernmental Panel on Climate Change). 2005. Workshop on new emission scenarios: Meeting report. Report of Working Group III Technical Support Unit, Bilthoven, The Netherlands.

Jorgenson, A. K. 2003. Consumption and environmental degradation: A cross-national analysis of the ecological footprint. *Social Problems* 50:374–394.

Jorgenson, A. K. 2004. Uneven processes and environmental degradation in the world-economy. *Human Ecology Review* 11:103–117.

Jorgenson, A. K. 2009. The transnational organization of production, the scale of degradation, and ecoefficiency: A study of carbon dioxide emissions in less-developed countries. *Human Ecology Review* 16:64–74.

Jorgenson, A. K., J. Rice, and J. Crowe. 2005. Unpacking the ecological footprint of nations. *International Journal of Comparative Sociology* 46:241–260.

Kahn, J. R., and J. A. MacDonald. 1994. International debt and deforestation. In *The causes of tropical deforestation*, ed. K. Brown and D. Pearce, 57–67. Vancouver, BC: University of British Columbia Press.

Kaya, Y. 1990. Impact of carbon dioxide emission control on GNP growth: Interpretation of proposed scenarios. IPCC Energy and Industry Subgroup, Response Strategies Working Group, Paris.

Kick, E. L., T. J. Burns, B. Davis, D. A. Murray, and D. A. Murray. 1996. Impacts of domestic population dynamics and foreign wood trade on deforestation: A world-systems perspective. *Journal of Developing Societies* 12:68–87.

King, G. 1997. *A solution to the ecological inference problem: Reconstructing individual behavior from aggregate data.* Princeton, NJ: Princeton University Press.

Krech, S. III. 1999. *The ecological Indian: Myth and history.* New York: W. W. Norton and Company.

Kuznets, S. 1955. Economic growth and income inequality. *American Economic Review* 45:1–28.

Lenski, G. 1986. Trajectories of development: A further test. *Social Forces* 65:794–795.

Lenski, G. 2005. *Ecological-evolutionary theory: Principles and applications.* Boulder, CO: Paradigm Publishers.

Lenski, G., and P. D. Nolan. 1984. Trajectories of development: A test of ecological evolutionary theory. *Social Forces* 63:1–23.

Liu, J., G. C. Daily, P. R. Ehrlich, and G. W. Luck. 2003. Effects of household dynamics on resource consumption and biodiversity. *Nature* 421:530–533.

Liu, J., T. Dietz, S. R. Carpenter, M. Alberti, C. Folke, E. Moran, A. N. Pell, P. Deadman, T. Kratz, J. Lubchencko, E. Ostrom, Z. Ouyang, W. Provencher, C. L. Redman, S. H. Schneider, and W. W. Taylor. 2007a. Complexity of coupled human and natural systems. *Science* 317:1513–1516.

Liu, J., T. Dietz, S. R. Carpenter, C. Folke, M. Alberti, C. L. Redman, S. H. Schneider, E. Ostrom, A. N. Pell, J. Lubchencko, W. W. Taylor, Z. Ouyang, P. Deadman, T. Kratz, and W. Provencher. 2007b. Coupled human and natural systems. *Ambio* 36:639–649.

Lomborg, B. 2001. *The skeptical environmentalist: Measuring the real state of the world.* Cambridge, UK: Cambridge University Press.

Longo, S. B., and R. York. 2009. Structural influences on water withdrawals: An exploratory macro-comparative analysis. *Human Ecology Review* 16 (1):74–82.

Lopez, R. 1994. The environment as a factor of production: The effects of economic growth and trade liberalization. *Journal of Environmental Economics and Management* 27:163–184.

Lopez, R. 2003. The policy roots of socioeconomic stagnation and environmental implosion: Latin American, 1950–2000. *World Development* 31:259–280.

Lough, T. S. 1999. Energy, agriculture, patriarchy and ecocide. *Human Ecology Review* 6:100–111.

MacKellar, F. L., W. Lutz, A. J. McMichael, A. Suhrke, V. Mishra, B. O'Neill, S. Prakash, and L. Wexler. 1998. Population and climate change. In *Human choice and climate* change, *Volume 1: The societal context,* ed. S. Rayner and E. Malone, 89–93. Columbus, Ohio: Battelle Press.

Marquart-Pyatt, S. T. 2007. Concern for the environment among general publics: A cross-national study. *Society and Natural Resources* 20:883–898.

Mayr, E. 1959. Typological versus population thinking. In *Evolution and anthropology: A centennial appraisal,* ed. B. J. Meggers, 409–412. Washington, DC: Anthropological Society of Washington.

McCay, B. J., and A. P. Vayda. 1975. New directions in ecology and ecological anthropology. *Annual Review of Anthropology* 4:293–306.

McKinney, L. A., G. M. Fulkerson, and E. L. Kick. 2009. Investigating the correlates of biodiversity loss: A cross-national quantitative analysis of threatened bird species. *Human Ecology Review* 16 (1):102–112.

McLaughlin, P. 1998. Rethinking the agrarian question: The limits of essentialism and the promise of evolutionism. *Human Ecology Review* 5:25–39.

Midlarsky, M. 1998. Democracy and the environment. *Journal of Peace Research* 35:341–361.

Mol, A. P. J. 1995. *The refinement of production: Ecological modernization theory and the chemical industry.* Utrecht: Van Arkel.

Mol, A. P. J. 1996. Ecological modernization and institutional reflexivity: Environmental reform in the late modern age. *Environmental Politics* 5 (2):302–323.

Mol, A. P. J., and G. Spaargaren. 2000. Ecological modernization theory debate: A review. *Environmental Politics* 9 (1):17–49.

Murphy, J. 2000. Ecological modernisation. *Geoforum* 31:1–8.

Myers, N., and J. Kent. 2003. New consumers: The influence of affluences on the environment. *Proceedings of the National Academy of Sciences, USA* 100: 4963–4968.

Neumayer, E. 2002a. Do democracies exhibit stronger international environmental commitment: A cross-country analysis. *Journal of Peace Research* 39:139–164.

Neumayer, E. 2002b. Does trade openness promote multilateral environmental cooperation? *World Economics* 25:815–832.

Nordhaus, W. D. 2006. Geography and macroeconomics: New data and new findings. *Proceedings of the National Academy of Sciences, USA* 103:3510–3517.

Norgaard, K., and R. York. 2005. Gender equality and state environmentalism. *Gender & Society* 19 (4):506–522.

O'Connor, J. 1994. Is sustainable capitalism possible? In *Is capitalism sustainable? Political economy and the politics of ecology*, ed. M. O'Connor, 152–175. New York: The Guilford Press.

Ogburn, W. F., and I. Goltra. 1919. How women vote: A study of an election in Portland, Oregon. *Political Science Quarterly* 34:413–433.

Palloni, A. 1994. The relation between population and deforestation: Methods for drawing causal inferences from macro and micro studies. In *Population and environment: Rethinking the debate,* ed. A. Lourdes, M. P. Stone, and D. C. Major, 125–165. Boulder, CO: Westview.

Parris, T. W., and R. W. Kates. 2003. Characterizing and measuring sustainable development. *Annual Review of Environment and Resources* 28:13.1–13.28.

Perman, R., and D. I. Stern. 2003. Evidence from panel unit root and cointegration tests that the environmental Kuznets curve does not exist. *Australian Journal of Agricultural and Resource Economics* 47:325–347.

Pigou, A. C. 1920. *The economics of welfare.* London: Macmillan.

Ponting, C. 1991. *A green history of the world.* London, England: Penguin Books.

Princen, T., and M. Finger. 1994. *Environmental NGOs in world politics: Linking the local and the global.* London: Routledge.

Ragin, C. C. 2000. *Fuzzy-set social science.* Chicago: University of Chicago Press.

Randall, A. 1987. *Resource economics: An economic approach to natural resources and economic policy.* New York: John Wiley and Sons.

Raupach, M. R., G. Marland, P. Ciais, C. Le Quéré, J. G. Canadell, G. Klepper, and C. B. Field. 2007. Global and regional drivers of accelerating CO^2 emissions. *Proceedings of the National Academy of Sciences, USA* 104:10288–10293.

Rayner, S. 1991. A cultural perspective on the structure and implementation of global environmental agreements. *Evaluation Review* 15:75–102.

Rayner, S., D. Lach, and H. Ingram. 2006. Weather forecasts are for wimps: Why water resource managers do not use climate forecasts. *Climatic Change* 69:197–227.

Rayner, S., and E. Malone. 1997. Zen and the art of climate maintenance. *Nature* 390:332–334.

Reid, W. V., H. A. Mooney, A. Cropper, D. Capistrano, S. R. Carpenter, K. Chopra, P. Dasgupta, T. Dietz, A. K. Duraiappah, R. Hassan, R. Kasperson, R. Leemans, R. M. May, T. A. J. McMichael, P. Pingali, C. Samper, R. Sholes, R. T. Watson, A. H. Zakri, Z. Shidong, N. J. Ash, E. Bennett, P. Kumar, M. J. Lee, C. Raudsepp-Hearne, H. Simons, J. Thonell, and M. B. Zurek. 2005. *Ecosystems and human well-being: Synthesis.* Washington, DC: Island Press.

Richerson, P. J. 1977. Ecology and human ecology: A comparison of theories in the biological and social sciences. *American Ethnologist* 4:1–26.

Richerson, P. J., and R. Boyd. 1997–1998. Homage to Malthus, Ricardo and Boserup: Toward a general theory of population, economic growth, environmental deterioration, wealth and poverty. *Human Ecology Review* 4:85–90.

Richerson, P. J., and R. Boyd. 2005. *Not by genes alone: How culture transformed human evolution.* Chicago: University of Chicago Press.

Roberts, J. T., and P. E. Grimes. 1997. Carbon intensity and economic development 1962–1971: A brief exploration of the environmental Kuznets curve. *World Development* 25:191–198.

Roberts, J. T., and P. E. Grimes. 2002. World-systems and the environment: Toward a new synthesis. In *Sociological theory and the environment: Classical foundations, contemporary insights,* ed. R. E. Dunlap, F. H. Buttel, P. Dickens, and A. Gijswijt, 167–196. Lanham, MD: Rowman and Littlefield.

Roca, J. 2003. Do individual preferences explain the environmental Kuznets curve? *Ecological Economics* 45:3–10.

Røpke, I. 1994. Trade, development and sustainability—A critical assessment of the "free trade" dogma. *Ecological Economics* 9:13–22.

Rosa, E. A., and T. Dietz. 1998. Climate change and society: Speculation, construction and scientific investigation. *International Sociology* 13:421–455.

Rosa, E. A., and G. E. Machlis. 1983. Energetic theories of society: An evaluative review. *Sociological Inquiry* 53:152–178.

Rosa, E. A., and R. York. 2002. Internal and external sources of environmental impacts: A comparative analysis of the EU with other nation groupings. Paper presented at *The European Union in international affairs.* National Europe Centre, Australian National University, Canberra, Australia, July 3.

Rudel, T. K. 1989. Population, development and tropical deforestation: A cross-national study. *Rural Sociology* 54:327–338.

Rudel, T. K. 2005. *Tropical forests: Regional path of destruction and regeneration in the late twentieth century.* New York: Columbia University Press.

Rudel, T. K. 2009. Succession theory: Reassessing a neglected meta-narrative about environment and development. *Human Ecology Review* 16 (1): 83–91.

Rudel, T., and J. Roper. 1997. The paths to rain forest destruction: cross-national patterns of tropical deforestation, 1975–90. *World Development* 25: 53–65.

Schnaiberg, A. 1980. *The environment: From surplus to scarcity.* New York: Oxford University Press.

Schofer, E., and A. Hironaka. 2005. The effects of world society on environmental protection outcomes. *Social Forces* 84:25–47.

Seager, J. 1993. *Earth follies: Coming to feminist terms with the global environmental crisis.* London: Earthscan.

Shandra, J. M., B. London, O. P. Whooley, and J. B. Williamson. 2004. International nongovernmental organizations and carbon dioxide emissions in the developing world: A quantitative, cross-national analysis. *Sociological Inquiry* 74:520–545.

Shandra, J. M., E. Shor, and B. London. 2009. World polity, unequal ecological exchange, and organic water pollution: A cross-national analysis of developing nations. *Human Ecology Review* 16 (1):52–62.

Sieferle, R. P. [1982] 2001. *The subterranean forest: Energy systems and the industrial revolution.* Cambridge: White Horse Press.

Simon, J. L. 1981. *The ultimate resource.* Princeton, NJ: Princeton University Press.

Simon, J. L. 1996. *The ultimate resource 2.* Princeton, NJ: Princeton University Press.

Sober, E. 1980. Evolution, population thinking, and essentialism. *Philosophy of Science* 47:350–383.

Spaargaren, G. 1997. The ecological modernization of production and consumption. Thesis. Landbouw Universiteit Wageningen.

Spaargaren, G., and A. P. J. Mol. 1992. Sociology, environment, and modernity: Ecological modernisation as a theory of social change. *Society and Natural Resources* 5:323–344.

Steenbergen, M. R., and B. S. Jones. 2002. Modeling multilevel data structures. *American Journal of Political Science* 46:218–237.

Stern, D. I. 2002. Explaining changes in global sulfur emissions: An econometric decomposition approach. *Ecological Economics* 42:201–220.

Stern, D. I. 2004. The rise and fall of the environmental Kuznets curve. *World Development* 32:1419–1439.

Stern, D. I., M. S. Common, and E. B. Babbier. 1996. Economic growth and environmental degradation. *World Development* 24:1151–1160.

Suri, V., and D. Chapman. 1998. Economic growth, trade and energy: Implications for the environmental Kuznets curve. *Ecological Economics* 25:195–208.

Sweezy, P. M., and H. Magdoff. 1972. *The dynamics of U.S. capitalism: Corporate structure, inflation, credit, gold and the dollar.* New York: Monthly Review Press.

Thompson, M., R. Ellis, and A. Wildavsky. 1990. *Cultural theory*. Boulder, CO: Westview Press.

Tole, L. 1998. Sources of deforestation in tropical developing countries. *Environmental Management* 22:19–33.

Turner, B. L. II, R. E. Kasperson, W. B. Meyer, K. Dow, D. Golding, J. X. Kasperson, R. C. Mitchell, and S. J. Ratick. 1990. Two types of global environmental change: Definitional and spatial scale issues in their human dimensions. *Global Environmental Change* 1 (1):14–22.

U.S. Climate Change Science Program. 2007. Scenarios of greenhouse gas emissions and atmospheric concentrations (part A) and review of integrated scenario development and application (part B). U.S. Department of Energy, Office of Biological & Environmental Research, Washington, DC.

Vayda, A. P. 1988. Actions and consequences as objects of explanation in human ecology. In *Human ecology: Research and applications,* ed. R. J. Borden, J. Jacobs, and G. L. Young, 9–18. College Park, MD: Society for Human Ecology.

Verweij, M., M. Douglas, R. Ellis, C. Engel, F. Hendriks, S. Lohmann, S. Ney, S. Rayner, and M. Thompson. 2006. Clumsy solutions for a complex world: The case of climate change. *Public Administration* 84:817–843.

Wackernagel, M., and W. Rees. 1996. *Our ecological footprint: Reducing human impact on the Earth*. Gabriola Island, BC: New Society Publishers.

Wackernagel, M., N. B. Schultz, D. Deumling, A. C. Linares, M. Jenkins, V. Kapos, C. Monfreda, J. Loh, N. Myers, R. B. Norgaard, and J. Randers. 2002. Tracking the ecological overshoot of the human economy. *Proceedings of the National Academy of Sciences, USA* 99:9266–9271.

Wernick, I. K. 1997. Consuming materials: The American way. In *Environmentally significant consumption: Research directions,* ed. P. C. Stern, T. Dietz, V. W. Ruttan, R. H. Socolow, and J. L. Sweeney, 29–39. Washington, DC: National Academies Press.

Wernick, I. K., P. E. Waggoner, and J. H. Ausubel. 2000. The Forester's lever: Industrial ecology and wood products. *Journal of Forestry* 98:8–14.

Wilbanks, T. 2006. How scale matters: Some concepts and findings. In *Bridging scales and knowledge systems: Concepts and applications in ecosystem assessments,* ed. W. V. Reid, F. Berkes, T. Wilbanks, and D. Capistrano, 21–35. Washington, DC: Island Press.

Wilk, R. R. 1997. Emulation and global consumerism. In *Environmentally significant consumption: Research directions,* ed. P. C. Stern, T. Dietz, V. H. Ruttan, R. Socolow, and J. L. Sweeney, 110–115. Washington, DC: National Academies Press.

Yamaji, K., R. Matsuhashi, Y. Nagata, and Y. Kaya. 1991. An integrated system for CO_2/Energy/GNP analysis: Case studies on economic measures for CO_2 reduction in Japan. Paper presented at the Workshop on CO_2 Reduction and Removal: Measures for the Next Century. Laxenburg, Austria, March 19–21, 1991.

York, R. 2008. De-carbonization in former Soviet Republics, 1992–2000. The ecological consequences of de-modernization. *Social Problems* 55 (3):370–390.

York, R., and E. A. Rosa. 2003. Key challenges to ecological modernization theory. *Organization and Environment* 16:273–288.

York, R., E. A. Rosa, and T. Dietz. 2002. Bridging environmental science with environmental policy: Plasticity of population, affluence, and technology. *Social Science Quarterly* 83:18–34.

York, R., E. A. Rosa, and T. Dietz. 2003. Footprints on the Earth: The environmental consequences of modernity. *American Sociological Review* 68:279–300.

York, R., E. A. Rosa, and T. Dietz. 2005. The ecological footprint intensity of national economies. *Journal of Industrial Ecology* 8:139–145.

Young, O. 2002. Institutional interplay: The environmental consequences of cross-scale linkages. In *The drama of the commons*, ed. E. Ostrom, T. Dietz, N. Dolsak, P. C. Stern, S. Stonich, and E. Weber, 263–292. Washington, DC: National Academies Press.

Yu, D. 1994. Free trade is green, protectionism is not. *Conservation Biology* 8:989–996.

Zhageni, E., and F. C. Billari. 2007. A cost valuation model based on a stochastic representation of the IPAT equation. *Population and Environment* 29: 68–82.

Zhang, Z. 2000. Decoupling China's carbon emissions increases from economic growth: An economic analysis and policy implications. *World Development* 28:739–752.

4

Progress in the Study of Land Use/Cover Change and the Outlook for the Next Decade

Emilio F. Moran

Introduction

Interest in the causes of land use change at local and regional scale is long standing in the social sciences (Thomas 1954; Sauer 1962; Steward 1955; Glacken 1973; Turner et al. 1990). It is in large part for this reason that the scientific community was quickly able to come to agreement that the issue on which both the physical sciences' and social sciences' research communities could quickly collaborate was in addressing land use/cover change science questions (NRC 1994). The global change research community has been able to make considerable progress in recent years on a number of land use/cover issues: the social causes of deforestation in regions such as the Amazon Basin and Southeast Asia (Skole et al. 1994; Dale et al. 1994; Kummer and Turner 1994; Moran et al. 1994; Moran and Ostrom 2005; Gutman et al. 2004; NRC 2005); the role of spatial distribution of human settlements in emergent forms of land use/cover (Behrens and Baksh 1994; Lambin 1994; Walsh and Crews-Meyer 2002; Lambin, Geist, and Lepers 2003); regional assessments of the impact of climate change on human communities (Liverman 1994; Ellis and Galvin 1994; Knight 1998; Mustard et al. 2004; Skole et al. 2004; Sader et al. 2004; Laporte et al. 2004; Krankina et al. 2004); and the relationship between population and land use/cover change (Meyer and Turner 1992; Entwisle et al. 1998; Walsh et al. 1999; McCracken, Boucek, and Moran 2002; Rindfuss et al. 2004; NRC 2005). These studies have, in turn, refined our understanding of the process of carbon emission from deforestation, and its uptake through processes of secondary succession (Houghton, Joos, and Asner 2004; Lu et al. 2004; Houghton 1994; Skole et al. 1994; Moran et al. 1994, 1996).

Transformation of land cover by human populations is among the most important factors contributing to biogeochemical changes taking place on earth (Houghton, Joos, and Asner 2004; Sponsel, Headland, and Bailey 1996; Ojima, Galvin, and Turner 1994; Turner et al. 1990). Tropical deforestation rates increased at an alarming rate of 50 to 90 percent in the 1980s (Myers 1991; Houghton, Callander, and Varney 1992), while forest cover increased by 25 to 30 percent since 1950 in North America and Europe (Moffat 1998). In addition to the unprecedented loss of species and genetic resources associated with tropical deforestation (Hansen, DeFries, and Turner 2004), regional weather patterns may be drastically changed as well (Bonan et al. 2004). In some regions of the Amazon, where pastures have replaced forests, for example, scientists estimate that "temperatures are about one degree Celsius higher and precipitation up to 30 percent lower in large deforested patches" (Couzin 1999, 317). The entire biogeochemical cycle may be dramatically altered by land use change and agricultural intensification (Detwiler and Hall 1988; Vitousek and Matson 1993; Rosenzweig and Parry 1994; Janetos 2004). Nevertheless, estimates of carbon emission are subject to high degrees of uncertainty, due in large part to difficulties in generalizing about the socioeconomic dimensions of land conversion across local to regional scales (Sorrensen 1998; Dixon and Brown 1994; Dietz and Rosa 1997; Moran, Brondizio, and McCracken 2002; Moran, Ostrom, and Randolph 2002; Brondizio et al. 2002). It is also a consequence of the fact that terrestrial vegetation and soils are extremely heterogeneous over the land surface, and estimates of the magnitude of carbon emissions during clearing and of carbon gains during regrowth of vegetation vary substantially (Woodcock and Ozdogan 2004).

Vitousek et al. (1997) point out that nearly half of the land surface of the earth has been transformed by human actions, and that already about one-quarter of the bird species have been driven to extinction. Nevertheless, almost all research by ecologists and other biophysical scientists studies ecosystems in isolation from human influence—and when included largely as a source of "disturbance." They conclude that understanding human actions and influences upon ecosystems is essential if we are to make progress in protecting and restoring ecosystems. Ecosystem dynamics occur at any one of several levels of complexity, from local to global, and understanding them requires a complex strategy of research that nests these different levels within each other (Moran, Brondizio, and McCracken 2002; Moran, Ostrom, and Randolph 2002; Gutmann 2000; Moran and Brondizio, 1998). To understand human use of the environment over time and in space is a fundamentally interdisciplinary enterprise. The study of land use and land cover is one domain in which the social sciences and the biophysical sciences come together to ensure a robust science of the environment—one in which humans are not only the problem but also essential to the solution (Moran 2006). *Land use* and *land cover* are distinct but complementary terms. Whereas land cover describes the land's physical attributes (e.g., forest, grassland), land use expresses the way such attributes have been transformed by human action (i.e., it provides a socioeconomic portrait of a landscape (LUCC 1995; Moran, Skole, and Turner 2004). Studies in the past five to ten years have contributed to our understanding of land use and land cover change by combining the skills of the social sciences with those of the physical and biological sciences (Meyer and Turner 1992, 1994; Gutman et al. 2004; Turner, Moran, and Rindfuss 2004; Moran and Ostrom 2005). This work has taken place at a number of scales, often consciously trying to understand how processes at the local scale are nested at regional, national, and global scales (LUCC 1995; Moran et al. 1994; Gibson, Ostrom, and Ahn 1998; Moran and Brondizio 1998; Fox et al. 2003; Moran and Ostrom 2005; Lambin and Geist 2006).

It is widely accepted that one of the first steps in analyzing land use/ land cover change is to understand its spatial patterns across a region. This essentially geographic information gains explanatory power by incorporating knowledge of how households and communities affect the condition of forest and other land cover types (Meyer and Turner 1992, 1994; Moran and Ostrom 2005), and how communities set rules for managing resources in order to achieve individual and community goals (Ostrom et al. 2002; Ostrom 1990, 2005; McCay and Acheson 1987).

To understand land use at the global and regional scale, one must take into account the importance of resource perception (Kempton 1993; Kempton, Boster, and Hartley 1995), the structure of opportunity costs (other alternatives available to a person, e.g., Kaimowitz and Angelsen 1998, Geist and Lambin 2002), the range of management practices known and historically practiced (Foster and Aber 2004; Turner, Moran, and Rindfuss 2004), the costs of exploiting different resources in land, labor, and capital terms, and the levels of risk that a population may entertain given its overall economic well-being or marginality. Human perception of the environment has contributed notable findings in recent years to our understanding of changing landscapes. How a farmer perceives or classifies soils plays a major role in determining his or her land clearing and pattern of land use (Conklin 1954; Moran, Brondizio, and McCracken 2002), no less a role than the Food and Agriculture Organization of the United Nations (FAO) map of the world influences how national policy makers and environmental planners give particular regional development plans specificity. Likewise, understanding how a local or regional population classifies or distinguishes between types of vegetation embodies a set of cultural criteria that usually shapes vegetation use (Brondizio 1996, 2005, 2008; Brondizio et al. 1994). Whether a category of vegetation is viewed as useful or as "a weed" determines whether it is used, overlooked, or removed. For example, it can be shown that the expansion in the number of species that have acceptance in international markets has shifted the behavior of logging companies in the Amazon, and expanded the impact of logging on forest cover, increased its flammability, and increased carbon emissions (Nepstad et al. 1999; Sorrensen 1998).

Biophysical Dimensions of Land Use/Cover Change

Climate, topography, soils, and vegetation interact to produce regional-scale patterns of distinguishable ecosystems (Turner, Moran, and Rindfuss 2004). Human impacts on these biophysical determinants of ecosystems have been increasing steadily, particularly since the industrial revolution. To understand the consequences of human activity in ecosystems, we need to understand biological and physical factors that influence the nature and composition of the ecosystems and determine the ways in which human actions shape the structure and function of these ecosystems. For example, analysis combining remotely sensed images and digital elevation models reveals a strong relationship between slope and land cover in the state of Indiana. At the state-wide level, Randolph et al. (2005) find that 70 percent of agriculture occurs on land of less than 10 percent slope, while 65 percent of deciduous forests are found on land with over 10 percent slope. Moreover, while the amount of public land is less than 4 percent of the total area of the state, topography strongly affects where these agencies acquire land. Much of the land acquired by federal and state agencies for the purpose of protecting forests was originally cleared and farmed by settlers. Due to poor soil quality and steep terrain, these lands were abandoned early in the twentieth century and are now old-growth forests available for conservation.

Our work in the Amazon has shown that soil fertility is a significant indicator of differences observed in the rate of growth of secondary forests, and by extension in the rate of carbon sequestration following deforestation of primary forests (Tucker, Brondizio, and Moran 1998; Moran, Brondizio, and McCracken 2002; Moran, Ostrom, and Randolph 2002). In more fertile sites, we have found a twofold difference in tree height over nutrient-poor sites, a difference that continues to amplify in the second decade of regrowth (see figure 4.1). This also leads to a very different species composition, with the more fertile sites being characterized by taller trees and less species diversity and density in the understory (see figure 4.2).

For interregional comparisons, we found differences in soil fertility explained more of the variance than other variables we tested. However, land use emerged as a more powerful variable for intraregional comparisons, explaining the differences in stand height and biomass (see

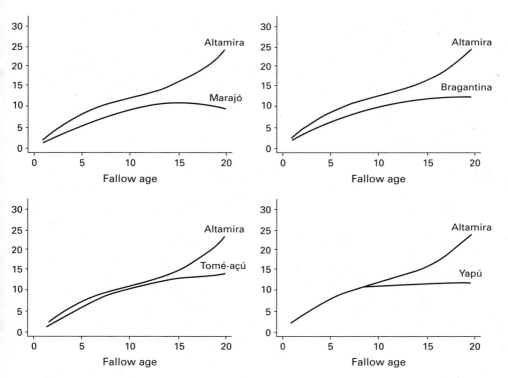

Figure 4.1
Height increment in secondary succession.
Source: Moran and Brondizio 1998, 108.

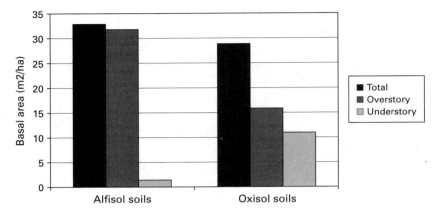

Figure 4.2
Comparison of basal area on soils of different fertilities.
Source: Tucker 1996.

figure 4.3). These findings show the importance of identifying the drivers at each level of analysis, and the challenge of discovering the linking mechanisms between levels of analysis to understand system dynamics (see figure 4.4).

An example of the applications of remote sensing to fundamental issues in social science is the study by Behrens and Baksh (1994) that has shown that settlement history mediates the effect of population pressure on indigenous land use (see also advances in Liverman et al. 1998; Fox et al. 2003; Moran and Ostrom 2005). Sedentism, and market opportunities promoting sedentism, seem more important drivers of land use intensification and tropical deforestation than population growth itself. Village formation and cattle ranching are associated with greater landscape heterogeneity but fewer woody species. Taking a population that is areally distributed over the landscape and concentrating it in large villages can intensify deforestation, particularly when exacerbated by development of pastures and irrigated rice cropping. Rice cultivation has grown in appeal because of the subsidized treatment it received in credit schemes that are as advantageous to borrowers as they are disastrous in the long term for national balance sheets. However, findings from the Wolong Panda Reserve in China suggest that those areas where settlements were concentrated led to a lesser impact on the panda bear habitat than other parts of the reserve where households lived in nonnucleated fashion (Liu et al. 2001).

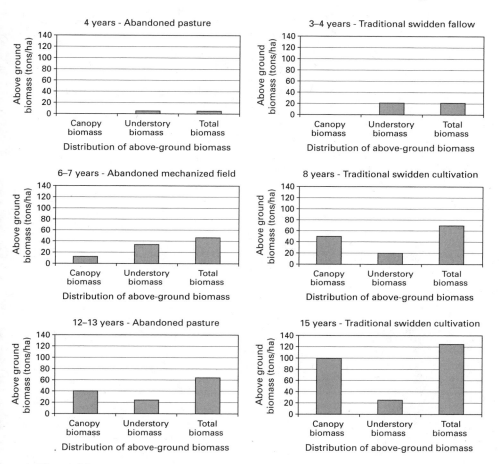

Figure 4.3
Impact of previous land use on above-ground biomass (canopy, understory, and total biomass), Ponta de Pedras, Pará State, Brazil. Traditional swidden fallow are compared to pasture and mechanized field uses.
Source: Moran et al. 2000.

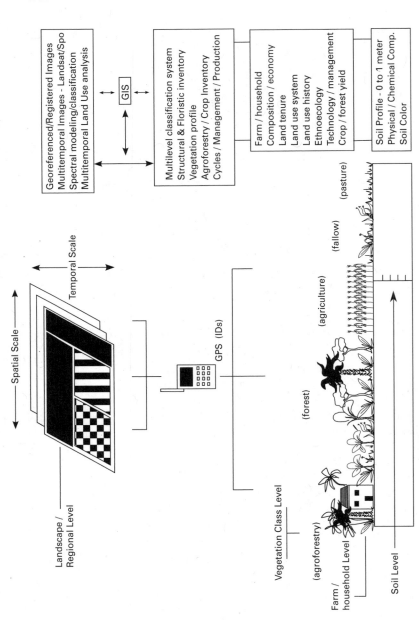

Figure 4.4
Method of multilevel analysis of land use/cover.
Source: Moran and Brondizio 1998, 101.

Social Science and Remote Sensing

Social scientists working on the human dimensions of global change have contributed to improved attention to the kinds of information that can be derived from orbital earth-observing satellites (Liverman et al. 1998; Rindfuss et al. 2004; Turner, Moran, and Rindfuss 2004; Gutman et al. 2004; Moran and Ostrom 2005). Because of their interest in understanding the behavioral dimensions of land cover change, social scientists have sought to develop algorithms that permit more detailed observation of spectral changes through time and infer human decisions from these shifts in reflectance values (Wilkie 1994; Moran et al. 1994; Mausel et al. 1993; Brondizio et al. 1996; Brondizio 2008). These advances have made it possible to monitor not only deforestation, but also up to three age-classes of secondary succession (see figure 4.5) in the Amazon (Mausel et al. 1993; Moran et al. 1994), as well as the changing patterns of agroforestry management in the Amazon estuary (Brondizio et al. 1994, 1996; Brondizio 2008).

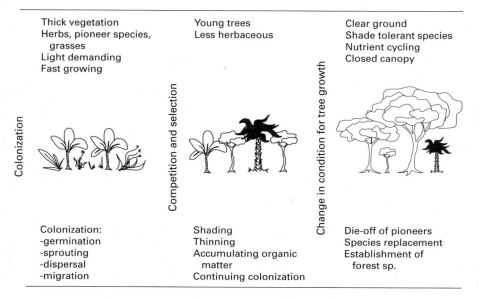

Figure 4.5
Diagram illustrating key features of secondary succession in Amazônia.
Source: Tucker, Brondizio, and Moran 1998.

Social sciences' participation on land use- and land cover-related research has raised important questions about the areal extent of secondary vegetation, and the likely miscalculation of biomass and carbon pools derived from overly aggregated analyses that cannot quantify the differences between mature and ten-year-old regrowth vegetation. This is a far from trivial issue: debates since Kyoto have and will continue to hinge on accurate carbon accounting. Thus, whether a forest is a six-year secondary forest with thirty-seven tons of carbon per hectare, or a seventeen-year secondary forest with 157 tons of carbon per hectare, or an ancient mature forest with many times that much carbon (even though at present this is not adequately valued in trade terms), has considerable significance in carbon emissions trading at international meetings. Global and even macroregional analyses are likely to have no less than a 30 percent error in their carbon accounts if they fail to distinguish between stages of secondary succession. As these areas continue to increase in areal extent, the significance of the error will only increase. It is often assumed that when forests burn in the Amazon, they are always pristine forests. Our research points out that after an initial period of clearing primary forest, most small farmers cut and burn relatively young secondary growth, rather than advanced successional or primary forests, thereby emitting considerably less carbon than global estimates have suggested (Moran, Brondizio, and McCracken 2002; Moran, Ostrom, and Randolph 2002; Moran et al. 1996, 1994; Sorrensen 1998). In the humid tropics, it has been difficult to distinguish mature from secondary forests when the assessment uses wall-to-wall methods with coarse-grained satellite imagery and limited ground-truth information (Lu, Batistella, and Moran 2007, 2008; Lu et al. 2002, 2008; Lu, Moran, and Mausel 2002).

Modeling and the Representation of Land Use/Cover Change

Work at regional and local scales raises issues that are critical to the future of global change research. For example, how should the variability present in landscapes be represented in global models? If alfisols (relatively fertile soils) comprise 10 percent of a grid cell in a global model in a region comprised of 20 cells, its importance to the human population's land use behavior would not be observable, since it is likely that the 10 percent occurrence of alfisols would be swamped by the dominant, nutrient-poor oxisols. However, this would seriously misrepresent land use and productivity potential since it is likely that close to 100 percent of the alfisols would be cultivated, whereas only 20 percent of the oxisols might be. It may be more accurate to include two grid cells as alfisols to ensure that the variability of soils in the larger region is represented and that the human behavior associated with them can appear in simulations of land use/cover change—rather than remain invisible as it often does in Global Circulation Models (GCMs) (Moran and Brondizio 1998; Moran 2008; Brondizio and Moran 2008).

By focusing on processes at local and regional scale, studies on the human dimensions of global change, or human-environment interactions as it is being called in recent years, have provided valuable information about the need to develop regional GCMs that can be used to test and improve the parameterization of global GCMs. This has been true for issues such as biomass variability in vegetation, precipitation, temperature, land tenure differences, institutions, and population size and distribution. Land use studies are essential to understanding the human role in altering terrestrial and marine ecosystems, and offer realistic answers to questions concerning the role humans play in protecting or destroying biodiversity, and what dimensions of human affairs are implicated in such a decision (Lambin and Geist 2006).

Although population growth is commonly seen as the major cause of land cover change, particularly through the clearing of land to grow food, its role is far more complex (Pebley 1998; Entwisle et al. 1998; Meyer and Turner 1992; Rindfuss et al. 2004; NRC 2005; Perz, Walker, and Caldas 2006). There are numerous cases that suggest that population growth and/or migration are indeed correlated with increasing rates of tropical deforestation (e.g., Allen and Barnes 1985), but there are just as many that suggest that population growth need not lead to increasing deforestation—when alternative employment, settlement concentration, and other processes are available as options to land clearing to provide a population with an acceptable standard of living (Moran and Ostrom 2005; Skole et al. 1994). In fact, there is considerable evidence that only at higher population densities does one find more intensive and efficient use of land (Hayami and Ruttan 1985; Boserup 1981) and that institutions to manage forests can develop effective enforcement under these conditions (Moran and Ostrom 2005; Ostrom 2005).

Modeling of global change tends to be divided into two unbridged worlds—the biophysical and the social—when what is needed are models that combine these two processes in terms of space, time, and decision (Turner, Moran, and Rindfuss 2004; Brown et al. 2004; Moran and Brondizio 1998; Constanza et al. 1993). Developing such integrated models is a massive undertaking and commonly has three major objectives: 1) to understand the causes and mechanisms governing land use and land cover changes; 2) to generate predictions about future changes; and 3) to help design better policies to reduce negative impacts (an excellent review article can be found in Verburg et al. 2006).

The processes of land use and land cover change are not necessarily driven by market forces (Lambin 1994) and therefore econometric models do not adequately deal with the driving forces of change (Kaimowitz and Angelsen 1998), despite the large number of such models that have been generated. Economic models have tended to underestimate the role of institutions, population, and biophysical factors.

One of the challenges of modeling land use and land cover change is how best to capture the complex biophysical and social drivers (Brown et al. 2004; Riebsame et al. 1994). Landscape dynamic models, based on transition probability matrices, logistic function-based models, spatial statistical models using GIS capabilities, ecosystem simulation models, and rule-based models of intelligent agents, are a set of alternatives available for modeling these processes (Moran and Ostrom 2005). A pluralistic and flexible approach to modeling is essential to adequately represent the variety of situations to be modeled—and their true complexity. Lambin (1994, 101) suggests that the major bottleneck of effective development of a hybrid, step-wise model is the availability of accurate empirical data at the appropriate level of spatial aggregation. The work of Land-Use and Land-Cover Change (LUCC) since the spelling out of the Science Plan in 1995 aimed to develop a world sample of land use situations against which to study trajectories of change. A synthesis volume is now available (Lambin and Geist 2006) and new activities are being undertaken under the Global Land Project (GLP), an heir to the LUCC program of the earlier decade (website: http://www.globallandproject.org/).

Progress in developing research in the past decade is evident in the International Human Dimensions Program/International Geosphere Biosphere Program (IHDP/IGBP) Core Project on Land-Use and Land-Cover Change, which lays a coordinated, comparative, and multilevel strategy for understanding, monitoring, and modeling land use (LUCC 1995). Examples of projects are "The Large-Scale Biosphere Atmosphere Experiment in Amazônia," "The Miombo Woodlands Project in Central Africa," and "The Regional Project in the Hindu-Kush Himalaya." Other important initiatives that have recently begun and take us into the next decade have developed at the Social Science and Population program at the National Institute for Child Health and Human Development (NICHD), which has allocated funds for population-and-environment research since 1995. A synthesis volume that includes papers from several of these projects is now available (NRC 2005). In 1996 the National Science Foundation funded a number of centers and teams on the Humans Dimensions of Global Change. Directly relevant to land use is the Center for the Study of Institutions, Population and Environmental Change (CIPEC) at Indiana University and the Center for Integrated Regional Assessment (CIRA) at Penn State University.

CIPEC's major objectives involve examining the causes, processes, and outcomes of variables associated with changes in forest conditions in the Western Hemisphere. To examine how and why some forests have disappeared, others have fragmented, and still others are regrowing requires the use of diverse disciplinary skills and a multilevel approach to processes that vary from the tree or patch level all the way to the national and international levels. We developed a five-tier framework (see figure 4.6) that helps us organize how human decisions at different levels are nested within each other (Moran and Brondizio 1998). Human decisions, while rational, are constrained by cultural values, the quantity and quality of available information, the incentives offered, and the learning and choice-making routines humans have been socialized into using (Ostrom 2005).

Methods, too, require careful attention to spatial and temporal variability. We collected five broad types of data: remotely sensed data, vegetation data, soils data, institutional data, and demographic data at a variety of scales, but in such a way that the data set being measured can be spatially georeferenced and linked to the level above and below it. Linking traditional tools of survey research and the national census with earth science tools offers an added capability than either tool set alone to capture the multilevel spatial and temporal causes and consequences of environmental change.

This has led to some useful advances in the study of land use/cover change and the human dimensions. These include methods that allow linking field surveys with land cover change at the level of the property for an entire landscape (see figure 4.7) by overlaying property boundaries on a time-series of satellite images within a GIS format and making this dynamic analysis part of the resources available in household field interviews (see figure 4.8). Considerable attention is being devoted to understanding the conditions under which private and communal

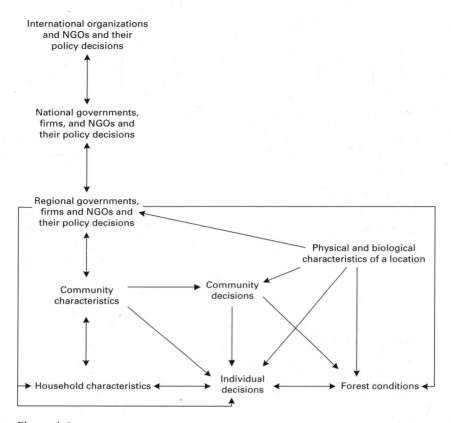

Figure 4.6
Five tiers of decision making.
Source: Moran, Ostrom, and Randolph 2002.

property regimes succeed or fail in sustaining forests through time under a broad array of local, regional, and international circumstances. A synthesis volume from the first six years of the CIPEC project is now available (Moran and Ostrom 2005).

Research Priorities on Land Use/Cover Change in the Next Decade

While considerable advances have been made in the past ten years in clarifying the human dimensions of land use/cover change, a great deal remains to be done. Janetos (2004) concurs with this assessment in the final chapter of the NASA synthesis volume of the land use and land

Figure 4.7
Farm lots along the TransAmazon Highway, Altamira, Pará State, Brazil.

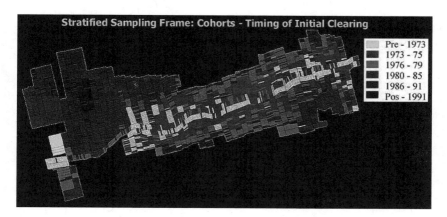

Figure 4.8
Integrating social survey data with parcel boundaries.
Source: McCracken, Boucek, and Moran 2002.

cover change program (Gutman et al. 2004). After all, the LUCC Science Plan was only articulated in 1995, NICHD began funding of land use-and-population issues in 1995, and NASA began support for land use/cover change research only in 1996. A new decade-long effort is being launched as the Global Land Project (GLP), which attempts to better integrate the social and biophysical sciences in the understanding of land-centric research (website for GLP Science Plan: http://www .globallandproject.org/Documents/report_53.pdf). As has been the case with climate change, funding for land use/cover change research needs to be increasingly articulated among all the agencies to ensure completeness of coverage on the many topics that deserve attention. NICHD will continue to emphasize population-and-environment studies that go beyond traditional demographic studies to incorporate GIS and remotely derived data from orbital satellites. NASA has now produced a synthesis volume (Gutman et al. 2004) and its focus remains firmly on understanding land use insofar as it informs atmospheric gas emissions from human activities. After giving emphasis to the Amazon for a decade in a special project called the LBA (Large-Scale Biosphere–Atmosphere Experiment in Amazônia [see synthesis volume by Keller, Gash, and Dias in press; and one focusing on human dimensions of the LBA Project, Batistella, Moran, and Alves 2008]), the program has turned its focus on Monsoon Asia and Boreal Forests. The economics program of the National Oceanic and Atmosphere Administration (NOAA) focuses on marine and coastal processes, and on climate impacts on human communities. There are many other issues that demand time and attention in the decade ahead, to which funding agencies need to give priority.

Understanding the historical development of major ecosystems remains an important goal. There have been excellent developments in environmental history and historical ecology in the past decade. Much of it has been focused on the United States (e.g., Gutmann 2000; Foster and Aber 2004), but environmental historians, geographers, and anthropologists have begun to set their sights on other regions, and global processes (Diamond 2005; Turner, Geoghegan, and Foster 2004; Redman 1999; Redman, James, and Fish 2004). Attention needs to be given to historical and prehistorical land use/cover change in critical areas such as the Amazon, boreal forests, temperate rain forests, and Southeast Asian forests, as well as the Argentine, Mongolian, and Russian savannas (chapters on these areas are available in Gutman et al. 2004). This issue dovetails with the emergent field of restoration ecology and the development of a paradigm for understanding "what" we are restoring (i.e., landscapes at the start of the twentieth century, the fifteenth century, the Paleolithic?). This work will benefit a great deal from interaction with the longer-standing work of the Past Global Changes Project (PAGES), made up of a sophisticated community of paleoclimatologists, archeologists, geologists, and historians (Bradley 1989; PAGES 1998).

This understanding of the historical development of landscapes needs to be connected to *the changing human population structure and distribution*. Over the next ten years the "field" of population and environment will expand rapidly and make important contributions to our understanding of global change (Pebley 1998; NRC 2005). No longer will attention focus merely on processes of population growth, fertility, and mortality, but will be devoted instead to understanding issues of spatial distribution (Gutmann 2000), to addressing spatially georeferenced household composition questions (McCracken, Boucek, and Moran 2002), urban/suburban linkages to adjacent rural areas (Boucek and Moran 2002; Meyer and Turner 1992), to understanding fertility decisions (Entwisle et al. 1998; NRC 2005), to documenting the scope of international migration flows, and to determining how space and time factors are evaluated in making resource use and reproductive decisions (Siqueira et al. 2007). The ebb and flow of population through time needs to be better understood. For example, the migration of population into the Midwest starting in the middle of the nineteenth century continued until about 1920. Since then, the population of the region has become increasingly urban—until the past decade when there has been a nationwide reversal with a growing number of households moving outside the cities and either commuting or working at home part of the time. This shift, if it continues, has considerable consequences in terms of fossil fuel use, lifestyle (and resource consumption), and allocation of resources such as roads, schools, and tax structures (McCracken, Safer, and Green 1997).

Joint work of social scientists with physical scientists needs to continue in order to quantify the amounts of carbon being sequestered in secondary successional vegetation and agroforestry systems. Both of these systems, as well as agriculture, are manipulated by human populations and require attention to better quantify the consequences to carbon pools and fluxes of different human land use decisions. Our recent work has shown that within ten years fallow vegetation in some parts of the Amazon has reached 70 percent of total basal area in adjacent forest, though only 38 percent of the mature forest species has returned (Moran et al. 1996). Future studies are needed to elucidate the role of land use on regrowth of secondary vegetation, the role of human use on species restoration after deforestation, and the interplay between land use choice and carbon emission and sequestration (Lu, Moran, and Mausel 2002; Lu et al. 2002, 2008; Lu, Batistella, and Moran 2005, 2008).

Now that orbital satellites with spatial resolution of one to three meters are available it is possible to link human behavior to environmental features whether in urban or rural areas (Cowen and Jensen 1998; Seto 2005; Redman 2005). This poses a challenge to ground-truthing since the finer-resolution data will require far more detailed field studies than have been common in remote sensing. Partnerships will be needed between the social and physical sciences to provide the necessary field detail to interpret the data and to take full advantage of these new platforms.

In the past the social science community found the data obtained using the Landsat Multispectral Scanner (MSS) too coarse to ask relevant questions of social science import. This began to change with the Landsat Thematic Mapper (TM) and the French Earth Observing Satellite (SPOT) (Behrens and Baksh 1994; Wilkie 1994; Moran et al. 1994; Brondizio et al. 1994, 1996). A greater number of social scientists will be available to help calibrate and test the accuracy of new sensors since they are now reaching a resolution that is more amenable to asking questions about behavioral processes (Cowen and Jensen 1998). Serious ethical and confidentiality issues are raised by these new satellite platforms that have hardly been addressed to date by the engineering community (Rindfuss and Stern 1998; VanWey et al. 2005). As of this writing, however, there is little evidence of a willingness by design engineers to incorporate the interests and expertise of social scientists in the design of new sensors capable of addressing questions of interest to human-environment integrative science.

Janetos (2004) points out correctly that a very important task ahead is to obtain more and better data, and I would add that one needs to find better ways to couple the social and the biophysical data. For example, census data (a primary source of social science information) is currently collected unevenly across the world every decade. This compares unfavorably with the continuous monitoring of land cover possible by satellites, and creates a temporal mismatch that has analytical implications. The current status of the Landsat program is in question, and thus the availability of comparable data across time may be limited in the future unless NASA and Congress take courageous decisions. Currently, we are looking to a possible two-to-five-year gap in data even under the most optimistic scenarios of a launch for Landsat 8 or equivalent. However, use of MODIS (another satellite of medium resolution), SPOT, and other platforms has increased and their resolutions tested against Landsat, sometimes with very good results (Lu, Batistella, and Moran 2008; Lu et al. 2008).

As we make progress in understanding regional-scale patterns of land use, and connect these processes to the national agricultural census and agricultural field surveys, it is possible to *understand municipal-scale processes of land cover transformation* (Gutmann 2000; Gutmann et al. 2005). However, such an understanding is insufficient to explain or can distort understanding of local-scale dynamics. The decision to clear mature forest, or secondary successional forest, remains poorly understood. We know that land tenure is implicated, as is the age/gender structure of households. However, work is needed to understand the role of credit policies, shifts in commodity production both globally and within larger nations, and shifts in interest rates (Skole et al. 1994; Wood and Skole 1998; Turner, Moran, and Rindfuss 2004; Brondizio 2008).

Human land use decisions are mediated by both internal household contingencies and by community institutions. Research is needed to tease out how individuals come together within institutions and negotiate common rules of resource access and strategic behavior. Research is needed to understand how institutions that mediate human interactions with environment and resources acquire knowledge of institutional shared understandings as members of those institutions are replaced over time. And research is needed on the structure of incentives that leads one community to degrade their forest resources, and another to conserve them. What role do population size and distribution play? Does ethnic homogeneity lead to more consistent conservation policies, and under what conditions do heterogeneous ethnicities successfully negotiate a shared understanding toward resource conservation (Ostrom 1999; Gibson, Ostrom, and Ahn 1998; Ostrom 2005)?

It has been customary in the past ten years to think of land use change as a product of population growth and economic activities (i.e., social driving forces). But this is a product of considering this process at a single scale of analysis. Variables that are statistically significant in cross-sectional studies are not statistically significant in panel studies in the same countries. In the coming decade it may be more productive to think of human actions not as "driving forces" but as human choices made around increasingly scarce resources. How human actors organize themselves to ensure their access to resources, and perhaps to ensure resource sustainability, need to have high priority (Tucker 2008).

As global models become more informed by regional approaches, in the next decade it will become possible to address aspects that have so far played a minor role in modeling land use/cover change above the local scale (Riebsame et al. 1994). This is one area where human and financial investments need to be made to go beyond descriptive models, to look at causal hypotheses, complexity, and predictive models. The surge of interest in agent-based models in the past three years (e.g., Brown et al. 2004; Parker et al. 2002, in press; Lim et al. 2004; Deadman et al. 2004) is indicative of this growth and potential, but results to date have been limited. Issues such as the structure of landholding, the tax and insurance regulations that influence decisions, the costs of alternative ways of protecting land resources, and assessment of short- versus longer-term management practices will need attention. In short, the next decade will be challenging. Priority needs to be given to integrative science, to training a new generation of young scientists able to achieve full human-environment integration in conceptualizing the questions, collecting the data, and analyzing that data in the context of extremely complex models.

Acknowledgments

The author thanks the many colleagues at the Anthropological Center for Training and Research on Global Environmental Change, and the Center for the Study of Institutions, Population and Environmental Change at Indiana University, whose ideas have influenced this paper. The research priorities were also influenced by my participation in the National Research Council's Committee on the Human Dimensions of Global Change and the Scientific Steering Committee of LUCC. My work on land use and land cover would not have happened without the support of the National Science Foundation through grants 9310049 and 9521918, and of NICHD through grant 9701386A. None of these agencies, or my collaborators, should be held responsible for the views espoused herein.

References

Allen, J., and F. D. Barnes. 1985. The causes of deforestation in developing countries. *Annals of the Association of American Geographers* 75:163–184.

Batistella, M., E. Moran, and D. Alves, eds. 2008. *Amazônia: Natureza e sociedade em Transformação*. São Paulo: Editora da Universidade de São Paulo (EDUSP).

Behrens, C., and M. G. Baksh. 1994. A regional analysis of Bari land use intensification and its impact on landscape heterogeneity. *Human Ecology* 22 (3): 279–316.

Bonan, G. B., R. S. DeFries, M. T. Cole, and D. S. Ojima. 2004. Land use and climate. In *Land change science: Observing, monitoring and understanding trajectories of change on the Earth's surface*, ed. G. Gutman, A. C. Janetos, C. O. Justice, E. F. Moran, J. F. Mustard, R. R. Rindfuss, D. Skole, B. L. Turner II, and M. A. Cochrane, 301–314. Dordrecht: Kluwer Academic Publishers.

Boserup, E. 1981. *The conditions of agricultural growth*. Chicago: University of Chicago Press.

Boucek, B., and E. F. Moran. 2002. Inferring the behavior of households from remotely sensed changes in land cover: Current methods and future directions. In *Spatially integrated social science*, ed. M. F. Goodchild and D. G. Janelle, 23–47. New York: Oxford University Press.

Bradley, R. 1989. *Global changes of the past*. Boulder, CO: National Center for Atmospheric Research, Office of Interdisciplinary Earth Studies.

Brondizio, E. S. 1996. Forest farmers: Human and landscape ecology of Caboclo populations in the Amazon Estuary. Ph.D. dissertation, School of Public and Environmental Affairs, Indiana University.

Brondizio, E. S. 2005. Intraregional analysis of land-use change in the Amazon. In *Seeing the forest and the trees: Human-environment interactions in forest ecosystems*, ed. E. F. Moran and E. Ostrom, 223–252. Cambridge, MA: MIT Press.

Brondizio, E. S. 2008. *The Amazonian Caboclo and the Açaí palm: Forest farmers in the global market*. New York: The New York Botanical Garden Press.

Brondizio, E., S. McCracken, E. F. Moran, A. D. Siqueira, D. Nelson, and C. Rodriguez-Pedraza. 2002. The colonist footprint: Toward a conceptual framework of land use and deforestation trajectories among small farmers in the Amazonian frontier. In *Deforestation and land use in the Amazon*, ed. C. H. Wood and R. Porro, 133–161. Gainesville: University Press of Florida.

Brondizio, E. S., and E. F. Moran. 2008. Human dimensions of climate change: The vulnerability of small farmers in the Amazon. *Philosophical Transactions of the Royal Society B* 363 (1498):1803–1809.

Brondizio, E., E. Moran, P. Mausel, and Y. Wu. 1994. Land use change in the Amazon Estuary. *Human Ecology* 22 (3):249–278.

Brondizio, E., E. Moran, P. Mausel, and Y. Wu. 1996. Land cover in the Amazon Estuary: Linking the thematic mapper with botanical and historical data. *Photogrammetric Engineering and Remote Sensing* 62 (8):921–929.

Brown, D. G., R. Walker, S. Manson, and K. Seto. 2004. Modeling land-use and land-cover change. In *Land change science: Observing, monitoring and understanding trajectories of change on the Earth's surface*, ed. G. Gutman, A. C. Janetos, C. O. Justice, E. F. Moran, J. F. Mustard, R. R. Rindfuss, D. Skole, B. L. Turner II, and M. A. Cochrane, 395–409. Dordrecht: Kluwer Academic Publishers.

Conklin, H. 1954. *Hanunóo agriculture*. Rome: Food and Agriculture Organization.

Constanza, R., L. Wainger, C. Folks, and K. Maler. 1993. Modeling complex ecological economics systems: Towards an evolutionary, dynamic understanding of people and nature. *BioScience* 43:545–555.

Couzin, J. 1999. Landscape changes make regional climate run hot and cold. *Science* 283:317–318.

Cowen, D., and J. Jensen. 1998. Extraction and modeling of urban attributes using remote sensing technology. In *People and pixels: Linking remote sensing and social science*, ed. D. Liverman, E. F. Moran, R. R. Rindfuss, and P. C. Stern, 164–188. Washington, DC: National Academies Press.

Dale, V., S. M. Pearson, H. Offerman, and R. O'Neill. 1994. Relating patterns of land-use change to faunal biodiversity in the Central Amazon. *Conservation Biology* 8:1027–1036.

Detwiler, R. P., and C. Hall. 1988. Tropical forests and the global carbon cycle. *Science* 239:42–47.

Diamond, J. 2005. *Collapse: How societies choose to fail or succeed*. New York: Viking Books.

Deadman, P., D. Robinson, E. Moran, and E. Brondizio. 2004. Effects of colonist household structure on land change in the Amazon Rainforest: An agent based simulation approach. *Environment and Planning B: Planning and Design* 31:693–709.

Dietz, T., and E. Rosa. 1997. Effects of population and affluence on carbon dioxide emissions. *Proceedings of the National Academy of Sciences* 94 (1): 175–179.

Dixon, R. K., and S. Brown. 1994. Carbon pools and flux of global forest ecosystems. *Science* 263:185–190.

Ellis, J., and K. Galvin. 1994. Climate patterns and land-use practices in the dry zones of Africa. *BioScience* 44 (5):340–348.

Entwisle, B., S. Walsh, R. Rindfuss, and A. Chamratrithirong. 1998. Land use/land cover and population dynamics in Nang Rong, Thailand. In *People and pixels: Linking remote sensing and social science*, ed. D. Liverman, E. F. Moran, R. R. Rindfuss, and P. C. Stern, 121–144. Washington, DC: National Academies Press.

Foster, D., and J. Aber. 2004. *Forests in time: The environmental consequences of 1,000 years of change in New England.* New Haven, CT: Yale University Press.

Fox, J., V. Mishra, R. Rindfuss, and S. Walsh, eds. 2003. *People and the environment: Approaches to linking household and community surveys to remote sensing and GIS.* Dordrecht: Kluwer Academic Press.

Geist, H., and E. Lambin. 2002. Proximate causes and underlying forces of tropical deforestation. *BioScience* 52 (2):143–150.

Gibson, C., E. Ostrom, and T. Ahn. 1998. *Scaling issues in the social sciences.* IHDP Working Paper No. 1. Bonn: International Human Dimensions Programme.

Glacken, C. 1973. *Traces on a Rhodian Shore.* Berkeley: University of California Press.

Gutman, G., A. Janetos, C. Justice, E. F. Moran, J. F. Mustard, R. R. Rindfuss, D. Skole, B. L. Turner II, and M. A. Cochrane, eds. 2004. *Land change science: Observing, monitoring and understanding trajectories of change on the Earth's surface.* Dordrecht: Kluwer Academic Publishers.

Gutmann, M. P. 2000. Scaling and demographic issues in global change research: The Great Plains, 1880–1990. *Climatic Change* 44 (3):377–391.

Gutmann, M. P., W. Parton, G. Cunfer, and I. Burke. 2005. Population and environment in the U.S. Great Plains. In *Population, land use and environment,* ed. B. Entwisle and P. C. Stern, 84–105. Washington, DC: National Academies Press.

Hansen, A. J., R. S. DeFries, and W. Turner. 2004. Land use change and biodiversity: A synthesis of rates and consequences during the period of satellite imagery. In *Land change science: Observing, monitoring and understanding trajectories of change on the Earth's surface,* ed. G. Gutman, A. C. Janetos, C. O. Justice, E. F. Moran, J. F. Mustard, R. R. Rindfuss, D. Skole, B. L. Turner II, and M. A. Cochrane, 277–299. Dordrecht: Kluwer Academic Publishers.

Hayami, Y., and V. W. Ruttan. 1985. *Agricultural development: An international perspective,* revised and expanded edition. Baltimore, MD: Johns Hopkins University Press.

Houghton, R. A. 1994. The worldwide extent of land-use change. *BioScience* 44 (5):305–313.

Houghton, R. A., B. A. Callander, and S. K. Varney, eds. 1992. *Climate change 1992: The supplementary report to the IPCC scientific assessment.* Cambridge: Cambridge University Press.

Houghton, R. A., F. Joos, and G. P. Asner. 2004. The effects of land use and management on the global carbon cycle. In *Land change science: Observing, monitoring and understanding trajectories of change on the Earth's surface,* ed. G. Gutman, A. C. Janetos, C. O. Justice, E. F. Moran, J. F. Mustard, R. R. Rindfuss, D. Skole, B. L. Turner II, and M. A. Cochrane, 237–256. Dordrecht: Kluwer Academic Publishers.

Janetos, A. C. 2004. Research directions in land-cover and land-use change. In *Land change science: Observing, monitoring and understanding trajectories of change on the Earth's surface*, ed. G. Gutman, A. C. Janetos, C. O. Justice, E. F. Moran, J. F. Mustard, R. R. Rindfuss, D. Skole, B. L. Turner II, and M. A. Cochrane, 449–457. Dordrecht: Kluwer Academic Publishers.

Kaimowitz, D., and A. Angelsen. 1998. *Economic models of tropical deforestation: A review*. Bogor, Indonesia: Center for International Forestry Research.

Keller, M., J. Gash, and P. S. Dias, eds. In press. *Amazônia and global change*. San Francisco: International Geophysical Union.

Kempton, W. 1993. Will public environmental concern lead to action on global warming? *Annual Review of Energy and Environment* 18:217–245.

Kempton, W., J. Boster, and J. Hartley. 1995. *Environmental values in American culture*. Cambridge, MA: MIT Press.

Knight, C. G. 1998. Globalization and global change research. *GeoJournal* 45 (1):27–32.

Krankina, O. N., G. Sun, H. H. Shugart, V. Khark, E. Kasischke, K. M. Bergen, J. G. Masek, W. B. Cohen, D. R. Oetter, and M. V. Duane. 2004. Northern Eurasia: Remote sensing of Boreal Forests in selected regions. In *Land change science: Observing, monitoring and understanding trajectories of change on the Earth's surface*, ed. G. Gutman, A. C. Janetos, C. O. Justice, E. F. Moran, J. F. Mustard, R. R. Rindfuss, D. Skole, B. L. Turner II, and M. A. Cochrane, 123–138. Dordrecht: Kluwer Academic Publishers.

Kummer, D. M., and B. L. Turner II. 1994. The human causes of deforestation in Southeast Asia. *BioScience* 44:323–328.

Lambin, E. 1994. *Modeling deforestation processes: A review*. TREES Report No. 1. Brussels: European Commission.

Lambin, E., and H. Geist, eds. 2006. *Land use and land cover change: Local processes, global impacts*. The International Geosphere Biosphere Programme Series. Berlin: Springer-Verlag.

Lambin, E. F., H. Geist, and E. Lepers. 2003. Dynamics of land-use and land cover change in tropical regions. *Annual Review of Environmental and Resources* 28:205–241.

Laporte, N. T., T. S. Lin, J. Lemoigne, D. Dever, and M. Homzak. 2004. Towards an operational forest monitoring system for Central Africa. In *Land change science: Observing, monitoring and understanding trajectories of change on the Earth's surface*, ed. G. Gutman, A. C. Janetos, C. O. Justice, E. F. Moran, J. F. Mustard, R. R. Rindfuss, D. Skole, B. L. Turner II, and M. A. Cochrane, 97–110. Dordrecht: Kluwer Academic Publishers.

Lim, K., P. J. Deadman, E. F. Moran, E. Brondizio, and S. McCracken. 2002. Agent-based simulations of household decision making and land use change near Altamira, Brazil. In *Integrating geographic information systems and agent-based modeling techniques for simulating social and ecological processes*, ed. H. R. Gimblet, 277–310. Oxford: Oxford University Press.

Liu, J., M. Linderman, Z. Ouyang, and L. An. 2001. The pandas' habitat at Wolong Nature Reserve. *Science* 293:603–605.

Liverman, D. 1994. Vulnerability to global environmental change. In *Environmental risks and hazards*, ed. S. Cutter, 326–342. Englewood, NJ: Prentice-Hall.

Liverman, D., E. Moran, R. Rindfuss, and P. Stern, eds. 1998. *People and pixels: Linking remote sensing and social science.* Washington, DC: National Academies Press.

Lu, D., M. Batistella, and E. Moran. 2005. Satellite estimation of aboveground biomass and impacts of forest stand structure. *Photogrammetric Engineering & Remote Sensing* 71 (8):967–974.

Lu, D., M. Batistella, and E. Moran. 2007. Land-cover classification in the Brazilian Amazon with the integration of Landsat ETM+ and Radarsat data. *International Journal of Remote Sensing* 28 (24):5447–5459.

Lu, D., M. Batistella, and E. F. Moran. 2008. Integration of Landsat TM and SPOT HRG images for vegetation change detection in the Brazilian Amazon. *Photogrammetric Engineering & Remote Sensing* 74 (4):421–430.

Lu, D., M. Batistella, E. F. Moran, and E. E. de Miranda. 2008. A comparative study of Landsat TM and SPOT HRG images for vegetation classification in the Brazilian Amazon. *Photogrammetric Engineering & Remote Sensing* 74 (3): 311–321.

Lu, D., G. Li, G. S. Valladares, and M. Batistella. 2004. Mapping soil erosion risk in Rondônia, Brazilian Amazônia: Using RUSLE, remote sensing and GIS. *Land Degradation and Development* 15 (5):499–512.

Lu, D., P. Mausel, E. Brondizio, and E. Moran. 2002. Above-ground biomass estimation of successional and mature forests using TM images in the Amazon Basin. In *Advances in spatial data handling: 10th International Symposium on Spatial Data Handling*, ed. D. Richardson and P. van Oosterom, 183–196. Berlin: Springer-Verlag.

Lu, D., E. F. Moran, and P. Mausel. 2002. Linking Amazonian secondary succession forest growth to soil properties. *Land Degradation and Development* 13 (4):331–343.

Land-Use and Land-Cover Change (LUCC). 1995. *Land use/cover science plan.* Stockholm: International Geosphere Biosphere Programme/International Human Dimensions Programme.

Mausel, P., Y. Wu, Y. Li, E. Moran, and E. Brondizio. 1993. Spectral identification of successional stages following deforestation in the Amazon. *Geocarto International* 8:1–72.

McCay, B., and J. Acheson, eds. 1987. *The question of the commons.* Tucson: University of Arizona Press.

McCracken, S., B. Boucek, and E. F. Moran. 2002. Deforestation trajectories in a Frontier Region of the Brazilian Amazon. In *Linking people, place, and policy: A GIScience approach*, ed. S. J. Walsh and K. Crews-Meyer, 215–234. Dordrecht: Kluwer Academic Publishers.

McCracken, S., C. A. M. Safer, and G. Green. 1997. Deforestation and forest regrowth in Indiana 1860–1990: A socio-demographic perspective. Paper presented at the Population Association of America, Washington, DC, March 26–28.

Meyer, W., and B. L. Turner II. 1992. Human population growth and global land use and land cover change. *Annual Review of Ecology and Systematics* 23:39–61.

Meyer, W., and B. L. Turner II, eds. 1994. *Changes in land use and land cover.* New York: Cambridge University Press.

Moffat, A. S. 1998. Temperate forests gain ground. *Science* 282:1253.

Moran, E. F. 2006. *People and nature: An introduction to human ecological relations.* Oxford: Blackwell Publishers, 2008.

Moran E. F. 2008. Population and environment in the Amazon Basin. Paper for Session: "New Directions in Land Change Science." Association of American Geographers annual meeting, Boston, MA, April 16.

Moran, E. F., and E. S. Brondizio. 1998. Land-use change after deforestation in Amazônia. In *People and pixels: Linking remote sensing and social science*, ed. D. Liverman, E. Moran, R. Rindfuss, and P. Stern, 94–120. Washington, DC: National Academies Press.

Moran, E. F., E. S. Brondizio, P. Mausel, and Y. Wu. 1994. Integrating Amazonian vegetation, land use and satellite data. *BioScience* 44 (5):329–339.

Moran, E. F., E. S. Brondizio, and S. McCracken. 2002. Trajectories of land use: Soils, succession, and crop choice. In *Deforestation and land use in the Amazon*, ed. C. H. Wood and R. Porro, 193–217. Gainesville: University Press of Florida.

Moran, E. F., E. S. Brondizio, J. M. Tucker, M. C. Silva-Forsberg, S. McCracken, and I. Falesi. 2000. Effects of soil fertility and land use on forest succession in Amazônia. *Forest Ecology and Management* 139:93–108.

Moran, E. F., and E. Ostrom, eds. 2005. *Seeing the forest and the trees: Human environment interactions in forest ecosystems.* Cambridge, MA: MIT Press.

Moran, E. F., E. Ostrom, and J. C. Randolph. 2002. Ecological systems and multitier human organizations. In *Knowledge, management, organizational intelligence and learning. UNESCO/Encyclopedia of life support systems*, ed. L. D. Kiel, 1–15. Oxford: EOLSS Publishers.

Moran, E. F., A. Packer, E. Brondizio, and J. Tucker. 1996. Restoration of vegetation cover in the Eastern Amazon. *Ecological Economics* 18:41–54.

Moran, E. F., D. L. Skole, and B. L. Turner II. 2004. The development of the international land use and land cover change (LUCC) research program and its links to NASA's land cover and land use change (LCLUC) initiative. In *Land change science: Observing, monitoring and understanding trajectories of change on the Earth's surface*, ed. G. Gutman, A. C. Janetos, C. O. Justice, E. F. Moran,

J. F. Mustard, R. R. Rindfuss, D. Skole, B. L. Turner II, and M. A. Cochrane, 1–15. Dordrecht: Kluwer Academic Publishers.

Mustard, J. F., R. S. DeFries, T. Fisher, and E. F. Moran. 2004. Land-use and land-cover change pathways and impacts. In *Land change science: Observing, monitoring and understanding trajectories of change on the Earth's surface*, ed. G. Gutman, A. C. Janetos, C. O. Justice, E. F. Moran, J. F. Mustard, R. R. Rindfuss, D. Skole, B. L. Turner II, and M. A. Cochrane, 411–430. Dordrecht: Kluwer Academic Publishers.

Myers, N. 1991. Tropical forests: Present status of future outlook. *Climatic Change* 19 (1–2):3–32.

Nepstad, D. C., A. Veríssimo, A. Alencar, C. Nobre, E. Lima, P. Lefebvre, P. Schlesinger, C. Potter, P. Moutinho, E. Mendoza, M. Cochrane, and V. Brooks. 1999. Large-scale impoverishment of Amazonian forests by logging and fire. *Nature* 398:505–508.

NRC (National Research Council). 1994. *Global environmental change: The human dimensions*. Washington, DC: National Academies Press.

NRC (National Research Council). 2005. *Population, land use, environment: Research directions*. Washington, DC: National Academies Press.

Ojima, D., K. Galvin, and B. L. Turner II. 1994. The global impact of land-use change. *BioScience* 44 (5):300–304.

Ostrom, E. 1990. *Governing the commons*. Cambridge, UK: Cambridge University Press.

Ostrom, E. 1999. *Self-governance and forest resources*. CIFOR Occasional Paper No. 20, Center for International Forestry Research (CIFOR), Bogor, Indonesia.

Ostrom, E. 2005. *Understanding institutional diversity*. Princeton, NJ: Princeton University Press.

Ostrom, E., T. Dietz, N. Dolsak, P. C. Stern, S. Stonich, and E. U. Weber, eds. 2002. *The drama of the commons*. Washington, DC: National Academies Press.

PAGES. 1998. Past global changes: Status report and implementation plan, ed. F. Oldfield. IGBP Report 45.

Parker, D., T. Berger, S. Manson, and W. McConnell, eds. 2002. *Agent-based models of land-use and land-cover change: Report and review of an international workshop*. Land Use and Cover Change Project Report Series No. 6, LUCC Focus 1 Office, Indiana University.

Parker, D., B. Entwisle, R. Rindfuss, L. VanWey, S. Manson, E. Moran, L. An, P. Deadman, T. Evans, M. Linderman, and G. Malanson. In press. Case studies, cross-site comparisons, and the challenge of generalization: Comparing agent-based models of land-use change in frontier regions. *Journal of Land Science*.

Pebley, A. R. 1998. Demography and the environment. *Demography* 35 (4): 377–389.

Perz, S., R. Walker, and M. Caldas. 2006. Beyond population and environment: Household demographic life cycles and land use allocation among small farms in the Amazon. *Human Ecology* 34 (6):829–849.

Randolph, J. C., G. M. Green, J. Belmont, T. Burcsu, and D. Welch. 2005. Forest ecosystems and the human dimensions. In *Seeing the forest and the trees: Human-environment interactions in forest ecosystems*, ed. E. F. Moran and E. Ostrom, 105–126. Cambridge, MA: MIT Press.

Redman, C. 1999. *Human impact on ancient environments.* Tucson: University of Arizona Press.

Redman, C. 2005. The Urban Ecology of Metropolitan Phoenix: A laboratory for interdisciplinary study. In *Population, land use and environment*, ed. B. Entwisle and P. C. Stern, 163–192. Washington, DC: National Academies Press.

Redman, C., S. James, and P. Fish, eds. 2004. *The archeology of global change.* Washington, DC: Smithsonian Press.

Riebsame, W., W. Parton, K. Galvin, I. Burke, L. Bohren, R. Young, and E. Knop. 1994. Integrated modeling of land use and cover change. *BioScience* 44 (5):350–356.

Rindfuss, R. R., and P. C. Stern. 1998. Linking remote sensing and social science: The need and the challenges. In *People and pixels: Linking remote sensing and social science*, ed. D. Liverman, E. F. Moran, R. R. Rindfuss, and P. C. Stern, 1–27. Washington, DC: National Academies Press.

Rindfuss, R. R., S. J. Walsh, B. L. Turner II, E. F. Moran, and B. Entwisle. 2004. Linking pixels and people. In *Land change science: Observing, monitoring and understanding trajectories of change on the Earth's surface*, ed. G. Gutman, A. C. Janetos, C. O. Justice, E. F. Moran, J. F. Mustard, R. R. Rindfuss, D. Skole, B. L. Turner II, and M. A. Cochrane, 379–394. Dordrecht: Kluwer Academic Publishers.

Rosenzweig, C., and M. L. Parry. 1994. Potential impact of climate change on world food supply. *Nature* 367:133–138.

Sader S. A., R. Roy Chowdhury, L. Schneider, and B. L. Turner II. 2004. Forest change and human driving forces in Central America. In *Land change science: Observing, monitoring and understanding trajectories of change on the Earth's surface*, ed. G. Gutman, A. C. Janetos, C. O. Justice, E. F. Moran, J. F. Mustard, R. R. Rindfuss, D. Skole, B. L. Turner II, and M. A. Cochrane, 57–76. The Netherlands: Kluwer Academic Publishers.

Sauer, C. 1962. *Land and life.* Berkeley: University of California Press.

Seto, K. 2005. Economies, societies, and landscapes in transition: Examples from the Pearl River Delta, China, and the Red River Delta, Vietnam. In *Population, land use and environment*, ed. B. Entwisle and P. C. Stern, 193–216. Washington, DC: National Academies Press.

Siqueira, A., A. Dantona, M. F. Dantona, and E. Moran. 2007. Embodied decisions: Reversible and irreversible contraceptive methods among rural women in the Brazilian Amazon. *Human Organization* 66 (20):185–195.

Skole, D. L., W. Chomentowski, W. Salas, and A. Nobre. 1994. Physical and human dimensions of deforestation in Amazônia. *BioScience* 44 (5):314–322.

Skole, D. L., M. A. Cochrane, E. A. T. Matricardi, W. Chomentowski, M. Pedlowski, and D. Kimble. 2004. Pattern to process in the Amazon Region: Measuring forest conversion, regeneration and degradation. In *Land change science: Observing, monitoring and understanding trajectories of change on the Earth's surface*, ed. G. Gutman, A. C. Janetos, C. O. Justice, E. F. Moran, J. F. Mustard, R. R. Rindfuss, D. Skole, B. L. Turner II, and M. A. Cochrane, 257–276. Dordrecht: Kluwer Academic Publishers.

Sorrensen, C. L. 1998. Biomass burning in tropical ecosystems: An analysis of vegetation, land settlement, and land cover change to understand fire use in the Brazilian lower Amazon. Ph.D. dissertation. Department of Geography, Ohio State University.

Sponsel, L. T. Headland, and R. Bailey, eds. 1996. *Tropical deforestation: The human dimensions*. New York: Columbia University Press.

Steward, J. 1955. *The theory of cultural change*. Urbana: University of Illinois Press.

Thomas, W. L., ed. 1954. *Man's role in changing the face of the earth*. 2 vols. Chicago: University of Chicago Press.

Tucker, C. 2008. *Changing forests: Collective action, common property, and coffee in Honduras*. New York: Springer.

Tucker, J. 1996. Secondary succession in the Brazilian Amazon: Investigation of regional differences in forest structure in Altamira and Bragantina, Para State. Undergraduate honor's thesis, School of Public and Environmental Affairs, Indiana University.

Tucker, J., E. Brondizio, and E. Moran. 1998. Rates of forest regrowth in Eastern Amazonia. *Interciencia* 23 (2):64–73.

Turner, B. L., II, W. Clark, R. Kates, J. Richards, J. Mathews, and W. Meyer, eds. 1990. *The Earth as transformed by human action*. Cambridge, UK: Cambridge University Press.

Turner, B. L., II, J. Geoghegan, and D. Foster, eds. 2004. *Integrated land-change science and tropical deforestation in the Southern Yucatan Final frontiers*. Oxford: Oxford University Press.

Turner, B. L., II, E. F. Moran, and R. R. Rindfuss. 2004. Integrated land-change science and its relevance to the human sciences. In *Land change science: Observing, monitoring and understanding trajectories of change on the Earth's surface*, ed. G. Gutman, A. C. Janetos, C. O. Justice, E. F. Moran, J. F. Mustard, R. R. Rindfuss, D. Skole, B. L. Turner II, and M. A. Cochrane, 431–448. Dordrecht: Kluwer Academic Publishers.

VanWey, L., R. R. Rindfuss, M. P. Gutmann, B. Entwisle, and D. L. Balk. 2005. Confidentiality and spatially explicit data: Concerns and challenges. *Proceedings of the National Academy of Sciences of the United States of America* 102 (44):15337–15342.

Verburg, P., K. Kok, R. G. Pontius Jr., and A. Veldkamp. 2006. Modeling land-use and land-cover change. In *Land use and land cover change*, ed. E. Lambin and H. Geist, 117–135. New York: Springer.

Vitousek, P., and P. Matson. 1993. Agriculture, the global nitrogen cycle and trace gas flux. In *The biogeochemistry and global change: Radiatively active trace gases*, ed. R. S. Oremland, 193–208. New York: Chapman and Hall.

Vitousek, P., H. Mooney, J. Lubchenko, and J. Melillo. 1997. Human domination of Earth's ecosystems. *Science* 277:494–499.

Walsh, S. J., and K. A. Crews-Meyer, eds. 2002. *Linking people, place, and policy: A GIScience approach.* Dordrecht: Kluwer Academic Publishers.

Walsh, S., T. Evans, W. Welsh, B. Entwisle, and R. Rindfuss. 1999. Scale-dependent relationships between population and environment in Northeastern Thailand. *Photogrammetric Engineering and Remote Sensing* 65 (1):97–105.

Wilkie, D. 1994. Remote sensing imagery for resource inventories in Central Africa: The importance of detailed field data. *Human Ecology* 22 (3):379–403.

Wood, C., and D. Skole. 1998. Linking satellite, census, and survey data to study deforestation in the Brazilian Amazon. In *People and pixels: Linking remote sensing and social science*, ed. D. Liverman, E. F. Moran, R. R. Rindfuss, and P. C. Stern, 70–93. Washington, DC: National Academies Press.

Woodcock, C. E., and M. Ozdogan. 2004. Trends in land cover mapping and monitoring. In *Land change science: Observing, monitoring and understanding trajectories of change on the Earth's surface*, ed. G. Gutman, A. C. Janetos, C. O. Justice, E. F. Moran, J. F. Mustard, R. R. Rindfuss, D. Skole, B. L. Turner II, and M. A. Cochrane, 367–378. Dordrecht: Kluwer Academic Publishers.

5

The Effectiveness of International Environmental Regimes

Oran R. Young

A striking feature of the recent past is the sharp rise in public interest concerning large-scale environmental problems and in the creation of international regimes as a means of addressing them (e.g., Young 1999a; Simmons and Martin 2002). Many see in this development a hopeful sign regarding the prospects for solving numerous problems ranging from the sustainable use of shared natural resources (e.g., transboundary water resources or straddling stocks of fish) to global environmental changes (e.g., the loss of biological diversity or the alteration of the earth's climate system). But how realistic is this hope? To ask this question is to launch an enquiry into the effectiveness or success of the institutional arrangements or regimes that have been established in recent decades to deal with a wide range of environmental problems arising at the international level. The purpose of this chapter is to report on this ongoing enterprise, assessing what we know about the effectiveness of international environmental regimes, asking what we need to know about these arrangements to increase their effectiveness in the future, and considering research strategies for obtaining this knowledge.

Conceptualized as sets of rules, decision-making procedures, and programs that give rise to social practices and govern interactions among the participants in these practices, international environmental regimes now cover a wide range of activities involving the human use of natural resources and the protection of ecosystems from anthropogenic disturbances.[1] While there are legitimate disagreements about the status of marginal cases and the precise point at which specific regimes are born or become operational, there is general agreement about the identity of the core members of this analytic category.[2] As a point of departure for this assessment, it is safe to say that the universe of international environmental regimes currently contains several hundred cases.[3]

Although the individual members of this universe share the defining features of all international regimes, they differ markedly among themselves along a variety of dimensions, including membership, geographical domain, functional scope, degree of formalization, balance between formal and informal elements, stage of development, and linkages to other regimes. Some regimes (e.g., the Great Lakes Water Quality Agreement) are bilateral; others are multilateral (e.g., the European transboundary air pollution regime); still others are global or nearly universal with regard to membership (e.g., the climate regime). Some regimes (e.g., the Antarctic Treaty System) are broad in functional terms but limited with regard to their geographical coverage. Others (e.g., the regime for whales and whaling) are functionally limited but broad in terms of geographical coverage. While many regimes are highly formalized in the sense that the agreements spelling out their constitutive provisions take the form of formally ratified conventions or treaties, others rest on declarations or informal agreements (e.g., the Declaration on the Establishment of the Arctic Council) that do not have the force of law.[4] Over time, most regimes evolve in such a way as to encompass a complex mix of formalized provisions and informal understandings that serve to amplify or modify their formal provisions.

Whereas some regimes are largely self-contained or stand-alone arrangements, others (e.g., the agreement dealing with straddling stocks and highly migratory fish) are embedded within or closely linked to other institutional arrangements in international society. Regimes also vary greatly in terms of their maturity or stage of development. Some (e.g., the arrangements for biosafety under the 2000 Cartagena Protocol to the Convention on Biological Diversity) are just getting underway. Others (e.g., the regime dealing with vessel-source pollutants) have gone through a number of distinct stages in the course of arriving at their current form. Like markets and political institutions operating in domestic settings, then, international regimes come in many shapes and forms. Yet this does nothing to negate the fact that they all belong to a single universe of cases or to undermine the effort to develop generalizations that hold across the entire universe.

Because environmental regimes normally arise in response to problems—real or perceived—that make their way onto the international political agenda, it is understandable that analysts have directed much of their attention initially to the processes involved in regime creation, asking why regimes form to deal with some problems but not others and what determines the shape or form that particular regimes take. This effort has yielded important results; it will undoubtedly constitute a focus of continuing interest among students of international regimes during the foreseeable future (Haggard and Simmons 1987; Young and Osherenko 1993; Hasenclever, Meyer, and Rittberger 1997). In recent years, however, analysts have come to realize that it is not enough to understand the forces governing regime formation. In the final analysis, we want to know whether regimes are successful or, in other words, whether they make a difference in efforts to come to terms with the problems that stimulate their creation. This realization has triggered a marked growth of interest in what is generally termed the effectiveness of regimes (Young and von Moltke 1994; Young 1996b; Haas, Keohane, and Levy 1993; Young 1999b; Breitmeier, Young, and Zürn 2006).[5] What do we know and what do we need to know about the effectiveness of international environmental regimes? That question constitutes the central concern of this chapter.[6]

What Do We Mean by Effectiveness?

At first glance, the meaning of effectiveness with regard to regimes seems intuitively obvious.[7] Regimes arise to solve problems. Effectiveness, therefore, is a measure of the extent to which they succeed in solving the problems that lead to their formation. Appealing as this approach to effectiveness is, it has severe limitations as a basis for analyzing the performance of international regimes. As numerous observers have pointed out, participants can and often do develop widely divergent perceptions of the nature or character of the problem to be solved, and regimes frequently come into existence in the absence of consensus in the realm of problem definition. The danger of ending up with spurious correlations is a constant threat to efforts to understand regime effectiveness construed as problem solving. The disappearance or amelioration of a problem following the formation of a regime does not constitute proof that the regime was a causal force in the process. Conversely, the failure of a problem to disappear following regime creation does not justify the conclusion that the regime had no effect at all; the problem could well have grown more severe in the absence of the regime. More generally, the operation of a regime is typically only one of a suite of factors—both intended and unintended—that plays some role in determining the course of international environmental problems. More often than not, the real problem is not a matter of determining whether a regime matters at all. Rather, the challenge is to find ways to determine the proportion of the variance in the realm of problem solving that can be attributed convincingly to the operation of the regime or to understand the interactions between institutional arrangements and other driving forces (Young 2002a). Given the limited size of the universe of cases and the amount of variance within this universe, finding ways to demonstrate the causal significance of international regimes as problem solvers is a tall order.

Faced with this somewhat daunting prospect, many analysts have sought to come up with alternative ways to think about the effectiveness of international regimes. An approach that is common—particularly among lawyers and political scientists—is to direct attention to issues of implementation and compliance in contrast to problem solving (see Chayes and Chayes 1995; Weiss and Jacobson 1998; Victor, Raustiala, and Skolnikoff 1998; Underdal and Hanf 2000). Do regime members take vigorous steps to implement regime rules or commitments and to turn them into enforceable regulations within their domestic jurisdictions? Do states or subjects operating under their auspices comply with regime rules or live up to the commitments they make in creating regimes? This approach has the virtue of being comparatively easy to operationalize; it is generally feasible to follow efforts to implement regulatory provisions or to get programmatic activities underway. But it leaves much to be desired as a way to think about effectiveness. Above all, there is no direct relationship between implementation and compliance, on the one hand, and solving pressing problems, on the other. Regimes can score high in terms of implementation or compliance without solving the problems that led to their creation in the first place. Conversely, regimes can have far-reaching consequences, even when their records seem mediocre with respect to conventional measures of implementation and compliance. Partly, this is attributable to the fact that some regimes are able to tolerate fairly extensive violations without becoming ineffectual. In part, it is a consequence of the fact that regimes may lead to substantial alterations in the behavior of key actors that have little or nothing to do with conforming to specific rules or commitments. Under the circumstances, the fact that a turn toward implementation and compliance as a way of conceptualizing effectiveness is also apt to lead to a loss of analytic rigor and a constant battle with empirical messiness looms large as a drawback of this approach to regime effectiveness.

Given these difficulties, many analysts have directed their attention toward behavioral consequences as a measure of the effectiveness of regimes (Young 1999b). International regimes are not actors in their own right, though they may lead to the creation of organizations whose function is to administer their provisions.[8] Under the circumstances, the question to be answered is whether regimes or governance systems play a role in shaping or guiding the behavior of those who are actors, including both the states that are ordinarily the formal members of international regimes and the government agencies, corporations, interest groups, and even individuals whose behavior is targeted by a regime's provisions. We want to know, in other words, not only whether the United States fulfills its obligations under the terms of the regime dealing with ozone-depleting substances, but also whether producers and consumers of such substances operating under the jurisdiction of the United States alter their behavior in response to the creation and operation of the regime.[9] Of course, it is important to observe that the behavioral effects of regimes include deterrence in the sense that actors are induced to refrain from taking steps they would have taken in the absence of the regime as well as compellence in the sense that the presence of the regime induces actors to take steps they would otherwise have failed to take.[10] As we shall see, moreover, there are both theoretical and methodological challenges associated with efforts to demonstrate the causal connections between the operation of a regime and the behavior of affected actors. Much depends, for instance, on the extent to which actors are properly treated as unitary utility maximizers or as more complex entities that respond to a variety of nonutilitarian stimuli.[11] And regimes are almost always merely one of a number of forces that operate—simultaneously or sequentially—to shape the behavior of relevant actors, a fact that makes it necessary to devise ways to sort out the relative impact of regimes from the impacts of other sources of behavior. Nonetheless, the focus on behavior lends empirical content to the study of regime effectiveness, and it has the added virtue of preserving a clear link to the underlying concern for problem solving.

In considerable measure, these approaches to effectiveness map onto the distinctions students of public policy commonly draw among outputs, outcomes, and impacts.[12] Outputs are regulations, programs, and organizational arrangements that actors establish to operationalize the provisions of regimes or, in other words, to move them from paper to practice.[13] Outcomes encompass changes in the behavior of those subject to the provisions of regimes, whether these changes involve bringing actions into conformance with the requirements of regimes or making other adjustments that become attractive as a result of the establishment of regimes. For their part, impacts have to do with problem solving in that they involve effects measured in terms of the concerns that lead actors to create regimes in the first place. Impacts may range from marginal to decisive; there is no need to think of them in all-or-nothing terms. In some cases, moreover, regimes give rise to new problems, whatever their impacts in terms of the problems leading to their creation.

Clearly, there are good reasons to take a lively interest in all three of these types of consequences in efforts to assess the success of individual regimes. Outputs have the virtue of being relatively easy to track. There is no doubt about the existence of a causal connection between international agreements and the implementing legislation and more detailed regulations promulgated to give these agreements traction within individual member countries. Yet outputs are the least consequential of the three types of consequences when it comes to problem solving. Focusing on impacts, by contrast, presents the opposite picture with regard to strengths and weaknesses. Impacts are what we really care about; they are what matter when it comes to problem solving. But the causal links between the operations of a regime and its impacts on the relevant problem are notoriously difficult to pin down convincingly. The danger of ending with spurious relationships is always present in this connection. A focus on outcomes represents a middle ground in both respects (Young 1999b). Behavioral changes lie somewhere between outputs and impacts in terms of their implications for problem solving; they also offer a middle ground with regard to demonstrating causal connections. As is the case in all studies of effectiveness, there is no prospect of coming up with a silver bullet in this field of study. There is much to be said, under the circumstances, for a strategy that encourages analysts to consider all three types of regime consequences in efforts to strengthen our grasp of the roles that regimes play in determining collective outcomes in international society.[14]

Two additional issues merit attention in this conceptual discussion. There is a critical difference in the goals of what we may call the pure theory of regimes and the contextualized theory of regimes or, for that matter, social institutions in general. Pure theory seeks to illuminate the logic of regimes on the assumptions that specific institutional arrangements are fully operational, accepted by all relevant subjects as facts of life to be complied with as a matter of course, and not subject to distortion resulting from the impact of outside forces. Analysis then focuses on the outcomes that can be expected to flow from the operation of these arrangements over time.[15] To take some concrete examples, this leads to assessments of the probable outcomes resulting from the operation of different electoral systems (e.g., proportional representation vs. single-member districts), different decision rules in legislative settings or committees, and different structures of property rights (see Buchanan and Tullock 1962; Duverger 1954).

Contextualized theory, by contrast, focuses on issues involving the extent to which regimes actually affect the behavior of those subject to their provisions and the relationship between the character of regimes as they are intended to operate in principle and the character of institutional arrangements as implemented or, in other words, as they operate in practice. The central concern here is to probe whether and to what extent regimes actually do determine the flow of collective outcomes in various social settings. Pure theory is largely an analytic exercise employing deductive reasoning and, in some cases, simulations to explore the dynamics of institutions as such; the results tend to be normative rather than descriptive. Contextualized theory is mainly an empirical exercise involving the use of a battery of techniques designed to determine the proportion of the variance in the outcomes flowing from social interactions that can be explained in terms of the operation of regimes (Underdal and Young 2004).

Both types of analysis are worthwhile. Many game-theoretic analyses as well as efforts to apply economic models to the analysis of regimes show the value of pure theory in this realm.[16] Barrett's discussion of the trade-offs between compliance and participation offers a concrete example (Barrett 2003). On the other hand, it is fair to say that the largest stream of research focusing on the effectiveness of international regimes takes the form of contextualized theory.[17] The central questions here are: do regimes matter and what proportion of the variance in world affairs is attributable to the operation of these institutional arrangements? The discussion in the remainder of this chapter directs attention for the most part to the contributions of contextualized theory.

In asking whether regimes matter, it is important to note as well that these arrangements—both singly and in combination—can generate broader consequences by altering the knowledge base available to actors in international society, the relative status of international actors, or even the constitutive features of international society as a whole, quite apart from their success in solving specific problems (see Levy, Young, and Zürn 1995, 308–312). Taken together, for example, the rise of international environmental regimes over the last several decades has surely played a part in enhancing the role of nongovernmental organizations in world affairs and in sensitizing us to the significance of global civil society as a factor in environmental problem solving.[18] The study of these broader consequences is obviously important. In the long run, their impact may even overshadow the effects of regimes in solving or alleviating any number of specific environmental problems arising at the international level (Underdal and Young 2004). But the study of broader consequences is an endeavor that is separate from the analysis of regime effectiveness as such. There is much to be gained from such a study (see Oberthür and Gehring 2006). But conflating the analysis of regime effectiveness and the study of broader consequences is a recipe for confusion. This chapter focuses explicitly on the issue of effectiveness, leaving the question of broader consequences to another occasion.

How Much Do Regimes Vary in Terms of Effectiveness?

Regimes clearly vary in terms of effectiveness. But how can we identify and measure this variance under real-world conditions? Given the preceding account of the conceptual difficulties associated with the idea of effectiveness, it will come as no surprise that we have yet to devise a straightforward way to operationalize the concept, much less to construct an index that will allow us to chart shifts in the effectiveness of individual regimes over time or to compare and contrast different regimes with respect to levels of effectiveness. This is a serious problem; it limits our ability to treat effectiveness as a dependent variable whose behavior can be followed in an unambiguous and uncontroversial manner. Ideally, it would be desirable to devise a method for developing an interval scale making it possible to track effectiveness in much the same way that we use gross national product (GNP) as a measure of the performance of economic systems or temperature as a measure of the behavior of weather systems. A group of analysts led by Detlef Sprinz has proposed and refined a procedure that would produce an index based on the proportion of the distance between the outcome that would have occurred in the absence of the regime and some measure of the social optimum that the operation of the regime has moved a system.[19] This index has some desirable analytic properties (e.g., it produces an effectiveness score ranging from 0 to 1 that can be compared across any number of cases). Nonetheless, any serious effort to make use of this index to measure the effectiveness of actual regimes faces hurdles that are virtually insurmountable, at least during the foreseeable future,[20] during which there is no prospect of turning this analytic construct into an empirically usable measure of effectiveness.

A more realistic goal over the short run is the development of an ordinal scale that would make it possible to rank regimes from high to low in terms of effectiveness and to monitor the performance of individual regimes over time in these terms.[21] Given the conceptual problems described in the preceding section, even the development of an ordinal scale allowing us to evaluate regime effectiveness with confidence is a tall order. Yet some such procedure is essential for those interested not only in measuring effectiveness but also in framing and testing hypotheses that can help to explain or predict variations in levels of effectiveness over time and across regimes.[22] Realistically, we should be aiming at this stage to devise a relatively simple ordinal scale that differentiates among four or five levels of effectiveness and that is usable by well-informed analysts to code the effectiveness of regimes with reasonable confidence. This is the approach underlying the development of the International Regimes Database (IRD), a large-scale relational database that relies on expert coders to provide judgments both about problem solving and about the roles that regimes play as forces contributing to problem solving (Breitmeier, Young, and Zürn 2006).[23]

Notwithstanding these problems of measurement, there is considerable agreement among students of international regimes, at least in general terms, regarding the effectiveness of specific arrangements.[24] No one is under any illusion that all—or even most—international environmental regimes are highly effective. Yet the evidence does not support sweeping judgments to the effect that "efforts to protect the global environment have largely failed in the sense that the trends in environmental deterioration have not improved and that more of the same will not get us where we want to be in time to head off an era of unprecedented environmental decline" (Speth 2004, xi). As is the case with similar analyses at the domestic level, both successes and failures are relatively common.

Among those regimes that are widely viewed as ranging from somewhat effective to highly effective are the Antarctic Treaty System, the Great Lakes Water Quality regime, the arrangement covering the dumping or incineration of wastes in the North Sea, and the regime for the protection of the stratospheric ozone layer (see Stokke and Vidas 1996; Botts and Muldoon 1996; Skjaerseth 2002; Parson and Greene 1995). Conversely, the list of regimes that most analysts would rank as ineffective or very ineffective includes the agreement on the conservation of migratory species of wild animals, the international tropical timber regime, many of the Regional Seas arrangements operating under the auspices of the United Nations Environment Programme (UNEP), and most species-specific and area-specific arrangements dealing with marine fisheries (see Lyster 1985; Weiss and Jacobson 1998; Miles et al. 2002; Peterson 1993). Most would concur as well in reaching mixed conclusions regarding the effectiveness of a number of other regimes, such as arrangements dealing with long-range transboundary air pollution in Europe, international trade in endangered species of wild fauna and flora, pollutants discharged into the Rhine River, and transboundary shipments of hazardous wastes. Imprecise as they are, these widely shared rankings offer some grounds for optimism regarding efforts to assess the effectiveness of international regimes.

Most observers would agree also that there are circumstances in which it is difficult to arrive at straightforward rankings regarding the effectiveness of regimes. It is common for specific arrangements to evolve over time, typically becoming increasingly effective with the passage of time and, in some cases, outliving their usefulness either because the problem is solved or because the character of the problem changes in some fundamental way. The regime dealing with intentional oil pollution at sea, for example, clearly became more effective following a shift from discharge standards to equipment standards (Mitchell 1994). Many traditional conservation regimes, which focus on efforts to regulate consumptive uses of living resources, have lost effectiveness with the rise of concerns for habitat protection and ecosystem-based management (EBM; for examples, see Lyster 1985). Beyond this, there are cases in which serious ambiguities impede efforts to arrive at judgments about regime effectiveness. Most observers agree that the regime for whales and whaling was ineffective during its early years but became more effective during the 1970s. But there are sharp differences of opinion about the effectiveness of this regime in more recent years attributable not to disagreements about the elements of the regime but rather to conflicting views regarding its basic purpose (see Andresen 2002). Of course, there are also cases in which judgments about the effectiveness of regimes must remain tentative until these arrangements have been in place long enough to compile a track record sufficient to provide a basis for assessment. Obvious examples include the arrangements established during the 1990s to deal with problems like climate change, the loss of biological diversity, and desertification. More generally, it is difficult to make early assessments about the effectiveness of regimes based on framework conventions that are intended to initiate a continuing process of regime formation.[25] All these issues complicate efforts to rate specific regimes in terms of effectiveness; they give rise to substantial differences of opinion in some cases. Unlike the conceptual difficulties discussed in the preceding section, however, these matters are largely empirical problems to be solved pragmatically rather than problems that point to disagreements about what we mean in speaking of the effectiveness of regimes.

There is a long way to go in the effort to construct an index of effectiveness that will allow us to explore success systematically as a key variable in regime analysis. But even at this stage, we know enough to lay to rest the sterile debate about whether international regimes matter at all or are properly understood either as epiphenomena that reflect deeper driving forces in international society or as arrangements that individual actors participate in only under duress.[26] The essential point to notice is that there is substantial variance in effectiveness both among individual regimes and within regimes over time. This is not to say that there is consensus among observers about the ranking of particular regimes even on a relatively crude ordinal scale of effectiveness. Still, virtually everyone agrees that some international environmental regimes have been highly successful, while others have turned out to be dismal failures. Even more common are cases in which levels of effectiveness lie somewhere between these extremes. This suggests that the appropriate course at this stage is to turn our attention to an examination of the sources or roots of institutional effectiveness. This exercise promises to be far more productive and illuminating than a continuation of sectarian battles over whether regimes matter at all.

What Do We Know about the Sources of Effectiveness?

Research on the effectiveness of international environmental regimes is still at an early stage. As the preceding discussion makes clear, moreover, serious methodological problems stand in the way of progress in this area. Even so, we already know a number of things about the determinants of institutional effectiveness in this domain, and we have some good leads concerning where to direct our attention in analyses of effectiveness during the next phase of research on environmental regimes. This section provides an overview of what we know already about factors governing the success of international environmental regimes under five headings: (1) problem structure, (2) regime attributes, (3) social practices, (4) institutional interplay, and (5) broader setting. In the process, it identifies major gaps in knowledge and paves the way for the next section's discussion of research strategies for broadening and deepening our current understanding of these matters.

Problem Structure   There is widespread agreement that some international problems are more difficult to solve than others. Coordination problems are easier to solve than collaboration problems, largely because participants have no incentive to violate the rules developed to solve coordination problems (Stein 1983). Thus, devising a successful governance system for air transport is less challenging than devising an effective regime to regulate transboundary air pollution. Situations featuring high levels of transparency in the sense that it is easy to tell whether those subject to regulatory rules are complying with their requirements are easier to deal with than situations in which subjects—including private actors as well as public agencies—can violate the rules clandestinely.[27] Consider the difference between equipment standards and discharge standards with regard to intentional oil pollution at sea as a case in point. Other things being equal, problems involving large numbers of actors, either as parties to the agreements themselves or as subjects of the regulatory arrangements devised, are harder to deal with than small-number situations (Oye 1986). Think of the differences between the protection of the stratospheric ozone layer and the earth's climate system in these terms. Similar remarks are in order about the length of the shadow of the future (Axelrod 1984). In cases where parties are engaged in interactions expected to last indefinitely (e.g., the governance system for Antarctica), incentives to cooperate will be stronger than in cases where the relationships are short-lived (e.g., short-term arrangements dealing with the exploitation of a finite resource).

What we lack at this stage is a comprehensive index to use in ranking and comparing problems in terms of the difficulty of solving them (Young 1999a, chapter 3). In fact, a number of analysts have made sustained efforts to develop an index of this sort. The most influential of these efforts involve the problem-structural approach of the Tübingen group, which looks at regime formation as a means of solving conflicts and rates problems in terms of what is called "regime conduciveness" (Rittberger and Zürn 1991), and the work of the Oslo group, which focuses on interests or preferences and looks to game-theoretical constructs as a way of differentiating among problems in terms of how hard it will be to solve them (Underdal 2002b). Although each of these approaches has added to our understanding of problem structure, both are fraught with analytical difficulties and problems of operationalization that limit their usefulness as procedures for rating real-world problems on a scale of hardness. The Tübingen approach, for example, overemphasizes the role of value conflicts and the pursuit of relative gains, and it pays little attention to the integrative aspects of regime formation. For its part, the Oslo approach suffers from the standard difficulties of mapping game-theoretic constructs onto real-world situations. Yet these pioneering efforts do point the way toward a more general assessment of problem structure in connection with efforts to evaluate the effectiveness of international environmental regimes.[28]

Regime Attributes   Because regimes are not actors in their own right, it is inappropriate to think of these constructs as agents that can succeed or fail in connection with assignments they receive from their creators.[29] Nevertheless, institutional arrangements do serve to channel the behavior of both their formal members and wider arrays of actors operating under the auspices of regime members. In the process, they affect the content of collective outcomes flowing from interactions among actors in international society. Here, too, we already have some knowledge of the roots of institutional effectiveness. A capacity to respond flexibly and to adapt to changing circumstances is particularly important to the success of regimes that deal with environmental issues, where our understanding of complex biophysical systems is developing rapidly, in some cases as a consequence of the operation of the regimes themselves. Well-constructed systems of implementation review (SIRs; Victor, Raustiala, and Skolnikoff 1998) appear to be important as methods of retaining the attention of policymakers and avoiding the onset of the "out of sight, out of mind" syndrome in almost every case. There is much to be said for approaching some problems of compliance with the rules and the decisions of regimes as matters of management rather than enforcement (Chayes and Chayes 1995). The extent to which regimes require secure sources of funding to prove successful depends upon the nature of the tasks they are expected to perform. Programmatic tasks like helping developing countries to avoid increases in the production and consumption of ozone-depleting substances, for instance, present greater funding requirements than procedural tasks like making annual decisions regarding allowable harvest levels for living resources.

Some recent research suggests that it is easy to overemphasize the importance of individual regime attributes, at least when treated as isolated variables in contrast to elements of interactive clusters of determinants of effectiveness. Research based on the International Regimes Database is raising important questions about specific attributes (Breitmeier, Young, and Zürn 2006). While many see the widespread use of consensus rules at the international level as a source of weakness, for example, the links between decision rules and regime effectiveness are poorly understood.[30] Similar remarks are in order regarding the role of what we now think of as noncompliance procedures (NCPs) in contrast to more formal dispute settlement procedures (DSPs), which are typically included in the constitutive provisions of international environmental regimes but which seldom loom large in the actual operations of these regimes (Werksman 1996). More generally, we need to improve our understanding of the relationships between regime attributes, on the one hand, and effectiveness construed in terms of outputs, outcomes, or impacts, on the other. Regimes that look impressive at the level of outputs are not necessarily successful when it comes to solving the problems that led to their creation. Regimes that produce striking results at the level of outcomes can generate unintended side effects that offset or even nullify the progress they bring about in terms of curbing or redirecting the behavior giving rise to the problem to be solved. Thus, it is difficult to provide a clear assessment of the effectiveness of a regime for the management of fish or marine mammals that succeeds only by shifting the attention of harvesters from one area or one species to another.[31] Overall, it seems clear that we need to reexamine our first-order assumptions about the role of regime attributes. Individual attributes seem likely to make a difference more as elements in causal clusters than as stand-alone determinants of effectiveness.

Social Practices   An important finding that follows from the discussion of attributes concerns the relationship between institutional arrangements in the narrow sense and the social practices that grow up around them. Regimes as such are sets of rules, decision-making procedures, and programs. But every successful regime gives rise to an encompassing social practice in which the members themselves become enmeshed in an increasingly complex web of interactive relationships, and in which a variety of actors with no formal roles in the regime emerge as players. It is the growth of a vibrant social practice that typically serves to legitimize a regime in the thought processes of various actors, to flesh out the constitutive provisions of a regime with a range of important informal understandings, to transform the rules of a regime into standard operating procedures, and to give rise to an informal but attentive community of actors interested in the success of the regime and prepared to function as watchdogs keeping track of its performance.[32] At this stage, our understanding of the connections between regimes in the narrow sense and social practices is limited. But it is already clear that the way forward will involve a sustained effort to integrate insights drawn from the new institutionalism of economics and public choice, which tends to focus on regimes in the narrow sense, and the new institutionalism of sociology, which directs attention to the character of social practices.[33]

Recently, we have become aware that civil society exists at the international level just as it does at the domestic level (Wapner 1997; Lipschutz 1996; Keane 2003; Kaldor 2003). Construed as a network of social connections that exists above the level of the individual (or the individual state in international society) and below the level of the state (or various governance systems in international society), civil society provides much of the social glue that holds governance systems together and allows them to operate effectively in a wide range of social settings.[34] There are large challenges facing those who take on the task of understanding the role of civil society as a backdrop for the functioning of specific governance systems. It is difficult to find ways to pin this concept down for purposes of empirical analysis in any setting, much less to develop well-formulated propositions about the role of civil society. Without doubt, these analytic challenges are even greater at the international or global level than they are at the domestic level. Yet it seems increasingly clear that the cost of ignoring the role of civil society as a determinant of the effectiveness of environmental regimes will be great.

Institutional Interplay   Until recently, students of international regimes exhibited a marked tendency to treat these entities as stand-alone arrangements and to conduct detailed case studies focused on individual regimes. Given the relative difficulty in grasping the concept of regimes and the complexity of specific arrangements, this practice is understandable. But with the growth in the population of regimes in international society, this procedure is no longer tenable; institutional interactions are widespread, and they clearly make a difference in terms of the effectiveness of individual regimes (Young 2002b, chapters 4 and 5; Oberthür and

Gehring 2006). It is helpful, in coming to terms with this phenomenon, to begin by drawing a distinction between horizontal linkages and vertical linkages (Young 2002b). Horizontal interactions involve connections between individual regimes and other institutional arrangements operating at the level of international society. Some observers have been struck by the dangers of individual regimes interfering with one another's operations in ways that reduce effectiveness; they have begun to speak of institutional congestion as a label for this phenomenon (Herr and Chia 1995; Weiss 1993). But the prospect of mutual reinforcement or synergy and other more positive connections seems equally important (Oberthür and Gehring 2006). This has given rise to an examination of nested regimes, as in the case of links between regional seas arrangements and the overarching law of the sea, clustered regimes, as in the case of the linked but differentiable components of the Antarctic Treaty System, and embedded regimes, as in the case of free-trade arrangements embodying larger principles of the neoliberal economic order.[35] It has also led to a consideration of structures of institutional arrangements and an examination of similarities and differences in structures of environmental institutions in contrast to economic institutions (von Moltke 1997; Raustiala and Victor 2004).

For their part, vertical linkages refer to connections between international regimes and institutional arrangements operating at lower levels of social organization. Many students of domestic institutions have observed that arrangements devised at the national level produce better results when they are compatible with regional or local practices than when they work at cross purposes with these practices. Studies of local arrangements centered on the use of common pool resources, for example, are replete with accounts of the disruptive consequences of national arrangements devised in ignorance of longstanding local procedures for "governing the commons" (Ostrom 1990; Ostrom et al. 2002).[36] The importance of these linkages is all the more important at the international level, where compatibility across several levels of social organization becomes an issue. Much of the criticism that has been leveled at the international regime for trade, currently embodied in the World Trade Organization, for instance, centers on claims pertaining to the destructive or exploitative impacts these global arrangements are alleged to have on the viability of longstanding resource regimes operating at regional and even local levels (Ross and Usher 1986; Young et al. 2008). Our knowledge of such matters remains relatively superficial at this stage. But we already know enough to say that there is a need to devote much more attention to institutional interplay in future efforts to understand the sources of regime effectiveness.

Broader Setting

International environmental regimes do not operate in a socioeconomic or biophysical vacuum. Rather, they arise and operate in broader settings that have obvious implications for their capacity to succeed in solving specific problems. Periods marked by economic recessions or depressions, for example, are likely to pose severe problems for efforts to solve environmental problems. The existence of political tensions or the occurrence of armed conflict exogenous to the environmental problems at hand among key players is apt to overshadow efforts to solve environmental problems. Consider, for example, the extent to which broader political problems impede efforts to devise effective regimes for international rivers in areas like the Middle East or the Indian subcontinent (Gleick 1993; Lowi 1995). At the same time, there is much that we do not understand well in this area. Is regime effectiveness a function of the extent to which members have similar or homogeneous domestic political systems, and does it matter whether these systems are democratic in some meaningful sense of that term? Do regimes work better when their members have what are known as "strong" states in terms of state-society relations?[37] Can effective environmental regimes arise in situations in which their creators are motivated more by political concerns than by a desire to solve environmental problems as such? Are there ways to immunize regimes dealing with specific problems from fluctuations in broader political and economic relations among their members?

With regard to environmental regimes more specifically, it is critical to consider the relationships between the institutional arrangements themselves and the character of the ecosystems to which they relate (Young 2002b, chapter 3). It is easy to speak, in general terms, about the need for congruence between regime attributes and ecosystem properties. But what does this mean in practice? Some answers to this question are beginning to emerge (Hanna, Folke, and Mäler 1996, part I; Young 2002c). The more resilient an ecosystem is, for instance, the less important it is to create monitoring mechanisms that can track changes in the system quickly and sensitively. The greater the homogeneity of the ecosystem, the less need there is for tailoring the components of a regime to the specific characteristics of the various subsystems that make up the overarching biophysical system. At the same time, it is clear that improving our understanding of the fit between ecosystems and institutional arrangements is a growth area in which the case is strong for investing resources intended to upgrade our ability to explain and predict the effectiveness of international environmental regimes.

In closing this section, let me step back and endeavor to put these comments about the various sources of regime effectiveness into perspective. There is little doubt, at this juncture, that regimes matter in the sense that they play a role in determining the content of collective outcomes at the international level (Barrett 2003; Breitmeier, Young, and Zürn 2006). As is the case with governance systems at all levels of social organization, the effectiveness of international regimes varies from striking success to outright failure. But the evidence drawn from the IRD as well as more conventional case studies makes it clear that the absence of a world government is not an insurmountable barrier in coming to grips with international environmental problems.

By itself, however, this observation is of limited interest. What makes the study of regime effectiveness both complex and intriguing is the fact that institutions constitute only one of a set of social drivers that typically interact with one another as determinants of collective outcomes at the international level and that assume different values in individual cases (Young 2002a). This makes it difficult to separate out the role of various categories of social drivers and to assess just what proportion of the variance in collective outcomes is attributable to institutional arrangements in contrast to other factors like material conditions and ideas (Young 1999b, chapters 1 and 5). It greatly reduces the prospects for constructing simple generalizations about the role of institutions couched in the form of statements specifying necessary or sufficient conditions for success in problem solving. And it raises questions about the extent to which it is helpful to treat some social drivers as underlying forces and others as intervening variables (e.g., Krasner 1983). None of this means that international regimes are of only marginal significance when it comes to solving environmental problems at the international level. But it does mean that future efforts to gain ground in understanding the effectiveness of international regimes must tackle multivariate relationships head on and anticipate the prospect that the same factors, like problem structure or regime attributes, that loom large under some conditions will produce no more than marginal effects under other conditions.

How Can We Improve Our Understanding of Effectiveness?

What more do we need to know about the effectiveness of international environmental regimes, and how can we go about obtaining that knowledge? The answer to the first part of this question depends on the objectives we are seeking to achieve. Our current understanding of effectiveness constitutes a good beginning toward illuminating this complex phenomenon. What is more, studies that pertain in one way or another to this subject currently constitute a growth industry among those interested both in international institutions and in environmental governance (Weiss and Jacobson 1998; Victor, Raustiala, and Skolnikoff 1998; Young 1999b; Social Learning Group 2001; Miles et al. 2002; Breitmeier, Young, and Zürn 2006; Biermann 2007; Young, King, and Schroeder 2008). From the point of view of learning how to design environmental regimes that have a reasonable prospect of solving the problems that motivate their creation, however, we have a long way to go. We know enough already not to overlook matters of compliance in efforts to solve collaboration problems or to ignore problems of flexibility and learning in dealing with biophysical systems whose dynamics are poorly understood. But this is hardly sufficient to support a robust and reasonably successful effort to engage in institutional design in the realm of environmental governance.[38] Assuming that this line of enquiry is concerned not only with understanding environmental problems as an end in itself but also with solving them, how should we proceed?

We need to acknowledge, at the outset, several analytical and methodological problems that amount to facts of life for those seeking to pinpoint the sources of regime effectiveness. Gauging or measuring effectiveness, treated as the dependent variable in this context, poses a real challenge due to the fact that judgments about causality are built into assessments of the success of regimes as problem-solving mechanisms (Levy, Young, and Zürn 1995, 290–308). Thus, to say that a regime has proven successful is to assert that a significant proportion of the variance in collective outcomes is attributable to its operation. It is not enough simply to observe a correlation between the creation of a regime and the disappearance or amelioration of the problem; the danger of spurious correlation is too great for that.[39] There is little prospect of conducting controlled experiments that are relevant to understanding international environmental regimes, though it is worth noting that natural experiments are feasible in some cases and that simulation exercises can play a useful role in illuminating issues that deserve more sustained attention in this field of study.[40] What is more, the universe of cases we have to work with is not large enough to allow for systematic applications of many familiar procedures involving statistical inference. It would be wrong to suppose that these problems are unique to the study of international regimes or to conclude that they pose insuperable barriers to the production of knowledge (King, Keohane, and Verba 1994). Students of the earth's climate system seeking to understand global warming face many of the same difficulties.[41] Nonetheless, we need to bear these constraints in mind in devising research strategies for the next phase of research dealing with the effectiveness of international environmental regimes.

That said, it is helpful to differentiate two streams of analysis that merit sustained attention during this next phase. One stream features an effort to consolidate, refine, and extend the current body of ideas about effectiveness. It features a commitment to using existing analytic frameworks and methods in the interests of generating cumulative knowledge. The other stream calls for an effort to break new ground and, in so doing, to shift this field of study onto a higher level of understanding.[42] Although the two approaches are quite distinct in terms of their research priorities, there is much to be said for an overarching research strategy that encourages both streams of analysis.[43]

Much of what we have learned so far about effectiveness is tentative or soft in nature. Partly, this is attributable to the fact that many of the relationships in question have not been formulated with sufficient precision to allow for rigorous testing. We know that certain simple propositions about effectiveness, like the notion that the existence of a dominant actor or a hegemon is necessary for regimes to prove successful, are not valid (Snidal 1985). But this hardly licenses the conclusion that power in the structural or material sense is unimportant in accounting for the effectiveness of specific regimes (Underdal 2002a). What we need in this connection is a definition of power that is easy to operationalize, avoids the pitfalls of circular reasoning, and is usable in efforts to test a battery of specific hypotheses about the links between power and effectiveness.[44] Similar comments are in order about the role of epistemic communities in the operation of environmental regimes (P. Haas 1989; E. Haas 1990). The idea of epistemic communities has struck a responsive chord in the thinking of many observers of environmental regimes, and it is relatively easy to point to specific cases in which groups exhibiting some of the characteristics of epistemic communities appear to have made a difference (Haas 1992). Yet the concept of an epistemic community has proven to be illusive when it comes to systematic empirical assessments. Observers frequently find themselves disagreeing not so much about the roles that epistemic communities play in actual cases as about whether or not we can say with confidence that an epistemic community is present. And these are not isolated examples. On the contrary, they exemplify a common problem plaguing efforts to turn interesting insights into a core of established propositions about the factors that determine the effectiveness of environmental regimes.

Where propositions have been spelled out with sufficient precision to allow for testing, moreover, we commonly discover that we are dealing with contingent relationships. It is relatively easy to disprove many—perhaps most—propositions about effectiveness that are stated as invariant relationships (e.g., statements purporting to identify necessary or sufficient conditions for the achievement of effectiveness; Young 1999b, chapter 5). The presence of a hegemon is not always critical to such achievement. The use of decision rules that call for consensus or even unanimity does not necessarily pose a problem for effectiveness. Uncertainty is not invariably a pitfall that needs to be mitigated or even eliminated altogether in the interests of achieving effectiveness. Yet none of this means that we can dismiss factors like the distribution of power among regime members, the nature of decision rules, and the state of knowledge about the problem at stake in our efforts to understand the determinants of effectiveness. What is needed, in this connection, is an effort to formulate a body of contingent propositions about such matters or, in other words, statements that both specify links and spell out as explicitly as possible the conditions or combinations of conditions under which these propositions can be expected to hold. Only in this way can we turn interesting speculation into usable knowledge about effectiveness.

These tasks of consolidation and refinement constitute a large and challenging research agenda for those interested in the effectiveness of international environmental regimes. We have made significant progress toward defining what is meant by effectiveness and taken some initial steps toward understanding its sources. With sufficient effort, this line of reasoning can yield a core of firmly established propositions that are useful to those responsible for designing or operating regimes. Impressive as it would be, however, this accomplishment would provide us with only a limited ability to make constructive contributions to the design and operation of effective environmental regimes. What is needed at this juncture are efforts to extend and even redirect the study of effectiveness in a manner that allows us to build on our initial accomplishments in order to move to a higher level of understanding of the sources of effectiveness.

Most students of effectiveness focus on states as the formal members of regimes and proceed to construct models in which these actors are treated as unitary and self-interested utility maximizers (e.g., Miles et al. 2002). There is much to be said for this procedure as a point of departure; additional insights may well flow from further work with such models. But to move forward in this field, we need to relax these behavioral assumptions in a controlled manner and to compare and contrast the insights that flow from a suite of differentiable models in contrast to a single stylized model. Three distinct steps in this realm seem particularly important to understanding the effectiveness of international environmental regimes.

There is, to begin with, a need to explore alternatives to conventional utility maximization as sources of the behavior of regime members. This involves opening up this research program to what sociologists call the normative and cognitive pillars of social institutions or to what others have labeled the logic of appropriateness and supplementing the logical rigor of economic models with the empirical insights of sociological analyses of institutions (Scott 1995; March and Olsen 1998).[45] An encouraging sign in this connection is the rise of what has become known as behavioral economics (Kahneman and Tversky 2000; Kahneman 2003). Although the new perspectives on behavior arising from this work are harder to model in a tractable manner, they do offer the prospect not only of improving empirical relevance but also of forging stronger links among the various groups of researchers interested in the significance of international institutions.

A second step turns on relaxing the unitary actor assumption embedded in many behavioral models in this field of study. This leads to a consideration of what Robert Putnam and others have characterized as the logic of two-level games, a perspective that highlights bargaining among different factions at the domestic level over the terms of positions to espouse at the international level (Putnam 1988; Evans, Jacobson, and Putnam 1993). Two-level games are not only hard to model; they also require the development of an analytic framework that sets the study of international institutions apart from mainstream concerns in game-theoretic and microeconomic models of bargaining.[46] This is not a trivial concern. Yet it does open up a wide range of important questions (e.g., issues relating to the implementation of international commitments in domestic legal and political systems) that are essential in any comprehensive effort to understand the significance of international environmental regimes (Victor, Raustiala, and Skolnikoff 1998).

The third step then features a move to extend the analysis to include roles that various nonstate actors play in determining the effectiveness of environmental regimes (Princen and Finger 1994; Charnovitz 1997; Mathews 1997).[47] Because most environmental regimes involve a two-step process in which states are the formal members but it is the behavior of a variety of other actors (e.g., corporations or even individual consumers) that actually causes the problems under consideration, those interested in international environmental regimes have recently directed attention to the efforts of states to implement commitments made at the international level as they apply to the behavior of private or semiprivate actors operating under their jurisdiction (Weiss and Jacobson 1998; Skjaerseth 2000). But it is increasingly clear that nonstate actors, such as the DeBeers Corporation in the case of diamonds or the Chicago Board of Trade in the case of commodities, can become major players in international environmental regimes; there are even regimes of some significance in which states are not among the major players.[48] Needless to say, relaxing all these assumptions at once is a recipe for theoretical confusion. Yet we cannot hope to make a successful transition to the next level of understanding regarding the sources of regime effectiveness so long as we remain unwilling to modify conventional models that assume all the important actors are states that can be treated as unitary and rational utility maximizers.

Quite apart from these underlying theoretical concerns regarding the actors and the sources of their behavior, there are some analytic issues that require attention in the next wave of studies of regime effectiveness. The preceding discussion made it clear that advancing our understanding of the effectiveness of regimes will require an analysis of multivariate relationships. In itself, this conclusion is unremarkable; similar observations are in order regarding many social phenomena. In the case at hand, however, the fact that there are severe limits on the use of most forms of statistical inference poses a major challenge. This is not to say that there is no place for inductive reasoning in the next phase of research on effectiveness. Several recent projects have used such reasoning to good effect (see especially Weiss and Jacobson 1998; Victor, Raustiala, and

Skolnikoff 1998; Social Learning Group 2001; Breitmeier, Young, and Zürn 2006). But this situation does lead to the conclusion that we need to engage in a sustained effort to understand the causal mechanisms or behavioral pathways through which regimes affect the behavior of various actors and, in the process, shape the content of collective outcomes in international society (Young 1999b). Like other social institutions, regimes are not actors in their own right. Accordingly, they can affect the content of collective outcomes only by influencing the behavior of regime members or other relevant actors.

How do they do this? One attempt to answer this question focuses on what have become known as the three "Cs"; regimes can increase the concern of relevant actors about the issues at stake, improve the contractual environment in the issue area, and enhance the capacity of key actors to carry out the terms of a constitutional contract.[49] Another study looks at regimes as (1) utility modifiers, (2) enhancers of cooperation, (3) bestowers of authority, (4) learning facilitators, (5) role definers, and (6) agents of internal realignment (Young 1999b). Clearly, these studies amount to nothing more than preliminary forays into a complex subject. But they do point the way toward an important line of enquiry for students of regime effectiveness. Given the constraints on the use of inductive procedures, one way to proceed is to focus more attention on tracing the causal chains through which institutional arrangements impact the behavior of various actors and through such impacts affect the content of collective outcomes in international society. Among other things, this line of thinking is likely to prove particularly helpful to those concerned with practical matters of institutional design.

Whether the focus is on consolidation and refinement or on extension and redirection, those seeking to improve our understanding of the effectiveness of environmental regimes must come to grips with some important methodological problems. The most critical of these is undoubtedly the need to develop reliable and harmonized data sets that are easily accessible to those desiring to explore a variety of hypotheses dealing with the sources of institutional effectiveness. The common practice of relying on stand-alone case studies in which the individual regime is the unit of analysis has served us well; there is certainly room for more work of this kind in the pursuit of knowledge about effectiveness. Yet a critical need during the next phase will be a capacity to subject both specific hypotheses about determinants of effectiveness and alternative models of the role of regimes to systematic empirical examination based on evidence drawn from relatively large numbers of cases.[50] Does the nature of the decision rules employed by environmental regimes, for instance, make a difference in terms of effectiveness? What is the connection between the establishment of noncompliance procedures and effectiveness? Is the presence of nonstate actors among a regime's members significant when it comes to the achievement of effectiveness?

Answering questions of this type calls for the development of a database containing comparable information on as large a number of individual regimes as possible. The construction of such a database is an expensive proposition that is difficult to justify to funding agencies as an end in itself. Once in place, however, a tool of this sort can become a public good available to all members of the relevant research community on convenient terms. Starting in 1993, the International Institute for Applied Systems Analysis (IIASA) supported an effort to develop an International Regimes Database (IRD) as part of its project on the Implementation and Effectiveness of International Environmental Commitments.[51] Although it has been time consuming and labor intensive to create, the IRD is now operational and available for use on the part of interested researchers. A first set of empirical findings based on data included in the IRD appeared in 2006 (Breitmeier, Young, and Zürn 2006). Although this work barely scratches the surface of the types of analysis made possible as a result of the creation of this database, the findings offer striking results regarding both the outcomes and impacts of the operation of a sizable collection of environmental regimes. The database opens up a wide array of opportunities to address other interesting issues.

The research strategies outlined in the preceding paragraphs offer no guarantee that we will succeed in developing a substantial collection of established propositions about the determinants of regime effectiveness. Much like the study of the earth's climate system, the theoretical, analytic, and methodological challenges facing students of effectiveness are great. But research in this field also resembles the study of global warming in the sense that the need for improved understanding is compelling and that the problems of formulating useful answers are worthy of the attention of the best and brightest analysts interested in international environmental issues. We have already made real progress in this field. But much remains to be done in order to arrive at results that will prove helpful to policymakers in a general way, much less serve as a useful guide for focused efforts in the realm of institutional design. Here, as elsewhere, the prizes will go to those who succeed in finding ways to overcome barriers pertaining to causal inferences and to relax problematic assumptions embedded in current models without incurring undue losses of analytical rigor.

Concluding Remarks

Since this chapter is itself a survey of ongoing discussions among research-ers working on regime effectiveness, there is no need to summarize the contents of the preceding sections, except to reemphasize that we are in need of well-crafted research strategies directed both toward consolidat-ing and refining existing knowledge and extending and redirecting our search for new insights about the determinants of effectiveness. Yet there is one point that deserves special attention in these concluding remarks. What we can realistically hope for in this realm is an ability to act like physicians who develop superb diagnostic skills rather than like chefs who are very good at following recipes (Young 2002b). Although varia-tions are certainly possible, recipes are expected to produce satisfactory results with a high degree of predictability and under a wide range of specific circumstances. In effect, they rest on a collection of statements spelling out sufficient conditions to transform collections of ingredients into finished products. The diagnostician, on the other hand, knows that there is a long list of factors that may play a role in explaining the con-dition of individual patients and that diagnoses based on necessary or sufficient conditions are few and far between. It is frequently possible to frame contingent or ceteris paribus propositions regarding the impacts of various factors and to observe complex interactions among a number of factors that are in play with regard to specific cases. But the role of the diagnostician is not to follow simple recipes that will ensure the health of individual patients. Rather, he or she must build up a convinc-ing interpretive account of each individual case based on a consideration of a variety of factors that taken together can account for the condition at hand. The prescription then follows from this interpretive account.

Applied to international environmental regimes, these comments suggest that we should never expect to be able to solve complex prob-lems through applications of simple recipes. What works in dealing with marine systems may not work in dealing with atmospheric or terrestrial systems. What makes sense in dealing with both ecosystems and social systems that are highly resilient may not work in dealing with systems that are vulnerable to nonlinear changes. What proves effective in cases where the behavior of the relevant systems is well understood may not work in cases where our understanding of this behavior is limited and subject to rapid change. None of this is to suggest that analyses of the sources of institutional effectiveness have nothing to contribute to the initial design or subsequent modification of international environmental regimes. But it does suggest that the most useful contributions of regime analysis to solving large-scale environmental problems will take the form of interpretive accounts based on efforts to join general knowledge with an in-depth understanding of individual cases in contrast to the application of simple recipes to complex problems of international governance.

Notes

This chapter builds on and updates an analysis presented initially in Young 1999b, chapter 5.

1. For a discussion of definitional and conceptual issues relating to international regimes (e.g., statements purporting to identify necessary or sufficient conditions for the achievement of effectiveness), see Levy, Young, and Zürn 1995.

2. A convenient source of information on the status of many of these regimes is the *Yearbook of International Cooperation on Environment and Development*, an annual publication edited by staff of the Fridtjof Nansen Institute in Oslo and published by Earthscan Publications in London.

3. Many other regimes produce environmental impacts, though they are not environmental regimes in their own right. This is particularly true of economic regimes, including broad arrangements like the international trade and monetary regimes and more focused arrangements like the regimes for various commodities.

4. These so-called soft law arrangements are on the rise in international society. See, for example, Burhenne 1993.

5. In addition, a European Union-funded Concerted Action on the Effectiveness of International Environmental Agreements has produced a number of relevant products.

6. For an account of recent scholarship on this subject, see Young, King, and Schroeder 2008.

7. For an extended account of these definitional matters, see chapter 6 of Young 1994. This account draws distinctions among (1) effectiveness as problem solving, (2) effectiveness as goal attainment, (3) behavioral effectiveness, (4) process effectiveness, (5) constitutive effectiveness, and (6) evaluative effectiveness.

8. A simple way to understand this point is to say that organizations are actors, while institutions are the rules of the game that guide their activities. See also Breitmeier 1997 and Peterson 1997.

9. For details on this case, see Parson and Greene 1995 and, more generally, Parson 2003 and Andersen and Sarma 2002.

10. The distinction between deterrence and compellence is discussed at length by Thomas C. Schelling (1967).

11. For an account that emphasizes normative and cognitive sources of behavior, see Scott 1995.

12. These concepts were introduced by David Easton (1965).

13. On the idea of a transition from paper to practice, see Mitchell 1994.

14. For an analysis of available methodologies, see Underal and Young 2004.

15. For well-known examples pertaining to domestic systems, see Downs 1957 and Buchanan and Tullock 1962.

16. For a range of examples, consult Axelrod 1984, Sandler 2004, and Kaul et al. 2003.

17. Contrast this orientation with the new institutionalism in economics as described by Malcolm Rutherford (1994).

18. Conversely, nongovernmental organizations have played increasingly important roles in shaping the character of environmental regimes. On the idea of global civil society, see Wapner 1997, Lipschutz 1996, and Keane 2003.

19. The initial formulations of this approach to index construction can be found in Sprinz and Helm 1999 and in Helm and Sprinz 2000.

20. To follow the debate about the usefulness of this proposed index, see Young 2001b, 2003, and Hovi, Sprinz, and Underdal 2003a, 2003b.

21. For a preliminary effort to develop such a scale, see Miles et al. 2002.

22. Compare the discussion of such matters in King, Keohane, and Verba 1994.

23. The IRD distinguishes between problem solving in general and the roles that regimes play in solving problems. It uses the following five-point ordinal scale to measure causal roles of regimes: (1) little or no causal impact, (2) modest causal influence, (3) balanced causal influence, (4) significant causal influence, and (5) very strong causal influence.

24. See the rankings in Miles et al. 2002 and Breitmeier, Young, and Zürn 2006.

25. For a study of the European Long-Range Transboundary Air Pollution (LRTAP) regime, which began in 1979 with a framework convention containing little substantive content but that has evolved steadily over the years, see Levy 1983.

26. For prominent examples of the argument that international regimes are mere epiphenomena, see the works of Susan Strange (1983) and John J. Mearsheimer (1994–1995) together with the responses by Robert O. Keohane and Lisa L. Martin (1995), Charles A. Kupchan and Clifford A. Kupchan (1995), John Gerard Ruggie (1995), Alexander Wendt (1995), and the rejoinder

by Mearsheimer (1995). An interesting variation on this line of thought can be found in Gruber 2000.

27. For more general accounts of compliance at the international level, see Mitchell 1996 and Raustiala and Slaughter 2002.

28. For a discussion that encompasses other perspectives on problem structure, see Young 1999a (chapter 3).

29. For a general discussion of agency, see Miller 1993.

30. For a general account of decision rules that contrasts the transaction costs of increasing the size of the majority needed to win with the welfare losses to those in the minority arising from reductions in the number needed to win, see Buchanan and Tullock 1962.

31. For a striking case in point involving pollock in the Bering Sea, consult Dunlap 1995.

32. For a case study that explores this theme in depth, see Botts and Muldoon 1996.

33. Contrast the economic perspective set forth in Rutherford 1994 with the sociological perspectives discussed in Scott 1995. For an account that addresses this issue in terms of a distinction between collective-action models and social-practice models, see Young 2001a.

34. For a range of perspectives on civil society, see Cohen and Arato 1992. The idea of global civil society is discussed in Mathews 1997.

35. An influential account of embedded regimes is Ruggie 1983. For more on the concepts of clustered, nested, and embedded regimes, see Young 1996a.

36. For a case study highlighting the disruptive consequences in question, see Jodha 1996.

37. On the distinction between "strong" and "weak" states, see Migdal 1988.

38. For a range of approaches to institutional design, see Goodin 1996.

39. To address this problem, the IRD protocol asks coders to provide separate answers to questions about problem solving and about the causal role a regime has played in the process.

40. There is sizable literature in the field of public choice dealing with simulations of institutional arrangements. For a good illustration, see Plott and Smith 1978.

41. For an account of the findings of the Intergovernmental Panel on Climate Change (IPCC) on this topic, see Houghton et al. 2001.

42. I am indebted to Arild Underdal for calling my attention to this distinction.

43. For an extended discussion of methodologies well suited to this field of study, see Young et al. 2006.

44. For an account that emphasizes the differences between power in the structural sense and bargaining power or leverage, see Young 1994 (chapter 5).

45. Young 1999b pursues this line of thinking with particular reference to international environmental regimes.

46. For a critical assessment of game-theoretic and microeconomic models of bargaining, see Young 1975.

47. Ringius 1997 provides a case study that helps to clarify the role of nonstate actors in the operation of environmental regimes.

48. Studies of regimes in which some or all of the key players are nonstate actors include Spar 1994, Haufler 1997, and Pattberg 2007.

49. The three "Cs" were introduced by Haas, Keohane, and Levy (1993) and used again to good advantage by Keohane and Levy (1996).

50. A useful, though limited, start in this direction is made by Miles et al. 2002. For those interested in pushing this agenda forward, the IRD offers a wealth of opportunities.

51. On the architecture of the International Regimes Database, see Breitmeier et al. 1996a, 1996b.

References

Andersen, S. O., and K. M. Sarma. 2002. *Protecting the ozone layer: The United Nations history*. London: Earthscan Publications.

Andresen, S. 2002. The International Whaling Convention (IWC): More failure than success? In *Environmental regime effectiveness: Confronting theory with evidence*, ed. E. L. Miles, A. Underdal, S. Andersen, J. Wettestad, J. B. Skjaerseth, and E. M. Carlin, 379–404. Cambridge, MA: MIT Press.

Axelrod, R. 1984. *The evolution of cooperation*. New York: Basic Books.

Barrett, S. 2003. *Environment and statecraft: The strategy for environmental treaty-making*. Oxford: Oxford University Press.

Biermann, F. 2007. "Earth system governance" as a crosscutting theme of global change research. *Global Environmental Change* 17:326–337.

Botts, L., and P. Muldoon. 1996. *The Great Lakes Water Quality Agreement: Its past successes and uncertain future*. Hanover, NH: Institute on International Environmental Governance.

Breitmeier, H. 1997. International organizations and the creation of environmental regimes. In *Global governance: Drawing insights from the environmental experience*, ed. O. R. Young, 87–114. Cambridge, MA: MIT Press.

Breitmeier, H., M. A. Levy, O. R. Young, and M. Zürn. 1996a. International Regimes Database (IRD): Data protocol, International Institute for Applied Systems Analysis, WP-96-154.

Breitmeier, H., M. A. Levy, O. R. Young, and M. Zürn. 1996b. The international regimes database as a tool for the study of international cooperation, International Institute for Applied Systems Analysis, WP-96-160.

Breitmeier, H., O. R. Young, and M. Zürn. 2006. *Analyzing international environmental regimes: From case study to database.* Cambridge, MA: MIT Press.

Buchanan, J. M., and G. Tullock. 1962. *The calculus of consent.* Ann Arbor: University of Michigan Press.

Burhenne, W. E., ed. 1993. *International environmental soft law.* Dordrecht: Martinus Nijhoff Publishers.

Charnovitz, S. 1997. Two centuries of participation: NGOs and international governance. *Michigan Journal of International Law* 18:183–286.

Chayes, A., and A. H. Chayes. 1995. *The new sovereignty: Compliance with international regulatory agreements.* Cambridge, MA: Harvard University Press.

Cohen, J. L., and A. Arato. 1992. *Civil society and political theory.* Cambridge, MA: MIT Press.

Downs, A. 1957. *An economic theory of democracy.* New York: Harper and Row.

Dunlap, W. V. 1995. Bering Sea. *The International Journal of Marine and Coastal Law* 10:114–135.

Duverger, M. 1954. *Political parties: Their organization and activity in the modern state.* New York: Wiley.

Easton, D. 1965. *A systems analysis of political life.* New York: Wiley.

Evans, P. B., H. K. Jacobson, and R. Putnam, eds. 1993. *Double-edged diplomacy: International bargaining and domestic politics.* Berkeley: University of California Press.

Gleick, P. H. 1993. Water and conflict: Fresh water resources and international security. *International Security* 18:79–112.

Goodin, R. E., ed. 1996. *The theory of institutional design.* Cambridge, UK: Cambridge University Press.

Gruber, L. 2000. *Ruling the world: Power politics and the rise of supranational institutions.* Princeton, NJ: Princeton University Press.

Haas, E. B. 1990. *When knowledge is power: Three models of change in international organizations.* Berkeley: University of California Press.

Haas, P. M. 1989. Do regimes matter? Epistemic communities and Mediterranean pollution control. *International Organization* 43 (Summer):377–403.

Haas, P. M., ed. 1992. *Knowledge, power, and international policy coordination,* a special issue of *International Organization* 46 (1).

Haas, P. M., R. O. Keohane, and M. A. Levy, eds. 1993. *Institutions for the Earth: Sources of effective international environmental protection.* Cambridge, MA: MIT Press.

Haggard, S., and B. A. Simmons. 1987. Theories of international regimes. *International Organization* 41:491–517.

Hanna, S. S., C. Folke, and K.-G. Mäler, eds. 1996. *Rights to nature: Ecological, economic, cultural, and political principles of institutions for the environment.* Washington, DC: Island Press.

Hasenclever, A., P. Meyer, and V. Rittberger. 1997. *Theories of international regimes.* Cambridge, UK: Cambridge University Press.

Haufler, V. 1997. *Dangerous cartels.* Ithaca, NY: Cornell University Press.

Helm, C., and D. F. Sprinz. 2000. Measuring the effectiveness of international environmental regimes. *Journal of Conflict Resolution* 45:630–652.

Herr, R., and E. Chia. 1995. The concept of regime overlap: Identification and assessment. Unpublished work, University of Tasmania.

Houghton, J. T., Y. Ding, D. J. Griggs, M. Noguer, P. J. van der Linden, X. Dai, K. Maskell, and C. A. Johnson, eds. 2001. *Climate change 2001: The scientific basis.* Cambridge, UK: Cambridge University Press.

Hovi, J., D. F. Sprinz, and A. Underdal. 2003a. The Oslo-Potsdam solution to measuring regime effectiveness: Critique, response, and the road ahead. *Global Environmental Politics* 3:74–96.

Hovi, J., D. F. Sprinz, and A. Underdal. 2003b. Regime effectiveness and the Oslo-Potsdam solution: A rejoinder to Oran Young. *Global Environmental Politics* 3:105–107.

Jodha, N. J. 1996. Property rights and development. In *Rights to nature: Ecological, economic, cultural, and political principles of institutions for the environment,* ed. S. S. Hanna, C. Folke, and K.-G. Mäler, 205–220. Washington, DC: Island Press.

Kahneman, D. 2003. Maps of bounded rationality: Psychology and behavioral economics. *American Economic Review* 93:1449–1475.

Kahneman, D., and A. Tversky, eds. 2000. *Choices, values, and frames.* Cambridge, UK: Cambridge University Press.

Kaldor, M. 2003. The idea of global civil society. *International Affairs* 79: 583–593.

Kaul, I., P. Conceicao, K. Le Goulven, and R. U. Mendoza, eds. 2003. *Providing global public goods: Managing globalization.* New York: Oxford University Press.

Keane, J. 2003. *Global civil society.* Cambridge, UK: Cambridge University Press.

Keohane, R. O., and M. A. Levy, eds. 1996. *Institutions for environmental aid: Pitfalls and promise.* Cambridge, MA: MIT Press.

Keohane, R. O., and L. L. Martin. 1995. The promise of institutionalist theory. *International Security* 20 (1):39–51.

King, G., R. O. Keohane, and S. Verba. 1994. *Designing social inquiry: Scientific inference in qualitative research.* Princeton, NJ: Princeton University Press.

Krasner, S. D. 1983. Structural causes and regime consequences: Regimes as intervening variables. In *International regimes,* ed. S. D. Krasner, 1–21. Ithaca, NY: Cornell University Press.

Kupchan, C. A., and C. A. Kupchan. 1995. The promise of collective security. *International Security* 20 (1):52–61.

Levy, M. A. 1983. European acid rain: The power of tote-board diplomacy. In *Institutions for the Earth: Sources of effective international environmental protection*, eds. P. M. Haas, R. O. Keohane, and M. A. Levy, 75–132. Cambridge, MA: MIT Press.

Levy, M. A., O. R. Young, and M. Zürn. 1995. The study of international regimes. *European Journal of International Relations* 1:267–330.

Lipschutz, R. D. 1996. *Global civil society and global environmental governance.* Albany: SUNY Press.

Lowi, M. 1995. Rivers of conflict, rivers of peace. *Journal of International Affairs* 49:123–144.

Lyster, S. 1985. *International wildlife law.* Cambridge, UK: Grotius Publishers.

March, J. G., and J. P. Olsen. 1998. The institutional dynamics of international political orders. *International Organization* 52:943–969.

Mathews, J. T. 1997. Power shift. *Foreign Affairs* 76 (January/February):50–66.

Mearsheimer, J. J. 1994–1995. The false promise of international institutions. *International Security* 19 (3):5–49.

Mearsheimer, J. J. 1995. A realist reply. *International Security* 20 (1):82–93.

Migdal, J. 1988. *Strong societies and weak states: State-society relations and state capabilities in the Third World.* Princeton, NJ: Princeton University Press.

Miles, E. L., A. Underdal, S. Andersen, J. Wettestad, J. B. Skjaerseth, and E. M. Carlin. 2002. *Environmental regime effectiveness: Confronting theory with evidence.* Cambridge, MA: MIT Press.

Miller, G. 1993. *Managerial dilemmas.* Cambridge, UK: Cambridge University Press.

Mitchell, R. B. 1994. *Intentional oil pollution at sea: Environmental policy and treaty compliance.* Cambridge, MA: MIT Press.

Mitchell, R. B. 1996. Compliance theory: An overview. In *Improving compliance with international environmental law*, ed. J. Cameron, J. Werksman, and P. Roderick, 3–28. London: Earthscan Publications.

Oberthür, S., and T. Gehring, eds. 2006. *Institutional interaction in international and EU environmental governance.* Cambridge, MA: MIT Press.

Ostrom, E. 1990. *Governing the commons: The evolution of institutions for collective action.* Cambridge, UK: Cambridge University Press.

Ostrom, E., T. Dietz, N. Dolsak, P. C. Stern, S. Stonich, and E. U. Weber, eds. 2002. *The drama of the commons.* Washington, DC: National Academy Press.

Oye, K. A. 1986. Explaining cooperation under anarchy: Hypotheses and strategies. In *Cooperation under anarchy*, ed. K. A. Oye, 1–24. Princeton, NJ: Princeton University Press.

Parson, E. A. 2003. *Protecting the ozone layer: Science and strategy.* Oxford, UK: Oxford University Press.

Parson, E. A., and O. Greene. 1995. The complex chemistry of the International Ozone Agreements. *Environment* 37 (March):16–20, 35–43.

Pattberg, P. H. 2007. *Private institutions and global governance: The new politics of environmental sustainability.* Cheltenham, UK: Edward Elgar.

Peterson, M. J. 1993. International Fisheries Management. In *Institutions for the Earth: Sources of effective international environmental protection,* eds. P. M. Haas, R. O. Keohane, and M. A. Levy, 249–305. Cambridge, MA: MIT Press.

Peterson, M. J. 1997. International organizations and the implementation of environmental regimes. In *Global governance: Drawing insights from the environmental experience,* ed. O. R. Young, 115–151. Cambridge, MA: MIT Press.

Plott, C. R., and V. L. Smith. 1978. An experimental examination of two exchange institutions. *Review of Economic Studies* 45:133–153.

Princen, T., and M. Finger. 1994. *Environmental NGOs in World Politics: Linking the local and the global.* London: Routledge.

Putnam, R. 1988. Diplomacy and domestic politics: The logic of two-level games. *International Organization* 42:427–460.

Raustiala, K., and A.-M. Slaughter. 2002. International law, international relations and compliance. In *Handbook of international relations,* ed. W. Carlsnaes, T. Risse, and B. A. Simmons, 538–558. London: Sage Publications.

Raustiala, K., and D. G. Victor. 2004. The regime complex for plant genetic resources. *International organization* 58:277–309.

Ringius, L. 1997. Environmental NGOs and regime change: The case of ocean dumping of radioactive waste. *European Journal of International Relations* 3:61–104.

Rittberger, V., and M. Zürn. 1991. Regime theory: Findings from the study of "east-west" regimes. *Cooperation and Conflict* 26:165–183.

Ross, D. P., and P. J. Usher. 1986. *From the roots up: Economic development as if community mattered.* Croton-on-Hudson, NY: Bootstrap Press.

Ruggie, J. G. 1983. International regimes, transactions, and change: Embedded liberalism in the postwar economic order. In *International regimes,* ed. S. D. Krasner, 195–232. Ithaca, NY: Cornell University Press.

Ruggie, J. G. 1995. The false premise of realism. *International Security* 20 (1):62–70.

Rutherford, M. 1994. *Institutions in economics: The old and the new institutionalism.* Cambridge, UK: Cambridge University Press.

Sandler, T. 2004. *Global collective action.* Cambridge, UK: Cambridge University Press.

Schelling, T. C. 1967. *Arms and influence.* New Haven, CT: Yale University Press.

Scott, W. R. 1995. *Institutions and organizations*. Thousand Oaks, CA: Sage Publications.

Simmons, B. A., and L. L. Martin. 2002. International organizations and institutions. In *Handbook of international relations*, ed. W. Carlsnaes, T. Risse, and B. A. Simmons, 192–211. London: Sage Publications.

Skjaerseth, J. B. 2000. *North Sea cooperation: Linking international and domestic pollution control*. Manchester: Manchester University Press.

Skjaerseth, J. B. 2002. Towards the end of dumping in the North Sea: The case of the Oslo Commission. In *Environmental regime effectiveness: Confronting theory with evidence*, ed. E. L. Miles, A. Underdal, S. Andresen, J. Wettestad, J. B. Skjaerseth, and E. M. Carlin, 65–85. Cambridge, MA: MIT Press.

Snidal, D. 1985. The limits of hegemonic stability theory. *International Organization* 39 (Autumn):579–614.

Social Learning Group. 2001. *Learning to manage global environmental risks: A comparative history of social responses to climate change, ozone depletion, and acid precipitation*, 2 vols. Cambridge, MA: MIT Press.

Spar, D. L. 1994. *The cooperative edge: The internal politics of international cartels*. Ithaca, NY: Cornell University Press.

Speth, J. G. 2004. *Red sky at morning: America and the crisis of the global environment*. New Haven, CT: Yale University Press.

Sprinz, D. F., and C. Helm. 1999. The effect of global environmental regimes: A measurement concept. *International Political Science Review* 20: 359–369.

Stein, A. A. 1983. Coordination and collaboration: Regimes in an anarchic world. In *International regimes*, ed. S. D. Krasner, 115–140. Ithaca, NY: Cornell University Press.

Stokke, O. S., and D. Vidas, eds. 1996. *Governing the Antarctic: The effectiveness and legitimacy of the Antarctic Treaty System*. Cambridge, UK: Cambridge University Press.

Strange, S. 1983. Cave! Hic dragones: A critique of regime analysis. In *International regimes*, ed. S. D. Krasner, 337–354. Ithaca, NY: Cornell University Press.

Underdal, A. 2002a. Conclusions: Patterns of regime effectiveness. In *Environmental regime effectiveness: Confronting theory with evidence*, ed. E. L. Miles, A. Underdal, S. Andersen, J. Wettestad, J. B. Skjaerseth, and E. M. Carlin, 433–465. Cambridge, MA: MIT Press.

Underdal, A. 2002b. One question, two answers. In *Environmental regime effectiveness: Confronting theory with evidence*, ed. E. L. Miles, A. Underdal, S. Andersen, J. Wettestad, J. B. Skjaerseth, and E. M. Carlin, 3–45. Cambridge, MA: MIT Press.

Underdal, A., and K. Hanf, eds. 2000. *The case of acid rain*. Aldershot: Ashgate.

Underdal, A., and O. R. Young, eds. 2004. *Regime consequences: Methodological challenges and research strategies*. Dordrecht: Kluwer Academic Publishers.

Victor, D. G., K. Raustiala, and E. B. Skolnikoff, eds. 1998. *The implementation and effectiveness of international environmental commitments*. Cambridge, MA: MIT Press.

von Moltke, K. 1997. Institutional interactions: The structure of regimes for trade and the environment. In *Global governance: Drawing insights from the environmental experience*, ed. O. R. Young, 247–272. Cambridge, MA: MIT Press.

Wapner, P. 1997. Governance in global civil society. In *Global governance: Drawing insights from the environmental experience*, ed. O. R. Young, 65–84. Cambridge, MA: MIT Press.

Weiss, E. B. 1993. International environmental law: Contemporary issues and the emergence of a New World order. *Georgetown Law Journal* 81:675–710.

Weiss, E. B., and H. K. Jacobson, eds. 1998. *Engaging countries: Strengthening compliance with international environmental accords*. Cambridge, MA: MIT Press.

Wendt, A. 1995. Constructing international politics. *International Security* 20 (1):71–81.

Werksman, J. 1996. Designing a compliance system for the UN Framework Convention on Climate Change. In *Improving compliance with international environmental law*, ed. J. Cameron, J. Werksman, and P. Roderick, 85–112. London: Earthscan Publications.

Young, O. R. 1975. *Bargaining: Formal theories of negotiation*. Urbana: University of Illinois Press.

Young, O. R. 1994. *International governance: Protecting the environment in a stateless society*. Ithaca, NY: Cornell University Press.

Young, O. R. 1996a. Institutional linkages in international society. *Global Governance* 2:1–24.

Young, O. R., ed. 1996b. *The international political economy and international institutions*, vol. 2. Cheltenham: Edward Elgar.

Young, O. R. 1999a. *Governance in world affairs*. Ithaca, NY: Cornell University Press.

Young, O. R., ed. 1999b. *The effectiveness of international environmental regimes: Causal connections and behavioral mechanisms*. Cambridge, MA: MIT Press.

Young, O. R. 2001a. The behavioral effects of environmental regimes: Collective-action vs. social-practice models. *International Environmental Agreements* 1:9–29.

Young, O. R. 2001b. Inferences and indices: Evaluating the effectiveness of international environmental regimes. *Global Environmental Politics* 1:99–121.

Young, O. R. 2002a. Are institutions intervening variables or basic causal forces? Causal clusters versus causal chains in international society. In *Millennial reflections on international studies*, ed. M. Brecher and F. P. Harvey, 176–191. Ann Arbor: University of Michigan Press.

Young, O. R. 2002b. *The institutional dimensions of environmental change: Fit, interplay, and scale.* Cambridge, MA: MIT Press.

Young, O. R. 2002c. *Matching institutions and ecosystems.* Paris: Institut du Développement Durable et des Relations Internationales.

Young, O. R. 2003. Determining regime effectiveness: A commentary of the Oslo-Potsdam solution. *Global Environmental Politics* 3:97–104.

Young, O. R., W. B. Chambers, J. A. Kim, and C. ten Have, eds. 2008. *Institutional interplay: The case of biosafety.* Tokyo: UN University Press.

Young, O. R., L. A. King, and H. Schroeder, eds. 2008. *Institutions and environmental change: Principal findings, applications, and research frontiers.* Cambridge, MA: MIT Press.

Young, O. R., E. F. Lambin, F. Alcock, H. Haberl, S. I. Karlsson, W. J. McConnell, T. Myint, et al. 2006. A portfolio approach to analyzing complex human-environment interactions: Institutions and land change. *Ecology and Society* 11 (2):31. http://www.ecologyandsociety.org/vol11/iss2/art31.

Young, O. R., and G. Osherenko, eds. 1993. *Polar politics: Creating international environmental regimes.* Ithaca, NY: Cornell University Press.

Young, O. R., and K. von Moltke. 1994. The consequences of international environmental regimes: Report from the Barcelona workshop. *International Environmental Affairs* 6:348–370.

6

Uncommon Ground: Critical Perspectives on Common Property

Bonnie J. McCay and Svein Jentoft

Global as well as local environmental problems are often explained in terms of a "tragedy of the [open-access] commons" whereby individual rationality with respect to common pool resources results in undesired and unintended social and ecological consequences. The best-known revisionist perspective on this approach underscores important conceptual and hence policy errors and has highlighted the importance of conditions in which collective action for common benefits can take place. We characterize both the model and the revisionist approach as "thin" or abstract, generalizing explanatory models, with strengths and weaknesses thereby, and we discuss a "thicker" or more ethnographic perspective that emphasizes the importance of specifying property rights and their embeddedness within discrete and changing historical moments, and social and political relations.

The "Tragedy of the Open-Access Commons"

It has long been appreciated that the lack of well-defined or exclusive property rights in resources may lead people to over-exploit them. The more intuitive and general understanding of this is encompassed in the maxim, "everyone's right, no one's responsibility." Aristotle recognized it two millennia ago: "what is common to the greatest number has the least care bestowed upon it. Everyone thinks chiefly of his own, hardly at all of the common interest" (*Politics*, book II, chapter 3; cited in Ostrom 1990, 2). Formalized in the 1950s by economists who focused on fisheries (Gordon 1954; Scott 1955; see also Warming 1911), it also found expression in Olson's analysis (1965) of the social dilemma whereby a group of people with the same interests will not necessarily act collectively to realize those interests because of the incentive each has to free-ride on the efforts of the others. The idea was popularized as "the tragedy of the commons" in 1968 by Garrett Hardin, who extended it to the problem of overpopulation.

The academic argument about the commons in the modern era derives from attempts to understand the political economy of capitalism and, more particularly, the "failures" of capitalist markets from the perspective of liberal economics. Why, if the capitalist economy generates so much wealth, are there so many poor people? That was the question prompting William Forster Lloyd's Oxford University lectures in the 1830s (Lloyd [1837] 1968, [1833] 1977). Lloyd explained poverty by virtue of an analogy between a pastoral commons and the English labor market, and between a calf and a human child, the calf armed with "a set of teeth and the ability to graze," and the child armed with a "pair of hands competent to labor" (Lloyd [1833] 1977, 11). Rights to enter the pasture or the labor market are freely obtainable common rights. Consequently pastures are overgrazed. By analogy, labor markets are oversaturated, resulting in the low wages and miseries of the laboring classes. Given free rights to put animals on a pasture or to procreate, replanting the pasture or raising wages would do little good because overstocking and overpopulation will only recur.

Lloyd's Malthusian view was picked up in the 1960s by Hardin ([1837] 1968). His exposition closely follows Lloyd's, as Hardin has acknowledged (Hardin and Baden 1977). Hardin added the language of marginal utility from economics to the pastoral analogy. Even though there might be signs of overstocking, it is rational for the individual cattle owner to add more animals to the pasture because his utility will be positive, say +1, whereas the negative utility to him is but a fraction of -1 because the costs of overstocking will be borne by his neighbors as well. The rational decisions of each individual accumulate to create an irrational dilemma for the group, and freedom becomes tragic: "The rational herdsman concludes that the only sensible course for him to pursue is to add another animal to his herd. And another, and another...but this is the conclusion reached by each and every rational herdsman sharing a commons. Therein lies the tragedy. Each man is locked into a system that compels him to increase his herd without minus in a world that is limited....Freedom in a commons brings ruin for all" (Hardin 1968, 1244).

The model that Hardin popularized had been developed formally by fisheries resource economists in the 1950s to explain the tendencies for fisheries to move toward overexploitation and overcapitalization (Gordon 1954) and to argue for the value of exclusive private ownership in managing fisheries (Scott 1955). It also was taken up by students of institutional and natural resource economics and the evolution of property rights (e.g., Hardin and Baden 1977; Stroup and Baden 1983; Anderson and Hill 1975; Anderson 1983). The main question had changed from why there are so many poor people to why natural and economic resources were wasted and depleted (implicitly relegating the issue of poverty as a side effect). Although based in theory on transactions costs and externalities in economics (Coase 1988; Cheung 1970), this work used Hardin's model to identify the institutional condition of "the commons" as the key source of disincentives and externalities. The commons became a metaphor for unregulated and open-access situations, and the phrase "common property" became coterminous with "open access" or "the absence of property rights," an important theorizing error as we will discuss.

Simplified models usually generate simple solutions, and in this case, based on the notion of open-access as the primary structural condition, the logical solutions are two-fold: either enclosure—creating exclusive and tradable property rights—to allow market forces to better align labor, capital, and resources; or, where privatizing enclosure is not feasible, government intervention to compensate for market failures. The alternative of "self-regulation" by users of the commons has no place in the model given the open-access condition (assuming that open access means both the lack of barriers to entry and the lack of regulation).

Government regulation is a major approach to managing the commons, especially for resources that are difficult to bound, enclose, and commodify. Indeed, a major rationale for government jurisdiction over the seas and navigable rivers, many forests, roads, the atmosphere, wildlife, and other such resources is that, for one reason or the other, they cannot or should not be privatized (cf. Rose 1994). If within state jurisdiction, they are treated as public property, and if beyond the jurisdiction of nation-states they are treated as truly open access, subject to control by international agencies, if at all. Government agencies and legislatures vary, however, in their capacities to manage "the commons" entrusted to them. Inequities, inefficiencies, and gross mismanagement are familiar results leading to searches for alternatives.

Partly in response to perceived problems with government management, economists, especially those carrying out the neoliberal agenda of "the new resource economics" (Anderson 1983), have pushed for the privatization solution, as in Gary Libecap's book *Locking Up the Range* (1981), which proposed privatization of the extensive public lands of the American West. From this perspective, privatization is a general and significant feature of complex, market-based societies and often viewed as inevitable in the course of human social evolution, a nineteenth-century ideology that persists. "The persistence of seemingly perverse property rights in the face of what would appear to be obvious alternatives" (Libecap 1989, 3) is therefore identified as an important point of entry to the study of processes of institutional change. The burden of scholarship is to explore why private property solutions have not yet come about, rather than why private property is chosen at all and what alternatives might there be.

This version of the idea of the tragedy of the commons is immensely popular, having become a folk and academic explanation for many social and environmental problems (for references, see McCay and Acheson 1987a, 2; Ostrom 1990, 3). One of its appeals is doubtless the fact that—like its close relative in political science, public choice theory—its prescriptions and assumptions can be congenial to those from the political "left" as well as the political "right" (DeGregori 1974). But it is contested, especially for its failure to recognize the role of community and the alternative of community-based approaches to common pool resource management.

Critiques

The impacts of the tragedy of the commons model on policy and research are numerous and profound. Despite this, many within the research community have mixed feelings about the model. Objections have been raised to some of its implicit and explicit assumptions. There also are serious questions as to policy recommendations that are deduced from the theory—questions that have contributed to a more community-based approach to resource management and conservation, as shown in recent works on forests (Gibson, McKean, and Ostrom 2000), African wildlife (Hulme and Murphree 2001), environmental protection (Cole 2002), and fisheries (Wilson, Nielsen, and Degnbol 2003; Weinstein 2000).

The assumptions of this model, like those of any model grounded in neoclassical economics, are "that common property is always of the open-access variety; that the users are selfish, unrestricted by social norms of the community, and trying to maximize short-term gains; that the users have perfect information; and that the resource is being used so intensively that overexploitation and depletion are possible" (McCay and Acheson 1987a, 7).

We address the first two points here (see Runge 1981 and Berkes 1987 for the second two). Hardin and others (e.g., Gordon 1954) may be criticized for reducing common property to open access, ignoring the wide variety of property relations that may be encompassed by the term. Ciriacy-Wantrup and Bishop (1975, 715) first pointed to the need to distinguish "common property" from "everybody's property," the latter being a condition of no property rights at all, a condition of completely open access or absence of management (cf. Hardin 1994).

"Sometimes both the institution and the resources subject to the institution are called the 'commons.' It is helpful, however, to differentiate between the concept, the institution,...and the particular resource that is subject to the institution" (Ciriacy-Wantrup and Bishop 1975, 715). The term *common pool* rather than *common property* should be used for the class of resources that are particularly problematic because of the difficulties of bounding or dividing them ("nonexcludability"), and the likelihood that one person's actions may affect another's enjoyment of the resource ("subtractibility") (Ostrom and Ostrom 1977).

In contrast, common property, like all other property, is a social institution, not an attribute of nature (Bohannan 1963; Furubotn and Pejovich 1972; McCay and Acheson 1987a). Moreover, common property refers to a highly variable class of property regimes. Among the features typically found are a right to use something in common with others, some expression of equality or equitability in the allocation of rights (Ciriacy-Wantrup and Bishop 1975, 714), and in some forms a right not to be excluded (Macpherson 1978). The individual owners may have use rights, but they may or may not have other property rights that they can exercise independently, such as the right to make changes or to transfer their rights to others (Schlager and Ostrom 1992). Such rights may inhere in the larger group or some governing body.

A key argument of the revisionist perspective on "commons" issues is therefore that one should distinguish between the features of the resource and how people choose to relate to the resource and to each other (Feeny et al. 1990; Berkes et al. 1989; Ostrom 1990). Just because a resource has properties that justify labeling it a common pool resource does not mean that people treat this resource as open access. Common pool resources can be treated as private property, the common property of a group, or as public property, owned by a state and used by members of the public, as well as combinations. Similarly, resources that have features lending themselves to easy privatization nonetheless can be treated as open-access, common, or public property.

Both environmental problems and solutions to them may be found under any property regime, whether common, state-based, private, or some mixture (Feeny et al. 1990). Moreover, the critique of Ciriacy-Wantrup and Bishop (1975) opened up the possibility of seeing common property as a positive, not negative, institution. As they and others since have observed, many institutions for regulating access and use of common pool resources have evolved, such as riparian institutions for water management, and some of these involve jurisdiction by a social community other than the state (Berkes 1987; Bromley 1992; Ostrom 1990; McCay and Acheson 1987b) within the framework of common property regimes.

This more optimistic view about social dilemmas of the commons is supported by simulation models and experiments (e.g., Axelrod 1984; Feeny 1992; Kopelman, Weber, and Messick 2002; Falk, Fehr, and Fischbacher 2002; Richerson, Boyd, and Paciotti 2002). Under various conditions of communication, trust, uncertainty, and other variables, coordination and cooperation among common resource users may occur even in the absence of external (i.e., state) governance.

Changes in such conditions can work upon a Hobbesian view of self-interested individuals to generate institutions that yield coordinated and cooperative social action or public choice (Bates 1992; Olson 1965). Nonetheless, many social researchers feel uneasy with the neoclassical economics perception of resource users as atomized, self-centered utility maximizers. "As a paradigm, it reduces human beings to predators, unrestricted by collective strategies and responsibilities" (Bjørklund 1990, 83). In contrast, social researchers underscore the social and moral aspects of user behavior. Users form communities. Natural resource extraction is guided by social values and norms, many of them "non-contractual" (Durkheim 1964), that may well stress moderation and prudence rather than excessiveness and recklessness. As even public choice-based scholars acknowledge, *community* in a moral and experiential sense is critical to the evolution of viable commons institutions (Ostrom 1992; Singleton and Taylor 1992; Jentoft 1999, 2000).

The revisionist perspective that under certain conditions resource users are capable of managing the resource themselves has lent a theoretical foundation to the rise in claims for the benefits of community-based natural resource management or environmental management. It also plays a theoretical role in advocates for governance reform toward more participatory governance, particularly the explicit sharing of management authority between local groups and the state, or "co-management" (Jentoft 1989; Pinkerton 1989; Wilson 2003; Jentoft, McCay, and Wilson 1998). Co-management may be strengthened when founded on common property rights that are held exclusively by well-identified corporate groups, as is for instance demonstrated among Japanese coastal fishing cooperatives (e.g., Ruddle 1989), but it may also function under conditions of relatively open access (Jentoft and Kristoffersen 1989).

The themes of decentralized and participatory management that are reinforced by revisionist "common property theory" have been adopted at many levels and in many forms of governance. They are echoed in the 2007 report of the Intergovernmental Panel on Climate Change: "Changes in development paths emerge from the interactions of public and private decision processes involving government, business, and civil society, many of which are not traditionally considered as climate policy. The process is most effective when actors participate equitably and decentralized decision making processes are coordinated" (IPCC 2007, 33).

For the IPCC, a more interactive approach to decision making is a means of enhancing the capacity of social systems such as local communities in adapting to climate change. If so, there is a need for social research to address which conditions are essential for such interactive arrangements to work, be they contractual or noncontractual in the Durkheimian sense.

The Mixed Value of Models
Ottar Brox (1990) points out that the tragedy of the commons model is nomothetic, an attempt to model the workings of general laws and principles, and that is its virtue. Even though the Hardin parable of herdsmen with cattle on the common pasture suggests a representative, empirical reality, Brox contends that the model portrays an "ideal type" in the Weberian sense, in other words, a model that "makes description of empirical phenomena in comparable and unambiguous terms possible" (Brox 1990, 230; Weber 1964). It should not be perceived as an idiographic description of a factual case. Accordingly, it is not falsified if in a particular case one or more of its assumptions does not hold true (but see Berkes 1987). It can be useful in comparative analysis.

In response to Brox, it must be observed that the critique of the tragedy of the commons model has resulted in models that similarly can provoke useful comparative research and critical thought. Best known is an evolving theoretical model of the conditions under which groups of resource users may be able to evolve and maintain viable and effective systems of common resource management. Ostrom (1990) has led contributions to this theory (see also McKean 1992 and Agrawal 2002), which for shorthand we can call the "comedy of the commons" (McCay 1995; Rose 1994; Boulding 1977). It makes room for self-governance and co-management approaches. For example Ostrom identifies situational variables that will affect judgment about the benefits of making an institutional choice for or against a particular kind of collection action. They include the number of appropriators, the size of the common pool resources, the temporal and spatial variability of resource units, and the amount and type of conflict (Ostrom 1990, 197); these and other variables, particularly those focused on the costs of monitoring and enforcing rules, are involved in institutional change. A related theoretical framework focuses on the conditions for successful co-management or collaboration among various groups of stakeholders ranging from resource users to government agencies and nongovernmental public interest groups (Pinkerton 1989, 1994; Jentoft 1989).

There is, nonetheless, danger in relying heavily on any model when trying to explain particular situations. A consequence of the popularity of the tragedy of the commons model, including the assumptions built into it and generalizations derived from it, is that numerous situations of resource use and abuse—but also of sustainability—are analyzed almost entirely in terms of common property or open access. This may be so even when property rights are not the issue at all (Emmerson 1980; Franke and Chasin 1980), where the social dilemma and free-riding features are not demonstrably at play, or where the property rights that make a difference are not those being analyzed.

An instance of misplaced analytic focus can be found in policy analyses of and responses to the problems of the fisheries of Newfoundland, Canada. In the early 1970s, the partly regulated but open-access regime of the inshore fisheries had little impact on the health of the fish stocks compared with the free-for-all regime of the international fisheries taking place farther off the shore (McCay 1978, 1979). Nonetheless, domestic policy restricting access to the inshore fisheries was recommended and eventually implemented based on the tragedy of the commons model

(The Kirby Report 1982) while insufficient policy attention was given to the task of managing the offshore and international fisheries (Steele, Anderson, and Green 1992; Matthews 1993). The authentically tragic consequence is that the cod fisheries were closed in 1992 because of the collapse of fish stocks largely due to offshore overfishing, contributed to by government failures in both science and policy (Finlayson 1994; Charles 1995). Nonetheless, policy continues to emphasize closing access to the inshore and nearshore fisheries (McCay and Finlayson 1995; Finlayson and McCay 1998).

Moreover, given the goal of better accounting for human/environment interactions and their social and ecological consequences as opposed to a goal such as supporting or challenging a particular model, there are philosophical reasons to be cautious about embracing grand or middling theories and models and making them the centers of our analyses (McCay and Vayda 1992; Vayda 2008). The "causal/mechanical" approach to scientific explanation (Kitcher 1985, 1989) emphasizes showing the causes actually operating in a particular situation; it may or may not call for use of a model such as the tragedy of the commons or the comedy of the commons. For the social sciences, this approach to explanation is preferred over the "unification" or nomothetic approach where the emphasis is more on showing conformity to laws or generalizations stemming from a broad theory (cf. Salmon 1984, 1989; Brandon 1990, 159–161).

Thick Analyses and Embedded Systems

Thin and Thick
The self-governance revisionist approach already described bears the risk of interpretation as being prescriptive (thou shalt be small-scale and self-governed) and overly optimistic (when left to their own devices people will reach viable solutions to their collective dilemmas). In addition, like the standard model of the tragedy, it is still squarely modernist, but with a shift in assumptions about human nature (more cooperative) and the degree of social interaction (more collective).

A more satisfying approach would add concerns about the interplay of conflicting interests and contested and agreed-upon meanings and definitions (Peters 1987). It would look at the specification of property rights and other institutional arrangements in particular intersections of history, politics, culture, time, and space: "Commons dilemmas must be explained in terms of the dynamics of conflict and competition between different social groups located in history and social systems rather than between the rational economizing individual unspecified and the group also unspecified" (McCay and Acheson 1987a, 22).

Both the tragedy of the commons model and the self-governance and co-management alternatives are what the philosopher Daniel Little (1991) would call "thin" or abstract, generalizing explanatory models. They can be very helpful in guiding the questions asked and providing frameworks for comparative analyses. Common property studies of the thin variety have been extremely valuable in culling out the criteria that seem to make a difference between success and failure in communal management (Ostrom 1990; McKean 1992; Agrawal 2002) as well as co-management (Pinkerton 1994; Pinkerton and Weinberg 1995; Singleton 1999). These studies recognize the importance of culture and community, although the nature of these "variables" is a matter of dispute (e.g., Singleton and Taylor 1992; Ostrom 1992) and is in any case abstract and generalized. The term *thin* is chosen to suggest its opposite: *thick*, which is meant to indicate a more ethnographic perspective, following the anthropologist Clifford Geertz's notion of the place of "thick description" in interpretive cultural anthropology (Geertz 1971; Little 1991). Here we take the liberty of tempering Geertz's use of the term to indicate a "thicker" or more ethnographic perspective that calls for careful specification of property rights and their embeddedness within discrete and changing historical moments, social and political relations, and environmental conditions, a methodological perspective that helps us avoid the twin perils of underestimating and overromanticizing the capabilities of people to manage the things they cherish and hold in common.

A relevant example of the cultural and historical specificity of the commons is the North American academic misuse of the term *common property* as the same thing as no property rights at all (McCay 1995). In North America common property has generally lost its status as anything other than specific legal arrangements, such as "tenants in commons," on the one hand, or the general power of the state over public lands and resources on the other. One intriguing explanation for loss of the possibility for truly community-oriented institutions for property management is Carol Rose's (1994) observation that the legal status of communal "custom" did not travel very well across the Atlantic, from English common law to American law, in part because Americans seemed determined to have nothing stand between the individual and his/her political representatives. More generally, in the Western world, the rise of radical individualism, capitalist practice, and liberal economic theory was linked to a shift in the understanding of property. Property came to be seen only as an individual right to exclude others from the use or benefit of something—that is, private property—when logically and historically it pertains to a broader class of individual rights, including the individual right not to be excluded from something (Macpherson 1978, 202). One can see the historical shift in, for example, early-nineteenth-century New Jersey, where a complex system of seine fishing rights along the Delaware River, whereby many individuals could hold various kinds of rights to use a particular fishing pool—rights not to be excluded by the owner of the land next to the pool—was reinterpreted by the courts such that the owner of the adjacent land's rights extinguished the others (McCay 1998).

Social Embeddedness

The analytical perspective previously advanced is well captured by the concept of social "embeddedness," originally introduced in the social sciences by Karl Polanyi who argued "that man's economy, as a rule, is enmeshed in his social relationships" (Polanyi 1957, 46). Similarly, Granovetter and Swedberg (1992) in a programmatic exposition of economic sociology argue that economic action is socially situated, in other words, enmeshed in economic and noneconomic institutions and networks of ongoing social relations. In their work, the term *embedded* has two often confused but distinct and valuable meanings. One is the methodological prescription that analyses of seemingly economic behaviors should focus on the social dimensions of those behaviors. This position reflects the fact that all economies are in some way embedded in other and larger structures (Barber 1995). Embeddedness is an ontological condition. The second is the claim that cultural systems differ in the extent to which economic transactions are embedded in kinship and other dimensions of social life and constructs of culture. Embeddedness is a variable.

The embeddedness position is an appropriate analytical perspective for the study of commons problems. It has been advocated and employed in work among fishers and herders. Gísli Pálsson criticizes the conventional approach, the "natural model," for only featuring the technical and ecological aspects of fishing and thus failing "to appreciate the ways in which production systems are differentiated with respect to their social relations." As an alternative, he proposes a model "which emphasizes the act of fishing, or any other extractive activity, as inevitably embedded in social relations" (Pálsson 1991, 157–158). In an investigation of the grazing lands of Botswana, Pauline Peters contends that the "definitions of rights, of relative claims, of appropriate uses and users are not only embedded in specific historical sets of political and economic structures but also in cultural systems of meanings, symbols and values" (1987, 178). She later writes, "Without a keener sense of the relations in which individual users are embedded, we cannot penetrate the dynamic of a commons, which is necessarily a social system" (193). Robert Paine's study of Sami reindeer pastoralism in Scandinavia brings the argument further: "The costs of disregarding the embeddedness factor (and in worse-case scenarios, terminating it by legislation) can be enormous even in economic terms" (1994, 193).

Contrary to the neoclassical economic perspective on rational behavior as motivated by the ambition to maximize individual gains, the embeddedness perspective would regard rationality as "anchored" within the social context within which the individual operates. As Selznick (1992, 57) argues, anchored rationality has the effect of multiplying commitments. The user is restrained by a number of concerns, for instance those pertaining to his roles as community member. It then follows that rather than taking individual rationalizing and optimizing as a fundamental assumption or heuristic about human nature, one would want to know why, in particular situations, people seem to be using individual rationalizing calculi of costs and benefits in making decisions. "It is an error to suppose that an individual calculus can explain a commons system— rather, one has to understand the socially and politically embedded commons to explain the individual calculus" (Peters 1987, 178). Thus, Davis and Jentoft (1993), criticizing the common assumption of individualism as a core trait of small-scale fishermen, take care to specify the nature of individualism among small-scale fishers of Nova Scotia. They discern two types ("utilitarian" and "rugged"), only one of which fits the tragedy of the commons scenario, and they attempt to show the conditions leading to an increase in one form over another, with hypothesized consequences for appropriate collective action.

The neoclassical economic model of the tragedy of the commons casts such tragedies as the result of market failure, due to imperfect property rights and hence incentive structures. The approach we are advocating might cast such tragedies as the result of "community failure" (McCay and Jentoft 1998). A working hypothesis is that the social conditions required for tragedies of the commons may result from processes of "disembedding," whereby resource users find themselves without the social bonds that connect them to each other and to their communities. If so, the tragedy of the commons is the product of social disruption and anomie rather than a "natural" outcome of individual rational behavior; it should be interpreted as a social pathology and an epiphenomenon rather than as a normal course of action.

The "community failure" perspective highlights the disembedding socioeconomic processes of modernity rather than converging on the single issue of property rights or their absence. The erosion of interpersonal commitments, solidarity, and moral standards characteristic of the embedded community has been triggered by global market forces as well as bureaucratic state practices. It should be seen as possible cause rather than probable consequence of tragedies of the commons. Further, restoring or recreating attributes of embedded communities is important if regulatory systems are to be effective in avoiding degradation of natural resources and in order to adapt to climate change (Jentoft 2009, forthcoming).

The notion of community is missing in the Hardin model (Fife 1977). Hardin does point out, however, that the community may confront the user with a difficult choice. Hardin argues that following the voice of the community ("If you don't do as we ask, we will openly condemn you for not acting like a responsible citizen") "is a causative factor in the genesis of the schizophrenia" (Hardin 1968, 1246). The embeddedness perspective would argue the reverse. As Amitai Etzioni points out: "While it is possible to think abstractly about individuals apart from a community, if individuals were actually without community they would have very few of the attributes commonly associated with the notion of an individual person. Such individuals typically are mentally unstable, impulsive, prone to suicide, and otherwise mentally and psychosomatically ill" (Etzioni 1988, 9). In other words, rather than confronting the user with an unsolvable dilemma, the community provides normative guidelines for and meaning in private sacrifice, which lessens the stress on the individual (Boulding 1977). The social matrix of users extends beyond the local community. Users are embedded in social systems of a larger scale that includes markets, organizational sectors made up of industries, professions, and national societies (DiMaggio and Powell 1991).

Increasingly, users are exposed to forces that are truly global. Not only are ecological crises spreading globally, so also are prescriptive models for problem solving. In this process, the sponsors of the Hardin model within the research community play a big role. Not only do they bring around a simple and easily recognizable definition of the common property problem, they are also advancing some explicit guidelines for political action. This is the power of the tragedy of the commons metaphor (Boulding 1977; cf. Leary 1995). Thus, the problem of Sami reindeer pastoralism is seen as structurally identical to the problems facing Maine small boat fisheries or Botswana cattle ranges, and in all settings the solutions advanced are basically similar: enclosure of the commons, preferably through privatization. The embeddedness perspective must therefore also highlight the impact of such extralocal forces on natural resource systems, including the roles of science and other expertise.

Typically, management systems are designed according to universal principles abstracted from local contexts. In these systems users are placed at the receiving end of a decision-making process that takes place at national and international levels. But management systems are also embedded at those levels. In an international comparative study of systems of user participation in fisheries management, we concluded that the specific organizational models reflect the broader institutional patterns and practices that prevail in each country (Jentoft and McCay 1995). With reference to Meyer and Rowan (1977) we argued that for reasons of legitimacy and efficiency, a particular management institution must be isomorphic with the broader institutional framework within which is embedded:

Fisheries management institutions do not originate in an institutional vacuum. ...The shape of fisheries management institutions is largely analogous to those that exist in other sectors of the society. For instance, the corporatist character of fisheries management in Scandinavia is parallel to institutions in other industries. Systems of consultation and negotiation between industry and government have been a crucial element in Scandinavian public administration. Neither are public hearings in the USA unique to fisheries. (Jentoft and McCay 1995, 236)

The Role of the State

In resource management the state often acquires the role of the external authority that is missing in game theory representations of commons problems such as "the Prisoners' Dilemma," where individuals on their own are unable to come up with optimal choices. The state is active in the design, implementation, and enforcement of resource regulations. To be institutionalized, a property rights system requires bureaucratic involvement and legislative voting. However well-intended, state initiatives frequently have ambiguous and unintended impacts. Social research has demonstrated that regulatory schemes often misfire or are directly counterproductive. Frequently, they also produce side effects such as social inequity and anomie. Sometimes the impacts of state involvement are even more subtle: "It is perhaps ironical that the state should be presented as the savior of people caught in the Prisoners' Dilemmas [and other collective-action problems] of a large society; for historically the state has undoubtedly played a large part in providing the conditions in which societies could grow and indeed in systematically building large societies and destroying small communities. The state has in this way acted so as to make itself even more necessary" (Taylor 1987, 167).

A similar criticism is raised in relation to fisheries management. Kasdan (1993, 7–8) argues: "Applying a 'tragedy of the commons' perspective which treats communities as if they are totally lacking in any ability to manage local resources because of unrestrained individual competition, results in politics which bring about the very conditions which that perspective presupposes." Davis and Jentoft (1989, 208) contend, "The redefinition of participation in fishing as a privilege granted to individuals by government through issuance of limited entry licenses countervails practices or attitudes among small boat fishermen that reference individual self-interest to collective organization and outcome." Thus, applying the Hardin model in real case management situations may well result in a self-fulfilling prophecy, as Maurstad (1992, 16) claims is unfolding in the Norwegian small boat fishery: "The tragedy is that there was not any tragedy until the solutions to counteract it were introduced. At least we do not know this for sure. What we know is that now the conditions for Hardin's tragedy are being created." From the perspective of the local community, bureaucratic involvement in resource management has a latent disembedding function. In effect it means a "'lifting out' of social relations from local contexts of interaction" (Giddens 1990, 21) of the responsibilities that were previously a concern of users. Vertical linkages of the individual user vis-à-vis government take precedence over horizontal linkages; in other words, those that users have with each other and that are lived out within their local community and on the commons. Former cooperative and symbiotic relations are transformed into competitive and "positional" (Hirsch 1976) relationships, bringing users into a position of dependency in their relationship with government. Thus, the social conditions that are conducive to social action—solidarity, trust, equality—are eroded.

Similar effects are attributed to market mechanisms. With reference to the Asia-Pacific region, Kenneth Ruddle (1993, 1) argues that "the commercialization and monetarization of formerly local and mainly subsistence or reciprocal exchange or barter economies, which now link them with external markets...leads to the breakdown of traditional management systems through the weakening or total collapse of traditional moral authority." In the final analysis, the process may evolve into a reversed situation where the market penetrates social relations. As pointed out by Polanyi (1957, 57): "Instead of economy being embedded in social relations, social relations are embedded in the economic system." This is also the argument of Jürgen Habermas (1984) on the "colonization life world": that the daily lives of human beings are increasingly being dominated by bureaucratic control and the logic of money transactions.

Ruddle and many other social researchers (e.g., Inglis 1993; Johannes 1989) have much faith in the role of co-management institutions and the inclusion of user knowledge in resource management in reembedding management responsibilities within the local community, arguments supported by the revisionist model of the comedy of the commons. However, commercialization and other forces may have weakened the capacities of local communities. Economists talk of the commons problem as one of "market failure," but in a very real sense the penetration of distant markets has contributed to the declining ability of local communities to manage local resources. Thus, in many tragedies of the commons the causes may be situations where market success has contributed to community failure.

On Sociology and Community

In the parable offered by Hardin, "each herdsman (entrepreneur) acts essentially alone for his own good without regard for the good of others; there is no community" (Fife 1977, 76). Criticisms of the Hardin model draw on perspectives and propositions that are basic to social science understandings of social communities. For instance: social actors have multiple goals and occupy a plurality of roles that sometimes are in conflict (Goffman 1969); both means and goals are infused with norms and values (Parsons [1937] 1968); people form multistranded networks and groups that are fundamentally moral in character (Durkheim 1964); they attribute meaning to their environments (Weber 1964); the community is not simply "added up" by its individual parts, but constitutes an integrated whole (Durkheim 1964). Thus, a fishing fleet is viewed as more than an aggregate of individual vessels; it is also a system of social relations that under certain circumstances may constitute a corporate group (Jentoft and Wadel 1984). The "lobster gangs" of Maine, portrayed by Acheson (1988), provide a good illustration: while lobstermen themselves often subscribe to the stereotype of the independent man at sea, they are in fact part of a complicated social network. To go lobster fishing, one must first become a member of a harbor gang. Once a person has gained admission, he can go fishing only in the territory "owned" communally by members of that gang. Fishermen identify with a particular harbor gang and are identified as members of it. Harbor gangs are also reference groups. Lobster fishermen in the same harbor gang ordinarily have long-term, multistranded ties with one another. Many are members of long-established families and share kinship ties as well (Acheson 1988, 48–49). Similarly, among the Sami of North Norway, pastoralists form households that form groups, such as the basic reindeer-herding unit, the *siida*: this is a form of cooperation among reindeer owners organized through kith relations. The term refers to a group of reindeer owners who live and migrate together and to the herd of reindeer they own and herd. As the herds differ in size through the year according to varying grazing conditions, so also does the demand for herding tasks and labor. Consequently the siida changes size and composition through the year, as the pastoralists divide and regroup their herds. The siida is in other words an alliance recruited through cognatic and affinal kinship relations, based upon mutual herding strategies among its members. This principle of organization provides each reindeer owner with potential access to pasture and herding partners over a large area (Bjørklund 1990, 80–81).

The groups that users construct are situated within a larger system, or within systems of different layers and scale, and must be analyzed accordingly (Ostrom 1995). As argued by Durrenberger and Pálsson (1987, 508) in relation to the fishery: "Rules of access to sea resources can only be understood in the context of the total socioeconomic system of which they form a part, including its land-based component." Hypothetically, then, when users compete their interaction is contained. There are rules of the game, for instance pertaining to territoriality. As members of a local community or an ethnic group, users are guided by ethical principles and/or social duties and responsibilities. Thus, competition may evolve without causing social disruption and disorder.

In fact, competition and cooperation should not be regarded as mutually exclusive activities (Taylor 1987). It could be argued that the former cannot take place without the latter. Among competitive users there must be some agreement as to what the competition is all about, who is allowed to participate, which strategies are permissible, and the rights of winners and losers. It could even be argued that cooperation is strengthened by competition. The rules of the game need to be confirmed. At a more general level, this is the point made by Georg Simmels who argued that social conflict should be thought of as an integrative mechanism and Lewis Coser who pointed out that conflict frequently helps to revitalize existent norms (see Rex 1961, 115–116). It is the task of the social researcher to describe what these restraining social mechanisms on resource extraction are and how they work in practice. Without ignoring the potential for social conflict, stratification, and disintegration, it should be assumed that fellow resource users are not always treated with affective neutrality and defined as a distant "they." As Etzioni (1988, 9) reminds us: "The society is not a 'constraint' or an 'opportunity,' it is us." Rather than perceiving the other as an outsider, if not intruder, users may often see themselves as "co-adventurers" of a socially integrated "we." Among user-group members there is solidarity, trust, and altruism. But as Portes and Sensenbrenner (1993) argue, these qualities are often "bounded"—in other words, limited to the specific community or group. Thus, user groups do not simply constitute aggregates of individual acts. They often result from deliberate collective action or have grown into a unity through social interaction over time. Communities often constitute organized activity of members who have social bonds and a common history, and who see themselves as sharing a common future. But one should be careful not to exaggerate the contained traits of unity, homogeneity, coherence, and stability. As Young (1995) remarks, communities are not static but change over time and they are often characterized by social fissures—as Barrett and Okudaira (1995) have shown even for Japanese fishery cooperatives, which are more widely thought of as the models for the success of local-level, community-based fishery management (e.g., Ruddle 1989). Communities should not only be thought of in structural and geographic terms; a community is also symbolically constructed (Cohen 1985). It exists in the minds of people as a repository of meaning and a referent of identity and belonging. This makes community more than a coalition and a transactional relationship. Hence, members' steadiness and loyalty result from involvement and commitment, and not only from a calculus. In other words, users sustain their community membership and adhere to norms and values not necessarily because it pays or from fear of sanctions. They do so because they feel morally committed.

The free rider in Prisoners' Dilemma experiments on the workings of common pool situations is someone whose rational choice is to let the other person shoulder the blame, or the costs; given that all actors have the same rational choice, the outcomes are suboptimal at best, often tragically so. Within the tragedy of the commons model, therefore, each actor is in the narrow sense of the word a rational actor, but he or she may be also acting immorally, and recognition of morality can be an important step toward cooperation in the commons.

Concluding Remarks

Scholars and practitioners who use the tragedy of the commons model to explain environmental problems and to advocate for particular solutions have implicitly or explicitly naturalized certain institutional and human conditions of open access, greed, and competition, and they have demonized common property and the commoners. The multidisciplinary critique over the past three decades has attempted to restore the cultural and situational relativity of the conditions of that tragedy and the values and potentials of rights held in common. The "thin" version of this critique has been extremely influential in underscoring the reality of and potentials for community-based self-regulation and co-management of common pool resources. The "thick" version of the critique, rooted firmly in the social sciences, gives greater attention to the social and cultural contents and contexts of situations framed as "the commons." Fundamental issues in the social sciences, including relationships between individuals and society, the nature of community, the embeddedness of economic behavior, and relationships between markets, states, and communities (Apostle et al. 1998), are played out in current debates about how to understand and deal with the human ecology of the commons.

In this context we call for a loose and expansive construct of community, one that would stretch from homesteads to townships to seats of central government and on to loose alliances among environmentalists or business leaders, the fragile institutions of international relations, the more robust institutions of global commerce, and even to "epistemic communities" of scientists and others engaged in trying to cope with common pool environmental problems (cf. Young 1989). The task is then to determine, for any given case of apparent abuse of common resources, where the failures lie and what can be done about them. To do this for any given situation requires exploring how various parties understand property rights and how those meanings are translated into behavior, custom, and law. It requires understanding the nature of conflicts over rights and responsibilities, the roles of science and other forms of expertise, and the larger global processes affecting land and natural resource management throughout the world. It also requires understanding, respecting, and building upon the social and political capacities of communities, key steps in "the struggle to govern the commons" (Dietz, Ostrom, and Stern 2003).

Acknowledgments

This chapter is based on a manuscript that was initially translated into German and published in 1996: Unvertrautes Gelände: Gemeineigentum Unter Der Sozialwissenschaftlichen Lupe (Uncommon Ground: Critical Perspectives on Common Property Theory), *Kölner Zeitschrift Für Soziologie und Sozialpsychologie* (*Cologne Journal of Sociology and Social Psychology*) 36:272–291. A later and much revised version was published in 1998: Market or community failure? Critical perspectives on common property research. *Human Organization* 57 (1):21–29. We have revised and updated the original manuscript, and we thank the reviewers of this book and the earlier papers for their comments and helpful suggestions.

References

Acheson, J. M. 1988. *The lobster gangs of Maine*. Hanover, NH: University Press of New England.

Agrawal, A. 2002. Common resources and institutional sustainability. In *The drama of the commons*, ed. E. Ostrom, T. Dietz, N. Dolsak, P. C. Stern,

S. Stovich, and E. U. Weber, 41–85. Washington, DC: National Academies Press.

Anderson, T. L., ed. 1983. *Water rights: Scarce resource allocation, bureaucracy, and the environment.* San Francisco: Pacific Institute for Public Policy Research.

Anderson, T. L., and P. J. Hill. 1975. The evolution of property rights: A study of the American West. *Journal of Law and Economics* 18:163–179.

Apostle, R., G. Barrett, P. Holm, S. Jentoft, L. Mazany, B. McCay, and K. Mikalsen. 1998. *Community, market and state on the North Atlantic Rim: Challenges to modernity in the fisheries.* Toronto: University of Toronto Press.

Axelrod, R. 1984. *The evolution of cooperation.* New York: Basic Books.

Barber, B. 1995. All economies are "embedded": The career of a concept, and beyond. *Social Research* 62 (2):387–413.

Barrett, G., and T. Okudaira. 1995. The limits of fishery cooperatives? Community development and rural depopulation in Hokkaido, Japan. *Economic and Industrial Democracy* 16:201–232.

Bates, R. H. 1992. Social dilemmas and rational individuals: An essay on the new institutionalism. Working Paper 164, Program in Political Economy, Papers in International Political Economy, Duke University, Durham, NC.

Berkes, F. 1987. Common-property resource management and Cree Indian Fisheries in Subarctic Canada. In *The question of the commons*, ed. B. J. McCay and J. M. Acheson, 66–91. Tucson: University of Arizona Press.

Berkes, F., D. Feeny, B. J. McCay, and J. M. Acheson. 1989. The benefits of the commons. *Nature* 340:91–93.

Bjørklund, I. 1990. Sami reindeer pastoralism as an Indigenous resource management system in Northern Norway: A contribution to the common property debate. *Development and Change* 21:75–86.

Bohannan, P. 1963. Land tenure. In *African agrarian systems*, ed. D. Biebuyk, 101–115. Oxford: Oxford University Press.

Boulding, K. 1977. Commons and community: The idea of a public. In *Managing the commons*, ed. G. Hardin and J. Baden, 280–294. San Francisco: W. H. Freeman.

Brandon, R. N. 1990. *Adaptation and environment.* Princeton, NJ: Princeton University Press.

Bromley, D. W., ed. 1992. *Making the commons work: Theory, practice, and policy.* San Francisco: International Center for Self-Governance.

Brox, O. 1990. Common property theory: Epistemological status and analytical utility. *Human Organization* 49 (3):227–235.

Charles, A. T. 1995. The Atlantic Canadian groundfishery: Roots of a collapse. *Dalhousie Law Journal* 18 (1):65–83.

Cheung, S. N. S. 1970. The structure of a contract and the theory of a non-exclusive resource. *Journal of Law and Economics* 13 (1):45–70.

Ciriacy-Wantrup, S., and R. Bishop. 1975. "Common property" as a concept in natural resources policy. *Natural Resources Journal* 15:713–727.

Coase, R. H. 1988. *The firm, the market, and the law.* Chicago: University of Chicago Press.

Cohen, A. P. 1985. *The symbolic construction of community.* London: Tavistock Publications.

Cole, D. H. 2002. *Pollution and property: Comparing ownership institutions for environmental protection.* Cambridge, UK: Cambridge University Press.

Davis, A., and S. Jentoft. 1989. Ambivalent co-operators: Organisational slack and utilitarian rationality in an eastern Nova Scotian fisheries co-operative. *Maritime Anthropological Studies* 2 (2):194–211.

Davis, A., and S. Jentoft. 1993. Self and sacrifice: An investigation of small boat fisher individualism and its implications for producer cooperatives. *Human Organization* 52 (4):356–376.

DeGregori, T. R. 1974. Caveat emptor: A critique of the emerging paradigm of public choice. *Administration and Society* 6 (2):205–228.

Dietz, T., E. Ostrom, and P. C. Stern. 2003. The struggle to govern the commons. *Science* 302 (5652):1907–1912.

DiMaggio, P. J., and W. W. Powell, eds. 1991. *The new institutionalism in organizational analysis.* Chicago: The University of Chicago Press.

Durkheim, E. 1964. *The division of labour in society.* New York: The Free Press.

Durrenberger, P., and G. Pálsson. 1987. Ownership at sea: Fishing territories and access to sea resources. *American Ethnologist* 14 (3):508–521.

Emmerson, D. K. 1980. Rethinking artisanal fisheries development: Western concepts, Asian experiences. World Bank Staff Working Paper 423, The World Bank, Washington, DC.

Etzioni, A. 1988. *The moral dimension: Toward a new economics.* New York: The Free Press.

Falk, A., E. Fehr, and U. Fischbacher. 2002. Appropriating the commons: A theoretical explanation. In *The drama of the commons*, ed. E. Ostrom, T. Dietz, N. Dolsak, P. C. Stern, S. Stonich, and E. U. Weber, 157–195. Washington, DC: National Academies Press.

Feeny, D. 1992. Where do we go from here? Implications for the research agenda. In *Making the commons work: Theory, practice, and policy*, ed. D. W. Bromley, 267–292. San Francisco: Institute for Contemporary Studies Press.

Feeny, D., F. Berkes, B. McCay, and J. Acheson. 1990. The tragedy of the commons: Twenty-two years later. *Human Ecology* 18:1–19.

Fife, D. 1977. Killing the goose. In *Managing the commons*, ed. G. Hardin and J. Baden, 76–81. San Francisco: W. H. Freeman.

Finlayson, A. C. 1994. *Fishing for truth: A sociological analysis of Northern Cod stock assessments from 1977 to 1990.* St. John's, Newfoundland: Institute of Social and Economic Research.

Finlayson, A. C., and B. J. McCay. 1998. Crossing the threshold of ecosystem resilience: The commercial extinction of Northern Cod. In *Linking social and ecological systems: Institutional learning for resilience,* ed. C. Folke and F. Berkes, 311–337. Cambridge, UK: Cambridge University Press.

Franke, R. W., and B. H. Chasin. 1980. *Seeds of famine: Ecological destruction and the development dilemma in the West African Sahel.* Montclair, NJ: Allenheld, Osmun.

Furubotn, E. G., and S. Pejovich. 1972. Property rights and economic theory: A survey of recent literature. *Journal of Economic Literature* 10:1137–1162.

Geertz, C. 1971. Thick description: Toward an interpretive theory of culture. In *The interpretation of cultures,* 3–32. New York: Basic Books.

Gibson, C. C., M. A. McKean, and E. Ostrom eds. 2000. *People and forests: Communities, institutions, and governance.* Cambridge, MA: The MIT Press.

Giddens, A. 1990. *The consequences of modernity.* Cambridge, UK: Polity Press.

Goffman, E. 1969. *The presentation of self in everyday life.* New York: Penguin Books.

Gordon, H. S. 1954. The economic theory of a common property resource: The fishery. *Journal of Political Economy* 62:124–142.

Granovetter, M., and R. Swedberg, eds. 1992. *The sociology of economic life.* Boulder, CO: Westview Press.

Habermas, J. 1984. *The theory of communicative action.* Boston: Beacon Press.

Hardin, G. 1968. The tragedy of the commons. *Science* 162:1243–1248.

Hardin, G. 1994. The tragedy of the unmanaged commons. *Trends in Ecology and Evolution* 9:199.

Hardin, G., and J. Baden, eds. 1977. *Managing the commons.* San Francisco: W. H. Freeman.

Hirsch, F. 1976. *Social limits to growth.* Cambridge, MA: Harvard University Press.

Hulme, D., and M. Murphree, eds. 2001. *African wildlife and livelihoods: The promise and performance of community conservation.* Portsmouth, NH: Heinemann.

Inglis, J. T., ed. 1993. *Traditional ecological knowledge: Concepts and cases.* Ottawa: Canadian Museum of Nature.

IPCC (Intergovernmental Panel on Climate Change). 2007. *Climate Change 2007: Mitigation. Contribution of Working Group III to the Fourth Assessment Report of the Intergovernmental Panel on Climate Change,* ed. B. Metz, O. R.

Davidson, P. R. Bosch, R. Dave, and L. A. Meyer. Cambridge, UK: Cambridge University Press.

Jentoft, S. 1989. Fisheries co-management: Delegating government responsibility to fishermen's organizations. *Marine Policy* 13:137–154.

Jentoft, S. 1999. Healthy fishing communities: An important component of healthy fish stocks. *Fisheries* 24:28–29.

Jentoft, S. 2000. The community: A missing link of fisheries management. *Marine Policy* 24:53–59.

Jentoft, S. 2000. Future challenges in environmental policy relative to ICZM. In *Integrated coastal zone management*, ed. E. Dahl, E. Moksness, and J. Støttrup. Malden, MA: Wiley-Blackwell Publishing.

Jentoft, S., and T. Kristoffersen. 1989. Fishermen's co-management: The case of the Lofoten Fishery. *Human Organization* 48 (4):355–367.

Jentoft, S., and B. J. McCay. 1995. User participation in fisheries management: Lessons drawn from international experiences. *Marine Policy* 19:227–246.

Jentoft, S., B. J. McCay, and D. C. Wilson. 1998. Social theory and fisheries co-management. *Marine Policy* 22 (4/5):423–436.

Jentoft, S., and C. Wadel, eds. 1984. *I samme bat: Sysselsettingssystemer i fiskerinaeringen.* Oslo: Universitetsforlaget.

Johannes, R. E., ed. 1989. *Traditional ecological knowledge: A collection of essays.* Gland: IUCN, The World Conservation Union.

Kasdan, L. 1993. Market rationality, productive efficiency, environment and community: The relevance of local experience. Paper presented at the International Congress on Ecology, Hermosillo, Mexico, April 15–17.

Kirby Report, The. Task Force on Atlantic Fisheries. 1982. Navigating troubled waters: A new policy for the Atlantic fisheries. Ottawa, December 1982.

Kitcher, P., 1985. Two approaches to explanation. *Journal of Philosophy* 82:632–639.

Kitcher, P. 1989. Explanatory unification and the causal structure of the world. In *Scientific explanation*, ed. P. Kitcher and W. C. Salmon, 410–505. Minneapolis: University of Minnesota Press.

Kopelman, S., J. M. Weber, and D. M. Messick. 2002. Factors influencing cooperation in commons dilemmas: A review of experimental psychological research. In *The drama of the commons*, ed. E. Ostrom, T. Dietz, N. Dolsak, P. C. Stern, S. Stonich, and E. U. Weber, 403–442. Washington, DC: National Academies Press.

Leary, D. E. 1995. Naming and knowing: Giving forms to things unknown. *Social Research* 62 (2):267–298.

Libecap, G. D. 1981. *Locking up the range.* Cambridge, MA: Ballinger Publishing Co.

Libecap, G. D. 1989. *Contracting for property rights.* New York: Cambridge University Press.

Little, D. 1991. *Varieties of social explanation: An introduction to the philosophy of social science*. Boulder, CO: Westview Press.

Lloyd, W. F. [1837] 1968. *Lectures on population, value, poor-laws, and rent, delivered in the University of Oxford during the years 1832, 1833, 1834, 1835, and 1836*. New York: Augustus M. Kelley.

Lloyd, W. F. [1833] 1977. *On the checks to population*. Reprinted in *Managing the commons*, ed. G. Hardin and J. Baden, 8–15. San Francisco: W. H. Freeman.

Macpherson, C. B. 1978. The meaning of property. In *Property: Mainstream and critical positions*, ed. C. B. Macpherson, 1–13. Toronto: University of Toronto Press.

Matthews, D. R. 1993. *Controlling common property: Regulating Canada's east coast fishery*. Toronto: University of Toronto Press.

Maurstad, A. 1992. Closing the commons—opening the "tragedy": Regulating North-Norwegian small-scale fishing. Paper presented at the 3rd Common Property Conference of the International Association for the Study of Common Property, September 17–20, Washington, DC.

McCay, B. J. 1978. Systems ecology, people ecology, and the anthropology of fishing communities. *Human Ecology* 6 (4):397–422.

McCay, B. J. 1979. Fish is scarce: Fisheries modernization on Fogo Island, Newfoundland. In *North Atlantic maritime cultures*, ed. R. Andersen, 155–189. The Hague, The Netherlands: Mouton.

McCay, B. J. 1995. Common and private concerns. *Advances in Human Ecology* 4:89–116. Greenwich, CT: JAI Press.

McCay, B. J. 1998. *Oyster wars and the public trust: Property, law and ecology in New Jersey history*. Tucson: University of Arizona Press.

McCay, B. J., and J. M. Acheson. 1987a. Human ecology of the commons. In *The question of the commons: The culture and ecology of communal resources*, ed. B. J. McCay and J. M. Acheson, 1–34. Tucson: University of Arizona Press.

McCay, B. J., and J. M. Acheson, eds. 1987b. *The question of the commons: The culture and ecology of communal resources*. Tucson: University of Arizona Press.

McCay, B. J., and A. C. Finlayson. 1995. The political ecology of crisis and institutional change: The case of the Northern Cod. Paper presented to the Annual Meetings of the American Anthropological Association, November 15–19, Washington, DC.

McCay, B. J., and S. Jentoft. 1998. Market or community failure? Critical perspectives on common property research. *Human Organization* 57 (1):21–29.

McCay, B. J., and A. P. Vayda. 1992. The ecology of natural resource and conservation management: A question-based approach to research in ecological anthropology. Paper presented to the Annual Meetings of the American Anthropological Association, December 3, San Francisco, CA.

McKean, M. A. 1992. Success on the commons: A comparative examination of institutions for common property resource management. *Journal of Theoretical Politics* 4 (3):247–281.

Meyer, J. W., and B. Rowan. 1977. Institutionalized organizations: Formal structure as myth and ceremony. *American Journal of Sociology* 83 (2):340–363.

Olson, M. 1965. *The logic of collective action: Public goods and the theory of groups.* Cambridge, MA: Harvard University Press.

Ostrom, E. 1990. *Governing the commons: The evolution of institutions for collective action.* New York: Cambridge University Press.

Ostrom, E. 1992. Community as the endogenous solution of commons problems. *Journal of Theoretical Politics* 4 (3):343–351.

Ostrom, E. 1995. Designing complexity to govern complexity. In *Property rights and the environment; Social and ecological issues,* ed. S. Hanna and M. Munasinghe, 33–46. Washington, DC: The Beijer International Institute of Ecological Economics and the World Bank.

Ostrom, V., and E. Ostrom. 1977. A theory for institutional analysis of common pool problems. In *Managing the commons,* ed. G. Hardin and J. Baden, 157–172. San Francisco: W. H. Freeman.

Paine, R. 1994. *Herders of the tundra: A portrait of Saami reindeer pastoralism.* Washington, DC: Smithsonian Institution Press.

Pálsson, G. 1991. *Coastal economies, cultural accounts: Human ecology and Icelandic discourse.* Manchester: Manchester University Press.

Parsons, T. [1937] 1968. *The structure of social action.* New York: The Free Press.

Peters, P. E. 1987. Embedded systems and rooted models: The grazing lands of Botswana and the commons debate. In *The question of the commons,* ed. B. McCay and J. Acheson, 171–194. Tucson: University of Arizona Press.

Pinkerton, E., ed. 1989. *Co-operative management of local fisheries: New directions for improved management and community development.* Vancouver: University of British Columbia Press.

Pinkerton, E. 1994. Local fisheries co-management: A review of international experiences and their implications for salmon management in British Columbia. *Canadian Journal of Fisheries and Aquatic Sciences* 51:1–17.

Pinkerton, E., and M. Weinberg. 1995. Fisheries that work; sustainability through community-based management. *A report of the David Suzuki Foundation.* Vancouver, BC: The David Suzuki Foundation.

Polanyi, K. 1957. *The great transformation.* Boston: Beacon Press.

Portes, A., and J. Sensenbrenner. 1993. Embeddedness and immigration: Notes on the social determinants of economic action. *American Journal of Sociology* 98 (6):1320–1350.

Rex, J. 1961. *Key problems of sociological theory.* London: Routledge and Kegan Paul.

Richerson, P. J., R. Boyd, and B. Paciotti. 2002. An evolutionary theory of commons management. In *The drama of the commons*, ed. E. Ostrom, T. Dietz, N. Dolsak, P. C. Stern, S. Stonich, and E. U. Weber, 403–442. Washington, DC: National Academies Press.

Rose, C. M. 1994. *Property and persuasion: Essays on the history, theory, and rhetoric of ownership*. Boulder, CO: Westview Press.

Ruddle, K. 1989. Solving the common-property dilemma: Village fisheries rights in Japanese coastal waters. In *Common property resources: Ecology and community-based sustainable development*, ed. F. Berkes, 168–184. London: Belhaven Press.

Ruddle, K. 1993. External forces and change in traditional community-based fishery management systems in the Asia-Pacific Region. *Maritime Anthropological Studies* 6 (1/2):1–37.

Runge, C. F. 1981. Common property externalities: Isolation, assurance and resource depletion in a traditional grazing context. *American Journal of Agricultural Economics* 63:595–606.

Salmon, W. C. 1984. *Scientific explanation and the causal structure of the world*. Princeton, NJ: Princeton University Press.

Salmon, W. C. 1989. *Four decades of scientific explanation*. Minneapolis: University of Minnesota Press.

Schlager, E., and E. Ostrom. 1992. Property-rights regimes and natural resources: A conceptual analysis. *Land Economics* 68:249–262.

Scott, A. 1955. The fishery: The objectives of sole ownership. *Journal of Political Economy* 63:116–124.

Selznick, P. 1992. *The moral commonwealth: Social theory and the promise of community*. Berkeley: University of California Press.

Singleton, S. 1999. Commons problems, collective action and efficiency: Past and present institutions of governance in Pacific Northwest salmon fisheries. *Journal of Theoretical Politics* 11:367–391.

Singleton, S., and M. Taylor. 1992. Common property, collective action and community. *Journal of Theoretical Politics* 4 (3):309–324.

Steele, D. H., R. Andersen, and J. M. Green. 1992. The managed commercial annihilation of Northern Cod. *Newfoundland Studies* 8 (1):34–68.

Stroup, R. L., and J. A. Baden. 1983. *Natural resources: Bureaucratic myths and environmental management*. San Francisco: Pacific Institute for Public Policy Research.

Taylor, M. 1987. *The possibility of cooperation*. Cambridge, UK: Cambridge University Press.

Vayda, A. 2008. Causal explanation as a research goal: A pragmatic view. In *Against the grain: The Vayda tradition in human ecology and ecological anthropology*, ed. B. Walters, B. McCay, P. West, and S. Lees, 317–367. Lanham, MD: Altamira Press.

Warming, J. 1911. *Grundrente af fiskegrunde*. Kobenhagen: National konomisk Tidsskrift.

Weber, M. 1964. *The theory of social and economic organization*. New York: The Free Press.

Weinstein, M. S. 2000. Pieces of the puzzle: Solutions for community-based fisheries management from native Canadians, Japanese cooperatives, and common property researchers. *Georgetown International Environmental Law Review* 12:375–410.

Wilson, D. C. 2003. The community development tradition and fisheries co-management. In *The fisheries co-management experience: Accomplishments, challenges and prospects*, ed. D. C. Wilson, J. R. Nielsen, and P. Degnbol, 17–30. Dordrecht: Kluwer Academic Publishers.

Wilson, D. C., J. R. Nielsen, and P. Degnbol, eds. 2003. *The fisheries co-management experience: Accomplishments, challenges and prospects*. Dordrecht: Kluwer Academic Publishers.

Young, O. 1989. The politics of international regime formation: Managing natural resources and the environment. *International Organization* 43 (3):349–375.

Young, O. 1995. The problem of scale in human/environment relationships. In *Local commons and global interdependence*, ed. R. O. Keohane and E. Ostrom, 27–45. London: Sage Publications.

7

Vulnerability of Coupled Human-Ecological Systems to Global Environmental Change

Jeanne X. Kasperson, Roger E. Kasperson, and B. L. Turner II

Introduction

In *Our Common Future*, its wake-up call to a world confronted by accelerating environmental changes, the World Commission on Environment and Development (WCED 1987) described a tapestry of global problems in which ecological and sociopolitical problems were deeply meshed. Global environmental threats and poverty were so interrelated, the commission argued, that a global risk assessment program was needed to discern the roots of the stresses emanating from human activities, as well as a new environmental ethic and an integrative attack on the dynamics of environmental degradation and poverty.

Various assessments since 1987 have confirmed this basic diagnosis. Taking climate change as an example, from the work of the Intergovernmental Panel on Climate Change (IPCC) we know that humans have altered the climates in which they live, and the evidence is growing that human activities are responsible for most of the global warming (IPCC 2007). A litany of effects that will unfold over the coming decades is likely to impose widespread stresses and perturbations on human and ecological systems, including an ongoing rise in global average sea level; increases in precipitation over most mid- and high latitudes of the Northern Hemisphere; increased intensity and frequency of droughts, floods, and severe storms; and unforeseen abrupt changes and extreme climatic events. We also know that the related effects will be strongly concentrated in particularly vulnerable regions as a complex array of other stresses—including growing populations, poverty and poor nutrition, accumulating atmospheric and water contamination, gender and class inequalities, the ravages of the AIDS epidemic, and inept or politically corrupt governments—also acts on these regions and shrinks capacities to cope. The ecosystems likely to be most vulnerable will be those already at the limits of their range, those in which barriers to species migration preclude or impede redistribution, those at the interface of ecotones (e.g., estuaries, coral reefs, seasonally dry forests, some fire-adapted systems), artificially simplified agro-ecosystems that contain less genetic diversity to adapt, and those ecosystems likely to experience further human-induced demands as a result of reduced production in other ecosystems on which humans are relying. Ecosystems highly dependent on social infrastructure or political stability are also likely vulnerable, where purposeful human actions that could be disrupted by climate change (e.g., artificial burning regimes to mimic natural processes, white-rhinoceros protection activities) have supplanted natural processes. The coalescence and interaction of social and ecological vulnerabilities may result in spirals of degradation that reinforce and even accelerate mutual vulnerabilities and damage. In short, the people, ecosystems, and regions already beset by a struggle to cope with a concatenation of stresses largely beyond their control are likely to bear most of the burden of climate and other global environmental changes. As the Millennium Ecosystem Assessment further noted, "Levels of poverty remain high, inequities are growing, and many people still do not have a sufficient supply of or access to ecosystem services" (MEA 2005, 61).

This should not be surprising, of course, based on what is already known about the changing global pattern of natural disasters and their effects on humans (Abramovitz 2001; IFRC 2001; UNISDR 2002; Wisner et al. 2004). Data from Munich Re, a German reinsurance company, reveal that natural catastrophes, those that tax the ability of the region to help itself and often necessitate interregional or international assistance, increased in number from 680 in 1994 to 950 in 2007 (Munich Re 2007). During the period from 1991 to 2000, natural disasters affected some 211 million persons per year, seven times the number affected by human conflict. Most revealing is the role of vulnerability in this toll. Of all those killed and affected by natural disasters, 98 percent was in developing countries, fully 86 percent in Asia, but only 1 percent in Europe. Meanwhile, the *World Disasters Report 2001* (IFRC 2001, 165) notes that of the 2.3 million people reported killed by conflict from 1991 to 2000, over three-fourths were from nations of low economic development. Although economic losses from natural disasters are concentrated in wealthy societies, the lower losses in developing countries carry far larger and longer-term negative effects on political, social, and economic productivity and stability. In 2004, some 235,000 persons died from natural catastrophes, as compared with 10,300 in 2000 (Munich Re 2007).

This intertwining of risk and vulnerability is a familiar theme in the field of risk analysis, the practitioners of which have long defined risk as a joint product. So, in 1942, Gilbert F. White wrote a Ph.D. dissertation in which he proposed to reduce damages from floods by decreasing exposure of peoples to floods and increasing their capacities to anticipate and cope with floods (White 1945). A long tradition of research on natural hazards (Mileti 1999; Mitchell 1989) has examined sources of vulnerability, extended by greater attention to social and economic structures and global processes predisposing human societies to high risk (Adger and Kelly 1999; Blaikie et al. 1994; Bohle, Downing, and Watts 1994; Cutter 1996; Ribot 1995, 1996; Pelling 2003b; Wisner et al. 2004; IPCC 2007). Studies of technological risk have examined the proneness of technological and industrial systems to failure (La Porte 1996; La Porte and Keller 1996; Perrow 1984, 1999), the vulnerability of critical societal infrastructure to natural disasters and human terrorism (Haimes 1990, 1998), and the factors propelling societies to greater energy insecurity (Khatib 2000; Stobaugh and Yergin 1979; UCS 2002; Yergin 1991; Yergin and Hillenbrand 1982). Meanwhile, concerns over food security and threats to small agriculturalists and fishers have sparked interest in the vulnerability of livelihood systems, especially in the South (Carney 1998; Carney et al. 1999; Chambers and Conway 1992; Scoones 1996; Vogel 2001). And the emerging field of ecological risk assessment has a developing methodology, derived from human risk analysis, focused on characterizing and reducing human-driven risks to ecosystems, including toxic wastes and pollution (Suter 1990, 1993).

This range of studies suggests one elemental insight largely missed in the evolving vulnerability literature: although writings typically champion a "right" model or approach, in fact vulnerability refers to widely different situations, differing complexes of stresses, varying complexes of predisposing vulnerability factors, and dissimilar sociopolitical and community contexts. Searching for the "right" theory or model for vulnerability is reminiscent of the prolonged sterile debate over the "right" political model for community politics until it finally dawned on researchers that there was in fact no single correct model—that different places had quite different power structures and that sound comparative studies required multiple models (Clark 1974).

At the same time, vulnerability has clearly "arrived" and become something of a buzzword, a highly visible topic in a wide expanse of global change and sustainability studies and assessments and in the agenda of international food and health organizations (FIVIMS 1999, 2000, 2001). It is also a prime issue in the years since September 11, 2001, as terrorism has become prominent on the international agenda. For hazards research, Mitchell (2001, 87–88) ascribes some of the appeal of vulnerability as an analytical concept to "its rhetorical connotations as well as its acuity as an intellectual device." Observing the mounting attention to vulnerability in studies of natural hazards and disasters, a recent review implicates increased vulnerability as overwhelming the effective use of knowledge. The IPCC produced a special volume from its second assessment on regional vulnerabilities to climate change (Zinyowera et al. 1998) and put vulnerability center stage in priority (if not actual work) in its third assessment (IPCC 2001; McCarthy et al. 2001), and continued this trend in its Fourth Assessment, especially in Working Group II (IPCC 2007). The United Nations Environment Programme (UNEP) and the United Nations Development Programme (UNDP) are actively developing vulnerability assessment procedures, indicators, and guidelines. Although the World Bank and regional banks have rediscovered poverty and undertaken extensive antipoverty programs, they have yet to integrate them into a broader framework of vulnerability analysis. Meanwhile, the International Federation of Red Cross and Red Crescent Societies (IFRC), in its strategic *Work Plan for the Nineties*, takes up the challenge of "improving the situation of the most vulnerable" (IFRC 1999b, 8). The Famine Early Warning System (FEWS) regularly produces two types of vulnerability assessments: "Current Vulnerability Assessments" of various populations' abilities to meet their current food needs, and "Food Security and Vulnerability Profiles" of long-term food security issues (http://www.fews.org). The Millennium Ecosystem Assessment (MEA 2003, 2005) has targeted vulnerability of human-ecological systems as a priority area of study. The International Human Dimensions of Global Environmental Change Programme (IHDP), taking stock of the centrality of vulnerability issues in its various initiatives, has also accorded vulnerability high priority as a cross-cutting issue in its various projects. The Global Land Project, shared by the IHDP and the International Geosphere-Biosphere Programme (IGBP), identifies the vulnerability of the coupled human-environment system as one of its principal research efforts (GLP 2005). The sustainability-science initiative has adapted vulnerability as an archetypal problem and accorded it major priority (Kates et al. 2000; Research and Assessment Systems for Sustainability Program 2001; USNRC 1999).

These are high expectations and priorities. What is the capability of current scholars and analysts, and the state of accumulated knowledge, to deliver? In the discussion that follows, we argue (1) that the existing research and assessment cupboard is filled with lots of things, but it is unacceptably cluttered and bereft of an integrative framework of theory and analysis; (2) that the truly integrative analysis envisioned by the World Commission on Environment and Development has been undermined by the failure to frame the analytic subject as coupled social-ecological systems; (3) that ideological squabbling in the social sciences has created an unproductive divergence between "structure" and "agency" in the framing of basic problems; (4) that the requisite funding sources and program for a sustained attack on an overriding set of issues of global importance have been lacking; and, as a result of the above, (5) that the cumulative progress over the past decade on understanding and analyzing vulnerability to global environmental change has fallen far short of what could and should have been achieved, and that a shift to coupled human-ecological systems can significantly enhance vulnerability analysis. That said, it is also the case that the carryover from the current state of scholarly knowledge into the arena of assessment and practice has fallen disappointingly short of what has been possible. From the highly revealing study of scholarly networks by Janssen and associates (2006) it is clear that conceptual and methodological fragmentation in vulnerability research remains a serious problem.

The goals, particularly for the next stage of work, must be realistic. Systematic studies of vulnerability cannot be expected to result in the near term in a quantitative understanding equivalent to that of the driving forces in the scientific arena of global environmental change (although see Luers et al. 2003; Luers 2005), but they can provide substantial qualitative understanding of the vulnerability of particular ecosystems, peoples, and places (Schröter, Polsky, and Patt 2005; Polsky, Neff, and Yarnell 2007). Several recent reviews of vulnerability research point the way towards the coalescing of much of this field of study (Adger 2006; Eakin and Luers 2006; Turner et al. 2003a).

Definitions

The term *vulnerability* derives from the Latin root *vulnerare*, meaning "to wound." Accordingly, vulnerability in simple terms means "the capacity to be wounded" (Kates 1985). Chambers (1989) elaborated this notion by describing vulnerability as "the exposure to contingencies and stress, and the difficulty in coping with them." Building on Cutter (1996), table 7.1 arrays the numerous meanings that have been attached to the concept of vulnerability. Here we define vulnerability simply *as the degree to which a system or unit (such as a human group or a place) is likely to experience harm due to exposure to perturbations or stresses.* It is apparent from relating the notion of vulnerability to a basic structural model of hazard that three major dimensions of vulnerability are involved in the evolution of hazard, as shown in table 7.1.

- *exposure* to stresses, perturbations, and shocks;
- *sensitivity*, of people, places, and ecosystems, to the stress or perturbation, including their capacity to anticipate and cope with the stress; and
- *resilience* of the exposed people, places, and ecosystems, that is, their ability to *recover* from the stress and to *buffer* themselves against and *adapt* to future stresses and perturbations

These dimensions also suggest the types of indicators needed to develop maps of vulnerability or "hotspots." Box 7.1 provides definitions of key concepts relevant to the discussions that follow in this chapter.

Foundational Theory: Sen, Holling, and Chambers

Although the vulnerability literature encompasses a diverse collection of writing and contributors, it also exhibits a remarkable degree of commonality among a few basic concepts and approaches (Adger 2006; Eakin and Luers 2006). This commonality arises from the influential work of the economist Amartya Sen, the ecologist C. S. Holling, and the developmental theorist Robert Chambers. It is important, therefore, to review briefly these ideas before distinguishing among the major existing conceptual approaches to vulnerability.

Amartya Sen and Entitlement Theory

"Why hunger?" Sen asks. Given the enormous expanse of productive power in agriculture, he notes, it is certainly possible to guarantee adequate food for all, and yet chronic hunger and severe famine persist. In 1977, Sen debuted his theory of *entitlements*, which he elaborated shortly thereafter in *Poverty and Famines* (Sen 1981). Put succinctly, the work is a deep analysis of the crucial roles of human endowment and exchange entitlements. Sen defines entitlements as "the set of alternative commodity bundles that a person can command in a society using the totality of rights and opportunities that he or she faces" (Sen 1983, 754). He ascribed the causal roots of entitlement failures as far removed from food production, residing instead in the social and economic system that governs the rights of people to exercise command over food and other necessities of life.

Sen contends that famine can occur without any loss in food availability (although often a reduction in food availability coalesces with entitlements failure, leading to famine conditions). In his view, access to food (food entitlement) arises from the ability to command it through legal and customary means. This theory of entitlement includes production of one's own resources, as well as exchanges and transfers through labor and markets in an exchange economy. According to Sen (1977), in an exchange economy, whether a family will starve depends on its *endowments*—what it has to sell (products, labor)—and its *entitlements*—whether it can sell what it has (opportunities for exchange), and at what prices (what the market will bear). The risk of starvation also depends on how much a family has to pay for food compared with its endowments. Thus, aspects of the exchange economy create family-specific abilities or lack of them (based on endowments), as well as externalities to which a family must respond (the price it must pay for food). Together, these elements create a "space" of famine vulnerability within which a household may find itself.

Exchange "entitlements" depend not merely on the relevant exchange rates but also on market imperfections and other institutional barriers and on the actual ability to sell or buy the commodities in question (Sen 1981). It is important to note that exchange entitlements depend on various institutional arrangements, in any given social or economic system, that affect people's command over commodities. Such institutional arrangements are based on rules governing "the rights that people...have to exercise command over food and other necessities" (Sen 1981, 375). The importance of exchange entitlements lies in their involvement at critical points in the chain of famine causation. In this sense, Sen's entitlement theory provides a structure for analyzing

Table 7.1
Selected definitions of vulnerability

Gabor and Griffith 1980
Vulnerability is the threat (from hazardous materials) to which people are exposed (including chemical agents and the ecological situation of the communities and their level of emergency preparedness). Vulnerability is the risk context.

Timmerman 1981
Vulnerability is the degree to which a system acts adversely to the occurrence of a hazardous event. The degree and quality of the adverse reaction are conditioned by a system's resilience (a measure of the system's capacity to absorb and recover from the event).

UNDRO 1982
Vulnerability is the degree of loss to a given element or set of elements at risk resulting from the occurrence of a natural phenomenon of a given magnitude.

Susman, O'Keefe, and Wisner 1983
Vulnerability is the degree to which different classes of society are differentially at risk.

Kates 1985
Vulnerability is the capacity to suffer harm and react adversely.

Pijawka and Radwan 1985
Vulnerability is the threat or interaction between risk and preparedness. It is the degree to which hazardous materials threaten a particular population (risk) and the capacity of the community to reduce the risk or adverse consequences of hazardous materials releases.

Bogard 1989
Vulnerability is operationally defined as the inability to take effective measures to insure against losses. When applied to individuals vulnerability is a consequence of the impossibility or improbability of effective mitigation and is a function of our ability to detect the hazards.

Chambers 1989
Vulnerability refers to exposure to contingencies and stress, and difficulty in coping with them. Vulnerability has thus two sides: an external side of risks, shocks, and stress to which an individual or household is subject; and an internal side which is defenselessness, meaning a lack of means to cope without damaging loss.

Mitchell 1989
Vulnerability is the potential for loss.

Liverman 1990
Distinguishes between vulnerability as a biophysical condition and vulnerability as defined by political, social and economic conditions of society...vulnerability is defined both in geographic space (where vulnerable people and places are located) and in social space (who in that place is vulnerable).

Table 7.1
(continued)

Downing 1991b
Vulnerability has three connotations: it refers to a consequence (e.g., famine) rather than a cause (e.g., drought); it implies an adverse consequence; and it is a relative term that differentiates among socioeconomic groups or regions, rather than an absolute measure of deprivation.

Dow 1992
Vulnerability is the differential capacity of groups and individuals to deal with hazards based on their positions within physical and social worlds.

Smith 1992
Risk from a specific hazard varies through time and according to changes in either (or both) physical exposure or human vulnerability (the breadth of social and economic tolerance available at the same site).

Alexander 1993
Human vulnerability is a function of the costs and benefits of inhabiting areas at risk from natural disaster.

Cutter 1993
Vulnerability is the likelihood that an individual or group will be exposed to and adversely affected by a hazard. It is the interaction of the hazards of place (risk and mitigation) with the social profile of communities.

Watts and Bohle 1993
Vulnerability is defined in terms of exposure, capacity, and potentiality. Accordingly, the prescriptive and normative response to vulnerability is to reduce exposure, enhance coping capacity, strengthen recovery potential, and bolster damage control (i.e., minimize destructive consequences) via private and public means.

Blaikie et al. 1994
By vulnerability we mean the characteristics of a person or group in terms of their capacity to anticipate, cope with, resist and recover from the impact of a natural hazard. It involves a combination of factors that determine the degree to which someone's life and livelihood are put at risk by a discrete and identifiable event in nature or in society.

Bohle, Downing, and Watts 1994
Vulnerability is best described as an aggregate measure of human welfare that integrates environmental, social, economic, and political exposure to a range of potential harmful perturbations. Vulnerability is a multilayered and multidimensional social space defined by the determinate, political, economic, and institutional capabilities of people in specific places at specific times.

Cannon 1994
Vulnerability is a measure of the degree and type of exposure to risk generated by different societies in relation to hazards. Vulnerability is the characteristic of individuals and groups of people who inhabit a given natural, social, and economic space, within which they are differentiated according to their varying position in society into more or less vulnerable individuals and groups.

Table 7.1
(continued)

Dow and Downing 1995
Vulnerability is the differential susceptibility of circumstances contributing to vulnerability. Biophysical, demographic, economic, social, and technological factors such as population ages, economic dependency, racism, and age of infrastructure are some factors which have been examined in association with natural hazards.

Cutter 1996
Vulnerability is conceived as both a biophysical risk as well as a social response, but with a specific areal or geographic domain. This can be geographic space, where vulnerable people and places are located, or social space—who in those places is most vulnerable.

Vogel 1998
Vulnerability is perhaps best defined in terms of resilience and susceptibility including such dimensions as physical, social, cultural, and psychological vulnerability and capacities that are usually viewed against the backdrop of gender, time, space, and scale.

IFRC 1999a
Vulnerability can be defined as: The characteristics of a person or group in terms of their capacity to anticipate, cope with, resist, and recover from the impact of a natural or man-made hazards.

UNEP 1999
Vulnerability is a function of sensitivity to present climatic variability, the risk of adverse future climate change and capacity to adapt....The extent to which climate change may damage or harm a system; vulnerability is a function of not only the system's sensitivity, but also its ability to adapt to new climatic conditions.

Adger 2000
Individual and collective vulnerability and public policy determine the social vulnerability to hazards and environmental risks, defined here as the presence or lack of ability to withstand shocks and stresses to livelihood.

Cutter, Mitchell, and Scott 2000
Broadly defined, vulnerability is the potential for loss of property or life from environmental hazards.

IPCC 2001
Vulnerability is defined as the extent to which a natural or social system is susceptible to sustaining damage from climate change. Vulnerability is a function of the sensitivity of a system to changes in climate and the ability to adapt the system to changes in climate. Under this framework, a highly vulnerable system would be one that is highly sensitive to modest changes in climate.

IPCC 2007
The degree to which systems are susceptible to, and unable to cope with, adverse impacts (Schneider et al. 2007, 781).

Source: Adapted and updated from Cutter 1996, 531–532.

Box 7.1
Definitions

---

vulnerability   the degree to which a person, system or unit is likely to experience harm due to exposure to perturbations or stresses.

exposure   the contact between a system and a perturbation or stress.

sensitivity   the extent to which a system or its components is likely to experience harm, and the magnitude of that harm, due to exposure to perturbations or stresses.

resilience   the ability of a system to absorb perturbations or stresses without changes in its fundamental structure or function that would drive the system into a different state (or extinction).

stress   cumulating pressure on a system resulting from processes within the normal range of variability, but which over time may result in disturbances causing the system to adjust, adapt, or be harmed.

perturbation   a disturbance to a system resulting from a sudden shock with a magnitude outside the normal vulnerability.

adjustment   a system response to perturbations or stress that does not fundamentally alter the system itself. Adjustments are commonly (but not necessarily) short-term and involve relatively minor system modifications.

adaptation   a system response to perturbations or stress that is sufficiently fundamental to alter the system itself, sometimes shifting the system to a new state.

hazard   the threat of a stress or perturbation to a system and what it values.

risk   the conditional probability and magnitude of harm attendant on exposure to a perturbation or stress.

---

famines rather than presenting a particular theory of "ultimate" explanation.

Entitlements represent the set of alternative commodity bundles that a person can command in a society using the totality of rights and opportunities that he or she faces. The rights and opportunities, including what one owns and what one earns, Sen terms "endowments." In Sen's theoretical framework, endowments serve to create entitlements that broaden one's power over commodities. Entitlement mapping is a key way to outline and understand the relation between endowments and entitlements. It provides an analytical schema of how entitlements arise from endowments, and moreover, how such entitlements reside at critical points in the chain of famine causation or avoidance.

Entitlement theory provides a powerful entry into the ways in which social relations, economic systems, and individuals create disasters out of moderately risky situations. The structures within economic systems, institutions, and society more generally become a primary tool to explain why certain people—and not others—experience disasters in particular areas at particular times. Entitlement theory also suggests that much of vulnerability is socially controllable. In other words, coping methods and responses to perturbations are often more instrumental in determining the eventual toll of the disaster than is the magnitude of the perturbation.

Various researchers have extended or expanded Sen's theory. Leach, Mearns, and Scoones (1999), for example, consider Sen's original theory too restrictive since it focuses primarily on the command over resources derived through market channels, reinforced by formal legal property rights. Instead, they argue, many ways of gaining access to and control over resources exist beyond the market, and many ways of legitimating such access and control reside outside of formal legal institutional mechanisms (Gore 1993). Furthermore, these routes of access and control can be more important influences on entitlements than the formal legal institutions that serve to dampen or magnify the vulnerability of different people at various times. Accordingly, Leach, Mearns, and Scoones (1999) extend Sen's entitlement analysis to emphasize the role of social institutions in mediating environment-society relationships at various scales. They argue that a set of interacting and overlapping institutions, both formal and informal, which are embedded in the political and social life of an area, mediate access to and control over resources. In this context, social institutions act as social contracts and relationships, including government and legal institutions, informal social relations, and kinship networks.

C. S. Holling and Resilience

Theoretical and empirical ecology has inherited much from classical physics and, according to Holling (1978); this legacy has created the tendency to focus on constancy in defining and understanding ecological systems. Ecosystem stability has often been assumed and change has had to be explained (van der Leeuw 2000). Holling (1986) maintains that we can better understand ecosystems if we shift the emphasis toward assuming change and then try to explain stability. He argues that ecosystems continually confront the unexpected, so that the constancy of the system's behavior or condition state is less important than the persistence of the relationships that define the system. Consequently, Holling's theory of ecological resilience focuses on the existence of those relationships. As he puts it, there are two sciences—the science of parts where analysis centers on specific processes that affect specific variables, and the science of the integration of parts (Holling 1996a). Individuals die, populations disappear, and species become extinct, but ecosystems endure only if relationships among ecosystem elements—both biotic and abiotic—persist. With the concept of dynamic stability and resilience theory, he sees sets of disturbances at different temporal and spatial scales not as problems but as an integral part of the development and dynamics of ecosystems. Disturbances open up opportunities for ecosystem renewal and reorganization, development, and evolution (Holling 1996b).

Ecosystem resilience—the capacity to buffer or absorb disturbance—is fundamentally important because it makes possible system reorganization after disturbance (Nyström and Folke 2001). Because the ability of ecosystems to reorganize after disturbance allows them to continue providing life-support services to humans and other species, resilience is the key to sustaining the flow of life-support services, even as ecosystems evolve and change (Folke, Colding, and Berkes 2003).

Resilience is predicated on redundancy and the overlap of function in systems. Resilience refers to the size of the valley, or basin of attraction, around a state, which corresponds to the maximum perturbation that can be taken without causing a shift to an alternative stable state (Scheffer et al. 2001, 591). Simplification of ecosystems can cause a loss of resilience. Human-dominated ecosystems, which now make up a large part of the earth, tend to be simpler and are often more efficient at producing goods. Consequently, however, they are also likely to be less resilient than nonhuman-dominated systems. Loss of resilience increases the likelihood of ecosystems shifting into entirely different states (Jackson et al. 2001; Nyström, Folke, and Moberg 2000). Abrupt shifts among very different stable domains are plausible in regional ecosystems (Schröter et al. 2005).

Human-dominated systems may reduce resilience because such systems are invariably managed to suppress, circumvent, or remove many natural disturbances, while foreign disturbances are introduced. Paine, Tegner, and Johnson (1998) have termed these fundamental changes in disturbance regimes "compounded perturbations." Management of human-environment systems for efficiency with elemental changes in disturbance regimes could lead to greater surprise and shocks, and potentially even interruption of life-support services (Fraser 2007). Indeed, Holling stresses the inherent unknowability and unpredictability to sustaining the foundations for functioning systems of people and nature (Holling 1996a, b, 1997).

In Holling's world of oscillating and ever-changing systems, the notion of *resilience* to perturbations is a key determinant of the persistence of systems. Resilience determines the persistence of relationships within a system and is a measure of a system's ability to absorb perturbations before the system changes its structure (Holling and Meffe 1996, 330). In this definition, resilience is a property of the system, and a system's persistence (versus its probability of extinction) is the outcome of its resilience. The "golden rule" of natural resource management is to strive to retain critical types and ranges of natural variation in ecosystems (rather than reducing or controlling such variation; Holling and Meffe 1996, 334).

The Gunderson and Holling (2002) volume *Panarchy* has summarized and synthesized the rich work of the Resilience Alliance, a network of collaborating scientists (http://www.resalliance.org). In particular it documents key conclusions from 120 scientific papers, probing the structure in which systems of nature and humans are interlinked in never-ending adaptive cycles of growth, accumulation, structure, and renewal. In those conceptions, fast cycles invent, experiment, and test, the slower cycles stabilize and conserve accumulated memory of past successful, surviving experiments. In a healthy system, each level is allowed to operate at its own pace, protected from above by slower, larger levels, of change invigorated from below by faster, smaller cycles of innovation.

Holling's theory of resilience has been highly influential in vulnerability studies in the human and ecological sciences (e.g., Adger 2006; Eakin and Luers 2006; Fraser 2007), but, unfortunately, few efforts in the vulnerability stream of work have fully exploited the detail, nuances, and more recent developments of the theory. Although the term *resilience* is now routinely used to describe the capacity of people and societies to cope with and recover from impacts, ideas of stability versus resiliency, brittleness, coevolution of society and ecology, reorganization, and renewal—all central concepts in resilience theory—still await full incorporation by vulnerability analysts outside the Resilience Alliance. Yet clearly this work is a strong motive force toward integrated ecological-social analyses, as we will discuss.

Robert Chambers: Coping Strategies, Empowerment, and Development
Robert Chambers, a development theorist, has written perceptively on issues of vulnerability in a development context and particularly enriched the analysis of coping and adaptability. Distinguishing between poverty and vulnerability, Chambers characterizes vulnerability as "defenceless-ness, insecurity, and exposure to risk, shocks and stress." Accordingly, in his oft-cited view, vulnerability has two sides: "an external side of risks, shocks, and stress to which an individual or household is subject; and an internal side which is defencelessness, meaning a lack of means to cope without damaging loss" (Chambers 1989, 1; also Bohle 2001). He also takes a broad view of such losses, including their cumulative nature, as entailing becoming physically weaker, economically impover-ished, socially dependent, humiliated, or psychologically harmed.

Chambers (1997) also emphasized that participatory assessment approaches enable the vulnerable to express their multiple realities, and thus extends his analysis into constructivist thinking (see Oliver-Smith 1996; Tansey and O'Riordan 1999). As these realities are local, complex, diverse, dynamic, and unpredictable, the participatory approach uses multiple, subjective indicators of poverty status that emerge out of the experience of the poor, collected through participatory techniques. Such considerations have been extended to the coproduction of knowledge and translation between science, policy, and local stakeholders (Reynolds et al. 2007; Vogel and O'Brien 2006). Chambers argues that participa-tory assessment methods seek to empower the vulnerable—women, minorities, the poor, the weak, and the disadvantaged—to enact reversals in who has power. As such, participatory research methods offer a better means for assessing poverty and capturing what people themselves iden-tify as its principal dimensions and indicators. Moreover, they help to identify what the poor have rather than what they do not have, and in so doing focus on their assets, including tangible assets such as labor and human capital, productive assets such as housing, and largely invisible intangible assets such as household relations and social capital. To reduce vulnerability, people can make certain substitutions among different assets. For example, households that keep children in school rather than send them out to work are poorer in income terms; however, in the longer term, their strategy can reduce vulnerability through consolidating human capital as an asset.

The main issue here is that large stocks of one kind of asset may be of little use; the more assets people command in the "right mix," the greater their capacity to buffer themselves against external shocks (see also Bebbington 1999 and Moser 1998). Chambers (1997) also distinguishes three different types of agriculture worldwide, each of which has a different vulnerability to global environmental change. The three are: "first agriculture" (with high technology inputs in industrialized countries), "second agriculture" (the Green Revolution areas) in developing countries, and "third agriculture" (with low mechanization but crucially important to the poor) in the South. The latter, which includes most of the poorest and most food-insecure people of the world, is, Chambers argues, the critical group for mounting attacks on global patterns of vulnerability.

Chambers also accords particular attention to the diversity of vulnerabilities and coping strategies of the poor. Contrary to popular misconception, he sees such strategies as complex, diverse, and activist in the face of threat. Most poor people, he argues, do not put their eggs in one basket but act to reduce risks, to increase their adaptability, and to seek greater autonomy, a line of argument, it might be noted, that is prevalent in the literature on pastoral nomadism (Johnson and Lewis 1995). Like hazard theorists, he sees the essence of such coping as creating and maintaining wider options, particularly through the willingness and ability of household members "to do different things in different places at different times" (Chambers 1989, 2). Generally, poor people use complex investment strategies in coping pools, seek to diversify their portfolios of assets to handle better varying contingencies and bad times and, over time, strive to minimize irreversible losses. All the same, as Chambers notes, external interventions during crises often come too late, after poor people have become poorer by disposing of productive assets or taking on debts or obligations that threaten the security of their livelihoods.

Noting the lack of a developed theory and accepted indicators and methods of measuring vulnerability, Chambers (1989, 6) set out key research needs to guide vulnerability work:

• developing "simple and sure" methods for enabling vulnerable people to analyze their conditions and identify priorities;
• developing and testing indicators of vulnerability;
• assessing the modes, costs, and benefits of reducing vulnerability and preventing impoverishment, as compared with recovery actions;
• assessing and comparing coping strategies under stress, including sequences of response, thresholds of different types of responses, and the value and use of different assets;

• examining the effects of civil disorder on vulnerability and coping strategies, including effects on economy and household strategies;
• evaluating relief and development policies, including ways of strengthening people's current coping strategies; and delineating the effects on adult disability and death on household viability, strategies, and behavior.

This priority list has lost none of its relevance over time and still demarcates essential lines of inquiry for advancing our understanding of vulnerability, and particularly coping under stress.

Conceptual Approaches

Analyses of vulnerability reflect differing approaches, ranging from those narrowly based in ecology, to others centered on vulnerability as a component of hazards, to yet others that see vulnerability primarily as an expression of political economy. These largely divergent perspectives on vulnerability have yielded a highly fragmented literature, unduly vitriolic disciplinary and ideological debate, and sparse empirical testing and application of the competing frameworks. Only recently has movement to bridge these differences become apparent, particularly in the work of the Resilience Alliance (Berkes and Folke 1998; Folke, Colding, and Berkes 2003; Gunderson, Holling, and Light 1995), but also extending beyond it (Adger 2006; Eakin and Luers 2006; Turner et al. 2003a). Here we survey the major conceptual approaches to vulnerability that have emerged over time and their salient elements (for thoughtful alternative treatments, see Birkmann 2006 and McLaughlin and Dietz 2008).

Hazard and Risk Analysis
The creation of a field of systematic hazard analysis is a phenomenon of only the past fifty years; prior to that, individual dangers and disasters were examined and probed but comparative analyses and formal methods of analysis were few. Gilbert F. White's *Human Adjustment to Floods* (White 1945) was a particular benchmark in stimulating subsequent work, owing to its careful analysis of the growing toll of floods in the United States and its concern for examining the range of human behavior and coping exercised in managing risks. Not until several decades later, however, did White (1961) develop a broader conceptual approach aimed at enlarging the array of coping measures used in efforts to reduce the toll of natural hazards upon society.

Stimulated by White's early work, extensive research on natural hazards during the 1960s and 1970s created a set of concepts and formats for analyzing natural hazards and human responses to them (White 1974; White and Haas 1975). The basic construct is that human-nature interactions produce both resources and hazards. The critical agent is human-induced change, which transforms nature into beneficial and threatening outcomes. Interactions lead to disasters when hazards are extreme in magnitude, exposed populations are large, and the human-use system is particularly vulnerable. This recognition that hazard is a joint product of events (or perturbations), degree of exposure, and what now would be called sensitivity or susceptibility is a construct still very current, and which the IPCC efforts took many years to recognize. The approach to vulnerability in this early work on natural hazards failed to provide an in-depth conceptualization of vulnerability, but it did offer an extended treatment of coping, termed *adaptive capacity* (a combination of resistance and adaptive capacity), and social resilience was also very much part of the analysis (Burton, Kates, and White 1978, 1993). Social resilience, for its part, was seen as a mix of coping measures—individual and collective, incidental and purposeful—and adjustments and adaptations that make up society's interaction with the flow of hazards that confronts society. This work remains valuable for its formats for assessing human behavior around coping actions and its attention to broadening the range of human choice in hazard management. What the body of work missed substantially was the social, economic, and political structures that shape patterns of human vulnerability and constrain choice, issues taken up by the political economy school that focused on social vulnerability (to be discussed) and its roots in political and economic structures (e.g., Hewitt 1983).

The several decades since the first edition of *The Environment as Hazard* have witnessed the evolution of a diverse body of theory and empirical analysis treating environmental and technological risk. Some of this work has probed aspects of vulnerability in great depth, such as the landmark assessment of differential susceptibility of humans to chemicals by Calabrese (1978), the role of organizational structure and technological complexity in the proneness of certain industrial systems to catastrophic failure (Perrow 1984, 1999), the insecurity of energy systems to economic and political change (Khatib 2000; UCS 2002), the vulnerability of critical societal infrastructure to catastrophic natural events and terrorism (Haimes 1990, 1998), and the obstacles facing communities in long-term recovery from industrial disasters (Erikson 1994; Mitchell 1996, 2000). Although not specifically focused on vulnerability, diverse theoretical work in hazards research provides important entry points into the cultural, social, and political processes operating in society's encounters with environmental change. Cultural theory (van Asselt and Rotmans 1995; Douglas and Wildavsky 1982; Thompson, Ellis, and Wildavsky 1990; Tansey and O'Riordan 1999), for example, offers a broad interpretation into how cultural biases enter into the types of hazards that are addressed and the types of coping and management systems that are employed. The "social amplification of risk" (Kasperson et al. 1988; Pidgeon, Kasperson, and Slovic 2003) provides a conceptual framework for examining the social and political processes by which different societies process threats and risks, allowing some (and their impacted peoples or ecosystems) to grow while assiduously reducing others, and a large body of empirical work now is available documenting these "amplification" and "attenuation" processes. Social processes generating "hidden hazards" and vulnerable groups concealed from society's scrutiny and action have also been delineated (Kasperson and Kasperson 1991). Gender issues associated with differential public concern and response to risk have been documented (Flynn, Slovic, and Mertz 1994), and broader social theory probing the splintering of societies and the world economy into risk winners and risk losers and a dynamic leading to ever-increasing environmental degradation in the risk society set forth (Beck 1992, 1995, 1999, 2000).

If hazard research was the focus of the first generation of natural-hazards studies, critical theory and political ecology have received much attention over the past two decades, and it is to this perspective we now turn.

From Critical Theory to Political Ecology

Vulnerability would appear to be a logical outgrowth of natural hazards approached through the lens of Marxian and, more broadly, critical approaches. Their intricacies and complexities notwithstanding, critical approaches are predicated on various assumptions that emphasize the socioeconomic structures that control individual and group action and that captured attention in early studies on natural hazards. Thus natural hazards are to be understood in terms of the social conditions (political economy) that place people in harm's way (e.g., living on hillsides that are prone to landslides) and that reduce their coping capacity for managing the hazard (Hewitt 1983). In this sense, natural hazards (environmental perturbations and stressors) are a social construction in which different social units are differentially "placed in harm's way" and have differential coping capacities. These approaches are grounded in the belief that no individual or group would voluntarily choose a more hazardous or risk-prone setting, and do so only when other options are unavailable, or in some cases, when social safety nets that provide a buffer to the risks taken disappear (e.g., insurance against floods). The more marginal economically and weaker politically, and the fewer the options, the more likely is the environment to be hazardous, and the greater are the difficulties in coping with stresses and perturbations (e.g., Wisner 1988, 1993a, b; Wisner et al. 2004). Following this logic, vulnerability, or at least the vulnerability that warrants social concern, is linked to economic and political impoverishment, and so the research lens focuses on social units that are impoverished and what makes them this way (Waddell 1983; Watts 1983; Watts and Bohle 1993; Wisner et al. 2004).

The sources of impoverishments occur largely within the relations that a social unit maintains with other units, and tracing these relations may lead well beyond the geographical location of an impoverished group (e.g., Wisner et al. 2004). Thus critical approaches seek causal chains or networks of causes, often historical in nature, that more often than not lead to causes that are geographically exogenous to the social unit and linked to it through layers of connections that obfuscate the connectivity (Blaikie and Brookfield 1987). For example, in south-central Mali, increased vulnerability of villages to catastrophic fires follows from state-directed fire policies that are, in turn, a response to international concerns about the deforestation and "desertification" of the Sahelian fringe that find their way into various international accords and, ultimately, the conditions for international loans to the country in question (Laris 2002). For much of the economically "have-not" world, these relations are traceable to colonialism and are redirected and amplified under "globalization."

These kinds of orientations in vulnerability work join those on land change, sustainability, environmental justice, indigenous knowledge and rights, and feminist concerns under the heading of "political ecology" (Blaikie and Brookfield 1987), an interdisciplinary field directed to human-environment relationships following a loose "structural" approach whose followers in the academic community share a common suspicion of what they term "mainstream" theoretical approaches (Turner 1991). Vulnerability studies make up a prominent subset of research in this field (Blaikie et al. 1994; Dow and Downing 1995; Ribot 1995; Vogel 1998, 2001; Wisner 1993b). The name of the subfield notwithstanding, the intellectual origins of this line of vulnerability studies shape its questions and focus its analysis primarily on "social vulnerability" (Ribot 1995, 1996). Rarely does this approach address ecological or environmental vulnerability independent of its resource implications for the human occupants, despite complementary work on environmental entitlements (Leach, Mearns, and Scoones 1999). Even food insecurity and malnutrition associated with climate change are driven as much by nonfood factors as the effects of climate change on food (Brown and Funk 2008).

Bohle's revised framework (Bohle 2001; see also Watts and Bohle 1993) illuminates these characteristics. For Bohle, three main approaches—internal-external, coping assets, and conflict-crisis—are central for understanding vulnerability. This last approach, of course, epitomizes critical and Marxian perspectives. Bohle (2001) credits Chambers (1989) and Giddens (1996) with enlarging vulnerability studies in political ecology beyond external and structural considerations to include internal and agent-based ones (but does not access the extensive literature outside political ecology on these themes). Likewise, vulnerability assessment is rich in treating coping capacity, although an in-depth conceptualization awaited Sen's entitlement theory (Drèze and Sen 1989; Sen 1981, 1990), which is consistent with the base precepts of political ecologists in its emphasis on the role of social structures in defining entitlements (Ribot 1995; Watts and Bohle 1993). These issues notwithstanding, the work by Bohle (2001) reworks the three-pronged configuration of vulnerability—entitlements, empowerment, and political economy—provided by Watts and Bohle (1993) into a more integrative approach, as discussed in the next section. The focus of the political-economy/political-ecology school, however, remains strongly aimed at vulnerability of the social unit (e.g., Blaikie et al. 1994; Bohle, Downing, and Watts 1994; Ribot 1995; Adger 1999), and it is not clear where critical theory/political ecology approaches rest in regard to coupled human-environment systems or ecological systems absent human considerations. Further, the more reductionist interpretations of political economy can undervalue the role of human agency and culture as well (Lobao and Meyer 2001; Pelling 2003a; McLaughlin and Dietz 2008).

Integrative Analysis

An encouraging sign in vulnerability research and assessment is the gradual emergence of more integrative approaches. Bohle (2001), drawing upon an impressive array of research by his graduate students over a decade, has proposed a research strategy that structures analysis, following Chambers, to focus on both the "external" and "internal" dimensions of vulnerability. The work of Downing (Downing 1991a, b; Bohle, Downing, and Watts 1994) stands out for the high degree of integration it achieves across ideological and theoretical perspectives. In addition, analyses have increasingly sought to bridge the divide between ecological and social analysis and to suggest more integrative pathways for assessing vulnerability. Here we note in brief several of the more prominent of these.

Bohle (2001) has set forth a template—less than a model—that covers both external and internal dimensions of vulnerability, and the interactions between them (figure 7.1). The first theoretical strand focuses upon the interactions between "structure" and "agency," with the question still open as to the explanatory power of each. A second strand focuses on the assets people control that allow them to buffer themselves from stresses and perturbations. Such control presumably is closely linked with the political economy of the region and the ways in which various populations are "embedded" in the basic structures and dynamics of economy and polity. The third strand—crisis and conflict theory—treats tensions over risk and criticality and seeks to solve conflicts in coping actions. This approach takes important strides to identify and illuminate the social-structural component of vulnerability but accords less attention to the human component and largely externalizes the environment (WBGU/GACGC 2000, 184).

In *Regions at Risk: Comparisons of Threatened Environments* (Kasperson, Kasperson, and Turner 1995), an interdisciplinary group of natural and social scientists examines the trajectories of nine regions around the world in regard to vulnerability and degradation. Eschewing a geocentric or anthropocentric view of environmental change, the authors center their analysis on environmental change over the past 50-to-100-year period, in each region linking the broad human drivers of environmental change and natural variability to the human and ecological outcomes they produce. These outcomes are qualitatively classified into levels of endangerment or "criticality." Disaggregated analyses are then used to

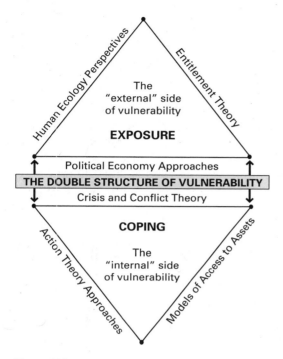

Figure 7.1
A conceptual model for analyzing vulnerability.
Source: Bohle 2001, 4.

identify the socioeconomic regional dynamics of change, ranging from social polarization, to exploitation of peripheries (marginalization), to "trickle-down" processes. Substantial attention is given to contextual effects and what the authors term "a rich tapestry of human causation." Ample evidence is offered of the differential speeds of ecological change and human response systems, propelling many of these systems toward trajectories of overshoot. Differential vulnerability is heavily implicated in the nature of human driving forces and the structure and effectiveness of human response systems.

The authors conclude that environmental "criticality" is a function of the speed and intensity of environmental degradation, the vulnerability of people and ecosystems affected, and coping capacities and resilience. They also conclude that environmental criticality emerges historically through a series of stages in which the decisive attributes are the regenerative capacities of affected ecosystems and the buffering and mitigative costs incurred by affected societies. They assign particular importance to the speed of progression through these stages and the extent to which nonlinearities, punctuated surprises, and threshold effects are present.

A highly ambitious analysis that internalizes vulnerability into a broader set of dynamics, linking stresses and effects across ecological and social science domains, is the work on *syndromes of global change* undertaken at the Potsdam Institute for Climate Impact Research (http:// www.pik_potsdam.de; Petschel-Held et al. 1999; Schnellnhuber et al. 1997; WBGU/GACGC 2000, 176–185). This approach to understanding global change seeks to be interdisciplinary, comprehensive, and integrative. The basic intent is to describe global change by assessing "archetypical, dynamic, coevolution patterns of civilization-nature interactions," termed *syndromes* (Schnellnhuber et al. 1997, 23; Lädeke, Petschel-Held, and Schellenburger 2004). These patterns represent different subdynamics of global change, which are modeled by the use of qualitative differential equations. The syndromes exhibit various *symptoms*, those qualities of global change that figure prominently in the ongoing problematic developments worldwide both in the natural environment and in society. Some eighty symptoms (e.g., urban sprawl, growing significance of NGOs, terrestrial run-off, increasing mobility) make up sixteen syndromes (box 7.2). A major goal is to detect geographical patchworks that sufficiently characterize syndromes on a global scale. The early analyses suggest promise not only for interrelating stresses, dynamics, and effects, but also for suggesting how key vulnerabilities enter. To reach the syndrome level, however, requires significant aggregation of highly complex components and processes operating in diverse ways. A critical issue for this approach is inherent in all global aggregation: how to reconcile generic properties or propositions with sufficient specificity so that they hold true at the regional scale. The names of the syndromes refer to functional patterns or characteristic features. These patterns of nonsustainable development can be grouped according to basic human use (and misuse) of nature: as a source for production, as a medium for socioeconomic development, as a sink for civilizational outputs.

A nearly decadal effort of work by ecological and social scientists under the auspices of the Resilience Alliance has generated a significant body of integrated work focused on coupled social-ecological systems. Enlisting theories of resilience and the evolution of ecosystems, this

Box 7.2
Syndromes of global change

Utilization Syndromes	
Sahel Syndrome	Overuse of marginal land
Overexploitation Syndrome	Overexploitation of natural ecosystems
Rural Exodus Syndrome	Degradation through abandonment of traditional agricultural practices
Dust Bowl Syndrome	Nonsustainable agroindustrial use of soils and bodies of water
Katanga Syndrome	Degradation through depletion of non-renewable resources
Mass Tourism Syndrome	Development and destruction of nature for recreational ends
Scorched Earth Syndrome	Environmental destruction through war and military action
Development Syndromes	
Aral Sea Syndrome	Damage of landscapes as a result of large-scale projects
Green Revolution Syndrome	Degradation through the transfer and introduction of inappropriate farming methods
Asian Tiger Syndrome	Disregard for environmental standards in the course of rapid economic growth
Favela Syndrome	Socioecological degradation through uncontrolled urban growth
Urban Sprawl Syndrome	Destruction of landscapes through planned expansion of urban infra-structures
Disaster Syndrome	Singular anthropogenic environmental disasters with long-term impacts
Sink Syndromes	
Smokestack Syndrome	Environmental degradation through large-scale diffusion of long-lived substances
Waste Dumping Syndrome	Environmental degradation through controlled and uncontrolled disposal of waste
Contaminated Land Syndrome	Local contamination of environmental assets at industrial locations

Source: Schnellnhuber et al. 1997, 23.

group has constructed a model of system coevolution. This conceptual model and resilience theory together form the foundations of Holling's extended theory of "panarchy," a framework for understanding the coevolution of ecological and social systems (Gunderson and Holling 2002). This model envisions a nested set of adaptive cycles, arranged as a dynamic hierarchy in space and time, that provide the novelty and persistence required for the sustainability of both human and ecological systems. According to the concept of panarchy, an ecological community passes through four phases:

• the *conservation phase*, with its great connectedness, energy stored in biomass, and low leakage of nutrients;
• the *release phase*, when some dramatic event disturbs the consolidated biomass, foodweb, and nutrient cycles;
• the *reorganization phase*, which is the most formless, with free-floating nutrients, less trapped energy, and many open niches; and
• the *exploitation phase*, in which species that can exploit these opportunities invade and increase, and over time, lock in new foodwebs and nutrient cycles (Holling 1998, 33).

Figure 7.2 depicts a stylized representation of the four phases.

The exit from the cycle is the stage where the potential can leak away and where a flip into a less productive and less organized system is most likely. The model, furthermore, contributes to Holling's five paradigms of nature: *nature cornucopian, nature anarchic, nature balanced, nature resilient*, and *nature evolving* (Holling 1998, 34).

Members of the Resilience Alliance have drawn on studies that have explored alternative stability domains in different ecosystems, including lakes, coral reefs, woodlands, deserts, and oceans, to assess large shifts that are apparent, feedback mechanisms, the role of stochastic events, and implications for management strategies (Scheffer et al. 2001; Berkes, Colding, and Folke 2003; Walker and Salt 2006). Among the more important findings are that contrasts among states in ecosystems are usually due to a shift in dominance among organisms with different life forms, that stochastic events (outbreaks of pathogens, fires, or climate extremes) usually trigger state shifts, and that feedbacks that stabilize different states involve biological, physical, and chemical mechanisms. The authors infer a number of management implications. Since systems often lack early-warning signals of massive change, societal attention tends to focus on precipitating events rather than on underlying loss of

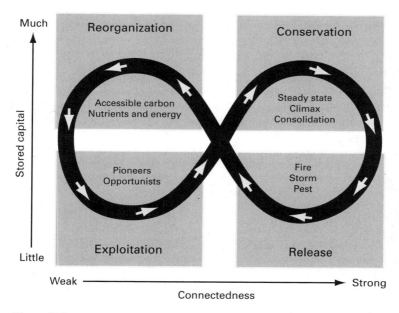

Figure 7.2
Schematic representation of panarchy.

resilience. But disturbance is a natural part of ecosystem change that promotes diversity and renewal processes. The authors conclude that management efforts to reduce unwanted state shifts need to focus much more on the slow and gradual changes (e.g., land use, nutrient stocks, soil processes, and the biomass of long-lived organisms) than on the more dramatic events (e.g., hurricanes, droughts, and disease outbreaks) that are inherently more difficult to predict or control.

Finally, it is worth noting the workshop of forty-four distinguished scientists convened in 2000 in Tempe, Arizona, in the United States to consider the needs and priorities for interdisciplinary environmental research. The results accorded particular attention to the issues surrounding the evolution and resilience of coupled social and ecological systems, and identified five principal research needs in this area: the evolution of social norms regarding the environment, past and future land-use change, feedback loops in social and ecological systems, disturbance and resilience in social and ecological systems, and developing coupled models of social and ecological systems (Kinzig et al. 2000, 18–22).

Structuring the Vulnerability Problem

Analyzing vulnerability entails confronting difficult issues in conceptualizing framing the vulnerability *problematique*. The literature abounds with treatments of a broad array of issues that fall into three main categories: exposure, sensitivity, and resilience. A series of key considerations must enter into the structuring of any sound vulnerability analysis. Here we identify the "essentials" of such an assessment. For a vulnerable alternative attempt, see Schröter, Polsky, and Platt (2005).

Choosing the Unit of Exposure

An initial decision involves selecting the exposure unit—who or what is at risk? (e.g., a social group, ecosystem, or place)—that is to be examined. In reality, many different entities may be at risk, so defining the purposes and scope of the analysis is a critical decision in structuring the vulnerability problem. If the problem is defined principally in terms of understanding the effects of a specific perturbation (e.g., climate change, economic downturn), selection among the wide array of affected systems and causal factors has already narrowed the scope of analysis to a single perturbation or set of perturbations. If the intent is to understand the vulnerability of a particular group, region, or ecosystem, then that unit or system can be the starting point but the analysis can be framed as a multistress or multiperturbation situation. A major pitfall lies in selecting the unit of exposure a priori, assuming that the social groups or ecosystems most at risk are known, and so the analysis ends up missing other highly vulnerable components or exposure units.

The work on the International Decade for Natural Disaster Reduction (Mileti 1999; UN 1988; USNRC 1991) and the IPCC assessments (Watson, Zinyowera, and Moss 1998) amply demonstrates that impact analyses have focused strongly on the vulnerability of natural systems, with some attention to economic implications. The Fourth Assessment, however, more seriously engaged human systems (Schneider et al. 2007). By contrast, environment-development approaches concentrated almost exclusively on "marginalized" human groups and the political economy involved in the "production" of "social vulnerability" (Blaikie et al. 1994), influencing particularly the World Food Programme (FIVMS 1999, 2000, 2001), the United Nations Environment Programme (UNEP 1999), and the United Nations Development Programme (UNDP 2000).

The effect of these different foci has been to drive a wedge between natural and social systems and to conduct segmentary analyses of what are in essence coupled human-environment systems. The major, and a highly noteworthy, exception to this trend has been the work of the Resilience Alliance, which starts with the essential hypotheses that resilience is important for both ecological systems and social institutions, that the well-being of both social and ecological systems is closely linked, and that resilience and flexibility are essential for forging capability to respond over time to surprises and crises (e.g., Berkes and Folke 1998; Gunderson and Holling 2002). The focus on coupled human-environment systems is only now beginning to attract wider attention but holds promise for more integrated assessments that unite rather than separate the work of social and ecological scientists (Kinzig et al. 2000).

Multiple Stresses/Multiple Vulnerabilities

Much of the past treatment of vulnerability has proceeded using established methods of environmental impact and natural hazards analysis in which the assessment begins with a particular developmental project (e.g., a new technology or facility) or a natural hazard event (e.g., a flood) and traces through the effects, positive and negative, likely to result. Accordingly, the analysis of vulnerability has largely been predicated upon a major type of perturbation or disturbance. Such structuring of the vulnerability analysis has occluded or concealed causal agents that are actually shaping the vulnerability of high-risk social groups, ecosystems, and places via multiple socioeconomic stresses and perturbations acting on the unit and the "normal" or "everyday" processes that are causing the unit to become more exposed to threats, more defenseless in dealing with the threats, and more prone to damage from the accumulating multiple stresses, perturbations, and shocks. Treating both human and natural hazards has been called the "double exposure" approach (O'Brien and Lubcheinko 2000), the challenge of which is now being further explored (e.g., Eakin 2006).

No matter what the unit of analysis, a complex of perturbations and stresses, both biophysical (e.g., climate change, sea-level rises) and socioeconomic and political (e.g., social inequalities, population increases, and civil strife), threatens the unit of exposure (Reid and Vogel 2006). An early example to capture such suites in a "multiple stress model of decision making" at the municipal level is available in Kasperson (1969). A more recent analysis of food security as a multiple-stress problem is available in Brown and Frank (2008). The suites of stresses and perturbations may interact, register their toll across differing exposure units, and call into play different types and levels of vulnerability (O'Brien et al. 2004). Moreover, the sequencing and temporal character of these suites of stresses shape the interactions and their ultimate impacts. At root, vulnerability assessment needs to grapple with the highly dynamic and interactive flow of multiple stresses and perturbations that can undergo analysis as complexes or constellations of threats. It is an imposing task for current assessment methodologies, which usually involve the typical divide-and-conquer procedures of the social sciences or risk analysis. In particular, a multiple-perturbation/multiple-vulnerability framing suggests that starting with the vulnerable people and systems and the outcomes to be avoided, working *backward* through major sources of vulnerability and *toward* suites of stresses may shed more, and perhaps different, light on vulnerability than the working-forward strategy of typical environmental impact assessment.

Cross-Scale Interactions

Much of the existing body of vulnerability research focuses on specific spatial and temporal scales of analysis (e.g., Füssel and Klein 2006), geared to the particular perturbation under study (e.g., impacts on agriculture in South Africa from a three-year El Niño Southern Oscillation [ENSO] event; Anyamba 1997) or to the availability of data on national-level "hotspots" (Brklacich and Leybourne 1999; Lonergan, Gustavson, and Carter 2000). Meanwhile, a significant dearth of information on effects at other scales presents a significant impediment to more sub-regional and localized analyses and applications (but see the local-global scale interactions in MEA 2005 and in Wilbanks and Kates 1999; Cash and Moser 2000). Cutter and Finch (2008) treat parts of the problem for social vulnerability to natural hazards in the United States.

The analyses in *Regions at Risk*, for example, found that in the shift from the global to small regional scales, the IPAT (Impacts = Population × Affluence × Technology) construct for explaining impacts gave way to a much richer and diverse set of explanatory variables, including multiple types of vulnerability and a greater role for technology (Ausubel 1996; Chertow 2001). Other studies of driving forces at finer local scales have found similar results (Angel et al. 1998; DeHart and Soulé 2000; Dietz and Rosa 1994; York, Rosa, and Dietz 2002), and Easterling (1997) has argued at length why regional-scale studies are essential. For political ecologists (Blaikie and Brookfield 1987, 27), the analysis often starts with the "land or resource managers" and follows the chain of causal connections that invariably leads to larger-scale drivers and processes (e.g., international timber companies operating through state agencies to create pressures on local land). The net effect of preselecting particular levels of scale, particular scale interactions, or particular "chains of explanation" is to assume away much of the potential richness of the operation of cross-scale dynamics in the production and amelioration of vulnerabilities. As Wilbanks and Kates (1999, 608) observe: "Where global change is concerned, it can be argued that a focus on a single scale tends to emphasize processes operating at that scale, information collected at that scale, and parties influential at that scale—raising the possibility of misunderstanding cause and effect by missing the relevance of processes that operate at a different scale." In short, the structuring of vulnerability analysis needs to take account of the dynamics of *cross-scale interactions*—those in which events or phenomena at one scale influence phenomena at other scales (Cash and Moser 2000; Cutter, Holm, and Clark 1996; Gibson, Ostrom, and Ahn 1998; Holling 1978, 1995; Turner et al. 1990; Wilbanks and Kates 1999).

Causal statements or "maps" of the sources of sensitivity and resilience invariably are predicated on phenomena at certain levels or scales or are typically focused on particular scale interactions (usually dyads). The crucial issue in linking scale to causal interpretations is identifying where the variables that explain a pattern or relationship are in fact located (rather than assumed) and whether they are fully captured in the scale chosen for the vulnerability analysis. And analysis needs to be sensitive to accelerated scale interactions, which, as Jodha (1995, 2001a, b) persuasively argues, are likely to distance resource users from the resource base, to disconnect production from consumption, and to separate the production of knowledge from its applications. Cash and Moser (2000, 113) suggest the use of hierarchy theory to capture scale issues in social-ecological interactions. Such theory views phenomena at a particular scale as the result of both the smaller/faster dynamics of system components at the next lower scale and the constraints imposed by the larger/ slower system dynamics at the next higher scale. Understanding cross-scale dynamics, they argue, requires simultaneously capturing *both* the driving and constraining forces at higher and lower scales.

Scale mismatches, such as the mismatch between the environmental system and the jurisdictional scope of the political authority, are a central issue in vulnerability analysis. Driving forces often emanate from macroforces, institutions, or policies set at higher-level scales—land tenure regimes, technological change, international financial institutions, and government policy—and are articulated through a finer pattern of local scales with highly variable local resource and ecological settings (Geoghegan et al. 1998; Pritchard et al. 1998). Political jurisdiction links to management by way of projects and hotspots, not via ecosystems or populations. Similarly, the time scale of political institutions stresses business cycles, electoral terms of office, and budget processes rather than spans of biological generation or ecosystem change (Lee 1993, 63). As a result, many environmental problems become exports to distant places (e.g., deforestation in Indonesia and the international timber trade) or to distant generations (e.g., the disposal of hazardous chemicals or radioactive materials). Moreover, the scope of political authority often matches poorly the scope of impacts and vulnerabilities, so that "transboundary" effects on vulnerable people and places are increasingly common (Linnerooth-Bayer, Löfstedt, and Sjöstedt 2001).

Internalizing such exports to the source and scale of problem generation is particularly difficult because vulnerable groups or groups controlling vulnerable ecosystems are commonly economically and politically marginalized. Meanwhile, the lack of cross-scale regimes and institutions encourages *policy pathologies* in which environmental and human systems proceed at difficult paces and at different scales, creating serious mismatches, and conflict, among ecosystems, social processes, and institutions (Cash and Moser 2000; Holling 1995).

Finally, a word about conjunctions that occur among processes that are operating at different time and spatial scales. Social-ecological systems have a cadence as they pass through seasonal, annual, and longer-term variability and fluctuations. They typically maintain rather different rhythms and patterns, but at certain critical times, conjunctions among processes occur and *windows of vulnerability* appear (Dow 1992, 432–433). Multiple stresses may then generate high-intensity perturbations and coincide with peaks of vulnerability, creating crises of damage and disturbance in the social-ecological system. Often these emerge as major "surprises" and as "shocks" to the institutions and managers of environmental systems (Brooks 1986; Kates and Clark 1996; Lawless 1977; Schneider, Turner, and Morehouse-Garriga 1998).

Endogenous Perturbations
Studies of natural hazards have mostly focused on the perturbations and stresses that develop outside the affected exposure unit or the

human-environment system, as in the case of tornadoes or drought (Cutter 1996; Glantz 1988; Wilhite 2000). Vulnerability assessment has maintained this emphasis inasmuch as the critical stressors identified operate in distant (distal) processes that play out in a particular locale (e.g., international factors drawing down local production systems; Blaikie and Brookfield 1987; Kasperson, Kasperson, and Turner 1995). Political-economic and entitlement perspectives that favor themes that locate the plight of the human system (environmental systems receive short shrift in this literature) on social structures beyond the influence of those affected have particularly influenced this direction of work. This emphasis has deflected attention away from those individual and societal actions that, no matter how limited, may exacerbate the perturbations and stressors, and even create new ones (Glantz 1988).

Endogenous stressors (Turner et al. 2003a) are those emanating within the coupled human-environment system that, with the help of exogenous forces, can accumulate to the tipping point of a perturbation. Salinization in the Tigris-Euphrates (Jacobsen and Adams 1958), deforestation in the Maya lowlands (Turner 2006) and on Easter Island (Acharya 1995), and the Great Plains Dust Bowl (Brooks et al. 2000, 74–77; Worster 1979), for example, are cases in which local land-use decisions apparently precipitated a "biteback" on the system. The environmental system, given sufficient time, often recovers (e.g., Maya lowlands; Turner 2006), but not without significant societal repercussions. Endogenous stressors may become less important as the human wealth of a coupled system provides substitutes for the drawdown of nature; new technologies reduce the impacts of effluents and wastes from high-consumption societies. Nevertheless, a full vulnerability treatment needs to treat endogenous linkages of potential perturbations and stressors.

Cumulative (Iterative) Vulnerability
These cadences and linkages over time and space suggest that vulnerability is better thought of and structured as an evolving set of processes than as a condition or state, or, as so often happens, a snapshot of an evolving process. Put slightly differently, vulnerability has its own history and its own trajectory, both of which must be understood. Rangasami (1985) has emphasized the problem in entitlement theory's depicting events when social groups collapse into starvation as "entitlement failures." She argues instead for viewing vulnerability in terms of long-term socioeconomic and political processes that conspire to

keep vulnerable members of the society prone to disaster when perturbations or accumulating stresses register their effects. Bohle, Downing,
and Watts (1994) have described the sequence of events involved in the
occurrence of a food crisis in which a concatenation of events combines
with structural vulnerability to produce an emergency or disaster. Building upon their portrayal of interacting forces, they depict vulnerability
as a sequential or iterative process in which shifting suites of stresses
intersect periodically with evolving vulnerability to draw down coping
resources and adaptive capacity at intervals of major perturbations,
making the social-ecological system increasingly prone to disaster over
time. The coping resources enlisted to recover from crisis events are
partially replenishable, through, for example, the changes in anticipatory behavior and adaptive strategies or through the acquisition (perhaps
across scale) of new entitlements, but the total stock of coping resources
in this case is also partially depleted. The production and amelioration
of vulnerability, through both "stores" of coping resources and through
social learning from experience, may be viewed as dynamic, uncertain,
and cumulative in nature.

But stresses are also multiple, complex, and cumulative. Consider the
case of chemicals in the environment. Some twenty thousand pesticide
products are typically on the market in the Toxic Substances Control
Act (TSCA) inventory in the United States. In addition, some eighty
thousand chemicals now on the market are in the inventory, and some
two thousand chemicals make their way to the market annually.
Examining the cumulative ecological and health effects of this mounting
chemical inventory is an overwhelming task. Even assessing the effects
of the much more limited set of chemicals at a particular site is daunting. Such an analysis needs to take account of the *accumulation* of
chemicals in the environment over time, across sources, across multiple
routes and pathways of exposure, to people and environmental components with widely differing susceptibilities to damage. Then potential
effects from the multiple stressors and exposures must be integrated
for the stressors acting together into a coherent picture of risk for
the different exposure units (people and ecosystems), for chemicals
whose toxicities we often know little about and even then only at high
levels of uncertainty. Still the job is not done, as the chemical threats
then need to be related to other substantially different social and economic stresses, and finally to often widely differing vulnerabilities to
individual stresses. Recognizing cumulative risk/vulnerability in logical

fashion aside, it is no easy task to develop the methodologies and approaches required to achieve a sound picture of differential cumulative vulnerability.

Causal "Maps" of Vulnerability

To understand the incidence and depth of vulnerability is to understand the sources of vulnerability and their causal linkages to the proximate factors—the roots—that shape the three dimensions of vulnerability—exposure, sensitivity, and resilience. In some cases, these roots are exogenous, lying in the basic social and economic structures that shape the differential endowments and access to entitlements of different populations. In other cases, the roots are endogenous in the social-environment system in which internal structures and processes generate both stresses and vulnerabilities that threaten the security of the system. In other cases, the roots lie in management systems and institutions. Management solutions intended to control near-term perturbations, as conventional natural-resources management tends to do, may increase the "brittleness" of institutions and the potential for larger-scale and more devastating disturbances (Holling 1995). In still other cases, the behavior of the local resource manager and the capacity to learn and fashion effective adaptive strategies is the key. Most typically, multiple sources of vulnerability exist, and it is necessary to demonstrate and to model—not to assume—analytic approaches to uncover the causal factors and the linkages in enlarging or reducing risk.

Such causal maps of vulnerability, and particularly those that capture social-ecological interactions, are rare and at an early stage of development. Bohle, Downing, and Watts (1994, 39–44) have described the causal structure of vulnerability as involving the intersection of three axes—*human ecology*, the way in which labor transforms nature and generates hazards; *expanded entitlements*, including endowments, social entitlements, and empowerment; and *political economy*, the national regimes of accumulation influenced by transnational processes. The triangle represented by connecting these axes is taken to be the "space of vulnerability" in which particular groups can be located (O'Brien et al. 2004). The framework is really an icon of vulnerability, however, rather than a causal framework, as causal linkages are not shown. Downing (1991a), drawing on the work of Hohenemser, Kasperson, and Kates (1985), has developed a causal structure of hunger that illustrates particularly connections across scale, domains (scales) ranging from national to individual levels, a simplified causal model of hazard (causes and consequences), and a set of directional linkages (figure 7.3).

Turning to energy as a key life-support system, the *World Energy Assessment* (Goldemberg 2000) suggests convincingly how extensively energy system-related vulnerabilities are intertwined with a host of social, democratic, and economic factors. Worldwide, two billion people lack access to electricity and another two billion people use traditional solid fuels for cooking. Smith (1993) estimated that burning solid fuels in poorly ventilated spaces caused about two million deaths per year, disproportionately concentrated among women and children in developing countries. Particulate matter and hydrocarbons are a growing serious global hazard. Hundreds of millions of people—mainly women and children—spend several hours daily gathering and transporting firewood and water to meet household needs. Affordable energy is a key lever in increasing household productivity and breaking out of the poverty cycle. Yet, poor households throughout the world, who pay a larger fraction of their income for energy than do the rich, are highly vulnerable to potential increases in the price of energy. Table 7.2 suggests some of the principal social, economic, and institutional interventions by which changed energy systems could reduce the vulnerabilities of many populations globally.

These various examples point to the need to develop a causal "map" of the factors, structures, and processes that produce differential vulnerability to stresses and perturbations. Such maps should consider both the proximate determinants of the three key dimensions of vulnerability—exposure, sensitivity, and resilience—and the extent to which these are linked to underlying social and economic structures and to ecosystem components and dynamics: in short, the causal maps need to be improved to capture cross-scale dynamics more adequately. Causal linkages among factors should be carefully established and documented empirically. Sensitivity analyses will then be required to assess where interventions may yield the greatest gain in vulnerability reduction.

Coping "Pools" and Strategies

Since we have argued that vulnerability is best conceived as a process, a set of cross-scale dynamics, and historical trajectories, it follows that learning and coping by the exposed system are essential ingredients in vulnerability. *Coping*, in our usage, refers to the wide-ranging set of mechanisms used and actions undertaken to reduce or ameliorate threats

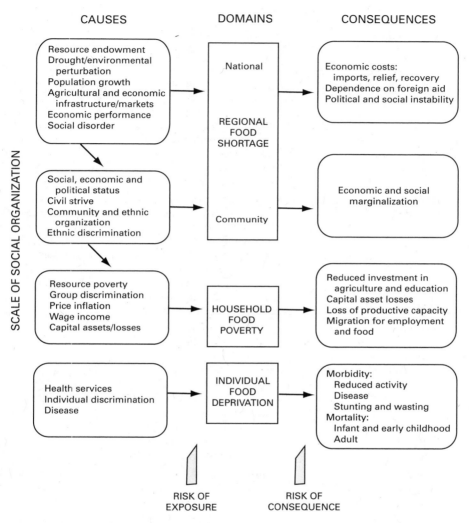

CAUSES   DOMAINS   CONSEQUENCES

Resource endowment
Drought/environmental
  perturbation
Population growth
Agricultural and economic
  infrastructure/markets
Economic performance
Social disorder

National

REGIONAL
FOOD
SHORTAGE

Economic costs:
  imports, relief, recovery
Dependence on foreign aid
Political and social instability

Social, economic and
  political status
Civil strive
Community and ethnic
  organization
Ethnic discrimination

Community

Economic and social
marginalization

Resource poverty
Group discrimination
Price inflation
Wage income
Capital assets/losses

HOUSEHOLD
FOOD
POVERTY

Reduced investment in
  agriculture and education
Capital asset losses
Loss of productive capacity
Migration for employment
  and food

Health services
Individual discrimination
Disease

INDIVIDUAL
FOOD
DEPRIVATION

Morbidity:
  Reduced activity
  Disease
  Stunting and wasting
Mortality:
  Infant and early childhood
  Adult

SCALE OF SOCIAL ORGANIZATION

RISK OF
EXPOSURE

RISK OF
CONSEQUENCE

Figure 7.3
A causal structure of hunger.

Table 7.2
Energy-related options to address social issues

Social challenge	Energy linkages and interventions
Alleviating poverty in developing countries	• Improve health and increase productivity by providing universal access to adequate energy services—particularly for cooking, lighting, and transport—through affordable, high-quality, safe, and environmentally acceptable energy carriers and end-use devices. • Make commercial energy available to increase income-generating opportunities.
Increasing opportunities for women	• Encourage the use of improved stoves and liquid or gaseous fuels to reduce indoor air pollution and improve women's health. • Support the use of affordable commercial energy to minimize arduous and time-consuming physical labor at home and at work. • Use women's managerial and entrepreneurial skills to develop, run, and profit from decentralized energy systems.
Speeding the demographic transition (to low mortality and low fertility)	• Reduce child mortality by introducing cleaner fuels and cooking devices and providing safe, potable water. • Use energy initiatives to shift the relative benefits and costs of fertility—for example, adequate energy services can reduce the need for children's physical labor for household chores. • Influence attitudes about family size and opportunities for women through communications made accessible through modern energy carriers.
Mitigating the problems associated with rapid urbanization	• Reduce the "push" factor in rural-urban migration by improving the energy services in rural areas. • Exploit the advantages of high-density settlements through land planning. • Provide universal access to affordable multi-modal transport services and public transportation. • Take advantage of new technologies to avoid energy-intensive, environmentally unsound development paths.

Source: Goldemberg 2000, 9.

and potential adverse impacts. Human coping may take various forms. Some coping measures involve *anticipatory actions* by which people seek to avoid exposure to threats or to increase their buffering or resistance to future stresses (and thereby lower their sensitivity to the hazards) that may occur. Coping also occurs as stresses unfold, accumulate, and (possibly) concatenate, and the exposed people or systems undertake short-term coping measures, referred to here as *adjustments*, which while adding to buffering capacity do not usually alter the social-environmental systems in fundamental ways. Finally, more fundamental interventions, referred to here as *adaptations*, typically occur after the perturbation or shock has registered its effects, as the coupled social ecosystem seeks to reduce its vulnerability to future perturbations and stresses.

Thus, it is essential in a vulnerability analysis to define the coping pool and resources available to a social-ecological system at risk. In his seminal piece on "choice of use in resource management," White (1961) set forth a template for assessing the range of choices open to an individual, group, or institution managing hazards. His particular interest was inquiring into the adequacy of decision processes in assessing such choices and in identifying ways of enlarging the range of choice. In this decision paradigm, attention was given to various behavior constraints after the writings of Herbert Simon (1957, 1979), such as *bounded rationality* and *satisficing behavior*, which led to suboptimal resource choices. This framework was subsequently extended to hazard and vulnerability analysis. We know, for example, that households and other exposed systems have portfolios of investments and other stores of coping resources that can be drawn down during periods of perturbation and stress. In such cases more vulnerable units are forced to expend important assets earlier and more completely than resilient units (Vogel 1998). Some years later, Brooks (1986) took up the question of *response pools*, arguing that surprises and shocks are inevitable in most systems and that the size and variegation of the human responses available to a threatened system are critical to its ability to respond to such events with minimal damage and disruption.

As with Holling, Brooks was particularly concerned over the tendency to create technological monocultures by focusing too heavily on efficiency at the expense of variety. He also observed that pruning the tree of technology, based solely on the first reasonably successful partial solution to a problem, is a common tendency in society—one that can reduce significantly the response pools available for dealing with surprise and increase the overall vulnerability of society to technological and environmental surprises. Learning curves, as a result, can actually contract response pools as society embraces near-term solutions at the expense of longer-term learning. Unfortunately, this promising line of inquiry into vulnerability has not been taken up as vulnerability analyses have focused on other issues.

One of those "other" issues has been how the broader social and economic structures have differentially shaped the magnitude of coping resources across society, empowering and endowing some members of society while weakening and depleting others. It has also been argued that more vulnerable people become marginalized to more hazardous environments at the same time their endowments and coping capacities are diminished and they are disenfranchised politically. This has led to considerable interest in *social vulnerability*, conceived as "a multi-layered and multi-dimensional social space defined by determinate political, economic, and institutional capabilities of people in specific places and at specific times" (Watts and Bohle 1993, 46). Various agencies have identified major types of "assets" that contribute to buffering against perturbations, increasing resilience, and providing livelihood security (Carney et al. 1999). Kelly and Adger (2000, 326) have argued for an analysis of the "architecture of entitlements," which they describe as "the influence levels of vulnerability within a community or nation that promote or constrain options for adaptation."

Finally, renewed interest in adaptive capacity and strategies of adaptation in relation to vulnerability is in full bloom. Like other forms of coping, adaptation is iterative, dynamic, and processual. Interactions occur throughout the coupled social and environmental system, involving an adaptation cycle that occurs in space and time (see figure 7.4). Smit and colleagues (1999) have proposed a framework for adaptation assessment with issues explored in some depth in R. J. T. Klein and associates (2007).

These stages and questions replicate those that occur in coping geared to sensitivity issues. It is useful, however, to distinguish between *adaptive capacity*, referring here to the potential to adapt to new circumstances and surprises, and the *adaptation that actually occurs*. (It should be noted that some ecologists would use a more specific definition, such as "system robustness to changes in resilience" Gunderson 2000, 435). Societal responses that take place in the face of growing environmental

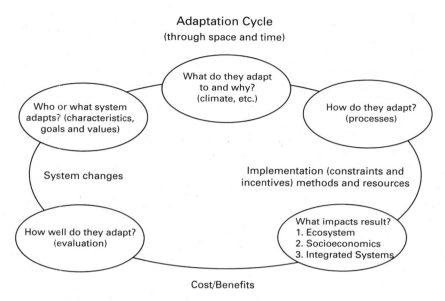

Figure 7.4
The adaptation cycle through space and time.
Source: Wheaton and Maciver 1999, 20.

degradation and threat typically lag seriously behind and fall well short of potential effectiveness across diverse threatened regions throughout the globe. Analyses are needed both to estimate and profile adaptive capacity and to explain the large gap that often exists between mitigative and adaptive capacity and actions actually undertaken.

With this discussion of the structuring of vulnerability analysis in hand, we now turn to a proposed conceptual framework, designed to guide a more integrative analysis of vulnerability.

Integrative Conceptual Framework

The authors, with input and advice from others in the Research and Assessment Systems for Sustainability Program (http://sust.harvard.edu), have created a framework for vulnerability that addresses coupled human-environment systems and their interactive vulnerabilities (see our briefer version in Turner et al. 2003a, b). This framework seeks to capture as much as possible of the "totality" of the different elements that have been identified and demonstrated in risk, hazards, and vulnerability studies and to frame them in regard to their complex linkages. It is not an explanatory framework; rather, it provides the components and linkages that must be addressed to capture the phenomena and processes that give rise to vulnerability. In this regard, it also serves as a definitional framework, identifying which component and linkages fall into the core arena of vulnerability. The framework recognizes that the components and linkages in question vary by the scale of analysis undertaken, and that the scale of the assessment may change the specific components but not the overall structure of the framework. As with complex agent-based modeling, full implementation of the framework will exceed the capacity and, in some instances, the needs of most vulnerability practitioners (i.e., agency use) who may focus on the development and simplification of the framework's subsystems. The framework, however, serves as a reminder of what is missing in assessments based on such simplifications.

The framework (see figure 7.5) recognizes two basic parts to the problem and assessment: perturbation-stresses and the coupled human-environment system. Of the two, vulnerability emerges from the attributes of the coupled system, comprised of sets of components that fall largely with the categories of exposure, sensitivity, and resilience. In the following we briefly describe each part and provide examples.

Perturbations and *stresses* are both human and natural in kind and are affected by processes often operating at scales larger than the event in question (e.g., local drought) and, in many cases, whose origins are exogenous to the ultimate location of the event. Of note, the social-environment system, in turn, can exacerbate the perturbations and stresses. For example, globally induced climate warming triggers increased variation in precipitation in a tropical forest frontier, while political strife elsewhere drives large numbers of immigrants to the frontier. These exogenous forces create new levels of land pressures that stress forest recovery, make cropping riskier, and increase the amount of forest cut and the local dependency on cultivation. The cropping strategies undertaken by economically marginal immigrants may intensify land degradation, which becomes an endogenous force that increases per-capita land clearance and reduces the capacity of the forest to recover.

The *coupled human-ecological system* maintains some level of vulnerability to these perturbations-stresses, related to the manner in which they are experienced. This experience is registered first in terms of the

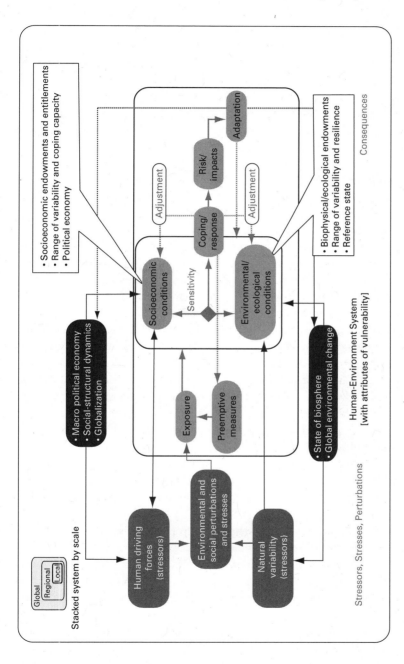

Figure 7.5
A framework for analyzing vulnerability.

nature of the *exposure* (e.g., intensity, frequency, duration), and involves measures that the human and environment subsystems may take to reduce the exposure. Take the case of slash-and-burn farmers in tropical regions who are experiencing increasing climatic aridity. Given the convective nature of tropical precipitation, these farmers may take preemptive measures to reduce exposure to drought by scattering cultivated plots in different niches across the landscape in the hope that some plots will gain more precipitation or take advantage of different soil-moisture regimes.

The coupled system experiences some level of harm to exposure (i.e., risk and impacts) determined by its *sensitivity*. Little work has been directed to the determinants and measures of sensitivity (at least in human subsystems). The level of harm experienced (e.g., human deaths incurred, cost of material damages, loss of ecosystem function) is usually taken as the measure of sensitivity to a hazard. The linkage between exposure and impact is not necessarily direct, however, because the coupled system maintains coping mechanisms that permit immediate or near-term adjustments that reduce the harm experienced, and in some cases, change the sensitivity of the system itself. Sensitivity is therefore a dynamic quality of the coupled system. Drought and land degradation, for example, reduce yields and household consumption, raising the potential for malnutrition in the human subsystem. To cope, a cash crop may be planted with low-yielding but drought-resistant varieties, producing food that becomes available as the regular harvest stocks dwindle. Where the opportunity exists, some segment of the household may seek off-farm employment, using the wages gained to purchase food. Likewise, the biophysical subsystem adjusts to the changing precipitation regimes by favoring more xeric species, changing the character of forest succession and recovery rates of soils whose nutrients have been reduced by cultivation.

If specific perturbation-stress persists over the long run (i.e., change in the external conditions in which the coupled system operates), the kind and quality of *system resilience* changes. This last change demands *adaptation* (fundamental change) in the coupled system. The human subsystem must be altered, or it ceases to function (e.g., abandonment of a place or region); the environmental subsystem changes by definition (e.g., climate and vegetation change). Consider the case of farmers responding to increasing aridity and a shift from tropical forests to savanna-woodlands by banding into communities that develop the infrastructure and institutions for small-scale irrigation. With improved water sources, a shift occurs to the commercial production of orchard products. Alternatively, the migrants move elsewhere, abandoning areas subsequently taken over by commercial cattle enterprises. Both of these adaptations, of course, carry with them implications for the environmental subsystem.

By definition, no part of a system in this framework is unimportant, and work directed specifically to each component and their linkages with other components is needed. Such work has begun, illustrated in assessment methods developed by Luers (2005) and Polsky, Neff and Yarnell (2007), and Schröter, Polsky and Patt (2005). Emergent vulnerable communities, however, signal the need for devoting much more attention to the base characteristics of coupled systems, because they hold the clues to the root causes of vulnerability and, hence, those elements that must be addressed in order to institute measures that reduce vulnerability.

Priorities for Next Steps

Vulnerability research has foundered amid the abstract theoretical discussion and acrimonious debate over alternative conceptual approaches and basic theory. The most pressing need for the next stage of work is for rigorous testing and concrete applications of the various conceptual frameworks (to this end, see our applications and testing of our framework in Turner et al. 2003b). This empirical work should continue to emphasize comparative case studies, for most extant evidence is limited unduly to single case studies that proceed from a particular conceptual approach. Vulnerability research has tended to be overly context- or case-specific, and, as a result, the development and the impacts of empirical findings have been distressingly noncumulative. The time is ripe for systematic cross-case and cross-theory analysis, designed to glean what a particular conceptual framework can and cannot deliver, and what aspects of our understanding are best established and supported by empirical evidence. A model meta-analysis (Geist and Lambin 2001) provides a useful guide for such comparative work. Frameworks promoting this effort have been constructed (Luers 2005; Polsky, Neff, and Yarnal 2007; Schröter et al. 2005), and attempts are now under way in several centers of vulnerability research to apply and further develop them.

Once comparative case studies yield lessons or general rules, a larger portion of vulnerability research must subject those lessons to strict "hypothesis" testing, replete with quantitative analyses. Such an orientation is imperative if applied and human-dimensions work on vulnerability is to link more usefully to research on its ecological and biophysical dimensions. Indeed, a major impediment to incorporating work on human vulnerability into research on global environmental change has been the paucity of research designs capable of contributing to model development and empirical tests, regardless of place-based orientation.

Fully applying and testing the framework we have set forth, or any alternative framework, will at first glance be daunting, owing to the setting of multiple stresses and multiple vulnerabilities and the complexity of linkages, scale interactions, and dynamics. Full application of the framework will exceed the resources and available time of most analysts and practitioners, and so comprehensive assessments or applications will perforce be rare. Yet even when the objectives of the study may be highly specific or the scope of analysis quite narrow, a major value of such a framework is to assist in structuring the problem and analysis. In the case of climate change, for example, where interest focuses on a particular set of perturbations or stresses, it will be useful to construct the analysis as a multiple-stress problem and to focus on climate perturbations but also to consider other stresses in the analysis. Or, alternatively, the concern may well be with marginalized, indigenous groups in society, but the analysis can be structured so that the unit of exposure is indigenous group-ecological interactions. Yet another case might involve a focus on local preparedness and coping, but the linkages with structural factors at higher scales (macropolitical economy, globalization) can still be considered as context. So the broad conceptual framework can play a significant role in framing studies and assessment in a more sophisticated form.

Another possibility is that analysis can proceed by making judgments on this question: what are the essentials that should be in any sound vulnerability analysis? Particularly for those seeking to use the conceptual framework we have set forth, if the full range of complexity is beyond the analyst's capability and resources, what are the essential elements of the framework to include? Appreciating that the answer will ultimately depend on the purposes of the study or assessment. We urge consideration of essentials that would include

- multiple stress/multiple vulnerability framing of the problem, including potential interactions among the stresses;
- exposure, sensitivity, and resilience as major dimensions for analysis;
- structuring of the exposure unit as a coupled system of ecological-social interactions;
- causal mapping of vulnerability, its social and ecological roots, and causal linkages;
- cross-scale interactions—the architecture of stresses, responses, and coping resources and strategies over multiple scales;
- vulnerability as evolutionary process—its history, iteration, and cumulative nature;
- coping and adaptation, by which human societies and ecosystems buffer themselves against perturbations, and their ability to recover or reorganize in modified or new systems.

(See also the eight steps outlined in Schröter, Polsky, and Platt 2005.) In any given case, of course, the list of "essentials" will differ, but we suggest the foregoing as a starting set for consideration.

It is also important to appreciate that the existing knowledge base of vulnerability is highly uneven. Since conceptual approaches have been very general in construction, and case studies typically quite specific in focus and approach, it is scarcely surprising that major gaps exist in the components of the conceptual framework we have elaborated. We have yet to determine, for example, how best to structure and implement multiple-stress types of analysis. We lack detailed causal maps of the factors and processes that shape vulnerabilities in a particular place. Few studies exist that detail the dynamics of human-environment interactions as systems degrade over time under stress. We know far too little about coping resources, adaptive capacities, and how they are mobilized and used in different places and the nature of linkages and interaction in coupled human-environment systems is still opaque. We need to target these voids in knowledge, to systematically begin to fill the empirical gaps, and to grow and deepen our conceptual structures.

Meanwhile, assessment and practice cannot wait; it is not possible to delay the next generation of vulnerability research coming to fruition. It is quite apparent that traditional environmental impact analysis lacks the conceptual and methodological capability to assess vulnerability issues; indeed such analysis typically obscures the situation of vulnerable ecosystems and human groups within the mass of aggregated data and

categories of effects derived from top-down assessments. Just as vulnerability assessments raise new questions and concepts, they also will
require new assessment processes and procedures. We may gain new
knowledge and insights by working backward—from the most vulnerable groups and those outcomes we seek most to avoid (from right to
left in figure 7.4), on to vulnerabilities and eventually suites of stresses.
Entering assessments at different scales of analysis, particularly the local
scales of place-based assessments, promises greater depth and texture—
and perhaps a fundamentally different format and presentation—than
existing analyses. These bottom-up assessments raise new possibilities
for collaborative data gathering, analysis, and how value issues enter
into vulnerability assessments. And since the local people at risk will also
be partners in these assessments, results will matter more in the policy-
and decision-making process. To these ends, we applaud the efforts on
applied vulnerability analysis in UNEP's (2002) *Global Environment
Outlook 3.*

Going forward with vulnerability analysis is, in its essentials, part of
the larger task of creating a sustainability science—dedicated to supporting the transition to a more sustainable world, and to forging new
interactions between science and the humanity it serves.

Acknowledgments

The writing of this chapter has relied on contributions from many
quarters. Support for the transatlantic collaboration of the authors,
based at the George Perkins Marsh Institute at Clark University
and the Stockholm Environment Institute (SEI), comes largely from
the Research and Assessment Systems for Sustainability Program
(http://sust.harvard.edu). Coordinated by William C. Clark and Nancy
M. Dickson at Harvard University, the program is supported by a core
grant from the United States National Science Foundation (NSF award
BCS-0004236) with contributions from the Office of Global Programs
at the National Oceanic and Atmospheric Administration (NOAA).
Under its auspices, several workshops have served to keep the topic
of vulnerability high on the research and political agenda. We are
immensely grateful to the participants at these workshops (for full lists
of these participants, see Clark et al. 2000; Research Assessment and
Systems for Sustainability Program 2001). We owe a particular debt of
gratitude to Robert W. Kates for his evaluation of an early draft of this

chapter. Also, we thank Jill Jäger, executive director of the International Human Dimensions Programme on Global Environmental Change (IHDP), for unwavering support of our efforts to advance the concept of vulnerability.

Many individuals merit special mention for their unflagging promotion of the various incarnations of our proposed framework for analyzing vulnerability. Pamela Matson and her team at Stanford University have been endeavoring to test the applicability of the framework in their case study in the Yaqui Valley in Mexico; and, at Harvard, Robert Corell and James McCarthy have done likewise for a case study in the Arctic. Meanwhile, a group at Clark University's Graduate School of Geography has worked closely with two of the authors to apply the framework to another Mexican case, the southern Yucatán peninsular region. A generous gift from the Howard and Leah Green Fund, The George Perkins Marsh Institute, Clark University, provided the initial support for Andrew Schiller's postdoctoral position.

Also at Clark University, Andrew Schiller, Ke Chen, Alex Pulsipher, and Wen Hsieh have enlivened our discussions, contributed their thinking, and challenged our conceptual lapses. An assemblage of two dozen researchers at SEI's workshop (Kasperson and Kasperson 2001) helped to sharpen our thinking. At SEI, Teresa Ogenstad cheerfully produced numerous early drafts of our manuscript. Erik Willis, in SEI's center at York (UK), performed magic on figure 7.4. Finally, we salute Clark University's indefatigable Mimi Berberian and Lu Ann Pacenka for transforming what appeared to be an irretrievably mangled penultimate draft into a real chapter.

References

Abramovitz, J. N. 2001. *Unnatural disasters.* Worldwatch Paper 158. Washington, DC: Worldwatch Institute.

Acharya, A. 1995. Small islands awash in a sea of trouble. *World Watch* 8 (6):24–33.

Adger, N. W. 1999. Social vulnerability to climate change and extremes in coastal Vietnam. *World Development* 27 (2):249–269.

Adger, W. N. 2000. Institutional adaptation to environmental risk under the transition in Vietnam. *Annals of the Association of American Geographers* 90: 738–758.

Adger, W. N. 2006. Vulnerability. *Global Environmental Change* 16:268–281.

Adger, W. N., and P. M. Kelly. 1999. Social vulnerability to climate change and the architecture of entitlements. *Mitigation and Adaptation Strategies for Global Change* 4 (3–4):253–266.

Alexander, D. 1993. *Natural disasters.* New York: Chapman and Hall.

Angel, D. P., S. Attoh, D. Kromm, J. DeHart, R. Slocum, and S. White. 1998. The drivers of greenhouse gas emissions: What do we learn from local case studies? *Local Environment* 3 (3):263–278.

Anyamba, A. 1997. Interannual variations of NDVI over Africa and their relationship to ENSO: 1982–1983. Ph.D. diss., Graduate School of Geography, Clark University, Worcester, MA.

Ausubel, J. H. 1996. Can technology spare the earth? *American Scientist* 84:166–178.

Bebbington, A. 1999. Capitals and capabilities: A framework for measuring peasant viability, rural livelihoods and poverty. *World Development* 27 (12): 2021–2044.

Beck, U. 1992. *Risk society: Toward a new modernity.* London: Sage.

Beck, U. 1995. *Ecological enlightenment: Essays on the politics of the risk society.* Atlantic Highlands, NJ: Humanities Press.

Beck, U. 1999. *World risk society.* London: Polity Press.

Beck, U. 2000. *What is globalization?* Cambridge, UK: Polity Press.

Berkes, F., J. Colding, and C. Folke, eds. 2003. *Navigating social-ecological systems.* Cambridge, UK: Cambridge University Press.

Berkes, F., and C. Folke. 1998. Linking social and ecological systems for resilience and sustainability. In *Linking social and ecological systems: Management practices and social mechanisms for building resilience,* ed. F. Berkes and C. Folke, with the editorial assistance of J. Colding, 1–25. Cambridge, UK: Cambridge University Press.

Birkmann, J. 2006. Measuring vulnerability to promote disaster-resilient societies: Conceptual frameworks and definitions. In *Measuring vulnerability to natural hazards,* ed. J. Durkmann, 9–54. Tokyo: United Nations University Press.

Blaikie, P. M., and H. C. Brookfield. 1987. *Land degradation and society.* London: Methuen.

Blaikie, P., T. Cannon, I. Davies, and B. Wisner. 1994. *At risk: Natural hazards, people's vulnerability and disaster.* London: Routledge.

Bogard, W. C. 1989. Bringing social theory to hazards research: Conditions and consequences of the mitigation of environmental hazards. *Sociological Perspectives* 31 (2):147–168.

Bohle, H. G. 2001. Vulnerability and criticality: Perspectives from social geography. *IHDP Update* 2:1, 3–5.

Bohle, H. G., T. E. Downing, and M. J. Watts. 1994. Climate change and social vulnerability: Towards a sociology and geography of food insecurity. *Global Environmental Change* 4:37–48.

Brklacich, M., and S. Leybourne. 1999. Food security in a changing world. *AVISO*, 4 (September):1–9. http://www.gechs.org.

Brooks, H. 1986. The typology of surprises in technology, institutions, and development. In *Sustainable development of the biosphere*, ed. W. C. Clark and R. E. Munn, 325–348. Cambridge, UK: Cambridge University Press.

Brooks, E., and J. Emel, with B. Jokisch and P. Robbins. 2000. *The Llano Estacado of the US Southern High Plains: Environmental transformation and the prospect for sustainability.* Tokyo: United Nations University Press.

Brown, M. and C. Funk. 2008. Food security under climate change. *Science* 319:580–581.

Burton, I., R. W. Kates, and G. F. White. 1978. *The environment as hazard.* New York: Oxford University Press.

Burton, I., R. W. Kates, and G. F. White. 1993. *The environment as hazard*, 2nd ed. New York: Guilford Press.

Calabrese, E. T. 1978. *Pollutants and high-risk groups: The biological basis of increased human susceptibility to environmental and occupational pollutants.* New York: Wiley.

Cannon, T. 1994. Vulnerability analysis and the explanation of "natural" disasters. In *Disasters, development and the environment*, ed. A. Varley, 13–30. Chichester: Wiley.

Carney, D., ed. 1998. *Sustainable rural livelihoods: What contributions can we make?* Paper presented at DFID's Natural Resources Advisers' Conference, July 1998. London: Department for International Development (DFID).

Carney, D., M. Drinkwater, T. Rusinow, K. Neefjes, S. Wanmali, and N. Singh. 1999. *Livelihood approaches compared: A brief comparison of the livelihoods approaches of the UK Department for International Development (DFID), CARE, Oxfam and the United Nations Development Programme (UNDP).* London: DFID.

Cash, D. W., and S. C. Moser. 2000. Linking local and global scales: Designing dynamic assessment and management processes. *Global Environmental Change* 10:109–120.

Chambers, R. 1989. Editorial introduction: Vulnerability, coping and policy. *IDS Bulletin* 20 (3):1–8.

Chambers, R. 1997. *Whose reality counts?: Putting the first last.* London: Intermediate Technology Publications.

Chambers, R., and G. Conway. 1992. Sustainable rural livelihoods: Practical concepts for the 21st century. IDS Discussion Paper 296. Brighton, UK: Institute of Development Studies, University of Sussex.

Chertow, M. R. 2001. The IPAT equation and its variants: Changing views of technology and environmental impact. *Journal of Industrial Ecology* 4 (4):13–29.

Clark, T. N., ed. 1974. *Comparative community politics*. Beverly Hills, CA: Sage.

Clark, W. C., J. Jäger, R. Corell, R. E. Kasperson, J. J. McCarthy, D. Cash, S. J. Cohen, P. Desanker, N. M. Dickson, P. Epstein, D. H. Guston, J. M. Hall, C. Jaeger, A. Janetos, N. Leary, M. A. Levy, A. Luers, M. MacCracken, J. Melillo, R. Moss, J. M. Nigg, M. L. Parry, E. A. Parson, J. C. Ribot, H. Joachim Schellnhuber, D. P. Schrag, G. A. Scielstad, E. Shea, C. Vogel, and T. J. Wilbanks. 2000. *Assessing vulnerability to global environmental risks: Report of the Workshop on Vulnerability to Global Environmental Change: Challenges for Research, Assessment and Decision Making*, May 22–25, Airlie House, Warrenton, Virginia. Research and Assessment Systems for Sustainability Program Discussion Paper 2000–12. Cambridge, MA: Environmental and Natural Resources Program, Belfer Center for Science and International Affairs (BCSIA), Kennedy School of Government, Harvard University. http://sust.harvard.edu.

Cutter, S. L. 1993. *Living with risk: The geography of technological hazard*. London: Edward Arnold.

Cutter, S. L. 1996. Vulnerability to environmental hazards. *Progress in Human Geography* 20:529–539.

Cutter, S. L., and C. Finch. 2008. Temporal and spatial changes in social vulnerability to natural hazards. *Proceedings of the National Academy of Sciences* 105 (7): 2301–2306.

Cutter, S., D. Holm, and L. Clark. 1996. The role of geographic scale in monitoring environmental justice. *Risk Analysis* 16:517–526.

Cutter, S. L., J. T. Mitchell, and M. S. Scott. 2000. Revealing the vulnerability of people and places: A case study of Georgetown County, South Carolina. *Annals of the Association of American Geographers* 90 (4):713–737.

DeHart, J. L., and P. T. Soulé. 2000. Does I = PAT work in local places? *Professional Geographer* 52 (1):1–10.

Dietz, T., and E. A. Rosa. 1994. Rethinking the environmental impacts of population, affluence and technology. *Human Ecology Review* 1:277–300.

Douglas, M., and A. Wildavsky. 1982. *Risk and culture: An essay on the selection of technological and environmental dangers*. Berkeley: University of California Press.

Dow, K. 1992. Exploring differences in our common future(s): The meaning of vulnerability to global environmental change. *Geoforum* 23:417–436.

Dow, K., and T. E. Downing. 1995. Vulnerability research: Where things stand. *Human Dimensions Quarterly* 1:3–5.

Downing, T. E. 1991a. *Assessing socioeconomic vulnerability to famine: Frameworks, concepts, and applications*. Research Report 91–1 (April). Providence, RI: Alan Shawn Feinstein World Hunger Program, Brown University.

Downing, T. E. 1991b. Vulnerability to hunger and coping with climate change in Africa. *Global Environmental Change* 1:365–380.

Drèze, J., and A. K. Sen. 1989. *Hunger and public action.* Oxford: Clarendon Press.

Eakin, H. 2006. *Weathering risk in rural Mexico: Climatic, institutional, and economic change.* Tucson: University of Arizona Press.

Eakin, H., and A. Luers. 2006. Assessing the vulnerability of social-environmental systems. *Annual Review of Environment and Resources* 31:365–394.

Easterling, W. E. 1997. Why regional studies are needed in the development of full-scale integrated assessment modelling of global change processes. *Global Environmental Change* 7:337–356.

Erikson, K. T. 1994. *A new species of trouble: The human experience of modern disasters.* New York: Norton.

FIVIMS (Food Insecurity and Vulnerability Information Mapping System). 1999. *The state of food insecurity in the world 1999.* Rome: Food and Agriculture Organization of the United Nations.

FIVIMS (Food Insecurity and Vulnerability Information Mapping System). 2000. *The state of food insecurity in the world 2000.* Rome: Food and Agriculture Organization of the United Nations.

FIVIMS (Food Insecurity and Vulnerability Information Mapping System). 2001. *The state of food insecurity in the world 2001.* Rome: Food and Agriculture Organization of the United Nations.

Flynn, J., P. Slovic, and C. K. Mertz. 1994. Gender, race, and perception of environmental health risks. *Risk Analysis* 14 (6):1101–1108.

Folke, C., J. Colding, and F. Berkes. 2003. Synthesis: Building resilience and adaptive capacity in social-ecological systems. In *Navigating social-ecological systems: Building resilience for complexity and change,* ed. F. Berkes, J. Colding, and C. Folke, 352–387. Cambridge, UK: Cambridge University Press.

Fraser, E. D. G. 2007. Travelling in antique lands: Using past famines to develop an adaptability/resilience framework to identify food systems vulnerable to climate change. *Climatic Change* 83:495–514.

Füssel, H.-M., and R. J. T. Klein. 2006. Climate change vulnerability assessment: An evolution of conceptual thinking. *Climatic Change* 75 (3):301–329.

Gabor, T., and T. K. Griffith. 1980. The assessment of community vulnerability to acute hazardous materials incidents. *Journal of Hazardous Materials* 8:323–333.

Geist, H. J., and E. F. Lambin. 2001. *What drives tropical deforestation? A meta-analysis of proximate and underlying causes of deforestation based on subnational scale case study evidence.* LUCC Report Series no. 4. Louvain-la Neuve, Belgium: University of Louvain.

Geoghegan, J., L. Pritchard Jr., Y. Ogneva-Himmelberger, R. R. Chowdhury, S. Sanderson, and B. L. Turner II. 1998. "Socializing the pixel" and "pixelizing the social" in land-use and land-cover change. In *People and pixels: Linking remote sensing and social science*, ed. D. Liverman, E. F. Moran, R. R. Rindfuss, and P. C. Stern, 51–69. Washington, DC: National Academies Press.

Gibson, C., E. Ostrom, and T. K. Ahn. 1998. *Scaling issues in the social sciences.* IHDP Working Paper no. 1. Bonn: IHDP.

Giddens, A. 1996. Affluence, poverty and the idea of a post-scarcity society. *Development and Change* 27 (2):365–377.

Glantz, M. H., ed., 1988. *Societal responses to regional climate change: Forecasting by analogy*. Boulder, CO: Westview.

GLP (Global Land Project) 2005. *Science plan and implementation strategy, IGBP Report 35/ IHDP Report 19*. Stockholm.

Goldemberg, J., ed. 2000. *World energy assessment: Energy and the challenge of sustainability*. New York: United Nations Development Programme (UNDP), United Nations Department of Economic and Social Affairs, and World Energy Council.

Gore, C. 1993. Entitlement relations and unruly social practices: A comment on the work of Amartya Sen. *Journal of Development Studies* 29 (3):429–460.

Gunderson, L. H. 2000. Ecological resilience: In theory and application. *Annual Review of Ecology and Systematics* 31:425–439.

Gunderson, L. H., and C. S. Holling, eds. 2002. *Panarchy: Understanding transformations in human and natural systems*. Washington, DC: Island Press.

Gunderson, L. H., C. S. Holling, and S. S. Light, eds. 1995. *Barriers and bridges to the renewal of ecosystems and institutions*. New York: Columbia University Press.

Haimes, Y. Y. 1990. *Hierarchical multiobjective analysis of large-scale systems*. New York: Hemisphere.

Haimes, Y. Y. 1998. *Risk modelling, assessment, and management*. New York: Wiley.

Hewitt, K., ed. 1983. *Interpretations of calamity from the viewpoint of human ecology*. Boston: Allen & Unwin.

Hohenemser, C., R. E. Kasperson, and R. W. Kates. 1985. Causal structure. In *Perilous progress: Managing the hazards of technology*, ed. R. W. Kates, C. Hohenemser, and J. X. Kasperson, 25–42. Boulder, CO: Westview.

Holling, C. S. 1978. Adaptive environmental assessment and management. *EIA [Environmental Impact Assessment] Review* 2:24–25.

Holling, C. S. 1986. The resilience of terrestrial ecosystems: Local surprise and global change. In *Sustainable development of the biosphere*, ed. W. C. Clark and R. E. Munn, 292–317. Cambridge, UK: Cambridge University Press.

Holling, C. S. 1995. Sustainability: The cross-scale dimension. In *Defining and measuring sustainability: The biophysical dimensions*, ed. M. Munasinghe and W. Shearer, 65–75. Washington, DC: Distributed for the United Nations University by the World Bank.

Holling, C. S. 1996a. Engineering resilience versus ecological resilience. In *Engineering within ecological constraints*, ed. P. C. Schulze, 31–44. Washington, DC: National Academies Press.

Holling, C. S. 1996b. Surprise for science, resilience for ecosystems, and incentives for people. *Ecological Applications* 6 (August):733–735.

Holling, C. S. 1997. Regional responses to global change. *Conservation Ecology* 1 (2):3. http://www.ecologyandsociety.org/vol1/iss2/art3/.

Holling, C. S. 1998. The renewal, growth, birth, and death of ecological communities. *Whole Earth* 93 (Summer):32–35.

Holling, C. S., and G. K. Meffe. 1996. Command and control and the pathology of natural resource management. *Conservation Biology* 10 (2):328–337.

IFRC (International Federation of Red Cross and Red Crescent Societies). 1999a. *Vulnerability and capacity assessment: An International Federation guide.* Geneva: IFRC.

IFRC (International Federation of Red Cross and Red Crescent Societies). 1999b. *Work plan for the nineties.* Geneva: IFRC.

IFRC (International Federation of Red Cross and Red Crescent Societies). 2001. *World disasters report 2001: Focus on recovery.* Geneva: IFRC.

IPCC (Intergovernmental Panel on Climate Change). 2001. *Climate change 2001: Synthesis report.* Cambridge, UK: Cambridge University Press.

IPCC (Intergovernmental Panel on Climate Change). 2007. *Climate change 2007.* Cambridge, UK: Cambridge University Press.

Jackson, J. B. C., M. X. Kirby, W. H. Berger, K. A. Bjorndal, L. W. Botsford, B. J. Bourque, R. H. Bradbury, R. Cooke, J. Erlandson, J. A. Estes, T. P. Hughes, S. Kidwell, C. B. Lange, H. S. Lanihan, J. M. Pandolfi, C. H. Peterson, R. S. Steneck, M. J. Tegner, and R. R. Warner. 2001. Historical overfishing and the recent collapse of coastal ecosystems. *Science* 293:629–637.

Jacobsen, T., and R. M. Adams. 1958. Salt and silt in Ancient Mesopotamian agriculture. *Science* 128:1251–1258.

Janssen, M. A., M. I. Schoon, W. Ke, and K. Borner. 2006. Scholarly networks on resilience, vulnerability, and adaptation within the human dimensions of global environmental change. *Global Environmental Change* 16:240–252.

Jodha, N. S. 1995. The Nepal middle mountains. In *Regions at risk: Comparisons of threatened environments*, ed. J. X. Kasperson, R. E. Kasperson, and B. L. Turner II, 140–185. Tokyo: United Nations University Press.

Jodha, N. S. 2001a. Interacting processes of environmental vulnerabilities in mountain areas. *Issues in Mountain Development* 2001/2 (September):1–6.

Jodha, N. S. 2001b. *Life on the edge. Sustaining agriculture and community resources in fragile environments.* Oxford: Oxford University Press.

Johnson, D. L., and L. A. Lewis. 1995. *Land degradation: Creation and destruction*. Oxford: Blackwell.

Kasperson, R. E. 1969. Environmental stress and the political system. In *The structure of political geography*, ed. R. E. Kasperson and J. V. Minghi, 481–496. Chicago: Aldine.

Kasperson, R. E., and J. X. Kasperson. 1991. Hidden hazards. In *Acceptable evidence: Science and values in hazard management*, ed. D. C. Mayo and R. Hollander, 9–28. Oxford: Oxford University Press.

Kasperson, J. X., and R. E. Kasperson. 2001. *International Workshop on Vulnerability and Global Environmental Change, 17–19 May 2001, Stockholm Environment Institute (SEI), Stockholm, Sweden: A workshop summary.* SEI Risk and Vulnerability Programme Report 2001–01. Stockholm: SEI.

Kasperson, J. X., R. E. Kasperson, and B. L. Turner II, ed. 1995. *Regions at risk: Comparisons of threatened environments.* Tokyo: United Nations University Press.

Kasperson, R. E., O. Renn, P. Slovic, H. S. Brown, J. Emel, R. Goble, J. X. Kasperson, and S. Ratick. 1988. The social amplification of risk: A conceptual framework. *Risk Analysis* 8 (2):177–187.

Kates, R. W. 1985. The interaction of climate and society. In *Climate impact assessment*, ed. R. W. Kates, J. H. Ausubel, and M. Berberian on behalf of SCOPE 27, 3–36. Chichester, UK: Wiley.

Kates, R. W., and W. C. Clark. 1996. Environmental surprise: Expecting the unexpected. *Environment* 38 (2):6–11, 28–34.

Kates, R. W., W. C. Clark, R. Corell, J. M. Hall, C. C. Jaeger, I. Lowe, J. J. McCarthy, H.-J. Schellnhuber, B. Bolin, N. M. Dickson, S. Faucheux, G. C. Gallopin, A. Grübler, B. Huntley, J. Jäger, N. S. Jodha, R. E. Kasperson, A. Mabogunje, P. Matson, H. Mooney, B. Moore III, T. O'Riordan, and U. Svedin. 2000. *Sustainability science.* Research and Assessment Systems for Sustainability Program Discussion Paper 2000–33. Cambridge, MA: Environment and Natural Resources Program, Belfer Center for Science and International Affairs (BCSIA), Kennedy School of Government, Harvard University. Modified version published in *Science* 292 (April 27, 2001):641–642. http://sust.harvard.edu.

Kelly, P. M., and W. N. Adger. 2000. Theory and practice in assessing vulnerability to climate change and facilitating adaptation. *Climatic Change* 47: 325–352.

Khatib, H. 2000. Energy security. In *World energy assessment: Energy and the challenge of sustainability*, ed. J. Goldemberg, 113–114. New York: United Nations Development Programme (UNDP), United Nations Department of Economic and Social Affairs, and World Energy Council.

Kinzig, A. P., J. Antle, W. Ascher, W. Brock, S. Carpenter, F. S. Chapin III, R. Costanza, K. L. Cottingham, M. Dove, H. Dowlatabadi, E. Elliot, K. Ewel, A. Fisher, P. Gober, N. Grimm, T. Groves, S. Hanna, G. Heal, K. Lee, S. Levin,

J. Lubehenco, D. Ludwig, J. Martinez-Alier, W. Murdoch, R. Naylor, R. Norgaard, M. Oppenheimer, A. Pfaff, S. Pickett, S. Polasky, H. R. Pulliam, C. Redman, J. P. Rodriguez, T. Root, S. Schneider, R. Schuler, T. Scudder, K. Segersen, M. R. Shaw, D. Simpson, A. A. Small, D. Starrett, P. Taylor, S. van der Leeuw, D. H. Wall, and M. Wilson. 2000. *Nature and society: An imperative for integrated environmental research.* A report from a workshop, Developing a Research Agenda for Linking Biogeophysical and Socioeconomic Systems, June 5–8, Tempe, AZ. http://lsweb.la.asa.edu/akinzig/report.htm.

Klein, R. J. T., S. Huq, F. Denton, T. E. Downing, R. G. Richels, J. B. Robinson, F. L. Toth. 2007. Interrelationships between adaptation and mitigation. In *Climate change 2007: Impacts, adaptation and vulnerability*, ed. M. L. Parry, O. F. Canziani, J. P. Palutikof, P. J. van der Linden, and C. E. Hanson, 745–778. Cambridge, UK: Cambridge University Press.

La Porte, T. R. 1996. High reliability organizations: Unlikely, demanding, and at risk. *Journal of Contingencies and Crisis Management* 4 (6):60–70.

La Porte, T. R., and A. Keller. 1996. Assuring institutional constancy. *Public Administration Review* 56 (6):535–544.

Lädeke, M. K. B., G. Petschel-Held, and H-J. Schellenburger. 2004. Syndromes of global change: The first panoramic view. *Gaia* 13 (1):42–49.

Laris, P. 2002. Burning the seasonal mosaic: Preventative burning strategies in the wooded savanna of southern Mali. *Human Ecology* 30 (2):155–186.

Lawless, E. W. 1977. *Technology and social shock.* New Brunswick, NJ: Rutgers University Press.

Leach, M., R. Mearns, and I. Scoones. 1999. Environmental entitlements: Dynamics and institutions in community-based natural resource management. *World Development* 27 (2):225–247.

Lee, K. N. 1993. *Compass and gyroscope: Integrating science and politics for the environment.* Washington, DC: Island Press.

Linnerooth-Bayer, J., R. Löfstedt, and G. Sjöstedt, eds. 2001. *Transboundary risk management.* London: Earthscan.

Liverman, D. M. 1990. Vulnerability to global environmental change. In *Understanding global environmental change: The contributions of risk analysis and risk management*, ed. R. E. Kasperson, K. Dow, D. Golding, and J. X. Kasperson, 27–44. Worcester, MA: The Earth Transformed Program, Clark University.

Lobao, L., and K. Meyer. 2001. The great agricultural transition: Crisis, change, and social consequences of twentieth century U.S. farming. *Annual Review of Sociology* 27:103–124.

Lonergan, S., K. Gustavson, and B. Carter. 2000. The index of human security. *Aviso* 6 (January):1–11. http://www.gechs.org/aviso.

Luers, A. 2005. The surface of vulnerability: An analytical framework for examining environmental change. *Global Environmental Change* 15:214–223.

Luers, A. L., D. Lobelle, L. Sklar, C. L. Addams, and P. Matson. 2003. A method for quantifying vulnerability, applied to the agricultural system of the Yaqui Valley, Mexico. *Global Environmental Change* 13:255–267.

McCarthy, J. J., O. F. Canziani, N. A. Leary, D. J. Dokken, and K. S. White, ed. 2001. *Climate change 2001: Impacts, adaptation, and vulnerability.* Cambridge, UK: Cambridge University Press for the Intergovernmental Panel on Climate Change (IPCC).

McLaughlin, P., and T. Dietz. 2008. Structure, agency and environment: Toward an integrated perspective on vulnerability. *Global Environmental Change* 18 (1):99–111.

MEA (Millennium Ecosystem Assessment). 2003. *Ecosystems and human well-being: A framework for advancement.* Washington, DC: Island Press.

MEA (Millennium Ecosystem Assessment). 2005. *Ecosystems and human well-being: Synthesis.* Washington, DC: World Resources Institute.

Mileti, D. S. 1999. *Disasters by design: A reassessment of natural hazards in the United States.* Washington, DC: Joseph Henry Press.

Mitchell, J. K. 1989. Hazards research. In *Geography in America*, ed. G. L. Gaile and C. J. Wilmott, 410–424. Columbus, OH: Merrill Publishing.

Mitchell, J. K., ed. 1996. *The long road to recovery: Community response to industrial disaster.* Tokyo: United Nations University Press.

Mitchell, J. K. 2000. Urban metabolism and disaster vulnerability in an era. In *Earth system analysis: Integrating science for sustainability, complemented results of a symposium organized by the Potsdam Institute (PIK)*, ed. H. J. Schnellnhuber and V. Wenzel, 259–377. Berlin: Springer-Verlag.

Mitchell, J. K. 2001. What's in a name? Issues of terminology and language in hazards research. *Environmental Hazards* 2 (3):87–88.

Moser, C. O. M. 1998. The asset vulnerability framework: Reassessing urban poverty reduction strategies. *World Development* 26 (1):1–19.

Munich Re. 2007. *Significant natural catastrophes in 2006.* Munich, Germany: Munich Re.

Nyström, M., and C. Folke. 2001. Spatial resilience of ecosystems. *Ecosystems* 4 (5):406–417.

Nyström, M., C. Folke, and F. Moberg. 2000. Coral reef disturbance and resilience in a human dominated environment. *Trends in Ecological Evolution* 15:413–417.

O'Brien, K. L., and R. M. Leichenko. 2000. Double exposure: Assessing the impacts of climate change within the context of economic globalization. *Global Environmental Change* 10:221–232.

O'Brien, K. L., R. M. Leichenko, U. Kelkar, H. Venema, G. Aandahl, H. Tompkins, A. Javed, S. Bhadwal, S. Barg, L. Nygaard, and J. West. 2004. Mapping vulnerability to multiple stressors: Climate change and globalization in India. *Global Environmental Change* 14:303–313.

Oliver-Smith, A. 1996. Anthropological research on hazards and disasters. *Annual Review of Anthropology* 25:303–328.

Paine, R. T., M. J. Tegner, and E. A. Johnson 1998. Compounded perturbations yield ecological surprises. *Ecosystems* 1:535–545.

Pelling, M., ed. 2003a. *Natural disasters and development in a globalizing world.* New York: Rutledge.

Pelling, M. 2003b. *The vulnerability of cities: Natural disasters and social resilience.* London: Earthscan.

Perrow, C. 1984. *Normal accidents: Living with high-risk technologies.* New York: Basic Books.

Perrow, C. 1999. *Normal accidents: Living with high-risk technologies, with a new afterword and a postscript on the Y2K problem.* Princeton, NJ: Princeton University Press.

Petschel-Held, G., A. Block, M. Cassel-Gintz, J. Kropp, M. K. B. Lüdeke, O. Moldenhauer, F. Reusswig, and H-J. Schellnhuber. 1999. Syndromes of global change: A qualitative modelling approach to assist global environmental management. *Environmental Modeling and Assessment* 4:295–314.

Pidgeon, N., R. E. Kasperson, and P. Slovic, eds. 2003. *The social amplification of risk.* Cambridge, UK: Cambridge University Press.

Pijawka, K. D., and A. E. Radwan. 1985. The transportation of hazardous materials: Risk assessment and hazard management. *Dangerous Properties of Industrial Materials Report* 5 (5):2–11.

Polsky, C., R. Neff, and B. Yarnal. 2007. Building comparable global change vulnerability assessments: The vulnerability scoping diagram. *Global Environmental Change* 17:472–485.

Pritchard, L., Jr., J. Colding, F. Berkes, U. Svedin, and C. Folke. 1998. *The problem of fit between ecosystems and institutions.* IHDP Working Paper no. 2. Bonn: International Human Dimensions Programme on Global Environmental Change (IHDP).

Rangasami, A. 1985. Failure of exchange entitlements, theory of famine: A response. *Economic and Political Weekly* 41:1741–1801.

Reid, P., and C. Vogel. 2006. Living and responding to multiple stressors in South Africa—Glimpses of KwaZulu-Natal. *Global Environmental Change* 16:185–206.

Research and Assessment Systems for Sustainability Program. 2001. *Vulnerability and resilience for coupled human-environment systems: Report of the Research and Assessment Systems for Sustainability Program 2001 Summer Study, 29 May–1 June, Airlie House, Warrenton, Virginia.* Research and Assessment Systems for Sustainability Program Discussion Paper 2001–17. Cambridge, MA: Environment and Natural Resources Program, Belfer Center for Science and International Affairs, Kennedy School of Government, Harvard University. http://sust.harvard.edu.

Reynolds, J. F., M. Stafford Smith, E. F. Lambin, B. L. Turner II, M. Mortimore, S. P. Batterbury, T. E. Downing, et al. 2007. Global desertification: Building a science for dryland development. *Science* 316:847–851.

Ribot, J. C. 1995. The causal structure of vulnerability: Its application to climate impact analysis. *Geo Journal* 35:199–122.

Ribot, J. C. 1996. Introduction. Climate variability, climate change and vulnerability: Moving forward by looking back. In *Climate variability, climate change, and social vulnerability in the semi-arid tropics*, ed. J. C. Ribot, A. R. Magalhães, and S. S. Panagides, 1–10. Cambridge, UK: Cambridge University Press.

Scheffer, M., S. Carpenter, J. A. Foley, C. Folke, and B. Walker. 2001. Catastrophic shifts in ecosystems. *Nature* 413 (October 11):591–596.

Schneider, S. H., S. Semonov, A. Patwardhan, I. Burton, C. H. D. Madadza, M. Oppenheimer, A. B. Pittock, et al. 2007. Assessing key vulnerabilities and the risk from climate change. In *Climate Change 2007: Impacts, adaptation and vulnerability*, ed. M. L. Parry, O. F. Canziani, J. P. Palutikof, P. J. van der Linden, and C. E. Hanson, 779–810. Cambridge, UK: Cambridge University Press.

Schneider, S. H., B. L. Turner II, and H. Morehouse-Garriga. 1998. Imaginable surprise in global change science. *Journal of Risk Research* 1 (2):165–185.

Schnellnhuber, H. J., A. Block, M. Cassel-Gintz, J. Kropp, G. Lammel, W. Lass, R. Lienenkamp, C. Loose, M. K. B. Lüdeke, O. Moldenhauer, G. Petschel-Held, M. Plöchl, and F. Reusswig. 1997. Syndromes of global change. *GAIA* 6:19–34.

Schröter, D., C. Polsky, and A. Platt. 2005. Assessing vulnerabilities to the effects of global change: An eight-step approach. *Mitigation and Adaptation Strategies for Global Change* 10 (4):573–595.

Schröter, D., W. Cramer, R. Leemans, I. C. Prentice, M. B. Araújo, N. W. Arnell, A. Bondeau, H. Bugmann, T. R. Carter, C. A. Gracia, A. C. de la Vega-Leinert, M. Erhard, F. Ewert, M. Glendining, J. I. House, S. Kankaanpää, R. J. T. Klein, S. Lavorel, M. Lindner, M. J. Metzger, J. Meyer, T. D. Mitchell, I. Reginster, M. Rounsevell, S. Sabaté, S. Sitch, B. Smith, J. Smith, P. Smith, M. T. Sykes, K. Thonicke, W. Thuiller, G. Tuck, S. Zaehle, and B. Zierl. 2005. Ecosystem service supply and vulnerability to global change in Europe. *Science* 310:1333–1337.

Scoones, I. 1996. *Hazards and opportunities: Farming livelihoods in dryland Africa. Lessons from Zimbabwe*. London: Zed Books.

Sen, A. K. 1977. Starvation and exchange entitlements: A general approach and its application to the great Bengal famine. *Cambridge Journal of Economics* 1:33–59.

Sen, A. K. 1981. *Poverty and famines: An essay on entitlements and deprivation*. Oxford, UK: Oxford University Press.

Sen, A. 1983. Development which way now? *Economic Journal* 93:745–762.

Sen, A. K. 1984. Rights and capabilities. In *Resources, values and development*, ed. A. K. Sen, 307–324. Oxford: Blackwell.

Sen, A. K. 1990. Food entitlements and economic chains. In *Hunger in history: Food shortage, poverty, and deprivation*, ed. L. F. Newman, W. Crossgrove, R. W. Kates, R. Matthews, and S. Millman, 374–386. Oxford: Blackwell.

Simon, H. A. 1957. *Models of man.* New York: Wiley.

Simon, H. A. 1979. *Models of thought.* New Haven, CT: Yale University Press.

Smit, B., I. Burton, R. J. T. Klein, and R. Street. 1999. The science of adaptation: A framework for assessment. *Mitigation and Adaptation Strategies for Global Change* 4 (3–4):199–213.

Smith, K. 1992. *Environmental hazards: Assessing risk and reducing disaster.* London: Routledge.

Smith, K. 1993. Fuel combustion, air pollution exposure, and health: The situation in developing countries. *Annual Review of Energy and Environment* 18:529–566.

Stobaugh, R., and D. Yergin, eds. 1979. *Energy future: Report of the energy project at the Harvard Business School.* New York: Random House.

Susman, P., P. O'Keefe, and B. Wisner. 1983. Global disasters: A radical interpretation. In *Interpretations of calamity from the viewpoint of human ecology*, ed. K. Hewitt, 263–283. Boston: Allen & Unwin.

Suter, G. W., II. 1990. Endpoints for regional ecological risk assessments. *Environmental Management* 14 (1):9–23.

Suter, G. W. II. 1993. *Ecological risk assessment.* Boca Raton, FL: Lewis Publishers.

Tansey, J. and T. O'Riordan. 1999. Culture theory and risk: A review. *Health, Risk and Society* 1 (1):71–90.

Thompson, M., R. Ellis, and A. Wildavsky. 1990. *Cultural theory.* Boulder, CO: Westview.

Timmerman, P. 1981. *Vulnerability, resilience, and the collapse of society: A review of models and possible climatic applications.* Toronto: Institute of Environmental Studies, University of Toronto.

Turner, B. L., II. 1991. Thoughts on linking the physical and human sciences in the study of global environmental change. *Research and Exploration* 7, no. 2 (Spring):133–135.

Turner, B. L., II. 2006. Culture, ecology, and the classic Maya collapse. 1491: Human-environment relationships and the collapse of the Maya. *Geographical Review* 96:490–493.

Turner, B. L., II, R. E. Kasperson, P. Matson, J. J. McCarthy, R. W. Corell, L. Christensen, N. Eckley, J. X. Kasperson, A. Luers, M. L. Martello, C. Polsky, A. Pulsipher, A. Schiller. 2003a. A framework for vulnerability assessment in sustainability science. *Proceedings, National Academy of Sciences* 100 (14):8074–8079.

Turner, B. L., II, R. E. Kasperson, W. B. Meyer, K. M. Dow, D. Golding, J. X. Kasperson, R. C. Mitchell, and S. J. Ratick. 1990. Two types of global environmental change: Definitional and spatial-scale issues in their human dimensions. *Global Environmental Change* 1 (1):14–22.

Turner, B. L., II, P. A. Matson, J. J. McCarthy, R. W. Corell, L. Christianson, N. Eckley, G. V. Hovelsrod-Brodd, J. X. Kasperson, R. E. Kasperson, A. Luers, M. L. Mortello, S. Mathiesen, R. Naylor, A. Pulsipher, A. Scheller, H. Selin, and N. Tyler. 2003b. Illustrating the coupled human-environment system: Three case studies. *Proceedings, National Academy of Sciences* 100 (14):8080–8085.

UCS (Union of Concerned Scientists). 2002. *Energy security solutions to protect America's power supply and reduce oil dependence.* Cambridge, MA: UCS.

UN (United Nations). 1988. *International decade for natural disaster reduction: Report of the Secretary General, United Nations.* New York: United Nations.

UNDP (United Nations Development Programme). 2000. *Overcoming human poverty: UNDP Poverty Report 2000.* New York: UNDP.

UNDRO (United Nations Disaster Relief Organization). 1982. *Disaster Prevention and Mitigation.* New York: United Nations.

UNEP (United Nations Environment Programme). 1999. Vulnerability and adaptation to climate change impacts. In *Newsletter of the United Nations Environment Programme*, ed. Rabi Sharma, 1–4. Nairobi: UNEP.

UNEP (United Nations Environment Programme). 2002. Human vulnerability to environmental change. In *Global environmental outlook 3*, chapter 3, 301–317. London: Earthscan. http://www.grida.no/geo/geo3/english/pdfs/chapter3_vulnerability.pdf.

UNISDR (United Nations International Strategy for Disaster Reduction). 2002. *Natural disasters and sustainable development: Understanding the links between development, environment and natural disasters.* Background Paper no. 5, DESA/DSD/PC2/BP5. New York: Department of Economic and Social Affairs, UNISDR.

USNRC (U.S. National Research Council). 1991. *A safer future: Reducing the impacts of natural disasters.* Washington, DC: National Academies Press.

USNRC (U.S. National Research Council). 1999. *Our common journey: A transition toward sustainability.* Washington, DC: National Academies Press.

van Asselt, M., and J. Rotmans. 1995. Uncertainty in integrated assessment modeling: A cultural-perspective based approach. GLOBO Report Series no. 9/RIVM. Bilthoven, The Netherlands: National Institute of Public Health and the Environment.

van der Leeuw, S. E. 2000. Land degradation as a socionatural process. In *The way the wind blows: Climate, history, and human action*, ed. R. J. McIntosh, J. A. Tainter, and S. K. McIntosh, 357–383. New York: Columbia University Press.

Vogel, C. 1998. Vulnerability and global environmental change. *LUCC Newsletter* 3 (March):15–19.

Vogel, C. 2001. Plenary: Vulnerability. 2001 Open Meeting of the Human Dimensions of Global Environmental Change Research Community, October 6–8. Hotel Gloria, Rio de Janeiro, Brazil.

Vogel, C., and K. O'Brien. 2006. Who can eat information? Examining the effectiveness of seasonal climate forecasts and regional climate-risk management strategies. *Climate Research* 33:111–122.

Waddell, E. 1983. Coping with frosts, governments, and disaster experts: Some reflections based on a New Guinea experience and a perusal of the relevant literature. In *Interpretations of calamity from the viewpoint of human ecology*, ed. K. Hewitt, 33–43. Boston: Allen & Unwin.

Walker, B. and D. Salt. 2006. *Resilience thinking*. Washington, DC: Island Press.

Watson, R. T., M. C. Zinyowera, and R. H. Moss, eds. 1998. *Regional impacts of climate change: An assessment of vulnerability*. Cambridge, UK: Cambridge University Press.

Watts, M. J. 1983. On the poverty of theory: Natural hazards research in context. In *Interpretations of calamity from the viewpoint of human ecology*, ed. K. Hewitt, 231–262. Boston: Allen & Unwin.

Watts, M. J., and H. G. Bohle. 1993. The space of vulnerability: The causal structure of hunger and famine. *Progress in Human Geography* 17:43–67.

WBGU/GACGC (Wissenschaftlicher Beirat Globale Umweltveränderungen/ German Advisory Council on Global Change). 2000. Specific vulnerabilities of regions and social groups. In *World in transition: Strategies for managing global environmental risks*, 176–185. Annual Report 1998. Berlin: Springer-Verlag. http://www.wbgu.de.

WCED (World Commission on Environment and Development). 1987. *Our common future*. Oxford: Oxford University Press.

Wheaton, E. E., and D. C. Maciver. 1999. A framework and key questions for adapting to climate variability and change. *Mitigation and Adaptation Strategies for Global Change* 4 (3–4):215–225.

White, G. F. 1945. *Human adjustment to floods: A geographic approach to the flood problem in the United States*. Research Paper no. 29. Chicago: University of Chicago, Department of Geography.

White, G. F. 1961. Choice of use in resource management. *Natural Resources Journal* 1 (March):23–40.

White, G. F., ed. 1974. *Natural hazards: Local, national, global*. New York: Oxford University Press.

White, G. F., and J. E. Haas. 1975. *An assessment of research needs on natural hazards*. Cambridge, MA: MIT Press.

Wilbanks, T. J., and R. W. Kates. 1999. Global change in local places. *Climatic Change* 43:601–628.

Wilhite, D. A., ed. 2000. *Drought: A global assessment*, 2 vols. London: Routledge.

Wisner, B. 1988. *Power and need in Africa*. London: Earthscan.

Wisner, B. 1993a. Disaster vulnerability: Geographical scale and existential reality. In *Worlds of pain and hunger: Geographical perspectives on disaster vulnerability and food security*, ed. H. G. Bohle, 13–52. Saarbrücken, Germany: Breitenbach.

Wisner, B. 1993b. Disaster, vulnerability: Scale, power and daily life. *Geo Journal* 30:127–140.

Wisner, B., P. Blaikie, T. Cannon, and I. Davis. 2004. *At risk: Natural hazards, people's vulnerability, and disaster*, 2nd ed. London: Rutledge.

Worster, D. 1979. *Dust bowl: The southern plains in the 1930s*. Oxford: Oxford University Press.

Yergin, D. 1991. *The prize: The epic quest for oil, money, and power*. New York: Simon & Shuster.

Yergin, D., and M. Hillenbrand, eds. 1982. *Global insecurity: A strategy for energy and economic renewal*. Boston: Houghton Mifflin.

York, R., E. A. Rosa, and T. Dietz. 2002. Bridging environmental science with environmental policy: Plasticity of population, affluence, and technology. *Social Science Quarterly* 83 (1):18–34.

Zinyowera, M. C., B. P. Jallow, R. S. Maya, and H. W. O. Okoth-Ogendo. 1998. Africa. In *The regional impacts of climate change: An assessment of vulnerability*, ed. R. T. Watson, M. C. Zinyowera, and R. H. Moss, 29–84. Cambridge, UK: Cambridge University Press.

8

Human Dimensions of Coupled Human-Natural Systems: A Look Backward and Forward

Eugene A. Rosa and Thomas Dietz

Introduction

We conclude this volume by returning to the two-part goal laid out in the opening chapter: to assess how and where our understanding of GEC—the human dimensions side of coupled human-natural systems (CHANS; Liu 2007a, b) in a global context—has advanced over the past two decades, and to bring into sharp relief not only the critical gaps in our understanding, but also the key opportunities, challenges, and limitations for further advances in knowledge. We deeply hope a review of the literature a decade hence will report a substantial and cumulative body of social science knowledge that is linked directly with knowledge in the traditional sciences.

The chapters in this edited volume focus on the human dimensions of CHANS. CHANS are inextricably interconnected in cycles of reciprocal causation via feedback loops that cause the human components to influence both each other and the natural system. The interaction of the two systems recurs in two conceptual locations: where the anthropogenic (human) drivers produce direct and relatively immediate ecosystem change; and where changes to physical and biological systems directly and indirectly affect what humans value, especially the natural capital and services necessary to ensure human well-being.

A handful of CHANS field studies have documented the feedback process. For example, fuel wood used in Wolong, China for cooking and heating resulted in the depletion of nearby forests. This alteration of that natural system forced local residents to collect firewood from further and further distances. Eventually, they encroached on the bamboo forests that sustain panda populations (An et al. 2005). The IHOPE project is attempting to examine such feedbacks at time scales longer than those used for most studies reviewed in this volume (Costanza, Graumlich, and Steffen 2007).

To organize coverage of the human dimensions we adopted the key proximate anthropogenic forces identified in the NRC/NAS publication, *Global Environmental Change: Understanding the Human Dimensions* (GEC92, discussed in chapter 1; Stern, Young, and Druckman 1992) as a template for the selection of chapters in this volume. The chapters attempt to reinvigorate the importance of the proximate drivers of coupled human-natural systems delineated in GEC92, while situating them in the larger context of PaSSAGE: the context of an accelerated pace, scale, and global spread of environmental impacts driven by a process of autocatalysis, globalization, and the interconnectedness of CHANS around the globe. The interplay of these fundamental forces, representing a dance between medium and outcome, between drivers and impacts, lies at the core of the recursive dynamic that characterizes CHANS within the larger context of global environmental change.

The chapters present a collection of exemplary works across a variety of domains in the social sciences devoted to understanding the dynamics of social and ecological systems shaping GEC. Each chapter can be summed up with the legal phrase, *res ipsa loquitor*—"the thing speaks for itself." And, indeed, each does—typically in considerable detail. We, therefore, do not recapitulate each chapter in depth here, but instead briefly review them in a context that emphasizes their role in shaping the direction of future research.

Horizontal Extensions

On a variety of the topics covered in this work are clear and considerable advances in knowledge in our understanding of CHANS. We can think of these topics as lying on a horizontal plane. And we are optimistic that future research will refine and deepen that knowledge even further. For example, we now have considerable knowledge of the role aggregate populations play in environmental impacts, but still have only a meager understanding of the factors that distinguish between rural and urban impacts, or of the effects of a world population increasingly dominated by urbanization rather than rurality. Our understanding of the relationship between population and land use and land cover, likewise, needs further refinement, as does our understanding of the other driving forces. Hence, the list of topics needing refinement remains long and attractive for productive research.

Vertical Extensions

More challenging, but more promising goals lie in the vertical direction; that is, where our understanding of anthropogenic drivers extends into the domains of the traditional sciences and modeling. One goal is the fuller integration of the types of social scientific findings reported here with the grand modeling efforts—of carbon, hydrological, atmospheric, and other cycles—now dominating the field of GEC. Another goal would be more systematic inclusion of human dimensions in projects devoted to integrating research by conducting large-scale assessments. Still another goal, perhaps beyond the reach of current data and methods but ponderable nevertheless, would be to develop integrated, aggregate metrics not only of stressors, such as the ecological footprint, but also of actual impacts—land use, climate change, shifts in biodiversity, and so on. And to achieve these, we clearly need the full engagement of a human dimensions agenda and by implication human dimensions researchers, in large-scale integrated data-collection efforts.

Looking Backward: Assessing Cumulative Social Science Research

Proximate Drivers

Our first goal as stated is to take stock of the cumulative social science research on the five driving forces impacting ecosystems identified in GEC92: population change, economic growth, technological change, political-economic institutions, and attitudes and beliefs. We also take stock of how social science knowledge is or is not incorporated into large-scale ecological assessments.

Population Change As a driving force of environmental impacts, population size has, without doubt, the longest and richest history. The STIRPAT research program, described in chapter 3, connects directly to the GEC92 recommendation: "Perhaps the most valuable research over the near term will come from comparative studies that involve ... a large number of representative data points" (Stern, Young, and Druckman 1992, 96). Furthermore, STIRPAT not only provides a framework for testing hypotheses about the role of population in CHANS dynamics and in global environmental change, but also disciplines the long-presumed or alternatively long-dismissed connections between population and impacts with a body of empirical studies (Dietz, Rosa, and York 2007; Rosa, York, and Dietz 2004; Shi 2003; York, Rosa, and Dietz 2003, 2005).

But such macrocomparative work is not the only approach to understanding the links between population and environment. The general findings can be modified or fine-tuned by CHANS case studies (Turner et al. 2003). And as Emilio F. Moran notes in chapter 4, scholars studying land use and land cover change have paid close attention to the dynamics of migration and family and household formation in their work (Caldas et al. 2007; Entwistle and Stern 2005; Liu et al. 2003; Perz, Walker, and Caldas 2006). In the future we would hope to see the courtship between the macro and the micro bloom.

Economic Activity   The macrocomparative research program described in chapter 3 not only systematically examined the role of population in stressing ecosystems and in driving GEC, but also the influence of economic activity. For example, it provided disciplined tests of the widely known idea of a Kuznets curve—as did a growing number of other studies (Grossman and Krueger 1995; Stern 1998, 2002; Cavlovic et al. 2000)—on the presumed benefits to the environment due to continued economic growth.[1] It also permitted empirical tests of the widely held belief that a structural change in national economies, from manufacturing to services, would alleviate impacts to the environment (Stern, Young, and Druckman 1992, 81). Empirical tests (e.g., Rosa, York and Dietz 2004) not only *disconfirmed* that hypothesis, but also led to the recognition that the infrastructure, upon which a service economy depends, especially the exponential growth in personal computers, contributes significantly to environmental impacts—both in their production process and in the wastes produced.

Land Use and Deforestation   The clearing of the richest tropical forests, especially in the Amazon Basin, has long been viewed as the principal cause of losses in the earth's biological diversity. Furthermore, the loss of moist forests, especially in the tropics, accounts for a significant amount of greenhouse gas (GHG) emissions. As noted in chapter 1, in connection with the colorful descriptor of "hamburger connection," the dominant source of deforestation is due to cattle raising, which covers nearly three-quarters of the cleared area (Browder 1989; Steinfeld et al. 2006). (The Browder reference speaks to the larger point in the preceding sentence, namely the connection between cattle raising and cleared rain forest.)

An understanding of patterns of land use and change, recognized early on as a priority issue for human dimensions research, is one of the topics that have attracted the most sustained investigator-initiated research. A key, counterintuitive finding from detailed studies at a local scale is that the presumed cause of land clearing and land cover change, population growth, is not always evident. While there are clearly instances where land cover change can be traced to population growth, there are many cases where population increase is not associated with exploitation of land, but instead is one factor in the dynamics of land use. Furthermore, the evidence shows that market forces do not always drive land cover changes, thereby drawing into question the presumptions of rational, self-interest beneath these forces (Jaeger et al. 2001).

Political-Economic Institutions

Common Property and Open Access   Private property, an outgrowth of industrialization and modernization in England in the eighteenth century, has spread around the world. Nevertheless, the older tradition of owner-less (or collectively owned or fictively owned) property with open access to some or all citizens or to other corporate entities (persona ficta), such as nation-states, persists in every corner of the world. Current research has clearly shown that the theoretical predictions in Garrett Hardin's (1968) oversimplified scenario often are not realized in practice.

Whereas Hardin claimed that neither rules nor technology could save the overexploitation of common property, there are many instances everywhere where institutions, local rules, or the thoughtful application of technology results in sustainable use. Bonnie J. McCay and Svein Jentoff, in chapter 6, add to this growing literature (Ostrom 1990; Ostrom et al. 2002; Dietz, Ostrom, and Stern 2003) demonstrating that the relationships between common property, resource use, institutional practices, and threats to sustainability are tied up in a complicated dynamic that results in a variety of outcomes—ranging from overexploitation to sustainable stewardship of environmental capital and services. The variety of common property practices reviewed by McCay and Jentoff show that the rational actor model underlying Hardin's analysis fails to predict many such practices.

International Environmental Regimes   A dramatic aspect of the ongoing process of globalization has been the unmistakable growth in the recognition of the interconnectedness of CHANS and GEC. Equally remarkable is the growth in this recognition not only by scientists and other experts only, but also by governments in all countries and at all levels and by citizens around the world. Because CHANS and established political systems are not coterminous, solutions to global environmental problems fall to national sovereignty and nation-state institutions.

Hence, the processes of developing rules, procedures, decision-making methods, and regulations and laws—environmental regimes—have led to a growth in international institutions. The key questions these processes pose include: What forms have these regimes taken? How are the form and processes of regime structures designed to match environmental problems within their purview? And, perhaps most important, how effective have institutional arrangements and regimes been in addressing global environmental problems?

Chapter 5, by Oran R. Young, addresses these questions succinctly but thoroughly. Young's response to these questions, with his review of international environmental regimes, does not come as an earth-shaking surprise: there have been notable successes and equally notable failures by international environmental regimes. But the core of Young's analysis is not the fact that some regimes have succeeded and some have failed. Rather Young provides many insights into why this is so and how we can best understand the emergence, implementation, and ultimate success and failure of international environmental treaties. One in particular is the need to develop greater clarity in conceptualizing key features—such as power—of the underlying processes of regime formation and operation. It is only from such clarity that variables and relationships can be analyzed and tested with precision.

Also important is the question: Which are the most promising metatheoretical frameworks for understanding international regimes? A sizable body of research on international regimes adopts, as do virtually all the social sciences in various forms, a version of the rational actor paradigm. Many international regime researchers have adopted utility theory as their framework of analysis. Young outlines the promise of that approach while pointing out the contingent and multilevel nature of actual decision making in the global context. Hence, as argued by Jaeger et al. (2001) the rational actor paradigm definitely has its place in explaining a circumscribed range of decisions, but there is no basis for claiming this paradigm provides the best purchase on all decisions.

The World as a Political Institution   The explosion at the Chernobyl nuclear power plant in the Ukraine in April 1986 produced deadly radioactive fallout in the immediate vicinity of the exploded reactor. It produced global fallout as well, of two very different kinds: the first was radioactive fallout, similar to that shrouding Chernobyl but at less lethal levels; and the second was a new form—political fallout over modern, transboundary environmental risks. German theorist Ulrich Beck was one of the first to recognize not only the coexistence of both forms of fallout, but also their mutual interdependency. And this mutual interdependency has become the defining core of the modern world, which Beck labeled "The Risk Society," the focus of the theory he expounds in chapter 2.

Chernobyl served notice that while societies contained many of their old divisions (rich versus poor, core versus peripheral regions), systemic risks, like nuclear power, did not abide by these traditional stratifications. Citizens' growing recognition of this reality also meant that the social groupings, especially social class, that once provided comfort and identity were no longer effective in serving these needs. According to Beck, citizens now lived in a reflexive, individualized world. This meant, too, that traditional means for expressing concerns and preferences— e.g., political parties—were irrelevant to satisfying people's concerns over the growing risks of advanced modernity. This complex of historical developments, and other aspects of sociotechnological change, resulted in an entirely new institutional form: subpolitics.

For Beck, subpolitics refers to political action outside of and beyond the representative institutions of the political system of nation-states. And because of the growing number of risks we all face, Beck claims we all can expect to see substantial growth in this form of political action. Whatever the validity of his conclusions, they coincide with a global sea change in the approach to public policy over environmental issues. Virtually every type of national government, every type of subnational government, and every type of environmental agency within government is committed to a broadening of stakeholder representativeness in environmental decision making (Stern and Fineberg 1996).

It is important to note a finding common to the foregoing drivers— land use and institutional factors (common property, international regimes, risk society). It is clear that the rational actor paradigm that pervades the social sciences, including neoclassical economics, cannot fully account for the relationship between drivers and environmental outcomes. While the paradigm does provide adequate explanations in some settings and some contexts, and while it leaves us with some tantalizing puzzles, it generally fails to provide a deep grasp of the reciprocal, feedback dynamics of CHANS.

For example, indirect effects of rational economic choice, via the market, typically fail to account for land use and cover changes. The use of common property sometimes conforms to the predictions of rational actor theory, but often does not. Similarly, international treaties and agreements sometimes reflect the aggregation of nation-states acting in their own self-interest, other times not. What makes these observations all the more compelling is that the failure of rational actor assumptions is neither conditioned by cultural or geographical settings, nor by dominant political regimes, but is found across the entire panoply of societies (Henrich et al. 2001). This finding not only elaborates our understanding (or lack thereof) of human dimensions of CHANS in the broader context of GEC, but also contributes to the larger social science literature by revealing strengths and limitations in alternative social science paradigms.

Large-Scale Assessments   Some of the most significant advancements in understanding globalized CHANS have taken place in the research and policy recommendations contained in a variety of large-scale assessments. The term *large-scale* here refers to studies where the underlying goal is to integrate a wide range of empirical and computer model findings into summary conclusions about environmental degradation or into scenario developments. Most well known among these are the IPCC (Intergovernmental Panel on Climate Change) assessments and the MEA (Millennium Ecosystem Assessment), with its focus on ecosystems and human well-being. In addition a number of research centers are focused on integrative assessment.[2]

Modeling is a key activity of each of these assessments. Yet despite the increased confirmation that anthropogenic drivers are principal causes of GEC, these modeling efforts do not take advantage of the best available social science (IPCC 2007). Generally missing from the large-scale assessments is the integration of current research on the anthropogenic drivers that underpin perturbations to the carbon, hydrological, and atmospheric cycles and that are threats to environmental capital and services. For example, climate models typically treat population, or economic and technological dynamics, either as exogenous, or as one factor in descriptive scenarios. Often the models either rely on the IPAT identity (where Impacts are accounted for by multiplying Population times Affluence times Technology) or, as in the IPCC, a slightly modified version of IPAT called the Kaya identity. As we noted in chapter 3 for these identities, the parameters are fixed by presupposition, not by empirical confirmation. Hence, even where the two principal components of the IPAT identity, population and economics, are included in physical models, the reliance on presuppositions about parameters rather than scientific confirmation raises questions not only about the precision and validity of model outcomes, but also about their predictive accuracy.

The Millennium Ecosystem Assessment, the most comprehensive survey of the ecological state of the planet, does explicate a variety of anthropogenic drivers (Nelson et al. 2006), referred to in the MEA as "indirect drivers." The consensus anthropogenic drivers explicated in GEC92—demographic, economic, sociopolitical, cultural, religious, and science and technology factors—are recognized. But they are not a central focus of the MEA's analysis. In the MEA, like many integrated assessments, the most comprehensive consideration of anthropogenic drivers is embedded in scenarios, where trajectories are not grounded in empirical social science but are postulated for a set of drivers. Often it is difficult to unpack the assumptions that link trajectories in population, affluence, and technology to environmental change. Sometimes the assumptions are simply those of the IPAT identity, subject to the multiple critiques reviewed in chapter 3.

Scenarios are useful as comprehensive thought experiments that ask conditional "if, then" questions (Carpenter et al. 2005; de Vries 2007; IPCC 2005; U.S. Climate Change Science Program 2007). But it can be argued that the two largest sources of uncertainty in integrated assessment models center on our limited ability to forecast future states of anthropogenic drivers and our equally limited ability to specify links between drivers and ecosystem change. Projections of population, economic activity, and technology will always be difficult. But systematic research here would allow us to base the specification of links between drivers and ecosystems on evidence rather than assumption. While social science knowledge can be effective in making scenarios more realistic, with a broader range of applications it can make a far more significant contribution to integrated assessments than has been the case up till now.

What is clear from our backward look at the cumulative research on the human dimensions of CHANS in a global context is that we know considerably more now than we did in 1992 when the GEC92 was published. But, where do we go from here?

Looking Forward: Prospects for Future Research

GEC92 outlined a U.S. national program for research priorities on the human dimensions of global environmental change. It consisted of five major priorities: (1) an enlarged program of investigator-initiated research on human dimensions of GEC, (2) a program of research targeted or focused on selected topics relating to the human dimensions of GEC, (3) an ongoing federal program for obtaining and disseminating relevant data, (4) a broad-gauged program of fellowships to expand the pool of talented scientists working in this field, and (5) a network of national centers dedicated to the conduct of research on the human dimensions of global environmental change.

As noted, considerable progress has been made in addressing some of these priorities. There has, indeed, been an enlarged program of investigator-initiated research (priority 1) as well as research targeted or focused on selected topics for understanding CHANS in the context of GEC (priority 2). There has been little progress, however, on priority 3, the development of federal programs designed for the collection, coordination, and dissemination of data. Yet even here there are signs of recent progress. The CIESIN (Center for International Earth Science Information Network), an established, ongoing program at the Earth Institute of Columbia University, is producing a steady stream of useful social data in coordination with biological and physical data.

Several incipient programs also promise progress toward meeting priority 3. Their principal mission is to create cyberinfrastructures, large repositories of data accessible to researchers via the Internet. For example, the NEON (National Ecological Observatory Network, www. neoninc.org) program, still in its early stages of planning, anticipates three intensive observation sites at each of twenty locations across the United States. The CLEANER (Collaborative Large-scale Engineering Analysis Network for Environmental Research, http://cleaner.ncsa.uiuc. edu/home/), representing a collaborative effort among engineers and natural and social scientists has a larger engineering emphasis than NEON. A key mission of CLEANER is to become a virtual repository of data and information technology for engineering modeling and for human-technology-environment interactions. We fervently hope that these data assembly efforts will include social as well as biological and physical science data, as their success depends on integrated analysis. But as of the time we write (spring 2008), such integration is not certain and the value of some of these programs for understanding anthropogenic environmental change is uncertain.

Priority 4 has barely attracted attention or resources. Yet the training and institutional accommodation of capable scholars devoted to CHANS research is essential to a deeper understanding and to cumulative knowledge in the field. Research has lagged in attracting established senior social scientists to the topic, as it has in the training of young researchers. The problem, while gaining in recognition (e.g., see Rosa, Kasperson, and Miles 2007), has yet to stimulate the concentrated efforts it requires.

Priority 5 has been supported to a modest degree by the U.S. National Science Foundation's programs to fund a handful of centers to study the human dimensions of GEC. But the excellent work that is the focus of these centers, including the Climate Decision Making Center at Carnegie Mellon University (http://cdmc.epp.cmu.edu/) and the Center for the Study of Institutions, Population and Environmental Change at Indiana University (http://www.indiana.edu/~cipec/), is centered primarily on narrowly scoped analysis. In contrast, the GEC agenda can be interpreted as calling for centers that would serve the entire human dimensions research and policy communities via data collection and integration, tool development, and decision-making support services. Our understanding of CHANS will be stunted insofar as further progress in knowledge of the human dimensions side remains dependent on an effective network of coordinated national centers focused on service to the research and policy communities yet to be established.

Reactive versus Proactive Framings

It is important to return to priority 1, investigator-initiated projects, since it not only comprises nearly a dozen research priorities, but also prefigured the overarching direction of human dimensions research. It specifically identified the need to study the robustness of CHANS in the face of global environmental change in its variety of manifestations (Stern, Young, and Druckman 1992, 242).This research priority, while summarizing insights from the social science synthesis, underscored recognition that an emphasis on building models to integrate social and physical models, due to the underinvestment in social models, was viewed as premature. Hence, GEC92 urged that the near-term research agenda focus on underlying human processes and especially responses to the stresses on CHANS due to global change. The global change research community seized upon this recommendation in the form of research on vulnerabilities, resilience, adaptation, and response—the topic of chapter 7 by Jeanne X. Kasperson, Roger E. Kasperson, and B. L. Turner II.

Climate Assessment   Climate assessments provide an instructive example of this orientation in vulnerability research. The common goal of a climate vulnerability assessment and subsequent plan of action is to reduce the impacts of climate change or its disruptive variability. A typical plan begins, implicitly or obliquely, with the expectation that continual warming of the climate is a *fait accompli*, and that it will occur for some decades even if greenhouse gases are curbed immediately. This focus preframes analyses toward reactive strategies—that is, toward post hoc assessments of potential impacts, of the conditions of vulnerability, and of the resources constituting the adaptive capacity of the impacted area—from local to global scales.

Whatever the scale, the assessment typically is elaborated with efforts to determine the triggers of impacts at the relevant scale and the trigger points where adaptive or responsive action might be taken. The assessment often is further elaborated with a portfolio of short-term and long-term responses to the impacts. Taken together, these and complementary analyses are tools used to help decision makers determine the range of actions available and to prioritize their adaptation and management choices. Benefit-cost analysis, one of the most widely used rational actor methods, usually is applied in the prioritizing. Furthermore, underlying the determination of the range of available actions are analyses that provide guidance on how to optimize the allocation of resources.

These considerations and others raise the question of where the most promising lines for future human dimensions research lie. Answering this question requires reflection on not only the progress that has been made in the social sciences, but also on the progress (or lack thereof) in the natural sciences addressing globalized CHANS. For despite the advances in our knowledge of the human dimensions, this knowledge has been undercapitalized by the natural sciences. While there are clear signs of progress in this essential integration, the pace of the progress can only be described as sluggish and is, therefore, disappointing.

The Ghost in the Models   A continuing challenge to the linking—let alone the integration—of human-natural system dynamics can best be illustrated with an example from modeling research. The challenge speaks across a much wider chasm in our understanding of global dynamics, those persisting large gaps in the integration of the drivers and consequences of GEC. While our understanding of consequences (effects) has advanced by leaps and bounds, the causes—which ultimately reside in human choice and action—are barely on the radar screen of effort and understanding.

> Models of environmental change at scales from local to global typically have much greater detail and sophistication in representing environmental dynamics than in representing social dynamics or the links between human and environmental variables. Climate change models are a good example: human population dynamics are typically represented as exogenous, and only verbal scenarios typically represent human economic and technological development. Such models do not employ the best available social science. (CHDGC 2006)

In short, the principal perturbation to the causal chain that connects human and ecological systems lies with anthropogenic forces, yet these remain in black—or worse—empty boxes in much global environmental change research.

Nonlinear Dynamics and Tipping Points

There are other challenges to deepening our understanding of GEC. From a very broad perspective GEC can be defined as the assessment of a large-scale uncontrolled experiment on the entire planet. One viable, frequently discussed possibility is to model all the major interconnected cycles of the global system—carbon, hydrological, atmospheric, and geologic—as a system of nonlinear dynamics. Capturing nonlinear dynamics with mathematical precision is a daunting challenge. More directly relevant to our point here, however, is the recognition that, whatever the proper mathematics for describing them, nonlinear systems nearly always contain phase transitions or tipping points—critical junctures where the dynamics of the system are categorically disrupted resulting in chaotic consequences manifest in shifts to emergent systems with entirely different configurations, structures, and parameters.

It is beyond the frontiers of current knowledge to know if and when earth systems will experience such tipping points. Even more uncertain are the panoply of consequences that would occur if tipping points were realized. Nonetheless, there is every reason to believe that the consequences to the earth system could be devastating. That being so, it further begs the question of whether an adaptive strategy, in the absence of a preventative and mitigating one, is the best choice for addressing threats to global CHANS.

Scientific Advances and Limits: Ecology's Heisenberg

An unavoidable constraint on future knowledge will be inherent limitations in the methods for scientifically investigating global processes. Physics has long enjoyed status as the exemplar of cumulative scientific knowledge. Advances in twentieth-century subatomic physics were often characterized by breakthroughs in an understanding of the atom's constituents. But advances were also characterized by a fundamental understanding of our limitations toward reaching a complete understanding of the atom.

Singular among those limitations was the uncertainty (or indeterminacy) principal of Werner Heisenberg, which states: "The more precisely the position [of a subatomic particle, like an electron] is determined, the less precisely the momentum is known in this instant, and vice versa" (Heisenberg 1927, 180). Despite this limitation provided by a conspiracy of forces in nature, great advances have occurred in knowledge of the fundamental building blocks of matter and unquestioned progress has been made toward developing a theory, called the Standard Model, for unifying the four basic forces of nature (gravity, electromagnetic, strong force, and weak force[3]). Currently, there is a universal theory for the first three forces, so the key limitation of the Standard Model is its failure to account for gravity (Weinberg 2001).

The field of ecology, too, has a precisely articulated limiting principle, attributed to ecologist Richard Levins (1966). With respect to mathematical and nonmathematical models, Levins pointed out that it is impossible to simultaneously maximize generality, realism, and precision. With this verity of model limitations as a foundation he went on to suggest three options: (1) sacrifice generality to realism and precision; (2) sacrifice realism to generality and precision; or (3) sacrifice precision to realism and generality. Levins's scheme not only reveals an inherent limitation in how we can understand environmental change, but also provides a guide to strategies for future research.

As noted in GEC92, option 1—sacrificing generality to realism and precision—characterizes most simulation models developed for policy analysis. While these models are realistic in the sense that their dozens to hundreds to thousands of equations provide a detailed structure of the systems being modeled, and while they are precise in the sense that the system relationships are represented by mathematical equations that yield exact values for variables of interest, the models lack generality. Thus we must be concerned about the ability of such models to handle excursions of the system outside the range of model calibration—outside the ordinary. Yet for understanding globalized CHANS, for understanding GEC, we are centrally interested in situations where what has been assumed to be a parameter of the model, a constant within an analysis, now becomes a variable whose dynamics we must understand. Global analysis is about "when the center cannot hold."

There is a parallel between lines of research focusing on one or a few local places whose goal is to examine them in great detail (e.g., many of our best studies of land use) and studies based on in-depth analyses of one or a few historical cases (e.g., many of our best studies of international treaties). Such studies are precise in the sense of providing detailed accounts and realistic in their tendency to avoid simplifications. But like many policy models, they do not optimize generalizability. Because the number of places or cases examined is limited, so too is the variation in social, cultural, political, and environmental context; and the limitation of variation in such key factors of necessity limits the ability to generalize.

Nevertheless, progress has been made over the past two decades— precisely by not following only one of Levins's three options but instead exploring all of them. The wisdom of Levins's analysis is that no single approach can optimize on all three dimensions. Rather, a triangulating approach comprising multiple methods can provide the global research community with more robust findings than any single approach would allow. That being so, globalized CHANS research might take the Standard Model in physics, including its incompleteness, as an exemplar to emulate. Despite the absence of gravity, the Standard Model represents a pivotal advance in theoretical knowledge. Similarly, the fact that our models of social systems have yet to escape Levins's limits should not be a barrier to incorporating aspects of these systems where progress has been made.

Option 2, emphasizing generality and precision while sacrificing realism, is faulted for the simplicity of models that choose this option. The models are so abstract, and so simplified that the question always remains of whether they provide only hypothetical results or can effectively inform policy decisions. The STIRPAT comparative research program described in chapter 3 ascribes, de facto, to this option.

However, there are good reasons to believe that the results of such models are useful in policy making, and not as unrealistic or ineffective as might be assumed. First, there is the issue of intellectual symmetry.

No model—whether explicated in formal logic, highly mathematical terms, systems terms, or ordinary language propositions—is isomorphic with the reality the model is intended to represent. Hence, a shortfall in realism characterizes all models. They differ here in degree only. Option 2 highlights models where concern with realism is not paramount. Nevertheless, models following this option provide a systematic approach to connecting the human dimensions with ecological systems, and are amenable to greater realism with the addition of parameters to test new hypotheses and the growing availability of data of unprecedented relevance.

Option 3, where precision is sacrificed for generality and realism, is typically associated with a broad range of theoretical and interpretive social scientific approaches. Chapter 2 by Ulrich Beck serves as an exemplar of this approach. Explanations tend to be descriptive and models tend to be discursive and are not mapped onto mathematical formulations. Characterizations such as this are often aligned with human dimensions social science. They also shine a light on one of the most widely adopted methods of integrated assessment—scenario building and analyses. While scenarios often incorporate a variety of formal analyses, including modeling, the results of the modeling are virtually always embedded in qualitative and descriptive interpretations. How, otherwise, could anyone—including policymakers—interpret and use the results?

That being so, analyses using this option (including scenario building) can be improved in a number of ways, for example, by adding precision from the advances in social science work coming out of options 1 and 2; or from additional work with qualitative and interpretive models and theories that are focused on the dynamic mutualities between social and ecological systems.

To sum up, there are clear logical, empirical, and logistic issues that must be addressed as we endeavor to further advance our understanding of the human dimensions side of CHANS. But the problems are not insurmountable. The research reviewed across the chapters of this volume shows that much progress has been made already and indicates clearly the paths we must follow for an enhanced understanding of the human dimensions of global environmental change.

Coda

The concluding section of this chapter pointed to the outcomes of the past consensus in the human dimensions community that the focus of research should be on vulnerability, adaptation, and response. We suggested an equally promising direction for future GEC research, a reinvigorated effort to integrate social science research with research in the biological and physical sciences. Next we developed, after Levins, recognition of the inherent limits in models and knowledge more generally. We had earlier described problems with data availability and with the logistics of making it available to researchers as another limitation on advancing our knowledge.

Going forward, we recommend that research and policy formation be reprioritized to focus on prevention and mitigation, not just adaptive response strategies. With the appearance of the Fourth Assessment of Intergovernmental Panel on Climate Change (IPCC 2007) and arguments by social scientists (Wilbanks 1984, 2003; Wilbanks and Romero-Lankao 2006), a policy shift is underway toward mitigation and adaptation. The application of this approach is straightforward in the case of climate. Given clear evidence the climate will warm over the next several decades regardless of what actions are taken to reduce the rate of GHG emissions, the only meaningful policy option is adaptive preparation. Despite the inertial inevitability of global warming there is also the need to soften the impacts as much as reasonably possible. This opens a significant policy space for mitigating actions.

The logic extends to the other dimensions of global environmental change and points to the need for coordinated analyses that can deepen our understanding of not only the sources of vulnerabilities and resiliency, but also the potential for mitigation and adaptation. The logic also creates an opening for social science research that advances our understanding of the human drivers of CHANS and pinpoints the trigger points for effective policy responses.

Notes

1. A similar argument is found in sociology as the ecological modernization theory (EMT; Mol and Sonnenfeld 2000).
2. The International Assessment Society (www.tias.uni-osnabrueck.de) and its journal *Integrated Assessment* provide access to these efforts. See also Costanza et al. (2007) for a review of integrated assessment models.
3. Electromagnetic forces include all forces between electrically charged particles, such those that produce light. The strong force binds the neutrons and protons together in the core of the atom. The weak force is responsible for the decay (Beta decay) of a proton into a neutron or other subatomic particle.

References

An, L., M. Linderman, J. Qi, A. Shortridge, and J. Liu. 2005. Exploring complexity in a human-environment system: An agent-based spatial model for multidisciplinary and multiscale integration. *Annals of the Association of American Geographers* 95:54–79.

Browder, J. O. 1989. *Fragile lands of Latin America: Strategies of sustainable development*. Boulder, CO: Westview Press.

Caldas, M., R. Walker, E. Arima, S. Perz, S. Aldrich, and C. Simmons. 2007. Theorizing land cover and land use change: The peasant economy of Amazonian Deforestation. *Annals of the Association of American Geographers* 97:86–110.

Carpenter, S. R., P. L. Pingali, E. M. Bennett, and M. B. Zurek. 2005. *Ecosystems and human well-being: Scenarios*, vol. 2. Washington, DC: Island Press.

Cavolic, T. A., K. H. Baker, R. P. Berrens, and K. Gawande. 2000. A meta-analysis of the environmental Kuznets curve studies. *Agricultural and Resource Economics Review* 29:32–42.

CHDGC (Committee on Human Dimensions of Global Change). 2006. *Statement of future research needs*. Washington, DC: National Research Council/ National Academy of Sciences.

Costanza, R., L. J. Graumlich, and W. Steffen. 2007. *Sustainability or collapse? An integrated history and future of people on Earth*. Cambridge, MA: MIT Press.

Costanza, R., R. Leemans, R. Boumans, and E. Gaddis. 2007. Integrated global models. In *Sustainability or collapse? An integrated history and future of people on Earth*, ed. R. Costanza, L. J. Graumlich, and W. Steffen, 417–445. Cambridge, MA: MIT Press.

de Vries, B. 2007. Scenarios: Guidance for an uncertain and complex world? In *Sustainability or collapse? An integrated history and future of people on Earth*, ed. R. Costanza, L. J. Graumlich, and W. Steffen, 379–397. Cambridge, MA: MIT Press.

Dietz, T., E. Ostrom, and P. C. Stern. 2003. The struggle to govern the commons. *Science* 302:1907–1912.

Dietz, T., E. A. Rosa, and R. York. 2007. Driving the human ecological footprint. *Frontiers in Ecology and the Environment* 5:13–18.

Entwistle, B., and P. Stern, eds. 2005. *Population, land use, and environment research directions*. Washington, DC: National Academies Press.

Grossman, G., and A. Krueger. 1995. Economic growth and the environment. *Quarterly Journal of Economics* 110:353–377.

Hardin, G. 1968. The tragedy of the commons. *Science* 162:1243–1248.

Heisenberg, W. 1927. Über den anschaulichen Inhalt der quantentheoretischen Kinematik und Mechanik. *Zeitschrift für Physik* 43:172–198. English translation: J. A. Wheeler and H. Zurek. 1983. *Quantum Theory and Measurement*, 62–84. Princeton, NJ: Princeton University Press.

Henrich, J., R. Boyd, S. Bowles, C. Camerer, E. Fehr, H. Gintis, and R. McElreath. 2001. In search of Homo economicus: Behavioral experiments in 15 small-scale societies. *American Economic Review* 91:73–78.

IPCC (Intergovernmental Panel on Climate Change). 2005. *Workshop on new emission scenarios: Meeting report.* Report of Working Group III Technical Support Unit, Bilthoven, The Netherlands.

IPCC (Intergovernmental Panel on Climate Change). 2007. *Climate Change 2007.* Report of Working Group I, of the Fourth Assessment. http://www.ipcc.ch/.

Jaeger, C., O. Renn, E. A. Rosa, and T. Webler. 2001. *Risk, uncertainty, and rational action.* London: EARTHSCAN.

Levins, R. 1966. The strategy of model building in population biology. *American Scientist* 54:421–431.

Liu, J., G. C. Daily, P. R. Ehrlich, and G. W. Luck. 2003. Effects of household dynamics on resource consumption and biodiversity. *Nature* 1359:1–4.

Liu, J., T. Dietz, S. R. Carpenter, M. Alberti, C. Folke, E. Moran, A. N. Pell, P. Deadman, T. Kratz, J. Lubchencko, E. Ostrom, Z. Ouyang, W. Provencher, C. L. Redman, S. H. Schneider, and W. W. Taylor. 2007a. Complexity of coupled human and natural systems. *Science* 317:1513–1516.

Liu, J., T. Dietz, S. R. Carpenter, C. Folke, M. Alberti, C. L. Redman, S. H. Schneider, P. Deadman, T. Kratz, J. Lubchencko, E. Ostrom, Z. Ouyang, W. Provencher, C. L. Redman, S. H. Schneider, and W. W. Taylor. 2007b. Coupled human and natural systems. *Ambio* 36:649.

Mol, A. P. J., and D. A. Sonnenfeld, eds. 2000. *Ecological modernization around the world.* London: Frank Cass.

Nelson, G. C., E. Bennett, A. A. Berhe, K. Cassman, R. DeFries, T. Dietz, A. Dobson, A. Doberman, A. Janetos, M. Levy, D. Marco, N. Nakićenović, B. O'Neill, R. Norgaard, G. Petschel-Held, D. Ojima, P. Pingali, R. Watson, and Z. Monika. 2006. Anthropogenic drivers of ecosystem change: An overview. *Ecology and Society* 11 (2):29. Available at http://www.ecologyandsociety.org/vol11/iss2/art29/.

Ostrom, E. 1990. *Governing the commons: The evolution of human institutions for collective action.* New York: Cambridge University Press.

Ostrom, E., T. Dietz, N. Dolsak, P. C. Stern, S. Stonich, and E. U. Weber, eds. 2002. *The drama of the commons.* Washington, DC: National Academies Press.

Perz, S. G., R. T. Walker, and M. M. Caldas. 2006. Beyond population and environment: Household demographic life cycles and land use allocation among small farms in the Amazon. *Human Ecology* 34:829–849.

Rosa, E. A., R. Kasperson, and E. L. Miles. 2007. Panel to address capacity building for research in human dimensions of global environmental change. Draft, Committee on the Human Dimensions of Global Change, National Academy of Sciences (May).

Rosa, E. A., R. F. York, and T. Dietz. 2004. Tracking the anthropogenic drivers of ecological impacts. *Ambio: A Journal of Human Environment* 33:509–512.

Shi, A. 2003. The impact of population pressure on global carbon dioxide emissions: Evidence from pooled cross-country data. *Ecological Economics* 44:24–42.

Steinfeld, H., P. Gerber, T. Wassenaar, V. Castel, M. Rosales, and C. de Haan. 2006. *Livestock's long shadow: Environmental issues and options.* Rome: Food and Agricultural Organization of the United Nations (FAO). http://www.fao.org/docrep/010/a0701e/a0701e00.htm.

Stern, D. I. 1998. Progress on the environmental Kuznets curve? *Environment and Development Economics* 3:173–196.

Stern D. I. 2002. Explaining changes in global sulfur emissions: An econometric decomposition approach. *Ecological Economics* 42:201–220.

Stern, P. C., and H. V. Fineberg, eds. 1996. *Understanding risk: Informing decisions in a democratic society.* Washington, DC: National Academies Press.

Stern, P. C., O. R. Young, and D. Druckman, eds. 1992. *Global environmental change: Understanding the human dimensions.* Washington, DC: National Academies Press.

Turner, B. L. II, P. A. Matson, J. J. McCarthy, R. W. Corell, L. Christensen, N. Eckley, G. K. Hovelsrud-Broda, J. X. Kasperson, R. E. Kasperson, A. Luers, M. L. Martello, S. Mathiesen, R. Naylor, C. Polsky, A. Pulsipher, A. Schiller, H. Selin, and N. Tyler. 2003. Illustrating the coupled human-environment system for vulnerability analysis: Three case studies. *Proceedings of the National Academy of Sciences* 100:8080–8085.

U.S. Climate Change Science Program. 2007. *Scenarios of greenhouse gas emissions and atmospheric concentrations (part A) and review of integrated scenario development and application (part B).* U.S. Department of Energy, Office of Biological & Environmental Research, Washington, DC.

Weinberg, S. 2001. *Facing up.* Cambridge, MA: Harvard University Press.

Wilbanks, T. 1984. Scale and the acceptability of nuclear energy. In *Nuclear power: Assessing and managing hazardous technology*, ed. M. Pasqueletti and D. Pijawka, 9–50. Boulder, CO: Westview.

Wilbanks, T. 2003. Geography and technology. In *Technology and geography: A social history*, ed. S. Brunn, S. Cutter, J. Harrington, 3–16. Dordrecht: Kluwer.

Wilbanks, T. J., and P. Romero-Lankao. 2006. The human dimensions of global environmental change. In *Sage handbook of environment and society*, ed. Jules Petty, 353–361. London: Sage.

York, R., E. A. Rosa, and T. Dietz. 2003. Footprints on the earth: The environmental consequences of modernity. *American Sociological Review* 68:279–300.

York, R., E. A. Rosa, and T. Dietz. 2005. The ecological intensity of national economies. *Journal of Industrial Ecology* 8:139–154.

About the Contributors

Ulrich Beck   Ulrich Beck is professor for sociology at the University of Munich, and has been the British Journal of Sociology Visiting Centennial Professor at the London School of Economics and Political Sciences since 1997. Beck is editor of both *Soziale Welt* and *Second Modernity* at Suhrkamp (Frankfurt am Main). His interests focus on risk society, globalization, individualization, reflexive modernization and cosmopolitanism. He is founding director of the Reflexive Modernization research center at the University of Munich (in cooperation with four other universities in the area).

Andreas Diekmann   Andreas Diekmann is professor of sociology at the Swiss Federal Institute of Science and Technology (ETH) in Zurich. He was awarded a Ph.D. in economics from the University of Hamburg and a Habilitation from the University of Munich. He conducts research in environmental sociology, rational choice, and game theory. His publications include sixteen books and over sixty research papers.

Thomas Dietz   Thomas Dietz is professor of sociology and crop and soil science, director of the Environmental Science and Policy Program, and assistant vice president for environmental research at Michigan State University. He was awarded a Ph.D. in ecology from the University of California at Davis. He served as chair of the U.S. National Research Council Committee on Human Dimensions of Global Change. He conducts research on environmental values, the relationship between democracy and science, and structural human ecology. His publications include ten books and over ninety research papers.

Carlo Jaeger   Carlo Jaeger is head of the Department of Transdisciplinary Concepts and Modeling and professor of modeling at the Potsdam Climate Institute. He was awarded a Ph.D. in economics by Goethe University and a Habilitation in human ecology by the Swiss Federal Institute of Science and Technology. He conducts research on climate change, public participation, and the application of modeling to risk and policy. His publications include twelve books and over sixty research papers.

Svein Jentoft   Svein Jentoft is a sociologist and professor at the Centre for Marine Resource Management, Norwegian College of Fishery Science, University of Tromsø, Norway. He specializes in social and institutional aspects of fisheries and coastal governance and development and their effects on indigenous communities. Among recent books he has coedited or coauthored are *Fish for Life: Interactive Governance for Fisheries* (Amsterdam University Press, 2005); *In Disciplinary Border Lands: On Interdisciplinarity* (Fagbokforlaget, 2007); and *The Rama People—Struggling for Land and Culture* (URACCAN, 2006), *Indigenous Peoples: Resource Management and Global Rights* (Eburon, 2008), and *Indigenous Peoples: Self-determination, Knowledge and Indigenism* (Eburon, 2008).

Jeanne X. Kasperson   Jeanne X. Kasperson, a longtime member of Clark University's faculty and staff, died August 27, 2002. From 1977 until her death she served as a research librarian for the Hazard Assessment Group and subsequently served as research librarian for the University's Center for Technology, Environment, and Development (CENTED), and later the George Perkins Marsh Library. Throughout her career, Professor Kasperson was an active scholar in the general areas of risk analysis and global environmental change. She was a key member of a highly productive research group at CENTED and its successor, the George Perkins Marsh Institute. She was the author of more than eighty articles, books, and technical reports, editor of several journals, and recipient of many research grants. The research library Jeanne X. Kasperson founded and built at Clark University offers one of the most extensive collections in North America on environmental risk and hazards, environment and development, and the human dimensions of GEC. In recognition, Clark dedicated the George Perkins Marsh Library to Kasperson in April 2003 and has established a fund in her memory.

Roger E. Kasperson   Roger E. Kasperson is research professor and Distinguished Scientist at the George Perkins Marsh Institute at Clark University. He received his Ph.D. from the University of Chicago and has taught at Clark University, the University of Connecticut, and Michigan State University. His expertise is in risk analysis, global environmental change, and environmental policy. Kasperson is a member of the U.S. National Academy of Sciences, and a Fellow of both the American Association for the Advancement of Science and the Society for Risk Analysis. He has served on numerous committees of the U.S. National Research Council. He chaired the International Geographical Commission on Critical Situations/Regions in Global Environmental Change and has served on EPA's Science Advisory Board. He now serves on the Human Dimensions of Global Environmental Change Committee of the U.S. National Research Council, is cochair of the Scientific Advisory Committee of the Potsdam Institute for Climate Change, and is on the Executive Steering Committee of the START Programme of the IGBH. He is a member of the National Academy of Sciences and the American Academy of Arts and Sciences. He has authored or coedited twenty-two books and monographs and more than a hundred and forty articles or chapters in scholarly journals or books and has served on numerous editorial boards for scholarly journals. From 2000 to 2004, Kasperson was executive director of the Stockholm Environment Institute in Sweden. He was a coordinating lead author of the vulnerability and synthesis chapters of the Conditions and

Trends volume of the Millennium Ecosystems Assessment and a member of the core writing team for the Synthesis of the overall MEA. Kasperson has been honored by the Association of American Geographers for his hazards research and in 2006 he was the recipient of the Distinguished Achievement Award of the Society for Risk Analysis. In 2007 he was appointed associate scientist at the National Center for Atmospheric Research in the United States.

Bonnie J. McCay Bonnie McCay is Board of Governors Distinguished Service Professor at Rutgers University, New Brunswick, New Jersey, where she chairs the Department of Human Ecology. Her graduate training was in anthropology at Columbia University (Ph.D., 1976), and her research and teaching have focused on challenges and policies for managing marine resources, particularly fisheries. She has done field research in Newfoundland and Nova Scotia, Canada, in New Jersey, and in Baja California, Mexico, with funding from the National Science Foundation, the New Jersey Sea Grant College Program, and the New Jersey Agricultural Experiment Station. Her books include *The Question of the Commons* (University of Arizona Press, 1988), *Oyster Wars and the Public Trust* (University of Arizona Press, 1998), and *Enclosing the Commons* (Institute of Social and Economic Research, 2002). She currently serves on the Science Advisory Committees for the California Current Ecosystem-Based Management Initiative and the NY Ocean and Great Lakes Ecosystem Conservation Council, and heads the Resource Policy Committee of the American Fisheries Society.

Emilio F. Moran Emilio F. Moran is Distinguished Professor and the James H. Rudy Professor of Anthropology, professor of environmental sciences, adjunct professor of geography, director of the Anthropological Center for Training and Research on Global Environmental Change (ACT), and codirector of the Center for the Study of Institutions, Population and Environmental Change (CIPEC) all at Indiana University. He is author of seven books, ten edited volumes, and more than a hundred and forty journal articles and book chapters. His research in the Amazon has been supported by NSF, NIH, NOAA, and NASA for the past two decades. His two latest books, *People and Nature* (Blackwell, 2006) and *Human Adaptability*, 3rd ed. (Westview, 2007) address broader issues of human interaction with the environment.

Eugene A. Rosa Eugene A. Rosa is the Edward R. Meyer Distinguished Professor of Natural Resource and Environmental Policy, professor of sociology, affiliated professor of environmental science, affiliated professor of fine arts, and faculty associate in both the Center for Environmental Research, Education, and Outreach and the Center for Integrated Biotechnology at Washington State University. He is a Fellow of the American Association for the Advancement of Science, has served on six committees and boards of the National Academy of Sciences, and is a frequent invited speaker in the United States and abroad. His research focuses on global environmental change, environmental and technological risk, and public perceptions of risk. He has published three books and numerous research articles, several of which have received awards of distinction.

B. L. Turner II   B. L. Turner II is the Gilbert F. White Professor of Environment and Society, School of the Geographical Sciences and Urban Planning, and School of Sustainability, Arizona State University. He is a member of the U.S. National Academy of Sciences and the American Academy of Arts and Sciences, a Fellow of the American Academy of Arts and Sciences and the American Association for the Advancement of Science, and the recipient of a Guggenheim Fellowship. He is a student of human-environment relationships, ranging from ancient Maya agriculture and environment in Mexico and Central America to contemporary global land-use change and sustainability science.

Richard York   Richard York is an associate professor of sociology at the University of Oregon and coeditor of the Sage journal *Organization & Environment*. He has published more than fifty articles, essays, and reviews, most of which examine environmental issues. He recently published *The Critique of Intelligent Design* (Monthly Review Press, 2008) with John Bellamy Foster and Brett Clark. He has twice (2004 and 2007) received the Outstanding Publication Award from the Environment and Technology Section of the American Sociological Association.

Oran R. Young   Oran Young is professor of environmental policy at the Bren School of Environmental Science & Management at the University of California, Santa Barbara. Specializing in the analysis of environmental institutions with particular reference to international regimes, Young also serves as codirector of the Program on Governance for Sustainable Development at the Bren School. He served for six years as founding chair of the Committee on the Human Dimensions of Global Change of the National Academy of Sciences in the United States and chaired the Scientific Steering Committee of the international project on the Institutional Dimensions of Global Environmental Change (IDGEC) under the auspices of the International Human Dimensions Programme on Global Environmental Change (IHDP). He is currently chair of the Scientific Committee of the IHDP. An expert on Arctic issues, Young served as vice president of the International Arctic Science Committee, chair of the Board of Governors of the University of the Arctic, and cochair of the Arctic Human Development Report. He is author or coauthor of many scholarly articles and more than twenty books, including *Institutions and Environmental Change: Principal Findings, Applications, and Future Directions* (MIT Press, 2008); *The Institutional Dimensions of Environmental Change: Fit, Interplay, and Scale* (MIT Press, 2002); *Governance in World Affairs* (Cornell University Press, 1989); *International Governance: Protecting the Environment in a Stateless* (Cornell University Press, 1994); and *International Cooperation: Building Regimes for Natural Resources and the Environment* (Cornell University Press, 1989).

Index